WE C

ANTHOLOGY

HERMANN SASSE

TRANSLATED BY
NORMAN NAGEL

CONCORDIA PUBLISHING HOUSE · SAINT LOUIS

6 7 8 9 10 11 12 13 14   12 11 10 09 08 07 06 05 04 03

WE CONFESS

JESUS CHRIST

Contents

Translator's Preface

Student, pastor, scholar, teacher, and confessor, Hermann Sasse (1895—1976) is recognized as one of the leading voices of confessional Lutheranism in the 20th century. Born in Sonnewalde, Germany, his theological activity extended through the decay of the Weimar Republic and the rise and fall of the Nazi regime. In the midst of such disruption he became and remained a staunch confessor of the *Una Sancta*, the one holy catholic and apostolic church. His confession was grounded in that earliest of all Christian confessions, "Jesus is Lord."

"Jesus Christ Is Lord" in this volume is Sasse at his brilliant best in the service of confessing Jesus Christ, the burning heart of all his work. This leitmotif has its early setting in *Mysterium Christi: Christological Studies by British and German Theologians*, edited by Bishop G. K. A. Bell in 1930. Two of the essays in this volume are taken from Sasse's "Letters to Lutheran Pastors," ("Briefe an lutherische Pastoren"), which he began to write after World War II and continued after his emigration to Australia.

Throughout this volume we have incorporated Sasse's footnotes into the text, sometimes with parentheses, sometimes without. We have generally broken up his long paragraphs into several smaller ones. Where we have added references, etc., in various places, these are indicated with brackets.

Dr. Sasse throughout his life, both in Germany and later in Australia, was involved in the whole Christian scene. He kept astonishingly well informed and was able to illumine developments and events in scattered parts of the world with his far-reaching knowledge of the church's history and confession. For him, to be a loyal Lutheran was to be a catholic Christian, heir to all the treasures of the church. His historical perspective blended with his confessional integrity won him the respect of Lutheran, Catholic, and Reformed alike.

Hermann Sasse wrote in times of theological turmoil and political upheaval. In the midst of great adversity he brought a message that would strengthen and hold. Many and varied were the situations he addressed, and yet through them all it is the same message, the only message which finally holds, the message about Jesus Christ, our crucified and risen Lord. The three volumes of the "We Confess" series, of which this is but the first, give testimony that Dr. Sasse's work lives on.

JESUS CHRIST IS LORD The Church's Original Confession

1931

1. The Original Confession

Kyrios Jesous Christos, "Jesus Christ is Lord." This is the original confession of the church. With it the Christian faith once entered world history. To understand the sense of this confession ever more deeply is the great, yes, basically the only task of all Christian theology. To repeat this confession, to speak it in ever new forms, to translate it into the language of all times and peoples, to protect it against misunderstandings and reinterpretations, and to understand its meaning for all areas of life—that is the task of all confession building within Christendom. No later confession of the church can and wants to be anything else than a renewal of the original confession to Jesus as Christ and Lord. This is true of the Apostles' Creed, the Nicene Creed, the confessional writings of the Reformation, and any confession in which the Christendom of the future may want to speak its faith. As this confession stood at the beginning of the church's history, so it will stand at its end. Then will be fulfilled that great word of the apostle: "At the name of Jesus every knee shall bow, in heaven and on earth and under the earth, and every tongue confess that Jesus Christ is Lord, to the glory of God the Father" (Phil. 2:10 f.).

Whoever wants to understand the sense of this confession must first be clear as to what a church confession actually is. Nowadays

9

this is much forgotten, and also theologians seem to be little aware of it. Confession does not belong, as many have thought, to the essence of religion. It does not even belong to the essence of the higher religions. Mysticism, for example, knows nothing of confessions. But from the very beginning it belongs to the essence of the Christian faith, and that threefold: confession of sin, confession of faith, and acclamation of God. These are the meanings of *homologein* and *exhomologeisthai* in the New Testament, and of corresponding words in Greek and Latin church usage. It still echoes on in Augustine's *Confessions*.

This Christian usage of confession has moved deeply in men's souls. It has given its name to a whole class of literature. Consider the confessions of Augustine and of Rousseau, and how these have affected the writing of autobiography. If people in the modern world, in contrast to all other periods of history, understood and evaluated great poetry as "confession" in that sense in which Goethe spoke of his works as fragments of a great confession, if philosophical and political world views appear among us as "confessions," then this is an aftereffect of confessing in the sense of the Christian faith. During a thousand-year history it has helped form Western man, and it still remains a force when its content—forgiveness of sin, confession of faith, and acclamation of God—have long been forgotten.

A special kind of Christian confession is, already in the New Testament, *the church's confession of faith*. Its essence can be seen through the following marks. It is to be understood, first of all, as *the answer that is evoked by* God's *revelation* of Himself, faith's answer to the received Word of God. When Jesus asked, "Who do you say that I am?" Peter answered with the church's first confession of faith: "You are the Christ" (Mark 8:29). It is not by chance that in Matthew's account Jesus speaks of revelation. All true confessions of faith want to be response to revelation. In them faith bears witness, in spare, objective statements of fact, to the revelation that has occurred. Therefore parallels to Christian confessions can be found only in prophetic religions that know of a revelation that once happened (e. g., the *shahada* of Islam). The church's confessions tell objectively of facts, not of subjective experiences. For this very reason they are offensive to modern man. They speak of what was revealed in Christ, which happened at one time in history. Therefore in later time they always point to the past, to the "once" and "there" of salvation history, to that which happened "under Pontius Pilate."

Confession as response to revelation is, second, *the response of the church*. It is not the response of just a single believer, even though each believer confesses with the creed "I believe," as at Baptism. Jesus' question was addressed to all the disciples together: "Who do you [plural] say that I am?" Peter answers in the name of them all, and his answer immediately becomes the confession of them all. It is again not by chance that in Matthew's account there follows immediately the first mention of the church. Confession and church belong together. Christ's church is always a confessing church. Not only does each Christian confess his personal faith, but the church, the whole company of believers, gives testimony of the revelation that has happened. The individual Christian joins this testimony in his personal faith. Out of such consensus of faith, worked by the Holy Spirit, is true confession born. (Cf. "Our churches teach with great unanimity" [Augsburg Confession I, 1] and similar statements in the Preface to the Book of Concord.)

The third characteristic of confession of faith is that it belongs in the liturgy, in the *divine service*, in which the church appears as the hearing, praying, and confessing congregation. Right from the beginning we see that the earliest confessional statements have their place in the divine service. As the answer of the congregation the confession is directed to God. In this respect confession is similar to prayer, although the two must not be confused.

When the church confesses, she is speaking not only to God but also to the world. This is the fourth characteristic of the church's confession. Every genuine confession has a polemical character, even if it does not contain condemnations against false doctrine. It separates *pure doctrine* from false doctrine, the Christian faith from the religions of the world, the church from all that is not church.

In this sense the New Testament formulas "Jesus is Lord" (Rom. 10:9; 1 Cor. 12:3) and "Jesus Christ is Lord" (Phil. 2:11; cf. 2 Cor. 4:5; Col. 2:6) are genuine confessions of faith and the prototypes of all later confessions of the church. Of their origin we are ignorant. We may be grateful that we are given an account of the origin of the Messiah-confession, "You are the Christ." But the New Testament gives us nothing certain about the origin of "Jesus is Lord." The early Aramaic-speaking church already called upon Jesus in prayer as "Lord." That is proved by the old prayer formula *marana tha*, "Our Lord, come!" (1 Cor. 16:22; cf. Rev. 22:20). Despite Bultmann this can only be addressed to Jesus. After the Lord's Prayer it is the oldest piece of the Christian liturgy. We cannot say, however, whether the confession of faith "Jesus is Lord" was already used in Aramaic. We find it in Greek in the churches that were served by Paul. Here it appears as a confession of faith at Baptism (as can be deduced from Rom. 10:9 and Col. 2:6) and is in use in the divine service (1 Cor. 12:3).

It is in the Greek *Kyrios Jesous* ("Jesus is Lord") that this confession attains its full resonance. Everything that is in the word *Kyrios* ("Lord") is here said of Jesus. *Kyrios* is "the name which is above every name" [Phil. 2:9], the holy name of God used in the Greek Bible.

(The concepts *Theos* ["God"] and *Kyrios*, ["Lord"] belong together, as we see in John 20:28, "My Lord and my God," and in 1 Cor. 8:5-6, "many gods and many lords," and then "one God" and "one Lord." We see them also together in the later title of the emperor *dominus et deus* ["lord and god"]. This meaning of *Kyrios* derives from the East, where what was said of the ruler was said of the deity and vice versa.)

Kyrioi ("lords") is what the cultic deities of the Oriental-Hellenistic mystery religions were called. *Kyrios* is what the Roman emperor was called in the emperor cult. In the language of the Hellenistic Orient *kyrios* is applied to a deity in its revelation, the revealed god. When the early church confesses its faith that Jesus Christ is *kyrios*, it is confessing its faith in His true deity. It thereby says no less of Him than does the Nicene Creed: "God of God, Light of Light, very God of very God."

With the confession that Jesus is *kyrios* the Christian faith is marked off from all surrounding religions. The confession that Jesus is the Christ just may have been possible among the Jews. At least the early church in Palestine thought so, though not the rulers of the Jews (John 9:22). But the confession that Jesus Christ is Lord brought the irreparable separation of synagogue and church. What was seen on the one hand as deification of a creature and blasphemy against the one and only God was seen on the other as no infringement at all of the fact that there is but one God. Paul puts the latter beyond doubt in 1 Cor. 8:6. To religious Hellenism the statement that a historical man of the recent past is *kyrios*, and only He, appeared to be utter foolishness and absurdity. To the Roman imperium the confession of Jesus as Lord, *Kyrios Jesous*, was a repudiation of *Kyrios Kaisar* ("Caesar is lord"), and so high treason.

Such are the depths and dimensions of the original confession of the church that Jesus is Lord. With it the early church gave its answer to the revelation which had happened in the historical human being Jesus of Nazareth. Thereby it marked itself off from all the religions of the world. In order to probe this confession further, and the faith in Jesus Christ as true God that is bound up in it, we shall explore two of the things which are foundational for this confession: the *resurrection* and the *ascension* of Jesus Christ. It is understood that we are thereby dealing with only a small segment in the area of Christology.

2. The Risen One

"If you confess with your lips that Jesus is Lord and believe in your heart that God raised Him from the dead, you will be saved" (Rom. 10:9). This word of Paul inseparably links the confession that Jesus is Lord with faith in His resurrection. There can therefore be no proper understanding of this confession that Jesus is Lord without the proper understanding of His resurrection. Let us then try to answer the question: What does the New Testament mean by the message of Jesus' resurrection?

From the very beginning the message of Jesus' resurrection or, otherwise put, that "God raised Him from the dead," is at the heart of the apostolic proclamation. But, as the New Testament shows, during the time of the apostles there was no attempt to picture the event of the resurrection; the first such attempt appears in the apocryphal Gospel of Peter. Beside the proclamation of the resurrection the New Testament has only reports of facts that should encourage faith in the resurrection that has happened. Such facts are the empty grave and the appearances of the Risen One.

The oldest account of Easter that we have is a formulary that summarizes the proclamation about Christ which Paul cites in 1 Cor. 15:1 ff. as a tradition which he has received and has handed on. The death, the burial, and the resurrection of Jesus are stated. There is no mention of the grave having been found empty. For bolstering faith in the accomplished resurrection only the fact is cited that the Risen One was seen by a number of witnesses. From this we may conclude that the Easter faith had its foundation in the appearances of the Lord and that the empty grave at the most played a secondary role in the earliest apostolic proclamation.

The account of the empty grave is first found in Mark. In the original text of this gospel there is no report of an appearance of the Risen One, but an appearance is pointed to which will take place for the disciples in Galilee. Peter is named especially, and in Paul he is the one listed first. Only later were a number of appearances attached to the end of Mark. The other evangelists took over what Mark tells of the empty grave, and combined this with reports of the appearances of the Risen One in Galilee (Matthew, Luke, and John), and in Jerusalem (Luke and John). The pressures operative in retelling, in persuading, and in defending the Easter message may already be at work here.

It is no accident that Mark's account of the empty grave became the actual Easter Gospel of the early church. It is the form of the Easter message that comes home most readily to everyday people. For such people in the early Palestinian church the empty grave was a way of portraying the resurrection that made the fact of Easter more comprehensible. As they had to defend the objective truth of their Easter faith over against their Jewish compatriots, they were not slow in using the empty grave as a proof that the resurrection had happened. As the generation that still remembered the compelling force of the Easter experiences grew old and died, the empty grave all the more had to become the foundation for the resurrection message throughout the church.

The appearances of the risen Jesus were known from the first, and they always had a place in that proclamation, as we see from our gospels. But the gospels show an unmistakable tendency to connect these appearances more and more with Jesus' grave. This can also be seen in their tendency to localize in Jerusalem the decisive events of the Easter days. We may call this the Jerusalem tradition. What it traces is indeed very early and reliable, and yet it is clear from the gospels that there is another tradition which tells of decisive appearances of the Risen One—at least the basic Easter experience of Peter—far from Jesus' grave, in Galilee. The gospels tell us what happened in Galilee, and yet what happened in and around Jerusalem has greater prominence. This may be due to the gathering of the believers in Jerusalem. Thus we hear no more of the appearance to Peter, although it was an appearance of the highest importance for the Easter faith of the early church.

In this older tradition the empty grave cannot have played a role. This is confirmed by the Pauline accounts. They represent a stage of the Christian proclamation when the message of Easter did not deal with the empty grave, nor with the physics of the Lord's body, but with the overwhelming experiences that were described as seeing the resurrected Christ.

With the fact of these experiences every investigation of the resurrection must begin. According to the New Testament they are the source of the Resurrection faith. When the critical historian has done all his sorting of the accounts, there remains this fact that cannot be shaken: Among the first Christians these were experiences that were described as a seeing of the risen Christ. These occurred at various places (Galilee, in and near Jerusalem, near Damascus), within a defined time but at various specific times (from the Easter appearance to Peter until the appearance to Paul), and to various persons and groups of persons (the Eleven, the Emmaus disciples, the Five Hundred). The people who had these experiences became convinced that Jesus had risen from the dead.

What are we to make of these experiences? Not much is gained if they are called "visions" and then classified within that psychological category, although the New Testament itself might give an indication in this direction (in Acts 26:19 Paul's Damascus experience is called an *optasia*, "vision"). With this we may have said something about their form but not their content.

We may make more progress with the help of Rudolf Otto's fine study in which he compares what happened to the disciples at Easter with what happened to the prophets, particularly with the call visions of prophetic religion. They certainly do have something in common. But even the experiences of prophetic religion are not explained by considering them visions from the psychological point of view. For what is essential in them is exactly that in which they differ from everything else that is called "vision" in the history of religions. We shall not get far in attempting to understand the experience of the prophets unless we recognize at the outset that there are true prophets and false prophets, authentic prophets and inauthentic prophets. The tools of psychology are no help at all for making this distinction. The psychologist of religion cannot tell why the experiences of Jeremiah are true prophecy while those of the "lying prophets" are not.

Nor is this distinction something that has been inserted later on from a dogmatic point of view. Demarcation against false prophecy belongs to the nature of all prophecy, as it sets itself off over against the spirituality of the ecstatic religions. The prophets are afraid they themselves may fall into error. Hence Amos' refusal of the title *nabi* ("prophet"). Therefore the prophets of Israel struggle against "the lying prophets," as also does Zarathustra. Therefore Mohammed early in his career feared that he might be a *kahin*.

How is the line to be drawn between true and false prophecy, between an actual call and an imagined one, between authentic revelation and the manifestations of a pneumatic enthusiasm, between the pure and the impure proclamation of the received "word"?

That is the theological problem of prophecy, to which already a pertinent review of the history of religions leads us. Even a genuine prophet can cease to be an instrument and messenger of God. The history of religions tells of a host of visionary and similar experiences. That among these there should be a special category of genuine prophetic experiences in which human beings are called to an office, to be proclaimers of God's Word—that is the riddle of prophecy.

If we test the nature of the Easter experiences by comparing them with the category of prophecy, we immediately see the contrast. What the prophets experienced is something that happened ever and again through the centuries. The Easter experience was confined to a single generation. What happens to a prophet happens to an individual. This may be the case with Easter, but it can also be the experience of a group (the two from Emmaus, the Eleven, the Five Hundred).

On the other hand, both types of experience have this in common, that they involve a call and mission. An office is conferred, in the one case that of a prophet, in the other that of an apostle. Not everyone had who the Easter experience became an apostle; this experience can also make a group of people into a church. No one, however, could be an apostle, according to the strict sense of the word, who was not "a witness to His resurrection" (Acts 1:22), although the New Testament does have a broader use of the term than this strictly theological usage of an apostle as a bearer of revelation. The more general usage includes itinerant preachers. According to 1 Cor. 15:7 Jesus appeared "to all the apostles." The apostolate and the Easter experience are inseparable, no less close than prophecy and the prophetic experience.

For understanding the Easter experience it is important to see it as an apostolic experience. The office of apostle, confined to a single generation of history, is something quite new when contrasted with prophecy. It is very significant that after the coming of Christ prophecy, while it does not disappear, becomes something quite different. In Christendom the office of prophet is an office within the church, certainly subordinate to the apostolate. "Built upon the foundation of the apostles and prophets" is said of the church in Eph. 2:20. The apostles come first.

The exclusion of prophecy as an independent factor of equal rank with the apostles and their witness did not take place without a struggle. But Montanism showed how necessary this exclusion was, this struggle between "Spirit and office," as it is usually called. For

16

Montanus laid claim to what was promised of the Paraclete in John, as did later also Mani and Mohammed.

The recognition that the revelation in Christ is not something inconclusive or relative stands and falls with the primacy of the apostolate over prophecy. Wherever prophecy asserts its independence and power, it is a threat to the finality of the revelation that happened once in history, of which the apostolic office bears witness. Christ's church is an apostolic, not a prophetic church. This does not mean, as some today suppose, a quenching of the Spirit, a constriction of religion within an ossified institution. Rather it expresses the conviction that revelation has taken place, that the word of God is no longer only given and assigned to a human being here and there, but that the Word has become flesh.

The apostolate was given once in a single generation. The office of an apostle goes along with the office of a prophet, and yet it is something quite different. The apostolic office, which founded the church, has the primacy over the prophetic office, which served to prepare for the church. The apostolic experience must therefore be something quite different from the prophetic experience, something unique, something for which there is no parallel in history. What happened for the apostles was the completion of the revelation that occurred in Christ, the experience of a happening, of a fact by which it is substantiated that Jesus Christ is Lord. This fact is stated with "The Lord is risen."

If this is so, then we must set aside the common misunderstanding of Easter which asserts that the disciples had only visions of Christ which prompted them to an assurance that their Master was living on, which prompted them to draw the conclusion that He was risen. Visions of Christ, regardless of how they are to be evaluated, have not been confined to those days. How are the Easter experiences different from other "visions and revelations of the Lord" (2 Cor. 12:1), of which also Paul knows?

The disciples could have arrived at the assurance that Jesus was somehow living on without those Easter days when something happened that changed their whole lives. When a loved and honored master is taken from his circle, it seems almost natural to feel that he somehow lives on after death. We have only to recall the significance of the death of Socrates for what people in the European tradition have thought about immortality. No, what happened with the disciples must surely have had a different content. Not "Jesus lives" but "Jesus is risen" is the real Easter message of the New Testament.

Something happened, God did something, something never heard of, something unique. This unheard-of event, this fact that can only be designated with the word "resurrection," is not some conclusion drawn from the Easter experience, something deduced, not even the assurance that Jesus lives on. However true that may be, it is not the essential point. The essential content and heart of Easter is that "Jesus is risen."

But what is meant by "resurrection"? What does it convey in the New Testament? What did Jesus mean when He spoke of the resurrection of the dead (and perhaps also of the resurrection of the Son of Man)? We will find the answer by considering where it was that the New Testament message of the resurrection was opposed and why. We know of this happening in Athens and in Corinth when Paul's mission brought him there. Why did they mock the resurrection in Athens? Why did some in the church at Corinth deny the resurrection of the dead? For one thing, any thought that the body might live again was repugnant to the Greek doctrine of the immortality of the soul. Such a notion was too utterly unphilosophical, too utterly not of the soul but of matter and the body. In 1 Cor. 15 Paul goes to no end of effort to defend the doctrine of the resurrection against such Greek objections. He shows its high spirituality, over against the misunderstanding that it is a materialistic idea. We modern people, for whose view of the world the idea of resurrection is also strange, may therefore be grateful that Paul was here forced to develop more fully what was for him a self-evident concept.

It would, however, be a mistake to suppose that what repelled the Greeks was only the question of matter and the body. Recall the scene in Athens that is so vividly pictured for us in Acts 17:31-32. Why did the interruption come when Paul said that God had raised Jesus from the dead? Was the thought of rising again really so intolerable to the Greeks? Why was the dying and rising again of Attis and Osiris not regarded as intolerable in the Greek world? Why did the Greeks of Paul's day accept without trouble the myths and cults of dying and rising deities and combine them with their belief in immortality, just as the older Greeks had done with the Dionysius religion?

No, it was not the idea of resurrection that was intolerable, but the message of a resurrection that was no myth. What repelled them was to hear of a resurrection that had happened at a particular time, an event that was above history and yet reached into history. We must be clear about what it means that when Christ was proclaimed this was a historical message. Although some mythological terms may

have been drawn into use, what was spoken of was the historical fact of a particular man who lived at a particular time in a particular place and whose death was a verifiable historical fact. That this man should be *the* revelation, this was intolerable to the Greeks, just as it is for moderns. When and where did the death of Osiris take place? The question has no sense. A myth tells of things that did not happen in history. A myth tells, to use the modern phrases, of necessary truths of reason, not of chance facts of history. We must never forget that ancient heathen religion had no thought of historical revelation. The death and resurrection of Jesus as a myth, as a parable of an eternal truth, this the Greeks could have accepted quite cheerfully—but not as a one-time historical event.

This leads us to a further point. The historical message of faith in Christ is at the same time an eschatological message dealing with the end of history. The resurrection of Jesus is bound up with the resurrection of the dead. Paul tells of this unmistakably in 1 Cor. 15 and alludes to it when he preaches on the Areopagus (Acts 17:31). At this point a chasm opens between the two views of the world, between the religious worlds of the Christians and of the Greeks. And at this point we learn to understand the nature of the resurrection.

The doctrine of the resurrection is not yet there when people expect that those who have died may return from the grave or their bodies come alive again. There is plenty of this in many primitive religions. Resurrection of the dead in its real sense is known only where it is seen as the culminating event of history. This is the case in the prophetic religions: Outside of Christianity we find it among the Parsees, in Judaism, and in Islam. Characteristic of this apocalyptic hope of resurrection is that it is not only for the individual but for all people. Resurrection is a cosmic event. It comes at the end of the world and means the beginning of a new creation. Death is thereby judged differently than among the Greeks. It is viewed not only as the end of an individual human life but also as a power that dominates the world. According to the doctrine of the resurrection, death is not simply the passing of the soul from one form of existence to another, as in India and among the Greeks (although it is that too), but death is the abhorrent disintegration of a human being. This way of looking at things does not make dying easy, but hard. The aim of the philosophical doctrine of immortality is to make dying easy, but the doctrine of the resurrection takes death with complete seriousness. The natural man's dread of death is not chased away by the consolations of philosophy.

In all this we may observe a difference in the way the body is valued. For the Greeks the soul is imprisoned, entombed, by the body. For the people of the New Testament the body is the temple of the Holy Spirit, a creation of God, and therefore His possession. The whole Biblical concept must have seemed childish and primitive to the Greeks, as it does to moderns. But that does not yet settle the matter. May not the primitive view of death, of dying, and of the body be the right one? This view is charged with being materialistic. But we may ask whether the materialistic view is not the one which considers the body as merely matter. Paul answers the charge quite clearly. Insofar as the body is merely matter it cannot inherit the kingdom of God. But it is not merely matter, not merely *sarx* (flesh), but something more. It is not higher or lower than the *psyche* (soul). Body and soul can belong to God or the devil. The life of the soul is in bondage to sin just as much as is the life of the body. The antithesis of godly and ungodly is not indentical with the antithesis of soul and body. Above both soul and body is the Holy Spirit (*pneuma hagion*), the Spirit of God, who is to be carefully distinguished from the natural spirit (*pneuma*) of man, the "ground of the soul," as it has been called.

The resurrection is the calling of the whole man, soul and body, out of death into life in the Spirit, just as he once was called to existence in the flesh in this transitory world. The resurrection is a new creation. (The Jewish and Persian apologists therefore liked to indicate the possibility of the resurrection by pointing to the miracle of creation.) As the creation of man cannot be separated from the creation of the world, or his existence from the existence of the world, so also the new creation of man is inconceivable without the new creation of the world, a world of which we are told: "Death shall be no more" (Rev. 21:4). This world, a new heaven and a new earth, corresponds to the human beings on whom the curse of having to die no longer remains.

These were more or less the thoughts which the people of the New Testament connected with the concept of the resurrection. From here we return to the question of Jesus' resurrection. It can be understood only when viewed in connection with the resurrection of the dead. Time and again Paul speaks of these as inseparable. As the Risen One, Jesus Christ is "the firstborn among many brethren" [Rom. 8:29]. "If there is no resurrection of the dead, then Christ has not been raised" [1 Cor. 15:13]. If He did not rise, then the dead also do not rise. If this connection is so close, then it becomes clear what the resurrection of Christ means: It is *the turning of old world to new world, the end of the former age and the beginning of the new, the dawn of the new world of eternity and of the Spirit.* The resurrection of Christ can be understood only as the event which fulfills history, as future that has become present. *It begins God's new creation. It ushers in the universal resurrection of the dead.* Here we glimpse the power of those Easter experiences by which the disciples became convinced that Jesus had risen from the dead. What they experienced was the fulfillment of all prophetic and apocalyptic expectations. What are the experiences of the prophets compared with these experiences? Did a prophet ever experience what the apostles and the first church then experienced?

If the resurrection of Jesus is to be understood this way, then we see why it is not pictured in the New Testament, why it cannot be described. It is incomprehensible and inexpressible, like the creation of the world and the incarnation of the Son. "The great deeds of God" no man can see. Only in their effects do they in some way reach into our world, into our reality. Only God through His Spirit can make us human beings sure of them. Since this is so, we are unable to describe the resurrection in more detail. The impossibility of giving it expression on the one hand and the need to bear witness of it on the other create the tension we find in the different accounts of the New Testament. We cannot get a consistent picture of what is said of our Lord's risen body by Paul and in the Gospels. Our knowledge cannot encompass the empty grave or the risen body of Jesus. We cannot relive what the disciples lived through at Easter.

Even if we knew all this, we still would know nothing about the resurrection itself. The heart of Easter is not in those "miracles." This is a grievous misunderstanding, although a very old and understandable one. *The* miracle of Easter is not the fact of the empty grave or our Lord's body as seen by Thomas but, lying behind all that, the act of the living God, who raised Jesus from the dead. In those "Easter facts" the final event of history somehow reaches into history. How far? About this there are, and probably always will be, differences of opinion. Not these "facts" but the event lying behind them, the act of God, is what the first church referred to when it went out into the world with the message: "The Lord is risen!"

3. The Exalted One

Only on the basis of the resurrection message can the confession be understood that Jesus is Lord. Yet it is profoundly significant that the New Testament separates the exaltation of Christ from His resurrection. As the Risen One, Christ would only have been the firstfruits of the dead (1 Cor. 15:20, 23), "the firstborn among many brethren" (Rom. 8:29). His resurrection would then be only the beginning of the resurrection of all the dead. There would basically be no difference between His resurrection and ours. While His being Lord would be unthinkable without the resurrection, yet it does not have its sole foundation there. Hence the New Testament makes the logical distinction between the resurrection and the exaltation. It is only a logical distinction insofar as both are actually inseparably connected. The ascension account in Acts 1 is not to be understood as minimizing this fact. The Risen One is the Exalted One. In raising Him from the dead God also exalted Him and "made Him both Lord and Christ" (Acts 2:24, 32 f., 36; 5:31).

The meaning of the exaltation was very early and clearly expressed with the words of Ps. 110:1: "The Lord says to my Lord, 'Sit at My right hand till I make Your enemies Your footstool.' " These words appear already at Mark 12:35 ff., and the other two synoptic gospels also have them in a controversy between Jesus and the Pharisees (Matt. 22:41 ff.; Luke 20:41 ff.). Even those who regard these words as inauthentic must yet agree that they go back to the earliest days of the Christian community, reflecting as they do the early sundering of church and synagogue. The words are also quoted in Acts (2:34 f.), in Paul (1 Cor. 15:25), and in Hebrews (1:13). The weight they carried is evidenced by their inclusion in the creed: He "sits at the right hand of God, the Father Almighty." The picture of sitting at the right hand of God, combined with the concept of the Son of Man according to Daniel, is already found in Jesus' answer to the high priest's question as to whether He was the Messiah: "I am; and you will see the Son of Man seated at the right hand of Power, and coming with the clouds of heaven" (Mark 14:62).

From all this we see that even the earliest faith in Jesus as the Messiah is linked with the thought of His exaltation. The Crucified One has ascended to heaven. As Son of Man and Judge of the world He shares in God's almighty power. Here it becomes clear how closely the idea of Messiah is related to that of Lord (*Kyrios*). If the crucified Jesus was seen to be the coming Messiah/Son of Man, then one had to think of Him as ascended to heaven. And as soon as this exaltation was thought of according to Psalm 110, the title "Lord" was given to Jesus. We do not know whether this psalm prompted the description of Jesus as Lord, but it surely facilitated it. What then is meant by the exaltation is clear. It means that Christ since His resurrection shares in the eternity, omnipresence, and omnipotence of God.

a. The Eternity of Christ

As the Exalted One, Jesus Christ shares in the eternity of God. This is expressed most clearly in the New Testament when certain formal religious phrases used to describe God's eternity are transferred to Him: He is the First and the Last, the Beginning and the End, the Alpha and the Omega. He is the one "who is and who was and who is to come"; "the same yesterday and today and forever." These formulas (cf. Rev. 1:4, 8; Heb. 13:8) have their home in the religious language of the Hellenistic Orient. Some are very old. "I am the First and the Last" goes back to Is. 41:4.

To get at what is meant by eternity we need briefly to consider the Biblical usage. The Biblical idea of eternity was developed in contrast to that of ancient Oriental astrology. In the latter view eternity is equal to the infinite sum of all aeons. The eternity that is ascribed to the gods of the Hellenistic East is abstracted from observation of the movement of the stars with their immeasurable periods of time. The world is eternal. If there is talk of a beginning and an end, it is never an absolute beginning and an absolute end. As the heavenly bodies at great intervals always return to where they were before, so existence repeats itself over great periods of time. From this comes the crowning notion of this view of the world, the idea of eternal return. Eternity here is the infinite sum of all aeons; eternity is unending time. Although traces of this may be found in some terms found in Biblical usage, notably in Ecclesiastes, what the Bible as a whole says about eternity is something quite different. Biblical religion makes a clear distinction between the world's time and God's eternity.

This way of putting it is found also in Persian religion and may have come from there. See the Persian distinction between *Zarvan akarana* and *Zarvan daregho-chvadata*. Oriental speculation may lie behind Plato's distinction between timeless, divine eternity and earthly time (*Timaeus*, 37, D). Aristotle again gives up the Platonic doctrine of eternity and identifies eternity with the unending time of the world.

The Bible's view of eternity excludes the open or hidden pantheism inherent in the astrological view of time and eternity sketched

23

above. Since God and the world are not identical, God's eternity is something other than the world's time. *The world's time, its aeon, is not infinite. It is bounded by its creation and its end.* There is an absolute beginning and an absolute end. God's eternity reaches beyond the world's time: "Before the mountains were brought forth, or ever Thou hadst formed the earth and the world, from everlasting to everlasting Thou art God" (Ps. 90:2). Cf. Ps. 102:25 ff.: "Of old Thou didst lay the foundation of the earth, and the heavens are the work of Thy hands. They will perish, but Thou dost endure . . . Thou art the same, and Thy years have no end." It is very significant that in Heb. 1:10 ff. these words are referred to Christ.

God is the First and the Last. One sees how the ideas of creation and of the end are connected with the strict monotheism which is opposed to all open and hidden pantheism. All these thoughts, which belong to the great prophetic religions, appear at the same time in history. (They are fully developed in the second part of Isaiah.) According to this conception the distinction between the world's time and God's eternity, between aeon in the sense of the world's time and aeon in the light of eternity, is not merely a quantitative one. They are not related to one another like finiteness and infinity. Rather, the distinction is qualitative. The distinctions between *sarx* (flesh) and *pneuma* (spirit), between death and life, between that which passes away and that which does not, between world and God are inherent in the distinction between time and eternity. They are incommensurable. As Emil Brunner says, "Eternity is just as little the continuation of time as it is that which precedes time. Eternity and time are incommensurable. Our temporality is a curved fragment of eternity" (*The Mediator*, p. 572). Eternity is not unending time but the opposite of time; it abolishes time. Thus the Slavonic Book of Enoch can say: "When the creation, which the Lord created, shall end, and every man shall go to the Lord's great judgment, then the seasons shall perish, and thence forward there will be no more years, nor months, nor days, and there will be no more hours thence forward, nor will they be reckoned, but there shall begin one endless age" (2 Enoch 65:6-8. Charles, *Pseudepigrapha*, p. 467).

What the New Testament says of Christ's eternity is to be understood in the light of this Biblical concept. Because Jesus Christ as the exalted Lord shares in God's eternity, therefore past, present, and future, the measures and boundaries of earthly time, no longer exist for Him. What is said of the eternal God is true also of Him: "Before the mountains were brought forth, or ever Thou hadst formed the earth and the world, from everlasting to everlasting Thou art God" [Ps. 90:2].

Theologians have often marveled at how early the thought of Christ's preexistence, that He existed "before all worlds," was expressed. It has been regarded as a philosophical speculation that is actually alien to the Christology of the New Testament. But the preexistence of Christ of which the New Testament speaks has in fact nothing to do with philosophy. It would be better not to use the term "preexistence," which derives from philosophy, and to substitute something like "eternal or supratemporal existence." From the standpoint of our thinking and our earthly, time-bound existence, the eternal is that which was before time as well as that which will be after time. This, however, is only an illustration and not a definition of the eternal. For what we think and say we have only temporal terms which have altogether been derived from our earthly, time-bound existence. Consider only the tenses of verbs, without which we cannot speak a sentence.

Also the language of the Bible has no other resources than these, and so must speak of the eternal in terms derived from time. So it speaks of the eternal as of that which was "from the beginning," "at the first," and "before the world was." God and Christ, wisdom (Prov. 8:22 f.), and God's love (Ps. 25:6) are "at the beginning of His work," "before the beginning of the earth," and "from of old." "Before the foundation of the world" the Father loved the Son (John 17:24). "Before the foundation of the world" God chose us (Eph. 1:4). The "before" in these statements contains more than merely the temporal distinction between before and after. It expresses the distinction between God's eternity and the world's time that is inexpressible by means of human language.

The eternity of Christ, His being beyond the limits of time, is the presupposition for the way the New Testament sees Christ already in "pre-Christian" history, a way of looking at things that is hard for us historically oriented modern people to grasp. Here we are not thinking so much of how the history of Israel, indeed the whole Old Testament, is allegorically related to Christ. (By the way, these allegories as we find them in Paul and Hebrews are not creative imagination at play, but rather a way of disclosing the very heart of this history.) Rather, we are thinking of the fact that what is said of the Lord (*Kyrios*) in the Old Testament is simply referred to Jesus Christ. As words of the Lord they are set beside the sayings of the historical Jesus and beside the words of the Exalted One as they are heard in the

Spirit by the seer of Revelation and by Paul. Similarly such events as the death and resurrection of Jesus are "eternalized" in a peculiar way. It is not that Jesus was the Crucified One, then became the Risen One, and now is the Exalted One. Rather, as the Exalted One is the Risen One, so He is also the Crucified One. His death is not something that belongs only to history, although it is certainly a historical event. As the Crucified One He is present among us.

We have finally resolved the apparent contradiction that we are waiting for the coming of the Lord and also know of His presence. It is simply not adequate to explain this as an addition of Hellenistic mystery religion to Palestinian eschatology. The apparent contradiction between the Coming One and the Present One has been implied from the beginning by confessing Him as Lord. The *Maranatha*, the prayer to the coming Christ, shows this, for this prayer presupposes that He to whom it is directed is already present, though unseen, in the midst of His congregation. Also here the distinction between before and after is lifted, and present and future have become one. The exalted Christ, He who shares in the eternity of God, stands above the world's time. His eternal being goes beyond the limits and measurements of earthly time.

The extraordinary difficulty these ideas create for us modern people lies in the great question: "How can we think both of the eternal being of the exalted Lord and of the temporal appearance of Jesus Christ?" The theological effort to think this through confronts a double danger. Either the eternal Christ is lost for the sake of the historical Jesus, or the reverse. Everything depends on the recognition that in Jesus Christ time and eternity become one, that eternity enters time, that God's revelation takes place in the world, that God became man. This is the miracle of God's revelation in Christ: The finite is capable of receiving the infinite, time is capable of receiving eternity, this age is capable of receiving the age to come (*finitum capax infiniti, tempus capax aeternitatis, saeculum hoc capax futuri saeculi*).

If this assumption is not admitted, then the revelation of which the Bible tells has not happened. For this revelation is bound up with things that happened in time: with the historical figures of the prophets, with the historical fate of the people of Israel and of the ancient world in general, with the Jesus of history who suffered "under Pontius Pilate" and died "outside the gate" of Jerusalem (Heb. 13:12), with the history of the apostles. The revelation has a temporal side that no speculation may set aside.

26

It has, however, also another side. What we see as happening in time is seen by God as happening in eternity. "The mighty deeds of God": the creation, the revelation through the prophets, the incarnation of Christ, His life on earth, His death, His resurrection and ascension, the founding of the church, the return of Christ, the judgment—all these are events having a double side, a temporal and an eternal. In their eternal aspect they are for us inconceivable; in their temporal aspect they are recognizable as acts of God only to faith. For only the believer sees, behind the temporal event, the act of God which goes beyond all human comprehension: behind the beginning of the world, the creation; behind the experiences of the prophets, the voice of God; behind the birth of Jesus, the incarnation of the Son; behind the earthly life of Jesus, the voice and activity of God; behind the death on the cross, the atonement; behind the Easter experiences of the disciples, the resurrection and exaltation; behind the end of the world, the judgment. Only for faith is the history of salvation truly the history of salvation. Faith knows that this history, whose temporal side it perceives, is the history of the acts of God and that what happens for us in time happens for God in eternity. For faith it is no tortured contradiction that Jesus Christ belongs to both time and eternity, but rather only an expression of the fact that He is true man and true God, that in Him the eternal God truly entered history.

b. The Lord of the Church

As the exalted Christ shares in God's eternity, so He also shares in His omnipresence and omnipotence. What has to be said about this can best be said if we begin with those aspects of His being which alone are knowable to us. That is the fact of the church. So we continue our meditation on the exalted Lord by speaking of Him as the Lord of the church. Only because we know Him as Lord of the church do we know Him to be the Lord and know about His kingdom. Dogmaticians speak of Christ's kingly office, as well as of His prophetic office and His priestly office. They go on to speak of His kingly office as threefold: the kingdom of power, the kingdom of grace, and the kingdom of glory. This is possible only out of the kingdom of grace, for it alone is an object of our experience—that is, the experience of our faith.

The exalted Lord and His church belong together. Only when the church appeared was He confessed as Lord. It is not insignificant that the Lord's name first appears in the form *maran, ho kyrios hemōn* ("our Lord"). What Luther says in his explanation of the Second Article about the personal relationship of the individual to Christ is perfectly correct and is also valid for the very early church: "I believe that Jesus Christ . . . is my Lord." Early also is the personal confession of the individual: "My Lord and my God!" (John 20:28). In the sense of this confession Paul can call himself the "slave" of Jesus Christ. But this is something secondary. Jesus is Lord first for His church and then for His servant. Jesus is "my Lord" only because he is "our Lord." Only as members of the church do we belong to Him. The Lord and the church belong so much together that the one is unthinkable without the other. One cannot speak of the Lord without also speaking of the church; and conversely, as soon as I speak of the church, I speak of the Lord. They belong together as head and body, as cornerstone and house, as vine and branches.

To understand this relationship between the Lord and the church we will begin with the word of Matt. 18:20: "Where two or three are gathered in My name, there am I in the midst of them." To be sure, this saying handed on by the earliest Palestinian church does not use the word "church." Yet it gives a classic description of the organic relationship between Christ and the church, one that exactly matches what we read in the epistles of Paul. The presence of the living Christ is constitutive of the church. But what is meant by this presence? Is it only a figurative expression when we speak of Jesus Christ as present in the midst of His congregation? Do we mean that our imagination makes Him real to us and that some influences of His earthly life reach into our lives? Beyond all doubt, the New Testament means something else when it speaks of the presence of Christ.

There may be help for us in understanding Matt. 18:20 from a Jewish statement that says something quite similar: "When two sit together and words of the Torah are between them, then the *shekinah* [the glory of God's presence] is between them" (Pirqe Aboth, 3, 2; cf. Strack-Billerbeck I, 794, on Matt. 18:20). Both statements, the Jewish and the Christian, speak of the real presence of the divine Being. In both this real presence is bound up with the holy Word (in the one with the name of Jesus called upon in prayer, and in the other with the holy Word of the Torah) and with the congregation. The place occupied by the *shekinah* (the personified Spirit of God) in the Jewish saying is occupied by the living Christ in the Christian saying. This is enormously significant. It matches what we read everywhere in the New Testament about the connection between Christ and the Holy

Spirit. Christ is present in that He is one with the Holy Spirit. Christ "according to the Spirit" (*kata pneuma*) is the exalted Lord (Rom. 1:4). The experience of His presence is mediated through the Holy Spirit. Only "by the Spirit of God" can one confess that "Jesus is Lord" (1 Cor. 12:3).

Here again we come upon a concept that was self-evident to the people of the Bible but which has been lost to modern man. Just as the Biblical concepts of resurrection and of eternity are hardly any longer understood in modern Christianity, so also the understanding of the Holy Spirit has more and more disappeared. One does not yet know who the Holy Spirit is if one knows the workings of the Spirit or of spirits as reported in the epistles of Paul. He tells of speaking in tongues, of prophecy, of visions, of things heard, of gifts of healing, of the power to do miracles, and of all sorts of gifts. Most of these phenomena do not belong only to Christianity but are found in many a religion. They are native to ecstatic religion, which is found all over the world. Here a person thinks of his powers and capacities as intensified into the supernatural because divinity is at work in him. Such primitive expressions of ecstatic religion were much prized in Corinth as evidence of possessing the Holy Spirit. Paul himself had experience of them, and yet he ranks them less than the silent working of the Spirit of Christ.

In making this distinction he does the same as the prophets of the Old Testament. They had such experiences too, and yet they decisively marked themselves off from the ecstatic seers and professional prophets. What is the significance of this distinction? It is connected with the distinction between true and false prophets and so also the scrupulous distinction between God and man—between what is truly God's doing and what is not.

Ecstatic religion discovered the *pneuma* (spirit). Spirit is a third thing in man in addition to body and soul. It is something in man by which he actually belongs to a world other than the empirical one. It is thought of either as a divine kernel dwelling within man or as something that at times comes over a person in the form of "enthusiasm" or "inspiration." This explains why "spirit" is used in different ways in the New Testament. There is a human spirit, there is also the Spirit of God (cf. 1 Cor. 2:10 ff.), and there are demonic spirits.

All psychology, unless it is content with a superficial analysis of the human soul, comes upon this inexplicable factor in man, a realm where things happen which psychological explanations fail to reach. What psychology can explain such phenomena as the poet's inspiration, the metaphysician's intuition or the mystic's experiences, to name things by which "spirit" can be made clear to modern man?

Ecstatic religion is different from prophetic religion, whose great work is to distinguish God from the world, true religion from false, God's world from the world of demons. The criterion by which the prophets and apostles tested the spirits has been called "ethical religion." If this means a religion that has understood the reality of sin in the presence of the holy God, then perhaps this expression may be useful.

When the prophetic religion of the Old Testament distinguished between true prophecy and false prophecy, it brought about the distinction between the Holy Spirit of God and whatever else may be called spirit. With the great prophets the doctrine of the Holy Spirit begins, although the term "Holy Spirit" comes only after the exile. Before this the term *Ruach Yahweh* (Spirit of God) was used.

The Holy Spirit, the true Spirit of God, makes a prophet to be a prophet. He will rest upon the Messiah (Is. 11:2). In the end-time He will be poured out upon all Israel and will make them truly God's people (Joel 2:28 f.; Ezek. 36:27; 37:14; 39:29). With the doctrine of the Holy Spirit the religion of the Bible before Christ gives its answer to the God-world problem. This doctrine opposes, on the one hand, all pantheistic and mystical religion, in which God and the world, or God and man, are openly or secretly identified. On the other hand, it opposes dualism, which separates God and the world to such an extent that there is no longer a relationship between them. (In the second part of Isaiah there is an attack against Persian dualism, 45:7.) The doctrine of the Holy Spirit recognizes the unchangeable difference between God and the world, between God and man; but it also knows that through His Spirit God works in the world, in man.

Thus far we have observed a doctrine of the Holy Spirit in which the distinction between God and the world and between God and man is impregnably clear and in which there is the recognition that God through His Spirit is at work in the world and in man. How intensely this problem was struggled with among the Jews is shown by the efforts to probe it philosophically and at the same time make it clear. There are the conceptions of the Word (*memra, logos*), of wisdom, and of God's glory (*shekinah*). In the prolog of John's gospel these are referred to the preexistent Christ. Along with what was believed about the Messiah, they are a preparation for the later Christology. It is not by chance that these conceptions from the Old Testament played so important a role in the church's christological controversies. We have only to recall how Arius and Athanasius argued about the interpretation of Prov. 8:22 ff.

Remarkably little attention has been given to what the doctrine of the Holy Spirit meant for Jesus. The battle He waged against the demons, which He asked His disciples to carry on, must have had an entirely different meaning for Him than for modern interpreters, for the ideas that lie at the root of this part of Jesus' life and work are foreign to them. How can we understand this conflict without recognizing that behind it stands a consciousness of the reality of the Holy Spirit more powerful than that possessed by any before or since who have claimed to possess the Spirit? What great meaning Jesus' experience at His baptism must have had for Him, when He knew that the Holy Spirit was resting on Him! John 1:32 emphasizes that the Spirit "remained on Him." Later (14:17) the disciples are promised: "He dwells with you, and will be in you." Are the events of Easter and Pentecost, the Easter experiences of the disciples, the beginnings of the church in Jerusalem, and early Christianity in Palestine even conceivable unless one assumes that behind them all there are great new experiences of the reality of the Holy Spirit (*pneuma*)? The first pneumatic church was the original church in Palestine and not, as some have supposed, the Hellenistic church of Paul's day. Just because the church in Palestine knew itself to be God's holy people living in the endtime, it knew it was in possession of the Holy Spirit. It was Israel "according to the Spirit."

What is said of the Holy Spirit in the New Testament, then, must be seen in the light of what was so powerfully experienced of the Spirit at the church's beginning. Without this the beginning of the church is totally unthinkable. The New Testament's view of the Holy Spirit can be stated in one sentence: Where Christ is, there is the Holy Spirit; where the Holy Spirit is, there is Christ. Christ and the Holy Spirit belong together. Faith can have no experience of the reality of the Holy Spirit unless it is somehow also an experience of the true living presence of Christ. There can be no faith in the present Christ, no confession that Jesus is Lord, unless it is mediated through the Holy Spirit.

This casts a new light on the history of God's revealing Himself. When men of God spoke, "moved by the Holy Spirit" [2 Peter 1:21], it was the eternal Christ who spoke in them. Therefore the Old Testament is to be understood only in the light of Christ, and so the church can regard it as its Holy Scripture. Wherever the activity of the Holy Spirit is spoken of, there one could also speak of the activity of Christ.

31

If the creation of the world cannot be thought of without the Holy Spirit, then it also cannot be thought of without the eternal Christ. Here is the inmost reason why the New Testament ascribes to Christ a role in the creation of the world. There are other, more incidental reasons, such as the application of Ps. 102:25 to Christ (Heb. 1:10).

All that is said in the New Testament about the Lord and about the Spirit has its key in the recognition that where the Lord is, there is the Holy Spirit, and where the Holy Spirit is, there is the Lord. Yet it would be mistaken to identify the two. There is indeed the daring statement: "The Lord is the Spirit" (2 Cor. 3:17). Yet if this were understood as stating identity, either the historical Jesus would be reduced to little more than a symbol and have no meaning of His own in contrast to the reality of the Holy Spirit, or the Holy Spirit would be reduced to a mere power. Against this the Augsburg Confession rightly protests, rejecting the view that the Spirit is a "movement which is produced in things" (I, 6). The *pneuma* is the Holy Spirit only when He is God Himself in His work, and not merely a power conferred by God or some operation of God. To deny the reality of the Holy Spirit as that of God actually present is inevitably to deny also that Jesus Christ is Lord. He would then be only a man endowed with divine power. The unhappy historicism of modern theology, which knows Christ only "according to the flesh" [Rom. 9:5], only the historical figure of Jesus of Nazareth, is a necessary consequence of losing the Biblical view of the Holy Spirit. If the Holy Spirit is no longer truly God, then neither is Jesus Christ, nor is He any longer the present Lord of the church. He may perhaps still be its founder, but that is not likely to last very long then either. The church then becomes a strange human institution which actually has suffered an incomprehensible apostasy from the great prophet of Nazareth and what He taught.

The faith of the New Testament is that Jesus Christ the Lord is present in His church, for He is one with the Holy Spirit. This is not the oneness of identity, or unity of person, but unity of being, as is expressed by *homoousios*. He is present as Lord of the church—we cannot experience Him in any other way. If we have spoken correctly about the relationship between Christ and the Holy Spirit, then what we have said of the Holy Spirit is true also of Christ: He is there *for us* only where the Word of God is.

The prophets' recognition of who the Holy Spirit is came from the Word of God that was entrusted to them. The fullness of the Holy Spirit was given to the earliest church from the Word, the Word become flesh. Paul's congregations, Christendom of all ages, experienced the reality of the Holy Spirit through the Word of the proclaimed Gospel of Christ. Whatever else may have been experienced in the first congregations or in later centuries, independent of this Word, has nothing to do with the Holy Spirit. Such phenomena were incursions of ecstatic and mystical religiosity, against which the apostolic church, and the church of all times, had to defend itself, and did so.

We may now recall what was said above regarding the protest in modern religious theory against the narrowing of revelation to something that happened once in the past, regarding the place of prophecy in the church and its subordination to the apostolic office, and regarding the alleged struggle between "Spirit" and "office." The binding of the Spirit to the Word belongs to the essence of Christianity as the religion of a revelation that has occurred only once. Since the Son of God became man, we know the Holy Spirit only as "another Counselor" (Paraclete/Comforter) who, proceeding from the Father and the Son, is given to God's church and remains with it forever [John 14:16]. The witness of this Paraclete is inseparably linked with the Gospel of Jesus and the apostolic proclamation of Christ.

The battle waged by the apostles against Hellenistic mysticism and by the church of the second century against Montanism is the same battle the Reformers waged against the unchurchly mysticism of the Enthusiasts. These maintained that the Holy Spirit is "experienced" "immediately," without the "external Word," by an "inner word" or an "inner light." Against all such the Augsburg Confession affirms that through Word and sacrament the Holy Spirit is given, "where and when it pleases God," to "those who hear the Gospel" (Art. V). When evangelical theology in our day does battle against the mystic-idealistic religious notions of the modern world, it is carrying on the same struggle.

The correct understanding of the New Testament, the purity of the Christian faith, and therewith the existence of the church depend on whether we understand anew that for us the Holy Spirit and Jesus Christ the Lord are present only where the Word of God, where the Gospel is. Wherever the Gospel is rightly proclaimed and the sacraments are rightly administered, that is, "according to the Gospel," there Christ the Lord is actually present. There He Himself calls us to repentance and faith, forgives us our sins, and incorporates us into His church, the congregation of justified sinners.

Only from this point of view can the essence of the church be understood. Where Christ is, there is the church (*ubi Christus, ibi ecclesia*). The actual presence of Jesus Christ, the exalted Lord, is the secret of the church. It is the ultimate difference between the church and all the religious associations of the world. For this reason the confession that Jesus Christ is Lord is the foundational confession of the church, the confession by which the church stands and falls.

Only within the church can this be understood. That Jesus Christ shares in the eternity, omnipotence, and omnipresence of God, that He, the Crucified and Risen One, the exalted Lord, is truly and personally present in His church according to His divine and human natures—those are statements that for the world outside the church make no sense at all, or at most are judged to be assertions of an immoderate religious fantasy. Only when we are in His church and in faith have experienced His power over us can we confess that "Jesus Christ is Lord," for "no one can say 'Jesus is Lord' except by the Holy Spirit" (1 Cor. 12:3).

Only in His church is it known what it means that He is Lord, and how glorious a Lord He is. Only as Lord of the church can we human beings in this age of the world recognize Him in faith. Well do we know that the Kingdom of Power is His too, that He is not only Redeemer and Lord of the human world but also of the whole creation, which waits for its redemption. This, however, we do not see, and we would get lost in speculation if we wanted to say more about it. We know also that the Kingdom of Glory is His too, that its now-hidden glory will one day be revealed and that someday "every knee will bow, in heaven and on earth and under the earth, and every tongue confess that Jesus Christ is Lord" [Phil. 2:10 f.]. But about this too we cannot give many details, because the Kingdom of Glory is substance of our hope and not data of our experience. Only as Lord of the church do we know Him already now.

So the original confession of Christians that Jesus is Lord is the foundational confession of the church. It confesses the living God, not the abstract God-concept produced by some system of philosophy, but the real God as He has revealed Himself. Whoever confesses that Jesus Christ is Lord confesses also the Father, who sent His Son into the world, gave Him into death for us, raised Him from the dead, and gave Him "the name which is above every name" [Phil. 2:9], the name *kyrios* ("Lord"). Such a person also confesses the Holy Spirit, in whom Jesus Christ is with us "always, to the close of the age" [Matt. 28:20].

Here lies a deep riddle for all human thought, one which the church with its doctrine of the Trinity has tried not so much to solve

34

theologically as to state. It is the riddle of the revelation of the living God in human history, the riddle of God's incarnation. The church in the days of the apostles was already aware of it and gave an answer, not with a philosophical theory but with this paradoxical confession of faith: "For us there is one God, the Father, from whom are all things and for whom we exist, and one Lord, Jesus Christ, through whom are all things and through whom we exist" (1 Cor. 8:6). That is the church's answer to what has been revealed, its everlasting confession.

THE THEOLOGY OF THE CROSS
Theologia crucis

Letters to Lutheran Pastors, No. 18
Jubilate 1951

Overshadowing all nations are the dark storm clouds that loom with the threat of World War III. At such a time all human life is dominated by a sense of uncertainty, now bound up with a general and alienating disillusionment. All the expectations and hopes that allowed individuals and nations to survive World War II have, within a few years, proven illusory. This great disillusionment actually stretches out over everything by which modern man has lived. Now, finally, the belief in progress with which humanity entered the 20th century lies in shambles. All the ideas and ideals for which men have fought and suffered since 1914, for which millions have gone to their death and for which they are now expected to die again, have turned out to be phantoms: nationalism and internationalism, fascism and pacifism, democracy and totalitarianism, liberalism and socialism, communism and patriarchalism. Is there a politician left whom we can take seriously as still believing in the ideals for which he would let millions perish?

The results of this general disillusionment—this destruction of the last things that human beings, estranged from the Christian faith, still had as substitutes for the lost religion—will be fearful. What is a man when he has nothing left to believe in?

As church people we are tempted to look at this situation with a certain complacency. Are not we the ones who have been telling modern man for a long time that this is how things must end? How often have we unmasked those ways of understanding the world, both philosophical and political, which promised a substitute religion! We have sounded forth the call to return to the faith of our fathers. What masses of theological works has this last generation produced, both in Europe and America, which analyze these modern substitute religions! How earnestly the attempt has been made to persuade people with practical apologetics, with the results of all that work! Many indeed have listened and turned. Poets, philosophers, physicians, scientists, and politicians have returned to the church. Many a gripping soul-history with a genuine conversion in its background has become known.

With some of our contemporaries, alas, one has the uneasy feeling that Christianity is for them only a substitute for the substitute religion they have lost. That is not for us to judge. Much rather we in the church should ask ourselves how it is with our own repentance (*metanoia*). It may be that our call to the world to repent falls on deaf ears because our preaching and our Christianity are perceived as also not free of illusions. The world has a sharp eye for spotting this. Can the Roman Church really expect Russia and the world to hear the call to repentance from the Madonna of Fatima? Can and should the world hear this call from the Pentecostal movement or the Salvation Army? What hearing can we expect for the still-strong Social Gospel as it proclaims the salvation of mankind by obedience to the Sermon on the Mount? Is it only hardness of heart when people do not heed the earnest preaching of repentance of a fundamentalistic Methodism? Perhaps they suspect that in all these proclamations there are illusions, very human illusions, dressed up in Christian clothes.

How do things stand with the proclamation of the Lutheran Church? Can we seriously assert that the preaching this last generation has heard from the Lutheran Church is free of human illusions, that it has been and is today none other than the proclamation of the pure Gospel in the sense of the Reformation? The great renewal of the theological understanding of the Lutheran doctrine of justification in German and Scandinavian Lutheranism since 1917 has certainly influenced preaching. But it was not enough to keep us from offering sacrifices in the house of God to the heathen gods of nation and race. This idolatry even drew support from what was taught about the orders of creation by theologians of the Luther Renaissance, and it claimed to be genuine Lutheranism. We must leave it to the Lutherans of other lands to give the names of the Baals to which they have offered sacrifice in their churches. Much might be learned from an analysis of the clouds of incense which rise up at the great church convocations.

All Christian churches, also those of the Lutheran confession, must face the fact that as they are today they do not live from the Gospel alone but also from human illusions. It must be clear to us that only a church that is free of illusions in what it proclaims can today speak the Gospel to a disillusioned world—the pure, that is, the real Gospel, and not a gospel that men have fashioned for themselves.

The question whether that is possible, whether the church can return to the pure Gospel in a reformation that it is always in need of, as Luther taught, has its quite concrete answer every time a sermon is preached. That is the enormous responsibility that rests in our day upon us pastors and upon each one of our sermons. We can ask ourselves no weightier question in today's situation of the world than the fundamental question of our office, "What shall I preach?" (Is. 40:6).

1

"Preach one thing: the wisdom of the cross." This is Luther's answer, in a fragment of a sermon of 1515 (WA, 1, 52 [American Edition 51, 14]), to this vital question. The wisdom of the cross, the word of the cross [1 Cor. 1:18], which the world calls great folly, is the actual content of Christian preaching, is the Gospel itself. So Luther, and with him the Lutheran Church.

Many Christians regard this as gross one-sidedness. The cross is only a part of the Christian message, along with others. The Second Article is not the whole Creed, and even within the Second Article the cross is only one fact of salvation among others. What a constriction of Christian truth Luther has been guilty of! Nowadays you can even hear Lutherans saying this sort of thing. How can true Christian theology be limited to a theology of the cross, as if there were not also a theology of the resurrection, as if the theology of the Second Article were not in need of being amplified by the Third, by a theology of the Holy Spirit and His work in the church and its means of grace and in the saints then and now?

Luther had a great deal to say about all these things. We have only to think of all he said and taught about the incarnation and the sacraments. What theologian before him had a deeper understanding of the First Article, of creation? How is it then that the *theologia*

38

crucis (theology of the cross) is charged with constriction and blamed for its one-sidedness?

Obviously the "theology of the cross" does not mean that for a theologian the church year shrinks together into nothing but Good Friday. Rather, it means that Christmas, Easter, and Pentecost cannot be understood without Good Friday. Next to Irenaeus and Athanasius, Luther was the greatest theologian of the incarnation. He was this because in the background of the manger he saw the cross. His understanding of the Easter victory was equal to that of any theologian of the Eastern Church. He understood it because he understood the victory of the Crucified One. The same can be said of his understanding of the work of the Holy Spirit.

Always it is from the cross that everything is understood, because hidden in the cross is the deepest essence of God's revelation. Because this is so, Luther's *theologia crucis* (theology of the cross) wants to be more than just one of the many theological theories that have appeared in Christian history. It stands against its opposite, the prevailing theology in Christendom, the *theologia gloriae* (theology of glory), as Luther calls it, and claims to be that right and Scriptural theology with which the church of Christ stands and falls. Only of the preaching of this theology, Luther maintains, can it be said that it is the preaching of the Gospel. What is this theology of the cross?

2

It was a long journey the church had to travel until in Luther's theology of the cross it reached the full understanding of the cross of Christ. In the ancient church the cross seems, as has often been remarked, to have played no very great role. Certainly the church of the first centuries, as in all ages, lived from the death of Christ on the cross. And it was aware of this. Every Sunday, every celebration of the Eucharist, made the Lord's death a present reality. Hardly any passage of the Old Testament is quoted as often by the fathers as Isaiah 53. Already in the second century the making of the sign of the cross was firm Christian usage. However, the pictures which tell of salvation present the types of Christ from the Old Testament. The beginnings of the presentation of the Passion in the visual arts of the ancient church came hesitantly, and then as one of the many happenings in the gospels. Theology itself did not seem to know how to deal with Christ's death on the cross.

When the great question of theology was put, "Why did God

become man?" (*Cur Deus homo*), it was asking about the reason for the incarnation and not about the reason for the death of Jesus. The doctrine of the cross—not yet understood as a doctrine in its own right—was included in the doctrine of the incarnation. It is also included in the mystery of the resurrection. What we call Good Friday and Easter were celebrated together in the ancient church as the Paschal mystery (*Pascha*, Passover). For the ancient church the essential fact of salvation was the incarnation. As Irenaeus put it, "For the sake of His immeasurable love He became what we are, so that we might become what He is." And the beginning of our salvation, of our coming alive, is His resurrection.

For the ancient church, as still for the Eastern Church, the cross is hidden in the miracle of Christmas and in the miracle of Easter. It disappears in the bright light of these festivals. You can hardly see the cross for the brightness of the divine glory. Even long after artists began to portray Jesus as the Crucified One, the cross was still almost blotted out by this glory. When the ancient world gave way to the early Middle Ages and the omnipotent Christ (*Christos Pantokratōr*) was replaced by the Crucified One on the church's triumphal arch above the altar, He remained very much the triumphant King. The Christ whom we see in ancient churches and the Romanesque churches of the early Middle Ages does not suffer; He triumphs. When the cross appeared everywhere in public after the time of Constantine, it did not tell of Christ's suffering and death. It was a sign of victory. "In this sign you will conquer." (*In hoc signo vinces.*) "The royal banners forward go; the cross shines forth in mystic glow." (*Vexilla regis prodeunt, fulget crucis mysterium.*)

Why is this so? How can we explain this limitation of ancient Christianity and its theology? One reason, to be sure, is the immense wealth of God's revelation in Holy Scripture. Centuries cannot exhaust it. We cannot expect the church of the first ecumenical councils to have settled right away what troubled the Western Church in the Middle Ages. Yet the horizon of their lives and their thought did play a part in determining which questions the ancient fathers chose to deal with. They were Greeks, or Orientals who spoke and thought as Greeks. They still lived in the Greek world of thought and were not free of the idealistic way of looking at man. Even the great Athanasius did not realize "how great is the weight of sin" (*quanti ponderis sit peccatum*). You can find Pelagianism in them all. At bottom, as for Dostoevsky and all of Orthodox Russia, a sinner is a poor sick person who must be cured with patience and love. This in contrast with the Roman mind, which sees a sinner as a lawbreaker who needs "justification" and discipline. But how can the cross be understood without knowing who and what brought Christ to the cross: "I caused Thy grief and sighing by evils multiplying as countless as the sands"? Here is the reason why the ancient church and the Eastern Church have never come to a theology of the cross.

3

The theology of the cross belongs to the West. Like every proper theology it begins with the liturgy. These liturgical beginnings indeed have their roots in the East, but in the Syrian rather than the Greek church. Could the closer relationship of the Syrian church with the language and way of thinking of the Old Testament explain the better understanding of the Old Testament Gospel of the Lamb of God? The Agnus Dei was introduced into the Roman Mass about A. D. 700 by a pope of Syrian background; the inclusion of the "Lamb of God" in the Gloria also comes from the East.

The Syrian church is near Jerusalem, the place where our Lord's death is most naturally and particularly pondered. There the Church of the Holy Sepulcher, built by Constantine, housed what were regarded as relics of the holy cross. It became the goal of pilgrims from all parts of Christendom and prompted the veneration of the cross which now spread throughout the whole church. In the West it centered at Rome, in the Church of "Holy Cross in Jerusalem." This veneration of the cross is still today a part of the Roman liturgy for Good Friday. We might perhaps call it the oldest form of the theology of the cross. By the roundabout way of this veneration of the cross and of its relics, devotion to the Crucified One became an essential part of Western piety in the Middle Ages.

Still part of the Roman liturgy for Good Friday are the two great hymns of the cross, "Sing, My Tongue, the Glorious Battle" (*Pange lingua*) and "The Royal Banners Forward Go" (*Vexilla regis prodeunt*). They are hymns to the cross, not to the Crucified. Venantius Fortunatus, who wrote them around the year 600, was moved by the enthusiasm generated by the relics of the cross which at that time Emperor Justin II had given to the Frankish queen Radegunde. "Sing, My Tongue" exalts the cross as a trophy and sign of victory (*crucis trophaeum*), addressing it as the holy wood, the holy tree of Paradise which became the instrument of salvation. In this expression of an ancient Christian thought one may perhaps even find something of the cult of holy trees among the Germanic tribes:

> Sola digna tu fuisti
> Ferre pretium saeculi
> Atque portum praeparare
> Arca mundo naufrago,
> Quam sacer cruor perunxit
> Fusus Agni corpore.

> Thou alone wast counted worthy
> This world's ransom to sustain,
> That by thee a wrecked creation
> Might its ark and haven gain,
> With sacred blood anointed
> Of the Lamb that hath been slain.

In the same way the powerful song of victory "The Royal Banners Forward Go" addresses the holy tree:

> O crux, ave, spes unica,
> Hoc passionis tempore
> Auge piis iustitiam
> Reisque dona veniam.

> O cross, our one reliance, hail!
> So may thy power with us avail
> To give new virtue to the saint
> And pardon to the penitent.

It was a long, circuitous way that 500 years later led to the *Salve, caput cruentatum* ("O Sacred Head, Now Wounded"), the greeting of the High Middle Ages to the Crucified One.

If we reflect on these early expressions of a theology of the cross, we see that they are typical examples of what Luther later called a theology of glory. The cross is a direct revelation of the glory of God in the world. Triumphantly it leads on the victorious armies of the Christian emperor and the hosts of the church militant ready for battle. As the demons once fled from the sign of the cross, so now the enemies of Christ fall to the ground before the emperor's standards with the cross upon them, or before a reliquary with a piece of the cross inside. Who can withstand the power of this sign? With the sign of the cross victory is always yours, because in it God's power in the world becomes visible.

Something very profound happened in the inner life of Christendom when for the first time in the churches and monasteries of Europe the *suffering* of the cross was understood. This change becomes visible in the representations of the Crucified, who now no longer stands as victor at the tree of the cross but hangs there suffering, later even writhing in agony and dying. This change took place in the late Middle Ages, when the great realistic crucifixes hung in the high choir of the Gothic churches replaced the triumphing Christ. The depth of Christ's suffering is deeply felt and experienced. The lowly Christ, the God-man in His deepest humility, becomes mankind's Brother. It became an ideal of medieval Christian piety to fashion oneself like Christ (*imitatio Christi*), even to the point of mystically experiencing all the agonies of the cross. Certainly it was only a narrow stratum of church people who experienced this, but all were affected by this piety. The liturgy and the way churches were built made sure of this.

It is significant that the discovery of the suffering and death of Christ as a fearful reality went hand in hand with a new realization of the seriousness of sin and of its forgiveness. There is nothing to equal this in the ancient church. Much can be said against what was taught about sin and its forgiveness in the Middle Ages. No one at that time grasped the depth of the Biblical understanding of sin. The whole system of penance was faulty, yes, a denial of the Gospel. Yet the observation of Claus Harms remains true: At that time people at least still felt sin and let forgiveness cost them something, and therefore the Middle Ages stood higher than the modern world.

"How may I come to have a gracious God?" This question moved the theology of the Latin church for a thousand years before it became the question of the Reformation. For centuries this question brought into the monasteries the most pious people of the Middle Ages, until it became the life-and-death question of the last great monk of the Middle Ages. During those thousand years Christians learned *that* both belong together: the sin of the world and the Passion of Christ, my sin and Christ's death on the cross. It was not yet possible, however, to answer the question as to *how* they belong together. The probing of this question produced the medieval theology of the cross.

Its greatest work is the pious Anselm's, *Cur Deus homo?* ("Why Did God Become Man?"). It is small, chaste, with a childlike simplicity, and yet unspeakably deep. Much can and must be said against his theory, against the attempt to show that the wonder of all wonders is reasonable, the attempt to figure out how God had to act and how much forgiveness cost Him, and other things. What cannot be denied is that here for the first time the vicarious satisfaction of Christ (*satisfactio vicaria*) was set down with profound theological thought and penetration. There were already theologians in that day who objected to it, as also many in our day. But the church has always ignored this protest and gone on with its work.

It is a remarkable fact that the doctrine which states that the death of Christ renders satisfaction for the sins of all mankind is the only doctrine of the Middle Ages that has won general acceptance. The medieval doctrines of sin and grace have remained in dispute. The dogma of transsubstantiation has remained confined to the Roman Church. All doctrines of the 16th century are confined to parts of Christendom. Not so Christ's vicarious satisfaction. Without adopting it from one another this has been included in their confessions as a doctrine of the church by Lutherans, by the Reformed, by Anglicans, and by Catholics.

In earlier times this was nowhere the case. Indeed the Nicene Creed and all Christendom with it teaches that the eternal Son of God, "for us men and for our salvation came down from heaven ... and was made man." But as to what "for us men and for our salvation" means, no doctrine is set down until Art. IV of the Augsburg Confession declared that Christ "by his death made satisfaction for our sins." The Reformed confessions teach practically the same thing, and so did the Council of Trent, which says of Christ that He "made satisfaction for us to God the Father" (Session 6, ch. 7). This is the actual contribution of the Middle Ages to the theology of the cross.

5

What was Luther's contribution to the theology of the cross? We may at first be inclined to find it in the strength of faith with which the budding Reformer appropriated to himself the entire comfort of Christ's atoning work. We must not forget, however, that there was faith in the merit of Christ—and the comfort of such faith—also in the Middle Ages.

Thomas Aquinas, when he was not yet 50 years old, died on his way to the Council of Lyon. When he received the Lord's Supper for the last time, he said, "I receive you, ransom price of my soul. For love of you I have studied and worn myself out. You I have preached and taught...." Thus the greatest thinker of the Middle Ages took leave of the uncompleted work to which he had given his life. Forgotten is all the wealth of his philosophical and theological knowledge. His system, which takes in heaven and earth, world and super-world, has now shrunk to the "one thing needful." Now, like Paul, he knows only "Jesus Christ and Him crucified" (1 Cor. 2:2), whose body and blood he receives for the last time on this earth, the price paid to redeem his soul. This Christ is the content of all theology. Forgotten is the theology of glory of the half-heathen proofs for the existence of God at the beginning of the *Summa theologiae*. Forgotten is the belief in the abilities of the natural man. Forgotten is the "triumph of theology" which Thomas celebrated in overthrowing Averroism, which had become a subject of art.

We dare never forget this genuinely Christian, evangelical side of the Middle Ages if we would rightly understand the Reformation. The original evangelical elements that are preserved in the Mass, with its "You alone are the Holy One" in the Gloria, the "Not weighing our merits, but pardoning our offences" in the Canon of the Mass, the Kyrie and the Agnus Dei, the Words of Institution and the formula of Baptism, the "King of majesty tremendous, who dost free salvation send us" in the Mass for the dead, the constant pointing to the thief on the cross—all this, as Luther recognized, sustained the life of the church in the Middle Ages, and sustains it still in Catholicism today. We should never forget that "by grace alone" (*sola gratia*) is a possibility also in Roman Catholicism, though only one possibility among others, and only in such a way that it can never become "by faith alone" (*sola fide*). Whatever else the Roman Church may be, it wants to be—and is—church of the cross, church of the Crucified One. His sacrificial death means more in its life and thought than in the life and thought of many a Protestant church. Only God knows whether in our day there are not many more Catholics who die with faith in the saving merit of Christ than Protestants.

Luther, however, was obviously more than a Roman Catholic Christian who, like many of his fellow believers and perhaps with unusual strength, believed in the Crucified One as his only salvation. His theology of the cross is something different from that of devout Christians of the Middle Ages. Where does the difference lie? The difference becomes apparent where Luther distinguishes the theology of the cross from the theology of glory. While Luther in the deep experiences of his struggle for a gracious God was learning to understand what the cross of Christ means for us human beings, he came to understand, as no one before him, the deepest nature of the revelation of the cross. He saw something in the cross of Christ which before him, as far as we know, no one since the days of the apostles had noticed. He saw not only the depth of God's wrath and the magnitude of His love, but with a grasp of both he probed the deep secret of the way God comes to us human beings, the secret of how He deals with man, the mystery of revelation itself.

6

What is the secret of God's way of revealing Himself? We want to see God and cannot. Even God's great saints cannot. "Show me Thy glory," Moses begs God (Ex. 33:18). The answer he gets is: "You cannot see My face, for man shall not see Me and live" (v. 20). One thing God will grant His servant. God's glory will go past him, and then he may look. "You shall see My back, but My face you cannot see" (v. 23). We know how Luther used this passage to make clear how God may be known. We cannot see God's face, His glory, no matter how much we may want to or how hard we may try.

The attempt to know God as He is, whether by contemplating the world, by mystical experience, or by philosophical speculation, is the theology of glory. It is the theology of natural man, of heathen and Turk, of philosophers, and sadly, sadly also of professors of theology. As Christians they should really know better. But "we theologians," as Luther remarks in a scholium on Ps. 66:17, "commonly mention the holy name of God," in which we were baptized and before which heaven and earth tremble, "so irreverently, especially in our arguing and even in our praying. . . . We think that the same verbosity and boldness should be transferred to divine matters." We speak of the Holy Trinity "the way a cobbler argues about his leather" (WA 3, 382 [American Edition 10, 322]). God becomes subject matter, the topic about which we talk. But whoever talks about a subject must stand above it, must be "master of his subject." Thus all theology, as Luther rightly saw, stands in constant danger of losing the right relationship with God. "He who wishes to philosophize by using Aristotle without danger to his soul must first become thoroughly foolish in Christ" (... *necesse est, ut ante bene stultificetur in Christo*). Thus Luther says in Thesis 29 of the Heidelberg Disputation (WA 1, 355 [American Edition 31, 41]). Otherwise he will become a theologian of glory, and that is no true theologian at all.

These two theologies which Luther distinguishes, the theology of glory and the theology of the cross, are not two stages of one and the same theology. They do not enlarge each other as do the natural and the revealed knowledge of God in those systems, Catholic and Protestant, constructed by dogmaticians under the influence of Aristotle. Much rather they exclude each other as false and true theology.

"He is not worthy of being called a theologian who perceives the invisible things of God as intelligible through the things that He has made [Rom. 1:20]. Rather, he is worthy of being called a theologian who perceives the visible things of God, His backside [Ex. 33:23], as intelligible through sufferings and the cross." These are the famous Theses 19 and 20 of the Heidelberg Disputation. Luther does not deny that such invisible things of God as "His power, His wisdom, His justice, His generosity, and so on" can be seen in the works of His creation, as he clarifies in his explanation of Thesis 19. What he does deny is that such knowledge is useful. It makes "neither worthy nor wise." It does not change our relationship with God. The explanation of Thesis 20 develops the thought that men have misused the knowledge of God which they have from what He has made. They have thus become fools. The knowledge of God from His works has never kept anyone from falling away from God and becoming an idolater. So it has pleased God to save those who believe through the folly of what is preached. This preaching is the word of the cross (1 Cor. 1:18 ff.).

While the theology of glory understands and sees the invisible things of God by the works of creation, it is said of the theology of the cross that it sees and understands the visible and back-side things of God by the suffering and the cross. The theologian of glory observes the world, the works of creation. With his intellect he perceives behind these the invisible things of God, His power, wisdom, and generosity. But God remains invisible to him. The theologian of the cross looks to the Crucified One. Here there is nothing great or beautiful or exalted as in the splendid works of creation. Here there is humiliation, shame, weakness, suffering, and agonizing death. But this appalling and depressing sight shows the visible part—the back—of God (*visibilia et posteriora Dei*). He remains invisible in the things that He has made. Here on the cross (*per passiones et crucem*) He becomes visible, that is, as visible as God can become visible to man, the way He became visible to Moses when God let him look at Him after He had passed by. What is visible of God is the back of God.

Thereby the unique meaning of the cross is established. In creation we do not see God. But we see Him on the cross—that is, as much as a human being can see Him. Therefore the cross is *the* revelation of

God, and the theology of the cross is alone worthy to be called theology.

In the explanation of the 20th thesis of the Heidelberg Disputation Luther says: "In John 14 [:8] . . . Philip spoke according to the theology of glory: 'Show us the Father.' Christ forthwith set aside his flighty thought about seeing God elsewhere and led him to himself, saying, 'Philip, he who has seen me has seen the Father' [John 14:9]. For this reason true theology and recognition of God are in the crucified Christ" (WA 1, 362 [American Edition 31, 53]). This last thought is repeated in the explanation to the next thesis: "God can be found only in suffering and the cross" [ibid.]. Here is a bedrock statement of Luther's theology and that of the Lutheran Church. Theology is *theology of the cross*, nothing else. A theology that would be something else is a false theology.

7

The cross is *the* revelation. It is the only place where God makes Himself visible. What do we mean when we say that? What does Luther mean when he says we can find God nowhere else than in the Crucified One? What is unique about God's presence on the cross?

To understand this, let us ask, "What is revelation?" We might say that revelation happens when something that is hidden comes out of its hiddenness. The revelation of God would then be when God comes out of His hiddenness. For God is hidden, as is the entire content of faith, the "things not seen" of Heb. 11:1, so often quoted by Luther. God remains hidden for us as long as we live on earth. His Word tells us that He "dwells in unapproachable light" [1 Tim. 6:16]. He also said that He "would dwell in thick darkness" (1 Kings 8:12). He is a God who hides Himself (Is. 45:15). His face no one can see (Ex. 33:20; John 1:18; 1 John 4:12). Only in the light of glory "we shall see Him as He is" (1 John 3:2), "face to face" (1 Cor. 13:12; Rev. 22:4).

But although God is hidden from our eyes, He does reveal Himself through His Word. He speaks to us human beings, and we can hear His Word. So God's way of revealing Himself in this world is by way of His Word.

"In many and various ways God spoke of old to our fathers by the prophets; but in these last days He has spoken to us by a Son." He is more than a prophet, for "He reflects the glory of God and bears the very stamp of His nature" (Heb. 1:1-3). He is the eternal Word who from the beginning is the content of every proclaimed and written

48

word of God. Of Him it says: "The Word became flesh . . . we have beheld His glory" (John 1:14). So the revelation in the Word becomes the *incarnation*. Therefore Jesus Christ, the Word (Logos) become flesh, is *the* revelation of God in this world. Only in Him, the eternal Word, does God step out of His hiddenness. He is the content of all the divine Word; His incarnation makes the Word visible. The man Jesus Christ is the visible Word (*verbum visibile*). Whoever sees Him sees God as much as God can be seen in this world.

From this point of view we can now understand what Luther confesses of the cross. If God would reveal Himself, make Himself visible, He cannot show Himself "as He is." He cannot show His uncovered glory. No human being could bear the sight of the unveiled God (*Deus nudus*). He chooses the covering of human nature. So the incarnation is both a *revelation* of God and a *covering* of His glory. The hidden God (*Deus absconditus*), the God who is for us the eternal, invisible God, becomes the revealed God (*Deus revelatus*) in Jesus Christ. This revelation, this uncovering, for that is what revelation means, is at the same time a covering.

Hence we can see how Luther can speak of God as hidden in two ways—God is hidden to the extent that He has not revealed Himself, and God is hidden when He reveals Himself in Christ. When God became man He was revealing Himself and at the same time covering Himself. He was

> The everlasting font of good
> In garb of mortal flesh and blood.

Nowhere is God more deeply covered and hidden than in the Passion. Gethsemane and the cry of dereliction on the cross shatter every attempt to twist the Gospel into a triumphal epiphany of some savior-god in the manner of the ancient mystery religions, or into a heroic epic. How often the theology of glory has tried to control the Gospel! The miracles have been particularly misunderstood in this way. To be sure, Jesus "manifested His glory" in them, as we are told in the account of the wedding at Cana. But it says explicitly: "*His disciples* believed in Him." Not the wedding guests, nor the five thousand whom He fed, nor the sick whom He healed, nor even those whom He raised from the dead believed in Him. Also these deeds were both a revealing and a covering of His divine majesty; only in faith did His disciples see His glory. His resurrection also was no demonstration for the world. The empty grave as such convinced no one who did not believe in Him. It could be explained away, as were also His miracles of healing (Matt. 27:64; Luke 11:28).

Faith always deals with what is hidden. Also the faith of the apostles and of the apostolic church that Jesus is Lord was faith in His hidden glory, in God veiled in flesh, in the true God in the form of true manhood. Nowhere, however, is this hiddenness more profound than in the cross. *Cruce tectum* ("hidden under the cross") is Luther's formula for this fact. Hidden under the cross is the divine majesty of Christ before His resurrection and exaltation. Hidden under the cross is His kingdom, "whether it be revealed or hidden under the cross" (Apology VII & VIII, 18). So too is the church: "The Church is hidden, the saints are unknown" (WA 18, 652 [American Edition 33, 89]). It cannot be otherwise. "It is necessary that everything which is believed should be hidden" (WA 18, 633 [American Edition 33, 62]). The cross and faith belong together. Cross-theology is always faith-theology. The cross demands faith *contrary to what our eyes see.*

If the cross is the place where God reveals Himself in hiddenness, then it is also the place where God's revelation is most repugnant to our reason. Measured by everything the world calls wisdom, as Paul already saw, the word of the cross is the greatest foolishness, the most ridiculous doctrine that can confront a philosopher. That the death of one man should be the salvation of all, that this death on Golgotha should be the atoning sacrifice for all the sins of the world, that the suffering of an innocent one should turn away the wrath of God—these are assertions that fly in the face of every ethical and religious notion of man as he is by nature. Already the presupposed doctrine of universal sinfulness is for the world something that cannot even be discussed, because it would mean the end of philosophical ethics.

Now Holy Scripture declares that just this "foolish" preaching of the cross is the wisdom of God which "will destroy the wisdom of the wise" of this world [1 Cor. 1:18 ff.]. Here between the wisdom of God and the wisdom of the world there is a complete and unbridgeable contradiction. What is foolishness to man is regarded as wisdom by God and vice versa.

In his defense against every attempt of the theology of glory to wipe it out, Luther plumbed the depths of this contradiction deeper than any theologian before or after him. "A theology of glory calls evil good and good evil. A theology of the cross calls the thing what it actually is" (Heidelberg Thesis 21 [American Edition 31, 41]). What a man regards as good can be sin in the eyes of God, for instance an Aristotelian ethicist's striving for virtue. What human wisdom considers good fortune and therefore strives for— health, success, affluence—these things God in His wisdom may see as harmful for a person's good and so deny them. In God's judgment sickness, failure, and poverty may be far better. And God's judgment is not mistaken, even when it contradicts all human reason. There can be no good, as we see things, in someone lying for years in a sickbed with an incurable ailment and then slowly and painfully dying. Yet God may see something very good in such an apparently meaningless fate. "When God makes alive, he does it by killing, when he justifies he does it by making men guilty, when he exalts to heaven he does it by bringing down to hell," Luther says in *The Bondage of the Will* about God's dealings that cannot be comprehended by our reason (WA 18, 633 [American Edition 33, 62]).

"By putting to death He brings to life" (*occidendo vivificat*): This we learn to believe under the cross of Christ. Our eyes see there only the suffering, the weakness, the agony of being forsaken by God, the disgrace, the crushing triumph of evil, and the victory of death. But for faith all these things are only the *visibilia Dei*, what God lets us see. Hidden deep within it all is the great event of the reconciliation between God and mankind, the victory of the world's Redeemer, which must be believed against all appearances and against our reason's doubting question, "How can this possibly be?"

8

These are the basic thoughts of Luther's theology of the cross, although we have by no means exhausted its entire content. What has been said may be enough, however, to prompt us to immerse ourselves anew in the basic thoughts of Lutheran theology. To us in our day this theology has especially much to say, for we live in a time when the illusions of the world—and also very many illusions of the Christian world—are crumbling. How often have we not heard that the Christian message is antiquated, that what is preached in church does not impress people anymore? There is some truth in this. What came out of the theologies that were popular among Protestants at the beginning of this century, and was preached in many churches as if it were the Gospel, all this is now antiquated indeed. It is the theology of glory in all its forms—and every confessional grouping of Christians has developed its version of such theology—which has been put to confusion by the course of world history, by the mighty judgments of God, which fall also upon the church.

Consider for a moment the messages that have been coming out of the big world conferences and organizations since the beginning of this century. How God has judged these great proclamations inspired by a boundless theology of glory, from the "evangelization of the world in this generation" to the various forms of the "century of the church"! No confessional grouping escapes this judgment. God Himself has sent us into the hard school of the cross. There, on the battlefields, in the prison camps, under the hail of bombs, and among the shattered sick and wounded, there the theology of the cross may be learned "by dying" (*moriendo*), as Luther says. To those whose illusions about the world and about man, and the happiness built on these, have been shattered, the message of the cross may come as profoundly good news.

All that we think and do in the church has to be cleansed by the theology of the cross if we are to escape the perils of a theology of glory. As it is true of the church that "The Church is hidden, the saints are unknown" [Luther, American Edition 33, 89], so also is her inmost life "hidden under the cross." As the church of Christ is hidden, so also is the righteousness and holiness of the believers. Hidden is the working of God in the means of grace. Hidden under the human words of Scripture and its proclamation is the Word of God. In the Lord's Supper the body and blood of Christ are hidden under the earthly elements. Always, however, this hiddenness is the hiddenness of His actual presence. The cross of Christ is not just a sign, but reality, because the Crucified One is not just a picture of God, but God Himself, God incarnate, the revealed God in the hiddenness of true humanity.

Now our preaching of the cross will evoke faith only if people notice that it is not the proclaiming of earnest theoretical principles which we have arrived at amidst clashing world views. The theology of the cross is never a Christian *philosophy*, as is always the case with the theology of glory. I cannot stand over against the One on the cross as an objective observer and give my judgment on Him. Rather, it is He who judges me—condemns me, acquits me.

Here lies the reason why the theology of the cross has such a terribly practical side. To believe in the cross always means also to carry the cross. A yes to the cross of Christ is also a yes to my cross. If this is not so, we are only playing games. It is not by chance that whenever Jesus spoke of His cross to His disciples He also thought of the cross which they would have to bear in following Him (Matt. 16:21-24).

According to Luther [*On the Councils and the Church*] "the holy possession of the sacred cross" belongs to the marks by which one can recognize the church, the people of God: "They must endure every misfortune and persecution, all kinds of trials and evil from the devil, the world, and the flesh (as the Lord's Prayer indicates) by inward sadness, timidity, fear, outward poverty, contempt, illness, and weakness, in order to become like their head, Christ" [WA 50, 641 f.; American Edition 41, 164]. The theologians of the cross should be the first to say yes to this, for they teach with Luther that thereby "the Holy Spirit not only sanctifies his people, but also blesses them" [American Edition 41, 165].

Do we lead our congregations with our yes to the cross? If not, then we are no theologians in Luther's sense and should give up the name Lutheran. It is the hardest chapter in all of theology to learn to speak this yes with a clear understanding of what it includes. We hear it from Luther's explanation of Rom. 12:2: "And thus just as the wisdom of God is hidden under the appearance of stupidity, and truth under the form of lying (Luther means, of course: under the form of a statement which appears as untruth to us)—for so the Word of God, as often as it comes, comes in a form contrary to our own thinking, which seems in its own opinion to have the truth (Luther means: the Word of God always comes in such a way that it says what is opposed to our spirit, which considers its own judgment to be correct) . . . so also the will of God, although it is truly and naturally 'good and acceptable and perfect,' yet it is so hidden under the disguise of the evil, the displeasing, and the hopeless, that to our will and good intention, so to speak, it seems to be nothing but a most evil and most hopeless thing and in no way the will of God, but rather the will of the devil" [WA 56, 446; American Edition 25, 438 f.]. This means: As the wisdom of God seems foolishness to man, as His truth seems a lie, so also God's good, gracious, and perfect will appears in the form of an evil, ungracious, and hopeless will. God's will actually seems to be the devil's will—that's how hidden it is.

But it remains that way only so long as a person refuses to give up his own will and what he considers his good purpose, along with his ideas of justice, goodness, and truth. When this happens, then it is with us as with Peter, who was going to be led where he did not wish to go and who nevertheless was willing to be led because it was the way "he was to glorify God" (John 21:18 f.).

[Again Luther, *Lectures on Romans*:] "A marvelous thing! . . . At the same time he is both willing and unwilling. Thus Christ in His agony perfected His nonwillingness (so to speak) by a most fervent willingness. For God acts this way in all His saints, so that He makes them do most willingly what they most strongly do not will to do." And Luther adds: "Philosophers marvel at this contrary state of affairs, and men do not understand it. Therefore I said that a person will never grasp this unless he learns to know it by experience" [WA 56, 447; American Edition 25, 439].

This experience is the experience of faith, the faith that does not see, that does not understand, such faith as Luther attributes to the dying Abraham: "He closed his eyes and withdrew into the darkness of faith. There he found eternal light" [WA 42, 655; American Edition 3, 149].

THE 1,500th ANNIVERSARY OF CHALCEDON

Letters to Lutheran Pastors, No. 21
September 1951

The Fourth Ecumenical Council is being commemorated wherever Christians acknowledge the continuing cogency of the great Christian doctrine confessed there so long ago. It met from Oct. 8 to Nov. 1 in the year 451 in the ancient town of Chalcedon, which lies opposite Constantinople on the Asiatic side of the Bosphorus.

The Orthodox churches of the east remember this council as one of the most splendid of them all. Second in significance only to Nicaea in 325, more than 600 Fathers were present. The Eastern Church calls it a synod and finds great importance in the fact that it took place. This is because the Eastern Church regards the ecumenical synod, the representative of the whole church, as the organ of the Holy Spirit. Through it He leads Christendom into all truth by working the miracle of the consensus of all the participating Fathers.

For Rome Chalcedon is the great example of a council as the solemn assembly of the church in which the successor of Peter and vicar of Christ proclaims the truth to the whole church in the authority of his infallible teaching office. In keeping with this, the coming weeks of celebration in Rome will first of all be devoted to the great *pope*, Leo. It was his achievement to make of this council a triumph of the Roman Church—though not an absolute one. For the council in fact accepted Leo's doctrine as the voice of Peter.

For the evangelical churches, and in particular for the Lutheran churches, there is no halo around either the great synod or the great pope. The synod took place before the gates of Byzantium in the twilight of the emperor's church politics. Concern for the unity of the church was bound up with concern for keeping the Roman Empire going. Similarly Leo was not only the successor of Peter but also the clandestine heir of the Roman caesars. Only thus is it possible to understand his church-political dealings.

For those of the evangelical faith what makes Chalcedon indeed an event in church history and worthy of the church's remembrance is only this, that at that time—in spite of all secular and church politicians, "amid the confusion of men and under the providence of God"—a dogmatic decision was made in one of the most vital matters of the Christian faith, a decision that has not been forgotten as have most of the other decisions of this synod and so many dogmatic resolutions of other synods. On the contrary, the greatest part of Christendom still confesses it today. It is a decision which the Lutheran Church considers an expression of the pure doctrine of Holy Scripture from which the church lives.

It is of this doctrine that we shall speak, this doctrine of the Council of Chalcedon as it is found in the Chalcedonian Creed. We shall not attempt to pursue the meaning of the individual items within the history of dogma—that cannot be done in the framework of these letters—but we want to ask what the meaning of this doctrine is for us today.

1

What a troubled time that was, the four generations between the eruption of the Arian controversy (320) and the Council of Chalcedon, the epoch of the first four ecumenical synods, the great dogma-forming epoch of the ancient church. After the Era of Constantine's short-lived attempt once more to hold the empire together with the help of the church, in the middle of the fourth century the inexorable disintegration set in. When the Second Ecumenical Synod met in Constantinople in 381, the Goths had crossed the Danube, other Germanic tribes had crossed the Rhine, and the so-called Migration of Nations had begun. By the time the Third Synod met in Ephesus in 431 the Latin Church, from Britain to Africa, was partly destroyed, partly reduced to little clusters among the conquering Germanic-Arian tribes. A year earlier Augustine had died during the siege of Hippo Regius.

The year of the Chalcedonian Creed was a year of fresh horrors.

When Easter had passed, Attila crossed the Rhine with an army of something like half a million Huns. They went plundering through Gaul until the bloody battle of Chalons, where combined Roman and Germanic forces resisted the Asians and checked their advance. But now Italy was endangered and in the following year was visited, as Leo put it, by the "scourge"— until the great miracle happened that the conqueror left Italy after the pope, as a member of the Roman delegation, had parlay with him.

Do such memories perhaps play a part in the Roman Church's commemoration of the Chalcedonian Creed, prompting it—at a time of great threat to Christian Europe and Roman Catholicism through the danger from the east—to celebrate the great pope of the era of the Migration of Nations?

We must not forget this epochal history which is the background of the great Ecumenical Synods and their dogmatic decisions, not if we would understand their deeper meaning. The great political experiment of the Constantinian age, to save the empire by means of the church, had failed. What Constantine had seen as the promise of the church, the church did not fulfill. After the sacking of Rome Augustine felt compelled to devote his great work *The City of God* to refuting the accusation that the transition to Christianity had caused Rome's downfall.

But is it not really the case that the church had failed? Did it not have anything better to do in these world-transforming times than to argue about theological problems? Before Nicaea Constantine had warned the church against this. Did not the great synods of the empire face more compelling and practical tasks than the hammering out of theological formulas? Think of the enormous mission opportunity with which the church was suddenly confronted when Constantine laid a world at its feet. Think of the problems the Migration of Nations placed before it.

But the resolutions which modern churches and synods feel themselves compelled to make in taking a position regarding events in the world had not yet been invented. And so the Synod of Constantinople in 381 achieved "nothing more" than the enduring confession that the Son is "of one substance" with the Father and that the Holy Spirit is truly God.

But is this not actually much more than anything the synod could have achieved if it had put out some word for the hour, for the situation of the church, a message to the world, to the empire, and to the nations? Is not the Nicaeno-Constantinopolitan Creed perhaps the very word, the message which modern Christians yearn for in the church of that time? What greater, more important, and more vital message could the church have given to the world, to the old and the new peoples, and to its own members, than the message of the eternal Son of God, "begotten of his Father before all worlds, God of God, Light of Light, very God of very God, begotten not made, being of one substance with the Father, by whom all things were made; who for us men and for our salvation came down from heaven and was incarnate by the Holy Spirit of the virgin Mary and was made man . . ."? This confession, made by the Christians of a dying world, became the confession of those new peoples and the confession of all succeeding generations of the church.

Is that not something much greater than all the "relevant" and "practical" resolutions and releases produced by church meetings in our day? Where are all the pronouncements with which the ecumenical world conferences have accompanied the secular history of our day? The world never even heard them, and the churches have long since forgotten them. You will not even find them in the textbooks of church history. The creed of that ancient synod, on the other hand, is prayed in thousands and thousands of churches every Sunday. More martyrs have probably died for this creed in the 20th century than in all the foregoing centuries of church history combined. The same may be said of the Creed of Chalcedon. Everything else that happened in that fateful year of 451, if it is remembered at all, is quite dead and gone. The doctrinal decision of Chalcedon is today as vital as it was then. As an exposition of God's Word it shares in that immortality which is described by this word of Scripture: "The grass withers, the flower fades; but the Word of our God will stand forever."

2

What is the Scriptural truth that was at stake at Chalcedon? The first two ecumenical synods had confessed that the Son is truly God. This raised the question of the relationship between the divine and the human nature of Christ. The following generations, under the leadership of the schools of Antioch and Alexandria, struggled with this question in grave controversies which shook the church. Yet it was ever so that knowledge of the truth comes only as the prize of battle for the truth. The vital importance of the great controversy for Christendom today is not taken away by the sins which were committed on all sides in this struggle, not least among the orthodox Alexandrians, nor by the fact that the struggle was carried on with the tools of ancient philosophies: Aristotelian in Antioch, Neoplatonic in Alexandria.

Harnack, along with the whole Ritschlian school, thought he could evade the doctrine of the two natures by rejecting the term "nature" as an unallowable philosophical notion. He wanted to understand the relation between God and man in Christ ethically rather than as pertaining to "natures," physically. He is refuted by the fact that thereby he himself became a Nestorian. The Christology of modern, liberal Protestantism is Antiochene-Nestorian: divinity dwelling in the man Jesus as in a temple; the man Jesus standing in an ethical relationship to divinity. The only difference is that the ancient Antiochenes still took the divine in Christ with utter seriousness.

We may recall the Christmas hymn in the Nestorian liturgy which sings of the mystery of the Logos become flesh: "He was in the bosom of His Father before there was any world, from eternity, as true God. In the fullness of time He came to us, took for Himself our body, and redeemed us as true man. . . . He was in His mother's womb for nine months and was born as true man. The angels praise Him as true God. He was laid in the manger as true man. The star proclaimed Him as true God." And so it goes through His whole life, with what the gospels say of Him being allotted to the true man and to the true God. The true man "increased in wisdom and in stature and in favor . . . " The true God turned water into wine. He prayed as true man. He performed His miracles as true God. "He was nailed to the wood as true man; He shook the rocks as true God." He died and was buried as true man. At this point the hymn has nothing to say about Him as God, but goes directly to the Resurrection: "He ate and drank with His disciples after the Resurrection as true man; He passed through closed doors and gave the Twelve the greeting of peace as true God" (cited from Fr. Heiler, *Urkirche und Ostkirche*, pp. 430 f.).

If we leave out the statements about Him as true God, we have the Jesus of the liberals—the "demythologized" Christ. The unity of the Redeemer's person, which Nestorianism could not find, is achieved by this theology of modern Protestantism. It does this by setting aside the allegedly philosophical concept of "nature"—although it appears in the New Testament, 2 Peter 1:4—and with it also the concept of the *divine* nature, and makes Jesus a mere man.

Here we see clearly that one cannot get away from the concepts of the divine and the human nature. Nature here is not a physical category, but the word designates the essence, somewhat as the English phrase "the nature of the church" indicates what the church is. The human nature of Christ is the fact that He is truly man; the divine nature, that he is truly God. Who is Jesus Christ? He is truly God and He is truly man. This, and nothing else, is confessed by the doctrine of the Two Natures. Therefore no Christian theology can do without it. Hence the relevancy of the old christological questions. They appear again and again in new forms. We have only to recall how the old struggle between Antiochene and Alexandrian Christology broke out again in new form in the 16th century between the Lutherans and the Reformed, even though both acknowledged Chalcedon—a struggle which basically continues to this day.

If we must speak of the divine and the human nature of the God-man, then we cannot avoid asking about the relation of these to each other. In 431 the Council of Ephesus had rejected Nestorius and the separation of the deity and the humanity in Christ. Now the truth of the distinction between the divine and the human nature had to be defended against Monophysitism, which grew out of Alexandrian Christology.

Monophysitism, which by unspiritual means had triumphed at the "Robber Synod" at Ephesus in 449, solves the problem of the divine and human person of the Redeemer in the simplest and apparently most Christian manner—a problem the Antiochenes were unable to solve. It teaches that the human nature was absorbed by the divine. Thus after the union of the natures in the Incarnation only one nature remains—the divine. The human nature has been absorbed into it like a drop of milk in the ocean.

This doctrine is not far from the Docetism of the ancient Gnostics and Marcionites. It can no longer understand the praying of Jesus. Gethsemane and being forsaken by God on the cross lose their meaning. The flesh of the Incarnate One is no longer truly flesh.

In modern form this Monophysitism was proclaimed during the German church struggle by the German Christians. [Ed. note: The "German Christians" were the pro-Nazi group in the German churches.] There is, for instance, this statement from the 28 theses of the Saxon Church (1933): "The argument whether Jesus was a Jew or an Arian makes no contact at all with who He really was. Jesus is not a bearer of human nature but reveals to us in His person the nature of God" (K. D. Schmidt, *Die Bekenntnisse des Jahres 1933*, p. 101). This is a sign that Monophysitism is a continuing danger to the church as much as are Nestorianism and Arianism.

The answer which Chalcedon gave to the question of the relation between the divine and the human nature in the person of the God-man is the simplest conceivable. The confession of 451 simply sets down side by side the three truths that must be taught about the person of Jesus Christ. It does not attempt to explain them.

Since the text of the Decree of Chalcedon is not found in our symbolical books—although its doctrinal content finds expression there in the Athanasian Creed and is confirmed by the Augsburg Confession (Art. III) and the Formula of Concord (Art. VIII)—let the chief sentences of this lengthy decree of faith be cited here:

The holy and great ecumenical synod . . . opposes those who seek to tear apart the mystery of the Incarnation into a duality of Sons, excludes from the holy fellowship those who dare to assert that the Godhead of the Only-begotten is capable of suffering, stands against those who imagine a mixture and a confusion of the two natures of Christ, expels those who foolishly maintain that the form of a servant which the Son took from us is from a heavenly or any other kind of substance other than ours, and anathematizes those who fancy that our Lord had two natures before the union and only one after the union.

Following the holy fathers we therefore with one accord do teach and confess one and the same Son, our Lord Jesus Christ, complete in Godhead and complete in manhood. He is true God and true man, with a reasonable soul and a body. He is of one being with the Father according to His Godhead, and of one being with us according to His manhood, like us in all things except for sin. Before all time He was begotten of the Father according to His Godhead, but in these last days He was born for us and for our salvation of Mary the virgin, the bearer of God.

He is one and the same Christ, Son, Lord, Only-begotten, acknowledged in two natures, without confusion (*asunchutos, inconfuse*), without change (*atreptos, immutabiliter*), without division (*adiairetos, indivise*), without separation (*achoristos, inseparabiliter*). The difference between the natures is in no way denied by the union; rather, the characteristics of each nature are preserved and both come together into one person (*prosopon*) and one hypostasis (*subsistentia*). We do not confess a Son divided and torn into two persons, but one and the same Son and Only-begotten and God, the Word, the Lord Jesus Christ, even as already the prophets spoke of Him, as He Himself has taught us, and as the creed of the fathers has handed on to us.

61

Since we have now made this decision with great exactness and care, the holy and ecumenical synod has resolved that no one may put forward another faith, or write it, or harbor it, or teach it to others. (There follows the threat of removal from office and excommunication of those who teach otherwise.)

Such is the faith of the fathers of Chalcedon: the faith in the true deity, the true humanity, and the true unity of the divine-human Person.

3

The doctrine proclaimed by Chalcedon, together with the Athanasian Creed and the Formula of Concord, is regarded by modern Protestantism as a horrendous example of irreligious dogmatism and theological hair-splitting. What bothers the critics particularly is, as Harnack put it, "the bald, negative definitions which are supposed to say it all" (*Lehrbuch der Dogmengeschichte* II, 397). Only the recent reawakening of understanding for the church's confession and dogma has mollified this harsh judgment. There is again understanding for the fact that a negative in the church's dogma can have a highly positive meaning, for there are truths which can only be expressed by way of the negative. There is again understanding for the way in which the "without confusion, without change, without division, and without separation" function as boundary markers. They are like the buoys which mark the passage for a ship. The ship must keep within them if it is not to come to grief. The rediscovery of the role of dialectic and paradox in theology has even led to a renewed recognition of Chalcedon as an example of a genuinely theological way of speaking. In fact there is no serious theologian today who would dispute that this confession, especially in its careful marking of boundaries against possible errors, safeguards the Biblical truths that Jesus Christ is true God and true man and at the same time one person.

For this reason, and not because of some sort of traditionalism, the churches of the Reformation have committed themselves to Chalcedon. In his explanation of the Second Article, "the most beautiful sentence in the German language," Luther was able to translate Chalcedon into language a child can understand and speak: "I believe that Jesus Christ, true God, begotten of the Father from eternity, and also true man, born of the virgin Mary, is my Lord. . . ." Here is Chalcedon for children. Indeed it is the test of every authentic dogma that it can be expressed so simply that even the simplest human being can pray it.

Our acceptance of the confession of 451 dare not, however, keep us from seeing its limitations. From a purely formal point of view it is no masterpiece of credal formulation. We cannot pray it as we can the Nicene Creed. And it is not intended to be more than a commentary on the Nicene Creed, as also the Formula of Concord wants to be a commentary comment on the Augsburg Confession. *The* creed for the Fathers of 451 remains the Nicene Creed, that is, the creed of Nicaea (325) with the exposition given by the 150 fathers at Constantinople (381). Both texts are expressly quoted as the full expression of the Christian faith. It was only after Chalcedon that the creed of 381, the Nicaeno-Constantinopolitan Creed, prevailed.

Yet there is something more that must be said. How was it that Chalcedon did not prevail as Nicaea did? It did indeed save the unity of the Greek and the Latin churches, but only within the Empire. Everything outside the Empire—the Armenian, Syrian, Coptic, Ethiopian churches—did not accept it. In the East the non-Greek churches remained Nestorian, as also the East-Syrian Church, which later reached to China and South India. Or they became Monophysite like the rest.

There were certainly political reasons for this. These peoples and churches wanted nothing more to do with the orthodox christendom of the Greeks and Romans. Awakening Asia rejected the church of the Empire because it represented a "western Christianity."

Asiatic Christianity, Monophysite and Nestorian, was then either swallowed up or overshadowed by Islam. Why? What does Islam have in common with Monophysitism? with Nestorianism? There is an anti-Roman, anti-Greek feeling in Islam, the spirit of Asia, which rejects the western spirit. But probably most important is that all three are christological heresies, especially Islam. The history of the church in every age shows the ease of the movement from one heresy to another—even when they are contradictory. The fate of the churches in the Orient was sealed when they declined to take the step to orthodoxy, as was done by the Arian churches of the West, one after another, after the end of the fifth century. They wanted to remain orthodox. The Nicene Creed remained their confession. But their history shows that one cannot really preserve Nicaea if one rejects Chalcedon as its valid exposition. We may observe something similar at a later time: no one can hold to the

Unaltered Augsburg Confession and at the same time reject the Formula of Concord.

What was confessed at Chalcedon did not win its way throughout Christendom. The reasons for this must also lie in the confession itself. It is not necessarily a weakness that within the boundaries drawn by the four negatives there remained different possibilities of christological understanding. There are, for instance, different possibilities of understanding the Trinity: in the East, God as three in one (*Dreieinigkeit*); in the West, God as threefold (*Dreifaltigkeit*). But the question must be asked whether at one point more ought to have been said.

At the beginning of the sixth century the doctrine of enhypostasia was developed, the doctrine that the human nature has its personality (hypostasis) in the divine nature—in other words, that the person of the God-man is the person of the Logos. But this view came too late to win over the Monophysites. How differently would the history of doctrine have gone if this had been confessed already at Chalcedon? This doctrine of enhypostasia was meant to preserve what was true in Monophysitism, just as the concern of Nestorianism for recognition of the two natures had unmistakably been safeguarded at Chalcedon. The fact that here a gap remained—and perhaps had to remain, in view of the state of theological knowledge at that time—is the main reason why the council of 451 could not really end the christological controversy. Even among Christians who confessed Chalcedon the controversy between Nestorianism and Monophysitism lived on in ever new forms.

It is even very probable that the deepest divergence between Lutheranism and Calvinism may be best understood as a reawakening in the Reformation of the old christological schools. So the controversy between the Lutherans and the Reformed about the Lord's Supper became a struggle to understand Chalcedon. The question of the presence of the true body and blood of Christ in the Sacrament of the Altar leads to the question whether the human nature of Christ is so united with His divine nature that it partakes of its attributes. Lutheran christology, continuing the Alexandrian emphasis on the oneness of the God-man, affirms this, while Reformed christology, in the sense of the Antiochene understanding of the doctrine of the two natures with its "the finite is not capable of the infinite" (*finitum non est capax infiniti*), denies it. So what separates Lutherans and Reformed still today, even in such quite practical matters as liturgy and polity, is their divergence in the right understanding of what was confessed at Chalcedon, that Chalcedon which together with the Nicene Creed is the great, common doctrinal foundation of all of the churches of the West.

4

As we review these great interlocking issues, we become painfully aware of the division of Christendom. But we should be clear about one thing. The deepest distress of Christendom is not that Chalcedon and Nicaea are differently interpreted, so that there are Christian confessions in the sense of the Orthodox, the Roman, the Lutheran, the Reformed, and the Anglican churches. The profoundest distress of Christendom today is that to a great extent what was confessed at Nicaea and Chalcedon has been lost, and with it the common doctrinal foundation.

The division between East and West in the Middle Ages, the division within western Christendom at the time of the Reformation were indeed unspeakable tragedies, and yet they could not altogether destroy the unity of Christendom. How East and West were still able to talk with one another in the high and the late Middle Ages! What a profound knowledge of the Eastern Church had Thomas Aquinas! How his theological lifework always kept all of Christendom in view! Even in the 16th and 17th centuries the battling churches of different confessions still form a sort of unity across the chasms that divide them. Only because this unity in the great foundational doctrines of the ancient Christian faith existed was it possible for the theologians of Trent to talk with Martin Chemnitz, Bellarmine with John Gerhard, Jakob Andreae with Beza, the Tuebingen faculty with Patriarch Jeremias, even though they spoke polemically.

It is not by chance that that Confession of the Lutheran Church which most sharply expresses opposition to the Roman Church, and calls the pope the Antichrist, also acknowledges with the strongest possible words its solidarity with that church in confessing "the sublime articles of the divine majesty": "These articles are not matters of dispute or contention, for both parties confess them" (Smalcald Articles, Part I). Only those who take this seriously understand what the Lutheran Church is, particularly also in relation to other confessional churches.

The real unity of the quarreling confessional churches, given by Nicaea and Chalcedon, did not break down until Pietism and the Enlightenment disintegrated the understanding of the dogmas of the ancient church. It was the 18th and not the 16th century that split up the churches. Since that time the differing confessions have stopped talking with one another, knowing one another, and believing in their unity. There is a kernel of truth in Calixtus' thought of the consensus of the first five centuries (*consensus quinquesaecularis*) as a basis for church union, as well as in the related Anglican idea of the "ancient undivided church." The syncretism expressed by Calixtus and Anglicanism goes astray, however, in supposing that it is possible to forget the Reformation, to relativize what it stood for, and to pronounce as nonessential the differences and opposing positions of the 16th century.

This way of church union plays a great role in the world again in our day, especially since the Ecumenical Movement carried it to all mission fields. Against it we have to say that the Reformation was something more than a division of Christendom to be regretted and forgotten. It resulted in a division, but at its heart was a renewed understanding of the Gospel. This may be accepted, rejected, or perhaps also modified, but it cannot be ignored. Whoever refuses to take a stand, who does not dare say yes or no to the claim of the Reformation to have the correct understanding of these ancient confessions with their "for us men and for our salvation"—that person truly does not take these confessions seriously.

In fact, in all the attempts at church union which consider the ancient creeds as a sufficient basis of agreement these are no longer taken as binding expressions of doctrine. They are rather treated as ancient liturgical texts and texts of canon law which one uses without breaking one's head about what they mean. Not taking them too seriously is then made into a virtue, and it is said that creeds grow out of the liturgy and can only be used and understood as liturgical texts. As long as they resound in the church, there is a feeling of oneness with the church of all ages. What seems to be forgotten here is that for the fathers these creeds confessed the great objective truths of the faith for which they were ready to die, and that these great trans-subjective truths are the very thing that produces the unity of Christendom also beyond confessional boundaries.

Here lies the deepest tragedy of divided Christendom. In the last 250 years we have lost what belonged to all Christians even through the religious wars and the worst of the confessional strife. This is shown with shattering clarity by the Ecumenical Movement in the last generation.

It was a great moment when the World Conference on Faith and

Order at Lausanne in 1927 acknowledged the Nicene Creed as the common confession of the church. Only too soon did it become apparent that most of the churches participating in the Ecumenical Movement had no thought of taking this resolve seriously. The dogmatic foundation of the great ecumenical associations and of the World Council of Churches, which grew out of them in 1947, remained the confession of Jesus Christ as "God and Savior." All churches that accept Jesus Christ as their "God and Savior" can participate, whatever this confession may mean for them.

This theologically inadequate, yes, erroneous formula derives from the sectarian scene in America and is capable of covering over all sorts of false doctrine. It can never replace the clear confession that God is three in one and Jesus Christ is truly God and truly man, the confession that would have to provide the foundation for what the churches do together and for their doctrinal conversations with one another.

We cannot escape the significance of the failure of all efforts by Lutherans and Anglicans to place the Ecumenical Movement on this basis. New Delhi in 1961 again saw this failure when a "Basis" was adopted which was deliberately ambiguous. Many Reformed churches have long since set aside the confessions of the ancient church, and the "young churches" founded by them on all mission fields have never had them. But even for the Anglican and Lutheran churches these creeds have in fact largely lost their dogmatic meaning, and exist only as documents of historical and liturgical significance which may also appear in church constitutions.

We hear Protestant voices complaining of Rome's unscriptural new dogmas. However well intended or evidenced these may be, they cannot obscure the fact that the Roman Church has at least preserved the ancient Scriptural creedal heritage of the church, even if marred by later additions. One may well ask what might have happened to this great heritage of the church if during the last 250 years the Church of Rome had not been the guardian, as she was in the days of Chalcedon, of the great dogmas of the ancient church, continually reminding the evangelical churches of what they have lost or are in process of losing.

5

In closing, a word about the *task* of those who see this distress of the church and for whom the memory of the Fourth Ecumenical

Council is an occasion to confess afresh "the sublime articles of the divine majesty," the great heritage from the ancient church to the rightly believing church of all ages. There are still—God be praised!—evangelical churches that know what sound doctrine is. And in those churches which as a whole have grown weak in the faith or have even fallen from the faith there are Christians and in particular faithful servants of the Word who have not been part of this falling away and who daily ask God to guard them against this temptation.

When we ask what we are to do, we perhaps first need to hear a word of warning against making too much of such a confession as that of Chalcedon. In his *On the Councils and the Church* Luther observes how little was known of Chalcedon in his day, and then goes on:

> And what happened to the dear saints and Christians who throughout these many centuries did not know what this council established? For there must always be saints on earth, and when those die, other saints must live, from the beginning to the end of the world; otherwise, the article would be false, "I believe in the holy Christian church, the communion of saints," and Christ would have to be lying when he says, "I am with you always, to the close of the age" [Matt. 28:20]. There must (I say) always be living saints on earth—they are wherever they can be—otherwise, Christ's kingdom would come to an end, and there would be no one to pray the Lord's Prayer, confess the Creed, be baptized, take the sacrament, be absolved, etc. (WA 50, 593, 6 ff. American Edition 41, 107).

One can be a Christian though ignorant of Chalcedon and its technical expressions. But one cannot be a Christian without confessing the faith witnessed at Chalcedon, the faith in Christ, truly God and truly man, truly one in the person of the God-man. This is the faith of the New Testament, faith in the Incarnation; it is taking with complete seriousness the saving message the Gospel: "The Word was made flesh."

As witness to this faith Chalcedon has meaning for the church of all ages. Therefore its doctrinal content became binding doctrine for the western church, in the second part of the so-called Athanasian Creed, and was later acknowledged in the confessions of the Reformation. The experience of Christendom shows that wherever the authority of the ancient confessions has been set aside, there also the Biblical doctrine of the incarnation of the eternal Son has been lost. It is not possible to maintain the authority of Holy Scripture and reject the authority of these confessions. This is so because the authority of the confessions is none other than the authority of their Scriptural content. This is why if the "norm that is normed" (*norma normata*), the confessions, should fall, the "norming norm" (*norma normans*), Scripture, always falls with it.

This has been the sad experience of Protestant Christianity in recent centuries. That theory has been proved false which was represented by Reformed churches and by pietistic Biblicism, that to lessen the authority of the creeds is to make the authority of the Bible greater and more sure. Under the banner of "the Bible alone" (*sola scriptura*), those in the Reformed churches from Switzerland to America and the Far East who deny that Christ is both God and man, and that God is triune, receive equal recognition with those who confess the old doctrines.

[Ed. note: Here the author cites several examples of this, which we have omitted.]

Now let no one come with the excuse that confessional formulations and church regulations cannot guarantee pure doctrine, that to use these to bolster the church is evidence of little faith, that the Holy Spirit can do His work also in such a situation and lack of trust in His doing so is evidence of unbelief, and that things are no better in churches that are theoretically Lutheran. We must respond that no theologian expects the church to be saved by confessional writings or by church constitutions. We know that the Holy Spirit blows where He wills and that the means of grace are doing their work wherever they are in use. We trust that the Lord of the church, who awakens the dead, can also awaken churches that are dead or dying, just as He has awakened our hearts to faith that were dead in sin. However, we declare it superstition to suppose that He will produce a miracle to do what He has entrusted to us, the servants of the church, and what we in our laziness and cowardice, in our love of ease, and in our fear of men again and again fail to do.

He has commanded the servants of the Word, the shepherds of His flock, for the sake of the eternal truth and for the sake of the souls entrusted to their care, to testify against false doctrine and to exclude it from the church. We must call it blasphemy to expect the Holy Spirit to set aside the obstacles with which we willfully hinder His work. We know that no confession can guarantee purity of doctrine. What errors have infiltrated the churches that have actually preserved the creeds of Nicaea and Chalcedon, such as the churches of the East and the Roman Catholic Church! But we also know that where confession of the truth is forgotten the church's doctrine must suffer complete corruption, the Gospel must die.

To say this, to testify of it to the Lutheran Church and to all Christians, is the great task of confessing Lutherans today. They may not expect much thanks. The world, also the Christian, also the Lutheran world, does not want to hear it. Today there are only a few groups, mostly small, who say all this and are not ashamed to be called confessional and orthodox. Yet on their faithfulness depends far more than most of us can imagine. We certainly do not want to be ashamed to belong to them.

I greet you all with the words that lead into confessing the creed in the liturgy of the Eastern Church: "Let us have love for one another, that we may confess in unanimity of faith."

CHURCH AND CONFESSION

1941

1

The profound change that has occurred in Evangelical theology in Germany during the last generation is nowhere more evident than in the question of the nature of the authority of the church's confession. When in the summer of 1911 Jatho was relieved of his office because of false doctrine, the whole of liberal Germany was incensed at this outrage upon what was regarded as Evangelical freedom. Adolf Harnack wrote a word of comfort to his friend Gustav Krueger, saying that one had to accept the condemnation of Jatho because the church is still a confessional church; the majority of its members could not endure the thought that the territorial church should permit "a Christianity without the living God and without the Lord Christ." "The time will certainly come," he wrote, "when even the Positive theologians, as in Switzerland, will realize that they are not committing treason against the most holy thing when they remain in an external church fellowship that embraces everything that comes under the heading of religion among us, as long as it is not Catholic or Jewish." Progress had, however, not yet gone so far, since "the situation has not yet been reached where the territorial church is no longer a confessional church."

In our generation it is incomprehensible that 30 years ago the most celebrated and influential theologian of Evangelical Germany could so speak about church and creed, that a great church historian could be so blind to the history of the church which he himself lived through. Life has thoroughly led this concept of the church and of the

71

church's confession to its ultimate nonsense. Even the disciples of Harnack and of the theology represented by him have in the meanwhile learned what happens to a church which is no longer able to say what it believes, teaches, and confesses, which can no longer distinguish between truth and error, pure and false doctrine, church and heresy. Those whose spiritual fathers once could not cry loudly enough, "Away from the confession!" "Away from the Apostles' Creed!" now sing with deep conviction, "Let no false doctrine us pervert" and in the divine service joyfully speak the Apostles' Creed, which not long ago was a stone of stumbling to them.

As gratifying as this may be, the theology of our day must earnestly ask itself whether this turnabout actually expresses a profound change in theological thinking. Genuine theological reflection has alive in it the faith of the heart. We may, in fact, be seeing what is only the outgrowth of emotional propensities and practical conclusions drawn from experience. It does not yet mean a rediscovery of the church's confession if I am persuaded by the inner deprivation of the church that the church cannot exist without its creed and if I therefore intervene for the latter's maintenance. That may be no more than a purely pragmatic approval of a confessional position.

Here may lie the deepest reason why the great confessional movement we have experienced in Germany since the World War and particularly in the last decade has not yet led to a thoroughgoing inner renewal of the church. Saying yes to the confession has for many of us not meant what it meant to our fathers at the time of the "Awakening" 100 years ago. That was a renewal of faith in Jesus Christ that was born out of a deep convulsion of the human spirit. A merely pragmatic approval of the confession can any day be reversed—and must be, as soon as the difficulties and dangers of sincere confessional loyalty and of doctrinal discipline become evident.

The old liberalism, which demanded doing away with the Apostles' Creed as a binding confession because it was no longer able to confess the miracles of the virgin birth and the Lord's bodily resurrection, had at least one great advantage over the pragmatic confessionalism which does not believe these things either, but yet blithely confesses them as if they were believed: the advantage of honesty. If I before God and man confess with the mouth what I do not believe in my heart, I am a hypocrite. This is a truth which no dialectical skill can abolish. Yet attempts are made to argue away this self-evident fact. The content of faith is cut loose from the act of believing, or the liturgical meaning of the creed is used to rob it of its doctrinal meaning. In all such cases one is practicing a theology of "as if." Such a theology does not build the church but destroys it.

It takes no gift of prophecy to know that every such theology sooner or later falls victim to the old liberalism (the term is not used here in the sense of a party name), for basically it has never overcome it. Liberalism lives on in such theologies without their representatives being aware of it, a liberalism that makes the reason of the pious individual the final judge over the doctrine of the church. In time it will enforce its demands all the more decisively, since it now appears in the garment of confessional loyalty.

Who will contest that here lies the deepest sickness of the great confessional movement of our time? If just for once in the German churches which commit themselves to the Augsburg Confession only those would speak who hold the facts witnessed by the Apostles' and the Nicene Creed to be facts indeed, or perhaps only those who really know the Augsburg Confession and affirm its doctrine to be Scriptural, how still it would suddenly become in the theological conference chambers of our time!

More than 20 years ago we set out on the road away from religious and theological subjectivism toward the church's doctrine. It has proved to be a road longer and more difficult than was then supposed. To travel that road all the way and so to complete "the great turning of the axis of the spirit from subject to object" in the field of Evangelical theology remains a task for the future.

2

Among the many prejudices and misunderstandings which still stand in the way of a deeper understanding of churchly confession belong the false ideas about the origins of confessions. The view put by Schleiermacher was that creeds originate in the need for self-expression that inheres in religion. In theology this view, one would hope, has finally been overcome, although it still informed the great *Corpus Confessionum* of 1928, in which C. Fabricius began to gather together *The Creeds of Christendom*.

We do not dispute that there is such a need in all religion or that it is present in Christianity. Even mysticism is never weary of speaking of those things about which it incessantly asserts that they actually can never be expressed by the human tongue. What we do dispute is that the church's confession ever grew out of such confessing. Certainly the church's confession, if it is genuine, can only come from the deepest personal conviction of faith. But its essence is never to be sought in any subjective religious experiences that may be expressed therein.

The essence of a church confession lies, first of all, in the fact that it bears witness to *objective* truths. These, like the incarnation or the resurrection of Christ, cannot be derived from subjective experiences and are independent of all subjective opinions. Second, it belongs to the nature of such a confession that it is the creed of the *church*, that it is confessed not only by an *I* but by a *we*.

Such confessing as may flow from a religious person's need for self-expression can only produce a number of individual confessions. In the 19th century the view was popular that the church's creed had to be understood as the common denominator in all the different personal creeds of the individual members of the church: "the religion in which we all agree," as the Enlightenment called its minimal religion.

If we look at modern attempts at confessions of faith, as for example the preambles of recent church constitutions, we find generally little more than colorless formulas. The less they say the more general agreement they find, for there is not much there that could be disagreed with. In this way contemporary theology has lost the understanding of what makes a churchly confession. The church's creed is as little a synthesis of many individual creeds as the church is an association of the adherents of the Christian religion.

For a long time there has been an alternative view of how creeds came into existence. It looks to the church's need to put its doctrine together, principally for catechetical and apologetic purposes. But this theory already comes to grief on the indisputable historical fact that the church's confession is older than its work of instruction and theology. These grow out of what the church confesses, not the reverse.

Recently, in response to what the church is now experiencing, this theory has been defended in the altered form that the necessity of combating heresy that threatens the existence of the church is the decisive motive for formulating creeds. Appeal was made to the familiar words of the Formula of Concord according to which the propagation of heresy made it necessary to formulate the ancient creeds from the Apostles' Creed on.

This view of how the creeds came into existence meant for many the rediscovery of the normative doctrinal character of creeds. The

19th century had lost almost all understanding for this. From the beginning it is of the essence of a creed that it separates true from false doctrine, truth from error, church from what is not church. This is in fact the case even when the rejection of error is not explicitly stated. Every genuine creed contains implicitly the rejection of the opposing doctrine. When the Nicaeno-Constantinopolitan Creed no longer includes the anathemas of 325, this in no way indicates a weakening of its anti-Arian stand.

Already the oldest Christian confessions, those short statements in the New Testament in which faith in Jesus as Christ and Lord is confessed, mark the church off from the synagogue (John 9:22) and from the religions of the heathen world around (1 Cor. 8:5 f.). Very early this original creed needed more precise stating of the incarnation as defense against heretical interpretations (1 John 4:2 f.).

However, as much as the propagation of heresy has been the *occasion* for formulating creeds, so little dare we suppose that here we have found the final *reason* for producing them. The confession of the truth is always older than the false doctrine. Confronted by the false doctrine the truth only receives fresh formulation. For instance, such vital antiheretical confessions as the creeds of Nicaea and Chalcedon used, as much as possible, creedal formulations that were already in existence. The rejection of error is only the necessary reverse side of the affirmation of the truth. This is also the meaning of the Formula of Concord when it defines the old creeds as "brief and explicit confessions which were accepted as the unanimous, catholic, Christian faith and confession of the orthodox and true church" (Epitome I, 3).

Still another theory recognizes the fact that the confession of the truth is older than the false doctrine and that the origin of creeds cannot be explained as the church's struggle against heresy. This theory has emerged from recent liturgical studies. It has its starting point in the frequently noted fact that the New Testament uses the same expression (*homologein* or *exomologeisthai*) for the confession of the faith and the praise of God. (Compare, for instance, Matt. 10:32; John 9:22; Rom. 10:9 f.; 1 John 4:2, 15; Phil. 2:11 with Matt. 11:25; Rom. 14:11; and 15:9.) The same usage holds true also for the Latin *confiteri*. (One may think of the beginning of the so-called Ambrosian Hymn of Praise [the Te Deum], which Luther sometimes numbered among the Confessions: "We praise you, O God, we acknowledge you to be the Lord.") From this usage and from the fact that in the cases of the "confess" in Phil. 2:11 and the hymns in the Book of Revelation it is apparently impossible to decide whether we are dealing with creeds or expressions of praise, the conclusion has been drawn that confession of the faith and praise of the Lord are identical.

W. Maurer (*Bekenntnis und Sakrament* I [1939]) is certainly right when he says: "The creed is the church's answer to what God has given in revealing the Christ. To this the church cannot of itself answer yes. It is the gift of the Holy Spirit. . . . The creed is the Spirit-worked answer to God's gracious act." Maurer, however, goes too far when he asserts: "Creed worked by the Spirit is always prayer" and when he sets up the thesis: "The creed grows out of the Sacrament." To be sure, there cannot be creed without prayer. To that extent one may say: "The answering church is the praying church." Creed and prayer, confession of the faith and praise of God may flow into one another. However, they are not identical and must be clearly distinguished according to their content, just as confession of the faith and praise of God are to be distinguished from confession of sin (the third meaning of *homologein* and *exomologeisthai*). According to the New Testament (cf. 1 John 1:9; Mark 1:5) and according to the experience of the church, this latter kind of confession is closely tied to the other two. (The deep connection among confession of faith, confession of sin, and praise of God, by the way, can be seen not only in the Reformation but also in the Lutheran Church until 1700. This throws a new light on so-often-misunderstood Orthodoxy.) Of course, the three meanings are closely connected only for the church on earth. The spirits of the justified in heaven are freed from sin. They walk by sight and no longer by faith. For them there is only *one* kind of "confessing," the praise of God which we hear in the hymns of Revelation.

It is also a correct observation that creed belongs to sacrament, to Baptism and to the Lord's Supper. The "we" that speaks in confession of faith is not some sum of pious individuals, but the church of God. It is the "we... all" who "by one Spirit... were... baptized into one body ... and ... were made to drink of one Spirit" (1 Cor. 12:13). Of them it is true: "Because there is one bread, we who are many are one body, for we all partake of the one bread" (1 Cor. 10:17).

Celebration of Baptism and the Eucharist indeed contributed much to the development of creeds. Liturgical language, which grew out of early Christian prophecy, indeed contributed much to creedal formulation. Many creedal statements indeed were first prayed in the liturgy and only later received dogmatic formulation. Nevertheless creed does not derive from liturgy or sacrament; it is older than both. The church's confession was there before the Lord's Supper was instituted, before Christian Baptism was in use.

What is meant when it is said that confession of faith is "the church's answer to what God has given in revealing the Christ"? What kind of answer does this revelation demand? According to the Sermon on the Mount it is the answer of obedience. Above the mere confession of "Lord, Lord," Jesus Himself puts the doing of the Father's will (Matt. 7:21). "They followed Him" is also an answer to the revelation in Christ.

When to this confessing by doing is added the confessing of giving praise to God for His majesty and mercy, is that not enough? Why is the church not satisfied with this answer? Why does its confessing always contain something more, something that at first glance does not appear to be an answer to the revelation in Christ, namely doctrine and dogma? Is the dogmatic content, generally understood to be essential for the church's confession, not actually a blurring—indeed a perversion—of the Biblical understanding of what it means to confess the faith? For dogma appears to be an answer to human questions, an attempt of the human spirit to grasp God's revelation by the power of thought.

The decisive response to all these questions is given by the New Testament itself in the undoubtedly genuine report about the origin of the first confession of the church at Caesarea Philippi [Matt. 16:13 ff.]. It was not human curiosity and not the theorizing interest of speculative theology that put the question to which this confession was the answer. Jesus Himself asked His disciples, "Who do you say that I am?" It is not enough that they follow Him. He does not call for a hymn, or for giving praise to His person, or for an evaluation of Him, but for a thoroughly sober judgment of fact.

"You are the Christ." This statement is faith's answer. "You are the Christ" does not pray to Him or call upon Him; it is a genuine confession. It is not yet in the form of liturgical acclamation, like the "Jesus Christ is Lord" of Phil. 2:11. It is not yet in the form of the Apostles' Creed or in one of the varied forms in which the confession would appear in the future, down to a book of catechetical instruction or a theological Solid Declaration. Here we have a simple and clear statement of fact. It is a straightforward answer that matches the conversational situation. It is a statement of dogma, for dogma is the doctrinal content of confession.

What gives this first confession, as indeed all churchly confession, its weight is not the person who speaks it, or the emotion or conviction with which it is spoken. It is only its content, so great and overwhelming that no man and no human reason could ever have thought it out. *This* "flesh and blood has not revealed . . . to you, but My Father who is in heaven."

In this sense and only in this sense is a creed "the church's answer to what God has given in revealing the Christ." The church's confession is the answer to the question that is implicit in this revelation, a question Jesus Christ Himself put to the group of disciples that was growing into the church, and so it is the question He puts to the church of every age: "Who do you say that I am?" With this question our Lord Himself calls forth the making of creeds and thereby the church's formulation of dogmas. He did not wish to be followed as someone unknown, to be bowed to as some numinous appearance. He wanted to be believed in as the Messiah promised by the prophets, the Son of Man of Daniel 7 and the Servant of God of Isaiah 53.

To preserve this primal confession clear and whole, to understand it ever more deeply, to explain it, and to protect it against misunderstanding and misuse—this is why the church has continued to formulate confessions. The Nicene Creed, the Creed of Chalcedon, the Augsburg Confession, and the Formula of Concord want to do nothing more than this. There is no genuine churchly confession that does not intend to be an answer to the question which is put by our Lord to every generation of the church: "Who do you say that I am?"

The answer cannot and would never wish to be a rational explanation of the mystery of the divine revelation. It can only be given by the church that believes and does not see, only in the faith which the Holy Spirit creates. But such faith by its very nature cannot keep silent. It must confess, and not only in praise of God and in spiritual song but in all situations, also in the clear and factual dogmatic sentence.

3

Jesus put His question to the whole body of His disciples. The answer He received was at first that of Simon. Upon this quite personal confession Jesus speaks a quite personal blessing (Matt. 16:17 ff.) which singles this first confessor out of the multitude of those who will join in his confession. And yet that confession had been given in the name of them all. We see this in the "we" of John 6:69: "We have believed, and have come to know, that You are the Holy One of God."

78

Here we confront a noteworthy fact. Opposition between personal confession and the confession of the church is simply not known in the New Testament or in the later church in those great times when confessions were made. How could there be such opposition when both faith and confession are genuine? We confess with Luther: "The Holy Spirit has called *me* through the Gospel, enlightened *me* with his gifts, and sanctified and preserved *me* in true faith; just as he calls, gathers, enlightens, and sanctifies *the whole Christian church* on earth and preserves it in union with Jesus Christ in the one true faith." Only when the Christian church again understands these words in all their depth will it understand afresh the Spirit-wrought miracle of the consensus of the true church. Then it will understand the "we" that sounds forth in the great confessions of the past: in the "We believe" (*Pisteuomen*) of the original creed of Nicaea, which in no way stands in opposition to the "I believe" (*Credo*) of the Apostles' Creed; in the "Our churches teach with great unanimity" of the Augsburg Confession; in the "We believe, teach, and confess" of the Formula of Concord.

This consensus, that is, the work of the Holy Spirit out of which the confession of the church grows, has perhaps its most beautiful expression in the Orthodox liturgy when the deacon calls for the confession of the creed. "Let us love one another, so that we may confess the faith with one heart." In this we may discern what is the chief function of such confession in the church. It is not the separation of truth from error, of pure doctrine from false. As vital as this function is for the church, it is never more, as we have already seen, than the reverse side of its positive work: Around the confession the church gathers. As the creed has grown out of the church's consensus, so it ever and again renews this consensus as it brings it home to each individual.

In order to probe this consensus more deeply, we may ask whom it actually includes. Who are the "we" who speak the confession? Obviously the group of people who speak the confession, who acknowledge it as their own: the group of disciples who agree with Peter's confession, and later the untold millions of Christians of every time and place who have acknowledged it as their own; the 318 fathers of Nicaea and the 150 of Constantinople, as also all Christians who then and later have confessed agreement with their doctrinal decisions; the "churches [that] teach with great unanimity" [Augsburg Confession I, 1] in whose name the Augsburg Confession was presented, together with the pastors, congregations, and churches of a later time who acknowledge it as theirs, "not because this confession was prepared by our theologians but because it is taken from the Word of God and solidly and well grounded therein" (Solid Declaration, Rule and Norm, 5).

The "we" speaking the confession can, then, be a larger or a smaller group. It can include the whole Christian church—all Christians have made Peter's confession their own—or a larger or smaller part of the same. But also in this case the confession, if it is a genuine churchly confession, is expressed with the conviction that truth is being stated which has validity for all Christendom.

In this sense every genuine churchly confession claims to have ecumenical validity. The Book of Concord and the dogmatic decrees of the Council of Trent are confessions of particular churches both in the way they came to be and the acceptance they received. Yet both the Lutheran and the Roman confession want to be catholic in the sense that they express the doctrine valid for all Christians because it is the doctrine of the one and only Gospel of Jesus Christ. Both are intent upon guarding from falsification the original confession of the church that Jesus is the Christ and so want to be an answer to the question of our Lord, "Who do you say that I am?"

From here we can understand the special character of *Lutheran* confession. This is made clearer by a comparison with what is understood as confession in the *Reformed* Church. "A Reformed confession of faith comes to formulation spontaneously and openly in a locally circumscribed Christian community, which in this way defines its character for the time being to those outside and gives direction for the time being to its inner teaching and life. It is a statement of the insight given provisionally also to the universal Christian church concerning the revelation of God in Jesus Christ, which is witnessed alone in Holy Scripture." This is Karl Barth's definition of his church's understanding of a confession. He gave it in 1925 in a memorandum for the Reformed World Alliance on the "Desirability and Possibility of a General Reformed Confession of Faith." (To what extent the Reformed of past centuries would agree with Barth is a moot question. He speaks for the Reformed with whom we are dealing.)

Also in Barth's definition we find the thought that the content of a confession is not the product of human reason but derives alone from the revelation of God in Jesus Christ, and that this content belongs to the whole church. However, the content of a confession is said to be an insight that is given to the church *provisionally*, and so it is replaceable by a better and profounder one. We see from the repetition of the expression that the statement of this insight is valid only "for the time being." Accordingly, no attempt is made to formulate a confession that would have validity for the entire Reformed Church. Production of confessions is left rather to "a locally circumscribed Christian community," to a congregation, a combination of congregations, or the church of a country.

Here we see why the Reformed do not have symbolical books. We recall that all editions of Reformed confessional writings are private collections of confessions which have currency in an individual church body, or at least did have once. It becomes clearer too why there is not a single confession that is common to all of the Reformed churches—not even the Apostles' Creed. Each of the great Reformed confessions is, or used to be, current only for a church in a particular area: the Confessio Helvetica, the Gallicana, the Belgica, the Scotica, the Heidelberg Catechism, and the Westminster Confession. Salnar's well-known attempt in his *Harmonia Confessionum* to put together the doctrinal content of these individual confessions remained a private undertaking.

In contrast with this, the Augsburg Confession is the common confession of all the Lutheran churches of the world. The other confessions are also universally acknowledged, even though the Formula of Concord may not have been officially adopted in one or another of the churches. Among Lutherans confessions have a quite different meaning than among the Reformed. They express the churchly consensus that is integral for the life and unity of the church, the agreement "concerning the teaching of the Gospel and the administration of the sacraments" spoken of in Art. VII of the Augsburg Confession.

This consensus is understood not only in a spatial but also in a temporal sense. Confession of faith not only unites us with those who today confess with us the true faith, but also with those who confessed it before us, and with those of coming generations who will confess it after us. To the catholicity that is not limited by place (*ubique*) belongs the catholicity that is not limited by time (*semper*). This finds expression in the fact that the Lutheran Confessions always emphasize most strongly that they are not proclaiming anything new but only the same old truth. For this reason the Book of Concord begins with the three catholic or ecumenical creeds. For this reason the Augsburg Confession begins with affirmation of the Nicene Creed, and the Formula of Concord with that of the Augsburg Confession and the other Confessions. As the Lutheran Confessions look to the past, they look also to the future. They are "a certain and public testimony, not only to our contemporaries but also to our posterity" (Formula of Concord, Solid Declaration, Rule and Norm, 16). This witness is given "in the presence of God and of all Christendom among both our contemporaries and our posterity" (Formula of Concord, Solid Declaration, XII, 40).

Of this continuity in the formulation of confessions the Reformed Church knows nothing. Where in the Lutheran Confessions the ancient creeds are reaffirmed, there the Reformed confessions of faith set down the Biblical canon. A confession is then the attempt to express the living generation's understanding of Scripture within a particular church jurisdiction. Whether and how much this understanding of Scripture agrees with that of earlier generations is indeed an interesting question, but it is a purely historical question. As such it is not a question of theological or dogmatic importance.

According to the Reformed view church history in the strict sense, a history which God's church experiences in the world, does not, indeed cannot, exist. For the Reformed faith the true church is not a continuing fact on earth, in history. It is something that happens from time to time where, and only where, it pleases God to use the words which men preach and by His Holy Spirit to make them divine words calling the elect to His church. According to this view there can be no continuity between our confessing and that of the generations before us and after us.

The Lutheran Church, on the other hand, acknowledges the organic connection between the confessing of succeeding generations. Lutherans know a church that does not merely happen from time to time by the miracle of the Holy Spirit coming to the words, but a church that endures through the millennia of history where the means of grace, the Word and the sacraments, have the work of the Holy Spirit alive in them. This church has its own history, which faith reads in the history of the administration of the means of grace. If there is a history of the way of God's Word in the world, then there is also a history of the working of this Word. This is the history of the church, which is a history of the church's answer that is evoked by our Lord's question inherent in the Gospel.

Thereby, however, confessions like the Nicene Creed and the Augsburg Confession cease being confessions of a single generation. In reality none of the great confessions outside of the Reformed Church has ever so understood itself. None of them wanted to be valid only locally, provisionally, and for the time being. They all wanted to give expression to that great consensus which binds together the rightly believing church of all places and all times.

4

How many misunderstandings, how much talking past one another could have been spared in the Evangelical theology of the last decade if one had observed the fact that the Lutheran and the Reformed churches are of different opinion not only about a number of important doctrines of the confession but also about the very nature of churchly confession. No one is served when this difference is overlooked or belittled. Theologians who have done this and, claiming to stand on the ground of the Lutheran Confessions, have with great show of learning and even more of eloquence laid on Lutheran pastors and churches the Reformed idea of what makes a confession, as if it alone were the truly evangelical one, have much to answer for. It is indeed a deeply serious question as to which confession has judged correctly here, and we do not intend to evade the duty of examining it closely. But first there has to be a clear delineation of the difference.

The statement that the church is gathered about the confession is acknowledged in the Lutheran Church. In the Reformed Church it is acknowledged, if at all, only with drastic limitations. Among the Reformed it is Holy Scripture around which the church is gathered. This position does immediately strike one as the more evangelical. One can see why the Lutheran Church has always been reproached for valuing confessions too highly and indeed for putting them above the Bible. We would no longer be heirs of the Lutheran Reformation if we did not with utter seriousness probe what truth there may be in this reproach. No Lutheran theologian will deny the danger for our church, the preeminently confessional church, at this point and that ever and again individual theologians have fallen victim to it. However, we can never concede that our church takes "Scripture alone" less seriously than the Reformed and that it gives Scripture a lesser role for the church when it says that the church is gathered about the confession.

Also for us Holy Scripture occupies the central position in the church. However, there is no denying that in this sinful world Scripture can also be misunderstood and misused. For a century before there was a New Testament the church had the same Bible as the synagogue. As soon as there was a New Testament it was commandeered by all the heretics. Today we share the same Bible with the worst of the sects. *The true church is gathered not around Scripture but around the rightly understood, the purely and correctly interpreted Bible.* It is the task of the church's confession to express the right understanding of Scripture which the church has reached. (See W. Elert, *Schrift und Bekenntnis* [1936] and *Der christliche Glaube* [1940], pp. 40 ff.) Thus pastors are helped to proclaim only the pure doctrine, and congregations are protected against the whims of the preacher and the misinterpretation of Scripture. In this sense the church's confession is servant of the Word.

We hear much of the advantages which modern exegetes have in contrast with those who gave us the Formula of Concord and the other confessions of our church. No one would deny their greater knowledge of language and history. At some points, however, the old theologians of the 16th century undeniably did better. First of all, for them the Bible was still a whole. The Bible, the Old and the New Testament, was for them not a more or less chance conglomeration of individual writings and historical layers. Therefore they were still able to interpret the *Bible* and not just separate passages and documents. They also knew the meaning of "Scripture interprets itself." Second, Holy Scripture exercised an authority over them before which they bowed in humility. The appeal to the Bible was not, for them, what it sadly has so often become: an appeal to the reason of the exegetes. As confessional theologians they were Biblical theologians. The Confessions were for them, as always for our church, only a commentary to Holy Scripture and a help to its proclamation.

As a commentary makes no sense without the text which it is expounding, so also the Confessions make no sense without the Bible. As a map gets its meaning when it keeps the traveler on the right road and away from false turnings, so the church's confessions get their meaning when they help the preacher to proclaim the good news purely and correctly. Whether a church is still a confessional church is decided not by the number of old confessional writings it still possesses but by its living proclamation in preaching, instruction, and pastoral care. If it is a genuinely confessional church in this sense, then it is also a Biblical church.

It is the experience of more recent church history that Biblical authority stands or falls with confessional authority. Has not the fate of the Reformed churches, which in the 19th century for the most part gave up binding their ministers to the confession, shown what happens to a church that binds its pastors to the confession not because but only insofar as it agrees with God's Word? In contrast to the Lutheran *quia* (because), the *quatenus* (insofar as) had in fact long been characteristic for the Reformed confessions. Karl Barth puts it as the "pious and free relativism with which they regard their own statements." But *quatenus* can be taken in two different ways. It can mean that only those doctrines may be in a confession which are drawn from Holy Scripture. This is self-evident for both Lutherans and Reformed. But it can also mean: I accept the confession insofar as it is in accordance with Scripture and leave it as an open question to what extent that may be the case.

Here the "pious relativism" has become impious indeed; in removing the authority of the confession, it removes that of the Bible also. If it is no longer possible to say whether a confessional statement is in accordance with Scripture or not, or if I can say no more than, "Today it appears so to me; therefore I will allow it to stand provisionally," then my doubt is basically not toward the confession but toward Scripture. I have lost confidence in it to interpret itself. I hear then only the confusing throng of exegetical opinions as they contradict one another, but no longer the clear and unmistakable voice of God's Word.

Against this relativism which darkens the clarity of Scripture and destroys its authority stands the confessional principle of the Lutheran Church. To those who represent this relativism it must appear as frivolous or as titanic arrogance when Luther says in his Great Confession of 1528: "I am determined to abide by it until my death and (so help me God!) in this faith to depart from this world and to appear before the judgment seat of our Lord Jesus Christ" (WA 26, 499 [American Edition 37, 360]) and when the confessors of the Formula of Concord say:

> In the presence of God and of all Christendom among both our contemporaries and our posterity, we wish to have testified that the present explanation of all the foregoing controverted articles here explained, and none other, is our teaching, belief, and confession in which by God's grace we shall appear with intrepid hearts before the judgment seat of Jesus Christ and for which we shall give account. Nor shall we speak or write anything, privately or publicly, contrary to this confession, but we intend through God's grace to abide by it (Solid Declaration, XII, 40).

It is not a false security that speaks here, but the certainty of genuine faith, which knows what God's Word is and what it says. It is the same certainty which, according to Luther, enables the true pastor to say when he leaves the pulpit: "In this sermon I have been an apostle and a prophet of Jesus Christ ... for it is God's word and not my word" (WA 51, 517 [American Edition 41, 216]).

That is Lutheran confessing. Here there is no "provisional," no "for the time being." That can never be, for the confessor always stands at the threshold of eternity. Confession is always "in the presence of God," as the Formula of Concord says at the place quoted above. This means that the confessor is always aware of the final judgment. Because the Lutheran Church has understood the profound eschatological seriousness of all confessing, to which the New Testament bears witness, therefore it knows no "provisional" confession.

5

Here is not the place to demonstrate the Scripturalness of the Lutheran Confessions. When we assert it, we do not of course mean that they are infallible, unrevisable, or in no need of expansion. Also, we do not make every single one of their theological sentences our own—especially since various theological schools had a hand in their formulation. We submit them to constant testing against Holy Scripture, the "norming norm" (*norma normans*).

But just this testing has convinced us that the great doctrinal decisions reached in the symbolical books of our church are correct. And so there can be no development of the Confessions which would ignore these decisions. The attempts in our day at new confessional formulations, to be put beside or in place of the old, must face our reproof that they have not gathered but have scattered, that they have not served to clarify the faith but to confuse it, because they have not taken the claims of the old Confessions seriously enough. They have given up the consensus with the fathers through many centuries in favor of some hasty, modish consensus of the moment.

The old Confessions are indeed witnesses as to how "Holy Scripture ... was understood and expounded by those living at that time." But they are witnesses in a different sense than the exegetical and dogmatic works contemporary with them. For "those living at that time" gave their confession with not only their contemporaries in view. They confessed their faith "in the presence of God and of all Christendom among both our contemporaries and our posterity"— and so before us too. In the old Confessions they speak to us today and call upon each of us to test their decisions and their doctrine by Holy Scripture.

No theologian may evade this demand made by the Confessions. If he does, he has already cut himself loose from the church of the fathers. There, however, where the theology of our day has gained a new understanding for the seriousness of this demand, where one knows what it means to confess "in the presence of God and of all Christendom among both our contemporaries and our posterity" and is prepared, with a view to the final judgment, to speak a yes or a no to the confession of the church—there the church has been discovered anew.

"I BELIEVE IN THE APOSTOLIC CHURCH"

1936

1

"I believe in one holy, catholic, and apostolic church." These words of the Nicaeno-Constantinopolitan Creed (in the following abbreviated as NC) are confessed together by the churches of the East and of the West, by Catholics and most Protestants. There is, however, wide diversity in the way of interpreting these words, especially the four predicates of the church: one, holy, catholic, and apostolic.

It is a remarkable fact in the history of dogma in our day—the history of dogma, the history of the church's teaching, accompanies all of church history—that the question, "What is the church?" has assumed increasing importance. Not only is it coming to occupy the center of theological interest within the different confessions but this great question has more and more become the object of discussion between the churches in the ecumenical movement. Wherever such encounters take place and the conversation among Orthodox, Anglicans, Old Catholics, Lutherans, and Reformed turns to the doctrine of the church, we find that questions about the oneness, catholicity, and holiness of the church lead to the question of its apostolicity.

What do we mean when we say of Christ's church that it is apostolic? There is perhaps no other theological question which exposes more clearly the deep differences in the doctrine of the church that have existed among the confessions since the 16th century. What an important role the question of the apostolic succession is beginning to play in our time! Even on the mission field the argument between the Catholic and the Protestant churches leads to a discussion of the question, which today is being fought about in South India, as to what the nature of the church's apostolicity really is: Is it to be understood from the vantage point of the apostolic succession or from that of apostolic doctrine, and how do these two relate to each other?

Evangelical theology in Germany, if I see correctly, has not been much occupied with the question of the church's apostolicity. This may be in part because our thinking about the church has always been defined by the Apostles' Creed, which calls it holy and catholic. Traditionally drawn into this was the *one* from the NC, although the Apostles' Creed does not have it.

This may also serve to explain why Luther, as far as I know, never specifically dealt with the problem of the "apostolic" church, even though his theological and reformatory lifework is the greatest contribution that has ever been made toward the right understanding of the church's apostolicity. Also the Lutheran Confessions, which represent the church's yield from Luther's lifework in this respect, in that they formulate the renewed apostolic doctrine and fix the normative meaning of this teaching for the church, never speak of the apostolicity of the church the way they speak of its oneness, catholicity, and holiness.

All the more, therefore, must our theology prepare itself for interconfessional discussions by asking about the meaning of "apostolic church" in this double sense: How is this designation to be understood historically? What does it mean in the doctrinal teaching of the church? Like all the weighty problems in the history of doctrine, both parts of the question, the historical and the doctrinal, are inseparably intertwined. We shall attempt to answer both questions, although in the compass of this paper we can hope for little more than a sketch.

2

The word "apostolic" as a description of the church in confessional formulations is found first in the East. Wherever it appears in Western confessions—whether in later variants and particular forms of the Apostles' Creed, whether in other confessional formulations and synodical resolutions—it is due to the influence of the NC.

(Examples are given in Hahn, *Bibliothek der Symbole und Glaubens-regeln der alten Kirche*, 1897, p. 393.) The NC, that great ecumenical confession which won its triumphant way through both East and West, was responsible for the church being confessed everywhere as apostolic. Even the confessions of the Nestorians (Hahn, p. 146) and the Monophysite Armenians (Hahn, p. 153) bear witness to how comprehensive this victory was.

The history of the formula "apostolic church" before the NC—along with Ed. Schwartz and H. Lietzmann we again see in this creed the confession of the Second Ecumenical Council of 381—can no longer with certainty be reconstructed. The formulation in the NC can be found already in a series of Eastern confessions of the last third of the fourth century, for example in the *Hermeneia eis tōn symbolōn*, falsely ascribed to Athanasius (Hahn, p. 138), in Epiphanius (Hahn, pp. 135, 137), and in the *Apostolic Constitutions* (Hahn, p. 141).

The earliest proven instance of the expression "apostolic church" in a symbol is found in what Alexander of Alexandria wrote to Alexander of Thessalonica and all bishops in connection with the Arian matter in the year 324. (The addressee is Alexander of Thessalonica, not of Constantinople, as in Theodoret, where the writing is found, and as Hahn's heading has on p. 19.) In this document the Alexandrian bishop weaves together a number of statements from what is obviously a symbol in use in his church. From these it is possible to reconstruct the symbol (Hahn, pp. 19 f.).

It begins: "We believe, as seems good to the apostolic church, in one unbegotten God." The clause "as seems good to the apostolic church" may well be an addition of the letter writer. It is clear from this clause that he was accustomed to using the expression "apostolic church" in the sense of "orthodox church," much as "catholic church" was in general use. In the text of the confession he calls the church "one and only, catholic, the apostolic church" (*mian kai monēn katholikēn, tēn apostolikēn ekklēsian*). Besides the absence of "holy," the "only" (*monēn*) next to "one" (*mian*) is noticeable. That this "only" in addition to "one" was a settled part of Egyptian confessional formulations can be seen from the short Coptic baptismal formula: "And in one, only one, catholic, apostolic, holy church which is His." The Latin translation reads: "Et in unam unicam, catholicam, apostolicam, sanctam, quae illius est, ecclesiam" (Hahn, p. 158). The Ethiopian baptismal formula has correspondingly: "Et in unicam, sanctam, quae super omnes est" (paraphrase of "catholicam") "ecclesiam apostolicam" (Hahn, p. 159). The end of the First Article in the Coptic *Apostolic Constitutions* has "one Godhead alone, one lordship alone, one kingdom alone, one faith alone, one baptism alone in the holy, catholic, and apostolic church for eternal life. Amen" (Hahn, p. 157). Everywhere the "only, alone" (*monē*) is explicitly or implicitly the companion of "one" (*mia*), while the German translation of the NC, *eine einige* ("one and only one"), is only a clearer way of saying "one church, one Baptism" (*una ecclesia, una baptisma*). The "one and only one," by the way, is also found in the *Hermeneia* mentioned above. There we read concerning the church, "in one and only one, this catholic and apostolic church" (*eis mian monēn tautēn katholikēn kai apostolikēn ekklēsian*; Hahn, p. 138).

This confession was indeed wrongly ascribed to Athanasius, but it was found in a Vatican codex along with the works of Cyril of Alexandria. This points to an Alexandrian origin, and so we may see in what it says about the church a missing link between Alexander's confession of 324 and the NC of 381. The confessions of Epiphanius and of the *Apostolic Constitutions*, which speak of the apostolic church, may have gotten the expression directly or indirectly from this source. In any case, no other source is demonstrable. These documents which speak of the "apostolic church," by the way, are unlike the other confessions of the fourth century (Jerusalem, Caesarea, the Antiochene symbol of 341, the Arian confessions, and the symbols of Sirmium and Nice; see also the table in H. Lietzmann, *Symbolstudien*, ZNW 21 [1922], pp. 20 f.), none of which use this term.

We may have then a formula of Alexandrian origin in "one and only one, catholic and apostolic church" (*mia monē, katholikē kai apostolikē ekklēsia*). It is found in Alexander of Alexandria and with slight variation in the *Hermeneia*, from where it made its way into the Armenian confession (Hahn, p. 153). (In all three cases "holy" is also missing, which Epiphanius I and the *Apostolic Constitutions* have.) So Alexandria is to be considered the home of the expression "apostolic church" in the usage of the symbols. Hahn (pp. 127 ff.) took the view that "apostolic" was already applied to the church in the original form of the Eastern baptismal confession. The evidence adduced by Lietzmann makes this view no longer tenable (*Symbolstudien*, ZNW 21 [1922], pp. 1 ff., especially p. 23, where the probable original form is reconstructed; cf. RGG, I, 445.).

Not only the use of "apostolic church" in confessional formulas is attested for the first time in the letter of Alexander of Alexandria written in 324. This letter, or the Alexandrian symbol that it quotes, is the first evidence of any usage of the expression "apostolic church," if we disregard Tertullian's use of the plural "apostolic churches," to which we shall return later. The expression "apostolic church" is not found in the apostolic fathers, the apologists, Irenaeus, Hippolytus, Clement, or Origen. Even Athanasius, Alexander's deacon, who accompanied his bishop to Nicaea and became his successor, does not seem to have used it. When he speaks of the orthodox church in the controversy with the Arians he calls it the catholic church.

Only since the adoption of the word "apostolic" as a designation of the church at the end of the fourth century, above all since the adoption of the Constantinopolitan Creed, has it been customary to designate the orthodox church as the "catholic and apostolic" church. While according to Eusebius and Athanasius "the catholic church" speaks in the Nicene Creed of 325, the later church historians (Philostorgius, Theodoret, Sozomen, and Socrates) and the synodical resolutions since the Council of Ephesus make it the "catholic and apostolic" church.

The usage *catholic and apostolic church*, however, appears already in the first third of the fourth century. Evidence for this is the letter of Constantine to Eusebius regarding the construction of a basilica at Mamre which is to be worthy of "the catholic and apostolic church" (Eusebius, *Vita Constantini*, III, 53). If this document is reliably transmitted, then it is, next to Alexander's letter, the earliest evidence for the use of the expression "apostolic church." We may conclude, then, that already during the time of Constantine the expression *catholic church* was expanded to *catholic and apostolic church*, and that this usage went into a church confession in Alexandria. From there in the last third of the fourth century it spread widely through the Eastern church and won its way into the ecumenical creed of Constantinople in 381.

3

This brief review of the history of the expression "apostolic church" must suffice. What is the meaning of "apostolic" here? Why was it included in the Creed?

While the Western baptismal confession in the second century, the *Vetus Romanum*, already confessed the *holy church*, the original form of the Eastern creed does not seem to have mentioned the church. The "Third" Article has only "and in the Holy Spirit," which is still the case in the Nicaean Creed of 325. While the West was long content to confess only "holy church" (*sanctam ecclesiam*, reproducing the *hagian ekklēsian* in the old Roman baptismal confession), the East on the threshold of the fourth century came to make mention of the church in the creed and immediately began to amplify it (along with statements about the Holy Spirit) with new epithets: "one (only), catholic, and apostolic," until the new article about the church reached the completion it has in the NC.

In this amplification the East's very different feeling for liturgical language undoubtedly played a role. In the East there is a love for beauty of sound and opulence of expression. In contrast, the Apostles' Creed in the West uses factual language, avoids any word that is not absolutely necessary, and with each new word states a new fact. But the NC in the East has the tendency to amplify one expression with another (e. g., in the christological statements).

This alone, however, does not explain the new sayings about the church, no more than the ones about the Holy Spirit. The latter statements were taken into the creed for a dogmatic reason—for the theologically necessary doctrine that the Spirit is, like the Son, "of one substance with the Father"—after they already had their place in the liturgical service. This is indicated in the NC itself, when it says about the Holy Spirit: "who together with the Father and the Son is worshiped and glorified." Here one may indeed say: "The law of praying is the law of believing" (*lex orandi lex credendi*). Also the unfolding of the doctrine of the church in the creed must have its dogmatic promptings.

What grounds were decisive in each particular case we cannot now say. Perhaps the expression "one and only one church," which came to be characteristic of later Egyptian formulations, was prompted by the Meletian controversy. At that time, during the persecution by Diocletian, there were martyrs in prison, Bishop Peter of Alexandria among them. They refused church fellowship to each other and went unreconciled to their martyr's death. But whether this gave occasion to emphasize the unity of the church naturally remains pure conjecture.

With certainty we can say no more than that the fourth century, wracked with the most serious doctrinal controversies, just as the equally controversy-filled second century before it, caused the church to think about what is true and what is false church. In the earlier great struggle against the Gnostics and against Marcion the concepts of the church's catholicity and apostolicity were worked out and became the common possession of all Christians both of the East and the West. So the heavy battles against the heretics of the fourth century were the occasion for bringing these concepts into the creed, together with the doctrine of the church.

The question what is meant by "apostolic" when used of the church is, then, not difficult to answer. The meaning is no other than that which it had in the struggle against the Gnostics. (The earliest instance of "apostolic" in Christian literature, by the way, is at the beginning of Ignatius' *Letter to the Trallians* [LCC, 1, 98], where the author says that he writes "in apostolic manner." Here the word does not yet have theological content.) Since the second century we hear both in the West and in the East of the "apostolic faith" or the "apostolic doctrine." This is the faith which according to the New Testament "was once for all delivered to the saints" (Jude 3).

Tertullian already uses the adjective "apostolic," while Irenaeus uses the noun "apostle" to circumscribe the meaning in the expression "doctrine of the apostles" (*Adversus haereses* III, 12, 11 *et passim*; he does not use the adjective "apostolic" but speaks of the apostolic succession as "the succession from the apostles," IV, 26, 2). But the matter is always the "apostolic doctrine" of Tertullian (*De praescriptione haereticorum*, 32), the "evangelical and apostolic tradition" of Cyprian (Epistle 69, 3), concepts and expressions that are also current among the Alexandrian fathers since Clement. (For Clement see O. Stählin's index. As for Origen, we may recall his programmatic statement in the preface to *De principiis*, ch. 2: "Only that truth is to be believed which in no way disagrees with the ecclesiastical and apostolic tradition.")

As already in Tertullian the doctrine can be called either "apostolic" or "catholic," so also later we find both words used as virtual synonyms. When Alexander introduces the creed which he quotes with "as seems good to the apostolic church," he could just as well have said, "as seems good to the catholic church." When the two words are used next to each other in the fourth century and later, one has the impression of a redundancy, such as authors like to use in edifying discourse.

Yet each of these two words began with its own solidly defined meaning, and with these differing meanings they came into the NC. The word "catholic" tells of the universality of the church spread spatially over the face of the earth. The word "apostolic" tells of the identity of the church of all times with the church of the beginning. To catholicity belong "all nations" (Matt. 28:19) and "to the end of the earth" (Acts 1:8); to apostolicity belongs "always, to the close of the age" (Matt. 28:20).

That the church today is no other than the church of yesterday and of the day of Pentecost; that it today has no other doctrine than in the days of Luther and of the Formula of Concord, and then no other doctrine than in the days of Bernard of Clairvaux and Thomas Aquinas; that the church's proclamation in the time of Gregory the Great and in the time of Cyprian dare be no other than in the days of the apostles; that there is only one Gospel for all the centuries of history until the last day, just as there is only one Gospel for the people of all nations and all races; that the Gospel is given us in the witness of the apostles, and nowhere else, and that this witness cannot be supplanted by any other source of revelation; yes, that the anathema of the true church would have to strike even an angel from heaven who would proclaim to us another Gospel than that proclaimed by the apostles—such are the thoughts that are contained in the statement of the church's apostolicity. These are the truths of the faith to which we commit ourselves when we confess with Christians of all confessions the words of the ancient ecumenical creed: "I believe in the apostolic church."

4

The great truths of the faith to whose recognition the Holy Spirit led Christ's church in the heavy doctrinal struggles of the early centuries and which have been recognized by the orthodox church of all times as the true interpretation of Holy Scripture do not cease to be truths because they have been misused, mutilated, or even falsified. If there is one thing especially that Evangelical theology in our day has to learn from Luther and the Confessions of the Reformation, it is that the ancient church again be taken altogether seriously. The history of the church did not stand still, as many a young theologian these days seems to think, from the death of the last apostle until Luther came on the scene. The decline of the knowledge and study of patristics in the present generation of theologians threatens to become catastrophic for our theology unless it is somehow checked. A church without patristics becomes a sect.

The previous generations with their "historicism" must bear their share of the blame. The purely historical view of the ancient world of Greece and Rome, which with its changing of "classical philology" into "the study of antiquity" (*Altertumswissenschaft*) was heralded as the height of progress, actually was the death of vital involvement with that world and almost destroyed what was left of classical education as we still had it in Germany. (One might put the matter the other way round and ask whether from the death of classical studies the new historical school was born. But it is a fact of our history of education that enthusiasm for the world of the classics was extinguished by historicizing instruction.) Similarly patristics in Evangelical theology suffered severely from "the historical sickness." For when all is said and done does anyone, even the professional historian, study history only because he wants to know "how it actually was"? The matter only then genuinely moves us when we recognize that there was something in what happened there that is decisive for our lives. So it is also with the answer to the historical question as to when and in what way the expression "apostolic church" emerged. It all depends on our understanding the great doctrinal decision that lies hidden behind the emergence of that expression and its being taken into the creed.

It is the great doctrinal decision which was hammered out in the struggles of the second century and which has determined the life of the entire church, the faith of all Christians of all confessions. Every time the "I believe in the apostolic church" sounds forth before a Christian altar, the church acknowledges its involvement in that gigantic struggle which had to be fought against the most dangerous enemy it has ever faced. The struggle began during the last days of the New Testament period and continued for several generations. We customarily call this enemy Gnosticism, although with this name we do not come anywhere near describing what all there was in it.

The creed's "I believe in the apostolic church" is the monument to the great victory over that enemy. It also calls to remembrance the fathers of the church of that time, above all the two great theologians of the apostolic church, Irenaeus and Tertullian. Tertullian, the creator and master of the church's Latin, to whom Christian doctrine owes so many of its technical terms, was also the first to bind the adjective "apostolic" to the word "church." He calls those churches apostolic churches which were founded by an apostle. In his basic work against the heretics (De praescr., 20) he explains that Jesus Christ chose the Twelve and appointed them to be the teachers for the nations and gave them the right doctrine. After the place made vacant by Judas' betrayal was filled by the election of Matthias,

> they received the promised power of the Holy Spirit for the working of miracles and for preaching. They first bore witness in

96

Judaea of the faith in Jesus Christ, and founded churches. Afterwards they went throughout the world and proclaimed the same doctrine of faith also to the heathen. And so they founded churches in every city, from whom yet other churches borrowed a sprig of the faith and the seed corn of the doctrine in order to become churches, and daily they still do this borrowing. Because of this they are regarded as apostolic, as descendants of apostolic churches. . . . In this way so many and such great churches are one single church, that first church from the apostles (*illa ab apostolis prima*), from which they all came forth. So they are all first and all apostolic, for all are one (*omnes primae et omnes apostolicae, dum una omnes*).

According to Tertullian, then, an apostolic church is one founded by an apostle and holding to his doctrine. One may also speak of a church as apostolic even if it was not founded by an apostle but by an apostolic church and from it received the doctrine. A congregation can establish the claim to be an apostolic church, and so a legitimate and orthodox church, in two ways, and Tertullian challenges the heretics to do so. Either a church can demonstrate that it was undoubtedly founded by an apostle, or it can demonstrate that it is in harmony with the doctrine of the churches which were founded by an apostle, the apostolic churches of the first rank, so to speak. For Tertullian, the former could never be demonstrated without the latter. The many apostolic churches which are thus recognized throughout the world, old ones and young ones, are yet one church.

It is as if Tertullian has it on the tip of his tongue, and yet does not say it: one apostolic church. He certainly would have had no objection against calling the church as a whole the apostolic church. He would acknowledge this statement of the NC as the faith and the doctrine he had always stood for. Yet it cannot be a matter of chance that he always speaks only of apostolic churches, that is, individual churches (Christians living in the countryside belonged to the church of a nearby city, as in Paul's day at Corinth), but never of the apostolic church. Some hindrance from his well-developed feeling for language must have kept Tertullian from expressing the formula which lay hidden within his lines of thought and which was destined to surface several generations later in an entirely different place.

Wherever people speak of the apostolicity of the church, there the great theological achievement of Tertullian, as also that of his comrade in the struggle, Irenaeus, comes alive. They are the actual discoverers of the "apostolic church." They put into the blood and marrow of Christians of all centuries and of all confessions that Christ's church by its very nature is apostolic.

Many a weighty objection may be made to the details of how they understood and established this apostolicity of the church. One can blame them, like later Catholicism, of making true what Cardinal Manning once said in the name of Roman Catholicism: "One must vanquish history with dogma." What a dogmatic and unhistorical picture Tertullian gives of the Twelve and their labors. (See the detailed presentation in J. Wagenmann, *Die Stellung des Apostels Paulus neben den Zwölf*, 1926.) What are we to think of a definition of an apostle that is so strict as to exclude Paul? Yet it is possible to find something of this sort of dogmatic picture of the apostolic period in Acts. The Jerusalem understanding of the apostolate as we have it in Acts 1:21 f. could never have allowed Paul to take a place as one of the Twelve. What Tertullian says so triumphantly to the heretics could also be said against him and the Roman church, with the legends of apostolic foundation and the fabricated lists of succession for so many a metropolitan see:

> Let them fabricate something like that. After their blasphemies what would they shrink from doing? But even if they would fabricate something like that, they still would accomplish nothing. For their doctrine itself, compared with the apostolic doctrine, will through aberrations and departures bear loud witness that they have no apostle or apostolic man as their authority (*De praescr.*, 32).

And yet there is a historical reality behind the idea of succession and the most important of those old lists of succession. The list of Roman bishops which Irenaeus transmits as an example of the succession of bishops (*Adversus haereses* III, 3, 3 [LCC 1, 372 f.]) was in fact neither what Irenaeus supposed it to be (a list of bishops following Linus, who was put in office by the apostles), nor was it a list of popes (as Rome later wished to have it). Yet is has a genuine kernel. (See Erich Caspar, *Die älteste römische Bischofsliste*, 1926.) The names are genuine. Even if we cannot speak of a monarchic office of bishop before the year 140, yet the men who are listed before the time of Pius are very likely historical figures, on whom actually rested the responsibility for the teaching, the succession of pure doctrine.

This is the outcome of Erich Caspar's epochal study mentioned above. If, in the very nature of the situation, there was no office of bishop in the early days of the church, then there can only have been a sequence of those who in a particular place followed one another in the work of teachers (*didaskaloi*). This office, and that of the prophets, was later subsumed into the office of bishop. In the *Martyrdom of Polycarp* (16, 2) he, bishop of Smyrna, is called "apostolic and prophetic teacher"[LCC 1, 155]. We can see how the three charismas of apostle, prophet, and teacher live on in the office of bishop.

It was not a dogmatic fiction but a historical reality, for which there are parallels in Judaism and in early Islam, that the oral tradition, the transmission of the doctrine from generation to generation, was taken with extraordinary seriousness. How else could the Gospel be preserved in a time when the Holy Scriptures of the New Testament were not yet complete? Certainly it was unavoidable that superstitious and even heathen notions would be attracted to the idea of the "sure charisma of the truth" (*charisma veritatis certum*) which was said to be received with episcopal succession (Irenaeus, *Adversus haereses* IV, 26, 2). Yet behind this view there still stood faith in the unshakable truth of Christ's promises. For His promises do not cease to be true, even when we human beings misunderstand them!

It is from this vantage point that we must understand the church's great decision in the second century. When the church declined the temptations of Gnosticism, of Marcionite dualism, and of Montanism with its claims of new revelations, it became the apostolic church. That meant, seen from the perspective of religious and cultural history, an extraordinary impoverishment. Perhaps it also meant that a great many Christians, deeply disappointed, left the church and sank back into heathenism. The "apostolic church" is a poor church. It has no marvelous new revelations, no knowledge of higher worlds, no possibility of proving its faith by reason. It lives from the witness of a few men who were neither religious geniuses, nor ethical heroes, nor original thinkers. The only authority for the unverifiable things they said was that Jesus Christ had sent them and that they were witnesses of His resurrection.

To the witness of these men, these apostles, these bearers of an office that existed only once, in a single generation of history, the church commits itself when it calls itself apostolic. Right here lies the meaning of the great doctrinal decisions that are bound up with the concept of "the apostolic church" in the second and in the fourth centuries. As the church of the One who truly became man, was actually crucified, and truly rose again, the church is called apostolic. It is the apostolic church because it is the church of Jesus Christ.

Appendix
Biography of Hermann Sasse

Dr. Hermann Sasse, it is widely held in ecclesiastical circles, was one of the strong confessional Lutheran theologians of this century. He was born on July 17, 1895, at Sonnewalde, in Lower Lusatia, Germany, as the son of Hermann Sasse and his wife Maria Magdalene, nee Berger. He was baptized in his birthplace and was confirmed at Berlin-Friedenau on March 22, 1910.

His early days of education were spent at various localities, such as Laage in Mecklenburg, at Lübeck, at Krotoschin, at Breslau in Silesia, and in Berlin. It is not known what were the chief influences that led him to study theology and philosophy for three and a half years at the University of Berlin, where he passed his first theological examination in 1916. In a letter written to a book reviewer of *The Reformed Theological Review*, in which his work *In Statu Confessionis* was reviewed by Prof. Klaas Runia (January/April 1968, No. 1), he says: "I belong to that generation of theologians who were trained in the liberal theology of pre-war Berlin, though I had excellent teachers and was never a radical liberal."

During the period 1916—18 he saw war service and, significantly, at that early stage of his career he began to grow critical of the liberal theology of his time. "One could live with it, but one could not die with it," was his growing conviction, as it became the conviction of a number of younger theologians of that time.

While Dr. Sasse's main theological interests lay in the direction of the New Testament in those early days of his theological training—he had the advantage and privilege of studying under the famous Adolf Deissmann, with whom he took his licentiate degree (today the Dr. Theol.)—his penchant for church history was strongly stimulated by two towering German theologians of the time, Karl Holl and Adolf von Harnack, of whom he often spoke in glowing terms later on in life; at the same time, of course, he was aware of their all-too-obvious weaknesses and liberal tendencies.

Although he was already in the ministry—he was ordained on June 13, 1920, in the St. Matthai Church in Berlin—he appears to have loved theology so passionately that he continued his studies and even gained his S.T.M. following a stay at Hartford Theological Seminary, Connecticut, U.S.A. (1925—26). It was at Hartford, it appears, that he was deeply influenced by Wilhelm Löhe's famous work, *Three Books on the Church*, which profoundly deepened his understanding of the church and led him further into studies of patristics and Luther so that more and more he left his liberal moorings to become an unflinching confessional Lutheran.

In May 1933 he took up his work as professor of church history, history of dogma, and symbolics at the University of Erlangen, near Nürnberg, where such prominent and influential theologians as Elert, Althaus, and Procksch were active in those high days of that University. Students who attended it for their theological training testify to the extremely exciting years and stimulating impetuses that emanated from the professors there.

This was especially true since at this time the upsurge of Nazi ideology under Hitler and Rosenberg began to threaten Biblical and confessional teaching in Germany. Sasse himself took a leading role in the establishment of the "Bekennende Kirche" and demonstrated forcefully against the dangerous inroads of neopaganism with its "Herrenvolk" mentality and thrust. In these difficult struggles of the church Sasse came into contact and collaboration with leading churchmen and theologians such as Karl Barth and Dietrich Bonhoeffer, although he could not always consent to their advice and theology. The Barmen Declaration particularly angered Sasse; he was developing more and more into an antagonist of false ecumenism and Barthian church diplomacy based on Reformed theology.

Sasse as a polemical theologian deserves some attention if his strength and wide influence in theological and ecumenical circles is to be appraised. In the years before he emigrated to Australia in 1949, he was heavily engaged in trying to prevent his own church, the Lutheran Church of Bavaria, from joining the *Evangelische Kirche in Deutschland* (E.K.i.D), a federation of Evangelical churches in Germany including the United churches of that country. It was Sasse's firm conviction, which he never abandoned throughout his life, that the formation of the E.K.i.D. would spell the end of the Lutheran Church as a confessional church in Germany and that it was clearly an attack on the Scriptures and the Confessions. In an unequivocal manner he made his position clear through an open letter to Bishop Meiser of Bavaria. When he saw that he could not convince him of his erroneous ecclesiastical course, Sasse became a member of the Lutheran Free Church in Germany and resigned his position. His unrelenting stand on the Lutheran Confessions, his deep understanding and appreciation of Luther's stand on the Sacrament of the Altar, and his aversion to all church-political manipulation and maneuvering forced him to take this step. He never regretted it, for to him it was a matter of conscience bound to the Word of God.

After about a year in the Free Church he accepted a call to become lecturer at Immanuel Theological Seminary in North Adelaide, South Australia, the theological training center of the United Evangelical Lutheran Church in Australia. With his wife Charlotte Margarete nee Naumann (whom he married on Sept. 11, 1924) and family (two sons) he arrived in Melbourne on Sept. 11, 1949, and in the following month was inducted into his field of work, the lectureship in church history. It was at this seminary, later to become Luther Seminary of the new amalgamated Lutheran Church of Australia, that he was to finish his renowned service.

Dr. Sasse was an immensely erudite scholar and at no time lost any of his desire to learn, rethink, and produce relevant theology. In spite of severe physical disabilities towards the end of his life, his mental and theological acuity in no way declined, much to the amazement of those who knew and worked with him. Already in his days in Germany he was a contributor to the great *Theologisches Wörterbuch zum Neuen Testament*, edited by G. Kittel, and would probably have continued so had not his going to Australia curtailed his research on certain Greek New Testament words for that lexicon. Indeed, he had done extensive preparations for the article on *ouranos* (heaven) before he left Germany. Unable to complete it because of his departure, he left the material with a colleague, who wrote it with the help of Sasse's notes.

If his major works are considered and evaluated, then it becomes clear that there were two areas of theology on which he focused most strongly—the *Sacrament of the Altar* and the *church*. In the '40s he edited a number of important articles on the Sacrament in an invaluable work called *Vom Sakrament des Altars*. In his influential book *Here We Stand* the doctrine of the Eucharist plays a prominent role, while his fine work *Kirche and Herrenmahl* and later *This Is My Body* demonstrate how clearly and confessionally he held to the Biblical-Lutheran conception of the Sacrament. That, too, is why he could in no way tolerate any compromise and syncretistic theology that tended to affect the Real Presence in the Sacrament. He believed strongly that the future of the Lutheran Church in the world depends on a joyful confession of this great dogma and the celebration of the Sacrament in accordance with the clear and unmistakable Words of Institution of the Lord of the church. That is why he wrote vigorously against the Leuenberg Concordie (cf. *Luth. Blätter*, No. 107 [Oct. 1972], pp. 57 ff.) and chastised it as the work of dilettantes, predicting that from it there must inevitably result a fresh catastrophe for the churches.

In his many statements, letters, and articles concerning the church Sasse always emphasized powerfully that church and confession belong intrinsically together. By this he did not mean just any confession, for instance one based on tradition or on pious opinion, but only those confessions that are firmly based on Scripture.

Such a true and dependable confession bears witness to Scriptural truth.

Therefore Dr. Sasse is able to state categorically and without reservation (in the last part of the third essay in this book): "The experience of Christendom shows that wherever the authority of the ancient confessions has been set aside, there also the Biblical doctrine of the incarnation of the eternal Son has been lost. It is not possible to maintain the authority of Holy Scripture and reject the authority of these confessions. This is so because the authority of the confessions is none other than the authority of their Scriptural content."

Dr. Sasse's unshakable belief that the church is always one, in spite of external denominations with their differences in liturgies and languages and politics, made him concerned and active ecumenically. From his early days as pastor in a parish and as an active participant in the "Faith and Order" movement of the World Council of Churches (he produced the report on the Lausanne meeting of 1927) he was operative in bringing to bear the centrality of the Gospel on the discussions and negotiations of many churches, keeping in contact with them by means of his massive correspondence and personal discussion and intervention. He was no utopian on the ecumenical scene; neither was he a pessimist, though sometimes his remarks could be mistaken for a despairing outlook. The unity of the church was for him an object of faith: "As no one can see the body of Christ, so no one can see its unity." That does not mean that the church is some kind of platonic concept; on the contrary, through the one Christ, the one Holy Spirit, the one Gospel, Baptism, and Eucharist, the unity of the church is present as a reality in the world. He was, however, always vigorously opposed to a visible unity based on anything less than the truth of the Scriptures—unity and truth dare never be separated was his constant warning. Where truth is compromised or rejected, there the church and its true unity must suffer and decline.

His years in Australia, while curtailing his scholarship in the narrow sense of the word, were largely spent in lecturing, preaching (he often preached, particularly to congregations of refugees, for whom he showed great compassion), reading and writing, advising and counseling. A great contribution was his work on the Intersynodical Committee, that group of theologians, pastors, and laymen entrusted with negotiating the union between the two Lutheran churches in Australia. It was invaluable that he brought to the conference table not only his enormous theological and ecclesiastical knowledge but above all his passionate concern and untiring zeal for the union of the two churches, both of which he could address with authority. He also took up the dialog with the Roman Catholic Church with enthusiasm and was a member of the dialoging committee set up by the Lutheran Church of Australia for this purpose. His erudition and incisiveness (also stimulated perhaps by the fact that his younger son had joined that church while in Adelaide), his inside information about that church (he corresponded with the Vatican, notably with Augustin Cardinal Bea), and his great belief in the power of God's Word that had changed Dr. Martin Luther and led to the Reformation of the 16th century—these made him a force at the interchurch discussions and further enhanced his reputation as "Australia's most distinguished acquisition from the Continental theological scene."

The last decade of his life—his wife predeceased him on March 4, 1964—he lived in comparative loneliness but unabating theological activity on the Adelaide scene. Due to disabilities he was no longer able to serve as guest lecturer, as he had previously at Wartburg (Dubuque) and Concordia Theological Seminaries both at St. Louis and Springfield, the latter giving him a D.D. Instead, he began to concentrate strongly on the theme "Concerning Holy Scripture" and indeed was well on the way to producing a work on this subject when he was suddenly taken out of this life on Aug. 9, 1976. Friends of his collected a number of essays and with some fiscal aid (apparently from his brother) were able to have these printed in a collection called *Sacra Scriptura*.

Several years have elapsed since Dr. Sasse's death; his works certainly follow him. An important part of the theological legacy he left to the Lutheran Church and the churches of the world will remain the memory of a theologian, pastor, teacher, and ecclesiastic who was firmly convinced of Augustine's dictum, which Sasse used as an introduction to Vilmar's *Dogmatik*: *In ecclesia non valet: Hoc ego dico, hoc tu dicis, hoc ille dicit, sed: Haec dicit Dominus* ("What counts in the church is not: This I say, this you say, this he says, but: Thus says the Lord").

J. T. E. Renner

In the year of Luther's 500th
birthday anniversary, November 1983
North Adelaide, South Australia

WE CONFESS

THE SACRAMENTS

Contents

Translator's Preface

Hermann Sasse's confession of Jesus Christ we have heard in volume one of the We Confess Series, *We Confess Jesus Christ*. In this volume he confesses that the salvation achieved by Christ alone is ours by His gift alone. His ways of giving are His to determine as He pleases. Only thus are they sure and liberating in their bestowal of what He says He is giving. We may in no way make His means of grace subject to our determinations. His are the words we are given to proclaim; His is the name put on us with the water of Baptism; His is the body and blood, which He gives into our mouths to eat and to drink; His is the forgiveness bestowed with the words of absolution; His are the keys entrusted to His ministry. All this Sasse confesses against every attempt to take them captive.

He speaks with powerful contemporary relevance because he knows the historical challenges. From its beginning the Gospel has suffered subversion, dilution, and addition. Men have attempted to make it more sure and more acceptable. Knowledge of these attempts is a resource for dealing with them, and Sasse recalls it for us as he points to Christ.

More than a defender of the faith, Sasse is at his happiest and best extolling his Lord. Jesus is the Lord. His salvation is ours only as His gift, and He gives it according to His good and gracious will. No necessity may be laid on Him in the ways of Scholastic or Enlightenment theology. Sasse's enormous learning and careful scholarship are put to this service.

He was so engaged in addressing the heavy needs of the day that his work comes to us mostly as a series of particular pieces, each with its own weight. The first of these essays, "Word and Sacrament: Preaching and the Lord's Supper," describes the life of the church as it moves forward from generation to generation. Its continuity is given only by the Lord and the continuity of His gifts. The church is where He gives His gifts, where the means of grace are made available. Only by them is it enlivened, sustained, and given a foretaste of the consummation to come. This first essay ends with a cry to the Holy Spirit: *Veni creator Spiritus*.

In 1949 Sasse wrote "Holy Baptism" in response to Barth's attack on Baptism. The progression of the essay is most instructive. First comes the contemporary church context, then history, theology, and Scripture. There is often a generating and focusing *Leitmotif* in Sasse's writings, and in this essay it is "Washing of Regeneration."

Sasse's primary study and training in the New Testament are witnessed in his thoroughgoing exegesis in "The Lord's Supper in the New Testament." Our Lord's life-giving Supper flows into the church, making it His body. Sasse extols the body and blood given and shed for us Christians to eat and to drink. Thereby we are enlivened for worship and work.

The vitality of these gifts is then confessed in "The Lord's Supper in the Lutheran Church." What is said of it in the Augsburg Confession is prompting for rejoicing and repentance. Again Sasse relates the discussion to the contemporary situation, history, theology, and Scripture. What our Lord says, does, and gives affects our lives, confession, and work.

What our Lord says and does is extolled in "The Lutheran Understanding of the Consecration." This may not be blurred or diminished by Protestant influences, Anglican ornamentation, or Roman infiltration. The enlivening gifts given by our Lord and confessed by our fathers direct our understanding, for we are captive to the Word.

The final essay, "Sanctorum Communio," points us toward the next volume, *We Confess the Church*. Sasse's understanding is rooted in his own profound ecumenical involvement. To forsake the doctrine of the Real Presence of the body and blood of Christ is to forsake the catholic tradition and what our Lord says. To be given His body and blood to eat and to drink is to be part of His body, the *una sancta*, which continues forever and is thus brought to the consummation. The faith that confesses this is not grounded in our observations or ideas but in the words of our Lord. Confessing His sacraments, we confess also His church.

WORD AND SACRAMENT
Preaching
and the Lord's Supper

Letters to Lutheran Pastors, No. 42
July 1956

(Published in *In Statu Confessionis: Gesammelte Aufsätze von Hermann Sasse*, ed. Friedrich Wilhelm Hopf [Berlin and Hamburg: Lutherisches Verlagshaus, 1966], 73–90.)

There is probably no question that leads so deeply into our office, its essence and its task, its necessity and its promise, as our present subject. Whenever theology becomes quite practical, it engages this problem. The profoundest Christian thinkers have pondered it, and it has affected all the churches of the world, the "Catholic" no less than the "Protestant." It is a problem not only for Protestantism, or for Lutheranism in particular. The Catholic churches of the East and West also have their problems with preaching and the Lord's Supper. The Eastern Orthodox Church, for example, which has gained a firm foothold in the West because of the massive migration of Orthodox Christians from Eastern countries, cannot be satisfied with continuing to celebrate its "Holy Liturgy" in the liturgical languages when it is no longer understood by the younger generation. They have to make use of their principle that the liturgy be celebrated in the language of the people. So an English translation has already been completed. But the liturgy must also be explained. Can the Eastern Church ever forget that its greatest preacher was John Chrysostom and that it is not enough to venerate his icon—that his example must also be followed?

Similar questions arise for Roman Catholicism, as the liturgical

11

movement indicates. It was born before the First World War out of a deep dissatisfaction on the part of the best young Catholics with the situation in their church. After 1918 it pointed out the shortcomings of the common Catholic worship so candidly that it had to be curbed and in part shut down by Rome. But the Curia had absorbed its great desire to elevate the major European languages to the position of liturgical languages with such vigor that we can still expect a major reform of the Roman liturgy in this century.

Is it a coincidence that the liturgical movement in Germany and other countries went hand in hand with a "Bible movement" and that the modern Roman church has produced masterpieces of Biblical translation? Is it a coincidence that the Roman church in the age of radio and television has again produced popular preaching that recalls the classical period of popular preaching in the Middle Ages?

But the encouragement of Bible reading and the special popular preaching are no substitute for the every Sunday parish sermon, especially if the latter is only a short lecture on a question of dogmatics or ethics. Truly, the problem of "Word and Sacrament: Preaching and the Lord's Supper" is not only our problem but that of all Christendom. Strictly speaking, it has been a problem throughout the history of the church, ever since Paul had to deal with the problems of the Lord's Supper (1 Cor. 10 and 11) and preaching (1 Cor. 14) in the church at Corinth.

1.

Old as the problem of Word and Sacrament is, it was first put as a theological question and given a theological answer by Augustine. Here, as in other matters, this great church father of the West is not always helpful, and we may not follow him as blindly as did the theology not only of the Catholicism of the Middle Ages but also of the Reformation. This can even be said of Luther himself, although he was able to break through the constructions of Augustine's sacramental doctrine at decisive points by bringing to light the witness of Scripture, a witness that was better maintained by the Eastern fathers. Since we have been reared in Augustine's sacramental teaching and even see Luther's teaching on the Sacrament through Augustinian spectacles, it is not easy. But should we just leave it to Roman Catholic theologians to recover something of the rich resources of the Greek fathers, who have such a great role to play in the Catalog of Testimonies at the conclusion of the

Formula of Concord (*Die Bekenntnisschriften der evangelisch-luther-ischen Kirche*, 6th ed. [Göttingen, 1967], 1101–35) as witnesses of Scriptural truth, just as they frequently appear also in the earlier Confessions?

Wherein lies the weakness of Augustine's sacramental doctrine? This may first of all be found in his attempt to establish *sacramentum* as a universal idea or category that applies to all religions [*Con. Faustum* 19. 11]. The Christian sacrament is then only a specific instance of a universal phenomenon common to all religions, both the true and the false. Now it is true that the Christian sacraments, such as Baptism and the Lord's Supper, have their parallels in many religions, as the apologists of the second century, and even Paul in 1 Cor. 10:18–21, have observed. No one denies that heathen rites and the myths they follow have echoes of the original knowledge of God, but through sin they have been perverted into the service of idols [Rom. 1:19–23]. In this sense, even the human sacrifices of the Teutons, the Aztecs, and the Syrians could be regarded as demonically perverted hints pointing to the sacrifice of the Son of Man. "Every dogma is as old as the world."

But to try to understand the Christian sacrament on the basis of a concept of sacrament derived from the history of religions is totally impossible. What constitutes the church's sacrament is something unique; it has no parallels. All the honor and love we owe Augustine as a great father of the Western Church may not obscure the fact that he had lived too long and too deeply in heathen religion and philosophy. He was not able to banish the old man from his thinking in the same way that he was from his life and faith. That is what it cost him to have "loved so late."

We may find something similar in what Augustine taught on Holy Scripture. Here also he has a universal idea or category of what "divine scripture" is and must be. This he applies to the Bible and shows how it matches his ideal instead of simply starting with what Holy Scripture has to say about itself. Had he done this, he would not have been able to put the Sibylline Oracles on a level with the prophets because they apparently correctly prophesied the coming of the Redeemer [*De. civ.* 18. 23]. As the Bible is not just a specific instance of what may be called "divine scripture" in the religions of the world, so also the Christian sacrament cannot be understood from a universal idea of *sacramentum*. The Christian sacrament is what it is because it was instituted by Jesus Christ and so is inextricably bound up with the incarnation of the eternal Son of God.

The theological tradition of the West has shown a remarkable stability through the Middle Ages into modern Catholicism. The same may be said of Lutheran and Reformed theology in the Reformation and through the period of orthodoxy. In doing theology, we simply may not spare ourselves the labor of differentiating between what the Bible says and the human mode of thinking. This is so even for so central a doctrine of the Christian faith as the doctrine of the Trinity. With the East one can think of it as three in one [*Dreieinigkeit*], with Augustine and the West as threefold [*Dreifaltigkeit*], without in any way diminishing the truth of the impenetrable mystery.

It was one of the mistakes of our fathers in the age of orthodoxy that they all too often identified the thought form with the Biblical content of a doctrinal statement. As a result they unconsciously and unintentionally clothed the eternal truth of Scripture in the transitory garb of a theological tradition. It should not be necessary to point out that this observation has nothing to do with the attempt of the Ritschlian School, above all of Harnack in his *History of Dogma*, to rob Christian dogma of its Biblical content by replacing what were taken to be the categories of Greek metaphysics with those of Kantian ethics. Nor does it have anything to do with the modern "demythologizing" of the New Testament by translating the Biblical statements into existential philosophy. What we have in mind here is what Luther did when he confronted the falsification of the Biblical faith by Aristotelian and Thomistic philosophy and when he told the Swiss, who so energetically appealed to Augustinian metaphysics in the Marburg Colloquy, where the limit of the authority of the church fathers is:

> We would indeed show the beloved fathers such honor that we read what they have written, which is so helpful to us, with the best understanding of which we are capable, insofar as they are in harmony with Holy Scripture. But where their writings are not in harmony with Holy Scripture, it is much better that we say they are mistaken than that because of them we depart from God's Word. (According to Osiander's report, which is confirmed by the reports of others, that Luther appealed to Augustine's own rule, according to which only the canonical books of Scripture have unqualified authority; see the texts, WA 30/III, 144–45, and W. Koehler, *Das Marburger Religionsgespräch: Versuch einer Rekonstruktion*, where several sources are cited on p. 177.)

It would have been better for the Lutheran Church if its theologians had always held to this rule in more rigorous self-criticism.

The practical consequence of the foregoing is that we must claim our freedom from the Augustinian school's universal idea of the *sacramentum*, as our Confessions essentially do when they do not first set down a definition of the nature of a sacrament and even leave the question of the number of sacraments open, in contrast with Rome (not more and not less than seven) and the Reformed Church (not more and not less than two). The way of the Confessions is in harmony with teaching of the early church, which was innocent of any such idea of sacrament. They spoke of particular "mysteries," using the word *mystery* quite broadly. In the 11th century the Latin *sacramentum* was still being used so broadly that Hugh of St. Victor, besides his other dogmatic works, wrote a dogmatics with the title *De sacramentis*, in which even the Trinity is called a *sacramentum*, that is, a mystery, something known only to faith. The classical dogmatician of the Eastern Church, John of Damascus, also knows no doctrine of the sacraments as such. He has chapters on "The Faith and Baptism" and on "The Holy Spotless Mysteries of the Lord," that is, the Eucharist [*De Fide* 4. 9. 13]. In harmony with this, when Luther uses the word *Sacrament* in the singular, he usually means "the Sacrament of sacraments," as the Sacrament of the Altar was first called by the fathers of the Greek church. There is an echo of this Lutheran usage in Justus Jonas's German text of the Apology when he renders Melanchthon's *eadem sacramenta* as "the same Baptism and Sacrament" (Ap VII/VIII 10). In this way also the Lutheran Church retained the freedom to call absolution a sacrament. Whether the office of the keys is called a sacrament or not is purely a matter of terminology, in which the church has and must have complete freedom if it wants to remain on the foundation of Scripture. Christ did not institute some abstract *sacramentum*. He instituted the office of the ministry, Baptism, Holy Communion, and the office of the keys. Only if we regain this freedom of the Lutheran Reformation will we be able to go all the way to the heart of what is uniquely referred to by the term "sacrament," whose essence is not to be found in any phenomena from the history of religions or in any human speculation about what God must do to redeem us. It is in the institution of the Lord that eludes every human why and in the incomprehensible wonder of the Incarnation. If we take that seriously, then the problem of Word and Sacrament takes on a completely different appearance.

2.

Augustine has left behind another difficult question for all the churches of the West in his definition of a sacrament as the "sign" [*sig-*

num] of a divine "thing" [res]. [*Signacula quidem rerum divinarum esse: visibilia, sed res ipsas invisibiles in eis (De Cat. Rud. 26. 50. Con. Faustum 19. 11) Ista, fratres, ideo dicuntur sacramenta, quia in eis aliud videtur, aliud intelligitur (Serm. 272. Ep. 138. 17). Aliud est sacramentum, aliud virtus sacramenti (In Joh. Tract. 26. 11).*] What we have here must first be recognized as a man's theological theory. It is quite noteworthy that the Eastern Church, which here, as always, represents an older form of Christianity, developed no such theory of sacrament as a sign of something divine. In the late Middle Ages and the century of the Reformation (Cyril Lucarius and his Calvinism) the Latin Scholastic doctrine, and with it the doctrine of sacrament as sign, did gain some entry into Eastern theology, but this private teaching today enjoys hardly any recognition, least of all by the Russian theologians. To be sure the sacraments (mysteries) are spoken of as symbols, as "the outward means of the unfathomable, hiddenly laden working of grace by the Holy Spirit through which the sanctification of man is again brought to completion" (Stef. Zankov, *Das Orthodoxe Christentum* [1928], 102 [*The Eastern Orthodox Church* (1929), 113]). What is characteristic however, is that even Dionysius the Areopagite sees what is termed sign and symbol more in the details of the celebration of the sacrament, the particular rites and ceremonies, the gestures and actions of the priest than in the sacraments as such. That is also to be understood when he speaks of the Eucharist in the plural: "the mysteries."

Thomas understands Augustine's definition of sacrament as a sign in such a way that it is spoken of as an effective sign (*signum efficax*). This is applied only to sacraments in the New Testament; the "sacraments" of the Old Testament have only a significative meaning. In the Eastern Church what is central is what they do. God works on man in a sacrament. "A Mystery or Sacrament is a holy act through which grace, or, in other words, the saving power of God, works mysteriously upon man." So Philaret in the *Christian Catechism* [284]. In such a doctrine of sacrament it can never come to that tearing apart of "sign" and "thing," *signum* and *res* that since Berengar, Wycliffe, the radical Hussites, the *Devotio Moderna* in the Netherlands, the Humanists, Zwingli, and Calvin has reduced sacrament to being only a *sign* of grace. This is probably not what Augustine had in mind. There are two levels in his sacramental doctrine—one, as presented in the liturgy, catholic realistic, the other spiritualizing. This split is the tribute he pays to Neoplatonic philosophy and is a burden that the churches in the West bear to this day. We in no way want to glorify the teaching of the Eastern Church

16

here or excuse its serious errors, but on this one point it stands nearer to the New Testament than what Augustine and those who followed him taught. *The New Testament does not know of the idea of sacrament as sign*. Perhaps the whole idea of sign originated in the designation of circumcision as a "sign of the covenant" [*signum foederis*] (Gen. 17:11). But despite the parallel drawn in Col. 1:11ff. between Baptism and circumcision—Paul was addressing Gnostics with a Jewish background—no one has ever found a place in the New Testament in which Baptism or the Lord's Supper or even the "elements" of water, bread, and wine are understood in the sense of the "sign" theory. None of the words that could be interpreted as such a "sign," such as *eikōn* (image), are used of Baptism or the Lord's Supper in the New Testament. Nowhere is it written that Baptism is an image or a sign of regeneration. It *is* the washing of regeneration (Titus 3:5). "We *were* buried therefore with Him by Baptism into death" (Rom. 6:4). "You *were* buried with Him in Baptism, in which you *were* also raised. . . . And you . . . God *made* alive together with Him" (Col. 2:12–13). Also the word *tupos* in the sense of model or image is not used of Baptism and the Lord's Supper or of their elements. There are "types" of the sacraments in the Old Testament, as when Paul in 1 Cor. 10:1ff., where we find Baptism and the Lord's Supper arranged together for the first time in the New Testament (cf. 12:13; John 19:34), points to certain experiences of the old people of God as "typological" [*tupikōs*] (1 Cor. 10:11, which the Vulgate accurately translates *in figura* [Tertullian, *figurate*, *Idol.* 5]) of the sacraments of the new people of God. So the "baptism" of the fathers in the cloud and in the sea, the "spiritual food" of the manna, the bread from heaven (cf John 6:31ff.), and the "spiritual drink" of the water from the rock are types, prefigurements of Christian Baptism and the Lord's Supper. But Baptism and the Lord's Supper are not "types," not prefigurements or parables. They do indeed point to the future, but it is a future already present with its gifts of grace. More will be said later on what it means that the future is present in the sacraments.

Here is where we find the heart of the Lutheran confession of the sacraments. Certainly Luther made much use, especially in his early period, of Augustine's idea of sacrament as a "sign." Here as in other patterns of theological thought he was bound by the theological schooling from which he came. We should not overlook the fact that until 1522 he had to carry on the struggle against Rome for the *sola fide* also in regard to sacrament according to the old formula: *Non sacramentum, sed fides sacramenti justificat* (Not the sacrament, but the faith of the one receiving the sacrament justifies). To that Luther always clung, with special emphasis at the point where he had to join the "through faith alone" in Baptism with the objectivity of the sacrament. "My faith does not constitute Baptism but receives it." This is from the Large Catechism, where Luther is defending the Baptism of infants (LC IV 53); it is sure for them, too. If the unqualified adherence to the *sola fide* is one side of the sacramental teaching of Luther and the Lutheran Church, the other is the insistence on the objectivity and reality of the sacrament, which was necessary over against the Enthusiasts. How serious this was for Luther is shown by the fact that he went beyond Thomas in his insistence on objectivity. Thomas stated, "An adult who lacked the intention [*intentio*] of receiving baptism should be rebaptized [*esset rebaptizandus*]," in order to receive Baptism validly and without question. But if the lack of intention is not certain, in case of doubt it should be conditional (*Summa theol.* 3. 68. 7. 3). Luther regarded the baptism of a Jew, who "should come today deceitfully and with an evil purpose," as a true baptism (LC IV 54), which under no circumstances is it to be repeated if the sinner should come to faith. This objectivity of the sacrament was settled for the Reformer from the very beginning, just as he always held fast to the Real Presence, even when he finally gave up transubstantiation in *The Babylonian Captivity*.

But the more he had to urge the objectivity of the sacrament against the "Sacramentarians," the more cautious he became in using the word *sign*. They were misusing it in a way that made of sacrament only a sign. In the Catechism he avoids the word *sign*, and we need only look at the Heidelberg Catechism to understand what that means. Here the sacraments (Question 66) are understood only as "signs and seals" [*Wahrzeichen und Siegel*] and no other effect is ascribed to them than of reminding believers of the actual salvation event and assuring them of it. This actual event is independent of the sacrament. Question 72 asks, "Is the outward washing with water itself actually the washing away of sins?" to which the answer is given: "No, for only the blood of Jesus Christ and the Holy Spirit cleanse us from all sin." The following question, why the Holy Spirit calls Baptism the washing of regeneration and the washing away of sins, is given the answer that He wants to teach us "that *just as* the filthiness of the body is taken away, so are our sins taken away by the blood and Spirit of Christ" and "that He wants to assure us through this divine *pledge* and *sign* [*Pfand und Wahrzeichen*] that we just as truly have been washed of our sins spiritually as we are washed with physical water." In the Lord's Supper

18

bread and cup are "*signs* [*Wahrzeichen*] of the body and blood of Christ" (Q. 75). Only "according to the nature and usage of sacraments" is the bread called the body of Christ (Q. 78). The bread *is not* the body, and so the body and blood of the Lord are not taken orally (Q. 76 and 77).

Under the pressure of such spiritualizing Luther more and more stepped back from the conventional word *sign* and also *pledge* [*pignus*], which was much beloved in the theology of the Middle Ages and had meant much to him in his early years. He was profoundly aware that sacrament has another side, the "external thing," which the Enthusiasts scorned (LC IV 7), the "gross, external mask," i. e., outward form [*Erscheinungsform*] (LC IV 19). However, as it is of the nature of divine revelation that God comes to us veiled, as the Incarnate One ("In our poor flesh and blood, Enclothes himself the eternal Good"), so is it of the nature of divine action "that God will not deal with us except through his external Word and sacrament" (SA III VIII 10). In this recognition of the indissoluble unity of "sign" and "object" [*Zeichen und Sache*] the danger of spiritualizing is overcome—the danger that lay in what Augustine taught and that since Berengar and Wycliffe captured so many Catholics of the late Middle Ages and since Zwingli and Bucer a large part of the Reformation movement. In this sense what Luther taught on sacraments is the great overthrow of Augustinianism in the church and the return to the essence [*Est*] of the New Testament.

3.

The third problem, which Augustine never fully found his way through, is the question of "Word" and "element." He first of all gave the solution that is quoted again and again in the Middle Ages, in modern Roman theology, and by the reformers: "Take the Word away, and what is the water but simply water? The Word is added to the element, and there results a sacrament, as if itself also a kind of visible Word" (*In Joh. Tract.* 80. 3). Of first importance here is the emphasis on the Word as that which constitutes the sacrament. It was a serious error to try to explain sacrament from the natural side [*Naturseite*], as was done in the 19th century under the influence of theosophical speculations, which even infiltrated Lutheran theology, and in the 20th century in the Berneuchener Movement influenced by Rudolf Steiner. The most impressive attempt to understand sacrament from nature was made by Paul Tillich in his early writings and in his dogmatics. He presents the view that in a sacrament an element from nature becomes the "bearer of the holy" [*Symbol und Wirklichkeit* (1966), 50; *Systematic Theology* (1963), 3:123]. That is supposed to be the essence of the Lutheran idea of sacrament. It is significant that Catholic theology must be brought to bear against him. It is not some mysterious quality of the water in Baptism or the bread and wine in the Lord's Supper but only the institution of the Lord that has designated just these elements, and His almighty Word alone makes them sacraments. Later as Scholasticism spoke of "Word" and "element" as "form" and "substance" and this was taken into Roman dogma, the constituting significance of the Word for a sacrament was underscored because the "form," the "idea," is always regarded as higher than the "substance." We should never forget that nor misunderstand it, as though the sacramental word in the Catholic sacrament is a kind of incantation with a magical effect, as Protestant polemic has often understood it. Johann Gerhard (Locus 21, 13) emphatically repudiates the Reformed understanding of the Roman and Lutheran consecration as a magical incantation [*magica incantatio*]. There may be a suggestion of "magic" in the Roman view that at ordination a power to consecrate [*potestas consecrandi*] is given to particular men as a *virtus*, a power in them. But even we would not acknowledge that, because today "magic" is generally understood as exercising coercion over the deity. In any case we must grant that the Roman Church also puts the Word above the element. What then is the relation of Word to element? What may be said of the element in the sacrament?

The answer that emerges may at first surprise us. The "element" does not at all belong to the essence of "sacrament." This follows from the fact that the medieval church had to abandon the idea of element and replace it with "substance" [*Materie*], which does not have to be an element, a thing of nature [*Naturding*] at all. So in the Sacrament of Penance what was done by the penitent (contrition, confession, satisfaction) was understood as the substance, while the absolution was its form. (Time will not allow us here to explore the magnificent attempt of Hugo of St. Victor, the first dogmatician of the medieval church, to construct a doctrine of the sacraments without the apparatus of Aristotelian philosophy. In spite of his beginning with Augustine's definition of sacrament as the "sign" of a holy "thing," he tries to keep clear of any philosophical system; *De Sacramentis* 1. 9.) Also the Augsburg Confession and its Apology do not know the idea of element with sacrament as such. This is shown by the inclusion of absolution among the sacraments (AC XIII): "The genuine sacraments, therefore, are Bap-

20

tism, the Lord's Supper, and absolution" (Ap XIII 4). In Gospel freedom the Apology (Ap XIII 11) declares that even ordination may be called a sacrament because Christ has instituted the office of the ministry and given it the promise of Is. 55:11. This freedom in speaking of sacraments in the Lutheran Church includes the freedom to regard the formula "Word and element" as what it is, a theological attempt to describe sacrament. The concept of *elementum* is dubious because of its ambiguity (consider the manifold meaning of the word in the New Testament) and vagueness, and we might well ask whether the reformers have done well in taking it over from Augustine's sacramental doctrine without more reflection.

4.

What is *our task* in view of this state of affairs? As Lutheran theologians we should follow the example of the Augsburg Confession in our theological thinking as in our teaching and preaching and never start from one common doctrine of the means of grace or the sacraments but deal with each of the means of grace by itself in its own particularity: Preaching the Gospel, Baptism, confession and absolution, the Sacrament of the Altar. Only then will we be able to understand the fullness of God's dealing with us, the different ways by which He comes to us, and the whole uniqueness of every single means of grace and so come to the proper use of each (consider the order of the articles of the Augsburg Confession and the arrangement of confession between Baptism and the Lord's Supper in the Small Catechism). Already with Baptism and the Lord's Supper it only causes confusion if we always try to draw parallels between them and to assert that what is true of the one sacrament must be said of the other. So it has been argued recently in the ecumenical movement even by Lutherans: Since the churches recognize one another's Baptism, they must also have reciprocal recognition of the Lord's Supper. As they put it, "altar fellowship" follows of necessity from "baptismal fellowship." But Baptism and the Lord's Supper, as immeasurably great as each of these sacraments is and as much as they cohere (1 Cor. 10:1ff.; cf. also the baptismal practice of the early church on Easter Eve and even the custom of the medieval church of giving infants the Lord's Supper, at least in the form of consecrated wine, right after baptism), are simply not the same.

What the Sacrament of the Altar is was told to us by the Lord Himself; what Baptism is we learn from His apostle. We know when the Lord's Supper was instituted from the account of the institution. The *institution* of Baptism, according to the common notion of the early church, and also of Luther ("To Jordan came the Christ, our Lord"), took place as a result of the Lord's letting Himself be baptized by John ("There He established a washing for us") and is not identical with the *command* to baptize. Baptism was performed in the apostolic age "in the name of Jesus" (e.g., Acts 2:38; 10:48; 19:5; cf. the command to baptize of Matt. 28:19 according to Eusebius in the apparatus of Nestle; 1 Cor. 1:13), later with the Trinitarian baptismal formula. The apostles often left the administration of baptism to others, and it is no devaluation of the sacrament for Paul to say that the Lord did not send him to baptize but to preach the Gospel. Baptism remains, with all the freedom and diversity of administration, the washing of regeneration, the full, complete sacrament, needing no completion in confirmation, as Anglican theology today says, not without effect on the Protestant churches.

We cannot go into the question here of what we would have to say today in our individual congregations about Baptism. It seems to me that the so urgently necessary instruction about the sacrament in Bible classes and sermons on the great texts of the New Testament that deal with Baptism should be taking place. Beyond that the fourth chief part of the Large Catechism should be treated in lectures and discussions. That applies especially to the question of infant baptism. We have to be aware of how ignorant the modern generation is, even in the Lutheran Church. We recognize far too seldom that religious and confirmation instruction and the Sunday school can in no way give what previous generations knew from home through Bible reading and what was learned from pious parents. Today the need of the hour for the Lutheran Church is to become a teaching church again. The success of Rome, of the sects, and of communism is based substantially on the fact that what they teach, they teach unflaggingly. And our congregations hunger more than we know for teaching. Why don't we give them the bread that they want? How often we have given the impression at the administration of baptism in the congregation or with a small baptismal party that an *opus operatus* has been administered. Who of those present knows what a miracle has happened here under the insignificant veil of the external sacrament? Who is aware that here a decision is made between the life and death, salvation and damnation of a person because this sacrament reaches into eternity? Are our congregations aware that they must pray in all seriousness for the newly baptized? Luther maintained that so many of the baptized are lost because this intercession has been lacking

(WA 19, 537f.; *Bekenntnisschriften*, "Taufbüchlein," 536, 20ff.). If this intercession were taken seriously, would it not also mean the beginning of a renewal of the office of sponsor that has become so secularized? Do we really believe that the members of our congregations take so much with them from a few hurried hours of confirmation instruction, in which something is said at the end about the sacraments—though they should really determine the whole content of confirmation instruction—that they are able to live on it throughout their whole lives as people who daily return to their baptism?

5.

Where Baptism is rightly taught, there the Gospel is rightly proclaimed, for the whole Gospel is contained in this sacrament: Christ's death and resurrection, our dying and rising with Him in repentance and faith, the bestowal already now of future heavenly treasures, eternal righteousness, innocence and blessedness. The same applies to the Sacrament of the Altar. Of it Luther once said: "This sacrament is the Gospel" ("Concerning the Veneration of the Sacrament of the Holy Body of Christ," 1523, directed to the Christians in Bohemia with a powerful emphasis on the Real Presence against every symbolic explanation). This is one of the Reformer's profoundest theological perceptions. Because this sacrament is the Gospel, the struggle over the sacrament was at the same time the struggle for the Gospel, and vice versa. That alone can explain what the world calls Luther's stubbornness and obstinacy in the controversy over the Sacrament, his inflexible seriousness on just this question. Neither for Zwingli nor for Bucer was the struggle for the Sacrament so important.

Why is the Sacrament of the Altar the Gospel for Luther? First of all simply because the Words of Institution contain the whole Gospel. To attack them is to attack the Gospel itself.

> Everything depends on these words. Every Christian should and must know them and hold them fast. He must never let anyone take them away from him by any other kind of teaching, even though it were an angel from heaven [Gal. 1:8]. They are words of life and of salvation, so that whoever believes in them has all his sins forgiven through that faith; he is a child of life and has overcome death and hell. Language cannot express how great and mighty these words are, for they are the sum and substance of the whole gospel. (WA 11, 432, 19 [American Edition 36:277])

It must be called an attack on these words if part of them is taken literally and another part figuratively, as when "Take and eat" and "Drink of it, all of you" are taken literally, "This is My body" and "This is My blood" figuratively, and then "which is given for you" and "which is shed for you" literally again. It is characteristic of Luther that right in the cited passage, as usual, he regards faith in the "for you" as most essential. It is what brings the blessing of the Sacrament. At the same time he stresses that this "for you" is inseparably bound with faith that the words "This is My body" and "This is My blood" are true and must be taken as they stand.

> Now beware of such a view. Let go of reason and intellect; for they strive in vain to understand how flesh and blood can be present, and because they do not grasp it they refuse to believe it. (WA 11, 434, 17 [American Edition 36:279])

With this understanding of the Sacrament the relationship between Word and sacrament is no longer a problem. They go together. The sacrament is the *verbum visibile* (visible Word); the Word is the *sacramentum audibile*, the audible and heard sacrament. The spoken and heard Word of itself is a thing of nature, sound waves that come from the voice box and are received by the ear. And yet we hear "in, with, and under" these sound waves, the Word of the eternal God Himself. The natural word becomes the Word of God, *is* the Word of God.

The Gospel comes to us in this twofold way, as Word and as sacrament. Thus absolution can also be counted among the sacraments: "Do you also believe that my forgiveness is God's forgiveness?" [the confessor asks]. As Christ's body and blood are hidden under the forms of bread and wine, so God's Word is hidden under the form of the human voice (and also Holy Scripture under the form of human writings). What the Word means for the Sacrament of the Altar becomes clear from the fact that nothing made such a profound impact on those who came from the Roman to the Lutheran Mass as the Words of Institution, which the German people had never heard before because they were spoken softly in the Roman Mass. Now they were chanted aloud at the altar in their own mother tongue. "Word" and "element" became one. In both God comes to us to give us *one* grace in different forms. This is surely the way of divine revelation. God does not come to us as *Deus nudus*, as Luther says, not naked, but always veiled. Thus in Christ divinity was veiled under His humanity and could only be recognized with the eyes of faith. This is the mystery of the Incarnation, in which the sacraments are rooted: "And the Word became *flesh* and dwelt among us, full of grace and truth; *we* have beheld His glory." "We," that is, the "witnesses chosen beforehand," the apostles and all those who by the Holy Spirit are to come to faith on the basis of the apostolic testimony. In faith they all are to see Christ's glory, which is hidden to the world until that day when it will be revealed to all people when He comes to judge the living and the dead.

6.

"This sacrament *is* the Gospel." Luther's recognition matches perfectly what the New Testament teaches. "For as often as you eat this bread and drink the cup, you proclaim (*kataggellete* is to be taken as present, not as imperative) the Lord's death until He comes." Thus Paul writes at the end of the first and oldest account we have of the institution of the Lord's Supper. Several of the ancient liturgies quote these words of 1 Cor. 11:26 as if they were a part of the account itself that Paul is quoting here [*Ap. Con.* 8. 12]. For the passage at 1 Cor. 11:23ff. belongs to the "traditions" that the apostle "received" and had faithfully passed on, just as the passage at 15:3ff., which reminds us of the Second Article of the Creed. That Paul received his Gospel directly from the Lord and not from men (Gal. 1:12) does not at all preclude his coming to know of details in the life of Jesus and the texts used in the liturgy by way of the church, probably in Antioch. The words "I received [*parelabon*] from the Lord what I also delivered [*paredōka*] to you" contain the same technical terms that we find in 1 Cor. 15:3 and probably mean no more than that what Paul hands on goes back to Jesus' Last Supper and what He Himself said and did there. Evidence of the utter reliability and great age of this account may be seen in the fact that it records an item that is no longer found in Mark. It was no longer regarded as essential that at the institution Jesus distributed the bread during the meal while the cup came at the end. Whether verse 26 belongs to the ancient account itself or is an authoritative commentary of the apostle, it does say with incisive brevity that the Lord's Supper is the Gospel itself.

Baptism is the Gospel, because the whole Gospel is contained in it, not only in words but also in what our Redeemer does in His mighty rescue of us from sin, death and the devil. Absolution is the Gospel, the forgiveness of sins, the anticipation of the verdict of justification that will come in the last judgment. The Lord's Supper is also the Gospel, and indeed in quite a special way. The Gospel is the Good News proclaimed in all the world in these last days (Matt. 24:14; Acts 2:17; Heb. 1:2). It is the message of the incarnation of the eternal Word, of His redeeming death, His resurrection and ascension, His sitting at the right hand of the Father and His return in glory for the final judgment and to complete our redemption in our own resurrection.

It is the will of Christ that this Gospel be proclaimed to all peoples. But this proclamation is not only to be the message of what God has done in the past and what He will do in the future. The proclamation of this "eternal Gospel" (Rev. 14:6) is always to be accompanied by the celebration of the Sacrament that our Lord instituted, by which His death is proclaimed until He comes. Without the celebration of this Sacrament the proclamation of the Gospel could be understood as just one of the many religious messages in the world. This does indeed happen where people are ignorant of the Sacrament. Without the continual proclamation of the Gospel this Sacrament may be understood as just one of the many fellowship rites that exist in the world of religions or as an unintelligible action of a mystery religion. But the Gospel is more than a religious message, the Sacrament of the Altar more than a religious ceremony. Both the Gospel that is preached and the Gospel that occurs in the Sacrament contain one and the same gift, though in different forms: the forgiveness of sins. This is not some doctrine about the possibility of a forgiveness of sins, not an illustration of such a possibility, but the actual forgiveness itself, this unfathomable miracle of God's mercy that blots out our guilt and gives us everything that comes with forgiveness: life and salvation, redemption of the whole person, both soul and body. Both the Gospel and the Sacrament bring this forgiveness, for in both the Lamb of God who died for the sin of the world is present.

7.

And so we come to the question of the *Real Presence*, which we must touch on here at least briefly. Why was this for Luther the question about the Gospel itself? The Lord Christ is present in all the means of grace. He comes to us in the preaching of the Gospel, in Baptism, and in absolution. In these He is present in His church, which is His body. Also where two or three are gathered in His name, gathered around His Word and Sacrament, there is the body of Christ, the whole body. For the body of Christ is not some sort of organism. It cannot be separated into pieces. It is always completely present, just as the sacramental body is always completely present in each part of the consecrated bread.

> Whether one this bread receiveth
> Or a thousand, still He giveth
> One sure food that does not fail.

Luther and our Lutheran fathers loved to quote these words from Aquinas's "Lauda Sion salvatorem." They ring on in the Communion hymns of our church. They can and must be applied in an analogous way to the "mystical body," the church, in order to avoid the unbiblical, romantic theory of the church as an organism. The presence in the Sacrament of the Altar, however, is not the same as the presence in the other means of grace.

There is today a most earnest struggle going on to understand this presence. There are Catholic and Protestant theologians who speak of it as making Christ's death, Christ's passion contemporary, a re-presentation of His sacrificial death. Among Catholic theologians such theories emerge from the effort to clarify the doctrine of Trent that identifies the sacrifice on the cross with the sacrifice in the Mass. According to the doctrine of Trent the sacrifice of Mass is to be understood as *memoria*, *repraesentatio*, and *applicatio* of the sacrifice on Golgotha. It was the late Benedictine monk, Odo Casel, who propounded the mystery theory that has engaged so much discussion. The point of departure for his exposition of the "cultic mystery" was the Hellenistic mysteries. These are then seen as "shadows" of the future mysteries of the church, corresponding to the relationship between nature and supernature [*Übernatur*].

> The *Kyrios* of a mystery is a God who has entered into human misery and struggle, has made his appearance on earth (epiphany) and fought here, suffered, even been defeated; the whole sorrow of mankind in pain is brought together in a mourning for the God who must die. But then in some way comes a return to life through which the God's companions, indeed the whole of nature revives and lives on. This was the way of pious faith and the sacred teaching (*hieros logos*), of society in the earliest mystical age. But the world, society is always in need of life; so the epiphany goes on and on in worship; the saving, healing act of God is performed over and over. Worship [*Kult*] is the means of making it real once more, and thus of breaking through to the spring of salvation. The members of the cult present again in a ritual, symbolic fashion, that primeval act. . . .

The mystery, therefore, embraces in the first place the broad concept of ritual *"memorial"—anamnēsis, commemoratio*—the ritual performance and *making present [Gegenwärtigsetzung]* of some act of the God's, upon which rests the existence and life of a community. (*Das Christliche Kultmysterium*, 2d ed. [1935]; emphasis added [*The Mystery of Christian Worship* (1962), 53]).

Justin and the early church could never have dreamed up something like this, certainly not if they remained in agreement with Paul, who did not regard these mysteries as earlier stages of Christian worship but as demonic perversion of divine truth. This whole theory falls to pieces before the simple fact that while the Hellenistic mysteries rest on myths, the Sacrament of the Altar is a matter of history. When did Attis and Osiris live? When did they die? The question is senseless because the myth does not tell of historical events. Jesus Christ, however, is a historical person. His death is a historical event that happened outside the gates of Jerusalem "under Pontius Pilate." The women who went to find His body did not have to wander all around like Cybele and Isis in the myth. They knew the place of His grave. And His resurrection was also a historical event: "On the third day He rose again from the dead." The whole theory was constructed to provide a foundation for the dogma of the identity of the sacrifice on the cross and the sacrifice of the Mass as defined by Trent. But where is there any such foundation in the New Testament? Is it by chance that the passage in the New Testament putting the high priestly work of Christ at the center has the word "once" [*ephapax*] right at the crucial place? He "entered *once* for all into the Holy Place, taking not the blood of goats and calves but His own blood, thus securing an eternal redemption" (Heb. 9:12). Who dares to interpret away this "once" in view of the words that conclude this great chapter: "Just as it is appointed for men to die *once*, and after that comes judgment, so Christ, having been offered *once* to bear the sins of many, will appear a second time, not to deal with sin but to save those who are eagerly waiting for Him" (Heb. 9:27f.).

Casel's theory is therefore untenable. It can be accommodated in the Roman Church because, for one thing, it has a different relationship with heathen religion than we do, and for another, because its doctrine of the real presence is not in any way challenged by it. That is not the case with similar theories that have sprung up in Protestant soil and today even make an impression on Lutherans. Casel betrays a very significant uncertainty regarding the Biblical concept of remembrance, as is shown by his opinion of Passover.

God's prescriptions were carried in exact ritual: the paschal lamb eaten in travelling clothes; *the history read recalling* how they left the land where they were slaves. So Israel's salvation and the founding of God's people was celebrated each year in ritual. . . . But the passover use was not properly a mystery because it was related first of all to human events and a *human deliverance.* (Casel, 60 [*Mystery*, 31])

What a misunderstanding this is of *salvation history* [*Heilsgeschichte*] and *salvation facts* [*Heilstatsachen*] in the Biblical sense!

In his thoughtful study, "The Salvation Event in the Proclamation of the Word and in Holy Communion" (in *Grundlegung des Abendmahlsgesprächs* [1954], 35–79 [for the English see his *Worship in the Name of Jesus* (St. Louis, 1968), 141–96]), Peter Brunner points out the realization of the presence of salvation history in the cultus that was first propounded by Rudolf Otto and developed by Old Testament scholars like Mowinckel, von Rad, and Weiser. It is expressed in the words of Moses in Deut. 5:1f.:

Hear, O Israel, the statutes and the ordinances which I speak in your hearing *this day*, and you shall learn them and be careful to do them. The Lord our God *made a covenant with us* in Horeb. *Not with our fathers* did the Lord make this covenant, but *with us*, who are all of us *here* alive *this day*. The Lord spoke with you face to face at the mountain, out of the midst of the fire, while *I stood between the Lord and you at that time, to declare to you the Word of the Lord.*

The interpretation that von Rad gives of this "actualization of the redemptive events" in the cultus and in God's holy Word that is part of the cultus is found in P. Brunner, p. 38 [*Worship*, 145]. It is really true that those who eat the Passover, in which they remember a historical event, are present at this event, because it is "salvation history," the history of what God had done, for which there is no temporal time. In addition to the way in which a past event is made a present reality through the Word, the Old Testament also has parabolic actions by the prophets, such as in Ezekiel 4 and 5, something still seen in the New Testament in the action of Agabus in Acts 21:10f. This *oth* [Hebrew], a holy sign (the word is also used of God's miraculous deeds), for the people of the Old Testament is really more than just a parable. R. Otto has called it "an effective representation" [*The Kingdom of God and the Son of Man* (Boston, 1957), 302]. He and others have used this then as the way to explain the Lord's Supper. The sacrifice of Christ's death, anticipated at the Last Supper, is re-presented in the celebration of the

Sacrament, just as also from the opposite perspective the messianic banquet in heaven is anticipated in it. This has been used by Anglican theologians, and even by some Lutherans, to take the hazardous step of seeing in the Sacrament the "re-presentation" of Christ's sacrifice and in this way seeing the Sacrament itself as a sacrifice. There was indeed a reality inherent in a prophetic sign, as also in the prophetic Word. It makes no difference whether the fall of Jerusalem is proclaimed by Jeremiah by "word" or by "action." But the category of parabolic action or of *oth* simply cannot explain the Lord's Supper. This is indicated by the fact that those theologians who explain it in this way no longer have any appreciation for the actual presence of the body and blood of Christ. Their doctrine of the Real Presence is Calvinistic, and that of the sacrifice is Roman Catholic. When it happens that they become Roman Catholic, they then have no difficulty in accepting transubstantiation.

There must be something else that is unique about the real presence in the Lord's Supper. The death of Christ is indeed a unique historical event. As with every actual event in earthly history, it is unrepeatable. But at the same time, like the exodus from Egypt commemorated in the Passover, it is also God's redemptive act, something that stands outside of earthly time, which does not exist for God. Rev. 13:8 calls Christ "the Lamb slain from the foundation of the world" [KJV]. He is the Crucified not simply as *staurōtheis* (aorist, which signifies a single event) but as the *estaurōmenos* (perfect, which means that what happened continues in effect). We note how Paul uses the aorist and perfect, comparing, for example, 1 Cor. 1:13 with 1:23; 2:2, 8; 2 Cor. 13:4 with Gal. 3:1; etc. From this we may see that with God a "temporal" event can be "eternal." But as a general principle this may be said of all God's deeds. What applies to Golgotha applies also to Sinai according to Deut. 5:2. However illuminating may be the recognition that in the Bible God's deeds in the past have also a present reality, this does not explain what is the *proprium* of the Sacrament. Brunner acknowledges this when he says that re-presentation and the Real Presence go together. "Through the real presence of Jesus' body and blood the *repraesentatio* carried out in Holy Communion receives its real and present concretion" (*Grundlegung*, 64 [*Worship*, 177]). The question that Brunner leaves open is what the actual "body" and "blood" are that are received under the forms of bread and wine. This is where I must part company with him, even though he quotes my statement in *Vom Sakrament des Altars* (p. 69) in support of his view (*Grundlegung*, 64 [*Worship*, 178]). The context of my statement shows that we are not in agreement.

Brunner says (p. 63 [*Worship*, 177]) "that the *sacrificed* body and the atoning and covenant-effecting *sacrificial* blood and, with this, Jesus' sacrifice on the cross, are present to us under the Eucharistic food and presented [*dargereicht*] with the bread and the wine" (Brunner's emphasis). Why is sacrifice stressed so much? There is no doubt that we receive the *sacrificed* body and the *sacrificed* blood. But why is it not said that the sacrificed body is at the same time the glorified body? It is certainly true that, along with the Christ who was sacrificed for us, His sacrifice on the cross is present—along with the one who suffered [*Christus passus*] comes also His suffering [*passio Christi*]. But can the sacrifice of the cross be *distributed* [*dargereicht*, that is, to the communicants]? If I have misunderstood Brunner, I would ask him in sincere friendship to clear up the misunderstanding. And I would put to him the question, What do unbelievers receive, that is, with the mouth? And how can something be possible today that the church regarded as impossible for 1,700 years and that is still today regarded by most of Christendom as impossible, namely, that there can be fellowship at the Lord's Supper between those who confess that the consecrated bread *is* the body of the Lord and those who confess no more than that the bread is a *sign* of the body, as is the case with those who hold to the Heidelberg Catechism. In his careful and conscientious investigation of the question (*Grundlegung*, 11–33) Brunner concedes that his approval of altar fellowship between Lutherans and those who confess the Heidelberg Catechism would not have been shared by Luther, had he known of this catechism (*Grundlegung*, 32 n. 25). But does this disagreement between Brunner and Luther perhaps relate to a deeper disagreement in understanding the essence of the Real Presence?

8.

Here we must break off the discussion of the Real Presence. Our intention was to substantiate Luther's statement: "This sacrament is the Gospel." If this is so, then it is clear that the church cannot exist without it. It had such vital place in the divine service in the time of the apostles, in the ancient church, in the Middle Ages, and also in Lutheranism before the incursion of Pietism. The divine service was the "Mass," a service of the Word and at the same time a service of the Sacrament. There is a growing conviction in all Protestant churches that with the conscious dissolution of the Mass among the Reformed churches and its decline in Lutheranism, something has been lost that is essential to the church. There is something of the truth to the saying often heard in America: "If a Protestant goes to church, he finds a preacher; if a Catholic goes to church, he finds Christ." Preaching can only decline, can only lose its essence as the proclamation of the *Gospel*, if the Sacrament of the Altar no longer gives us the objective presence of the incarnate Christ, if we no longer receive His true body and His true blood. On the other hand in the Roman Church the decline in the proclamation of the Gospel has changed the character of the Sacrament. It is something marvelous to behold in a Cistercian abbey when the monks, after choral prayer together early in the morning, go into the sacristy, take off their cowls, put on their chasubles, and each goes by himself to his altar in the great church to celebrate his Mass, to offer the Holy Sacrifice, as they say. But is this impressive celebration still the Mass of the early church, not to mention the Sacrament of the New Testament? No one has more effectively criticized this development of the Mass, in which the praying church [*ecclesia orans*] disappears, than the leaders of the liturgical movement in the Catholic Church. I know an Anglican monastery, which is also a theological seminary, where the students go to Communion every morning but for months on end hear no sermon. Can the Gospel survive in such churches? The early church was a preaching church, as was also the church of the Middle Ages at the high points of its history. Certainly the juxtaposition of preaching— in the early church there were often several sermons—and the Eucharist has always presented a practical problem, even in the East where there seems to be plenty of time. The pressure of time led either to the sermon's being cut short, as in today's Catholic High Mass on Sunday, or to the establishment of special preaching services without the Sacrament on Sunday afternoon as in the late Middle Ages or as is still the case today with Vespers. It is by no means the case that only we Lutherans are plagued with the problem of finding the rightful place for both preaching and the Sacrament of the Altar in the Sunday divine service.

Another question is closely related to this one, namely, the congregation's communion. In the ancient church all who took part in the Mass of the Faithful received communion. This later came to an end when masses of people came streaming into the church, and Communion was often replaced by the distribution of bread that was blessed but not consecrated at the end of the service. In the Middle Ages Communion was very infrequent. To receive Communion four times a year—at the three high festivals and at one lesser one—was a sign of the highest piety. Even of monks was no more required. I once greatly astonished a Dominican when I explained that Thomas certainly did not celebrate Mass every day. Receiving Communion was replaced by adoration of the host, a practice unknown in the ancient church and still not practiced by the Eastern Church.

Just as customs changed in the early church in connection with Baptism (the baptizing of infants and adults), so there was also a change in church customs with regard to the Lord's Supper. Over many centuries pastoral care has wrestled with the problem of whether frequent or less frequent but more devoutly prepared-for Communion is preferred. There were already debates about this in the Middle Ages. Later the Jansenists and the Jesuits were in controversy about it, until at the beginning of this century the decision came down in favor of frequent, and where possible, daily communion. But this was at the cost of not taking sin seriously, since according to Catholic doctrine no one may receive the Sacrament who is in a state of mortal sin. This same problem arises in the Lutheran Church when frequent communion, going to the Lord's Supper at each divine service is urged, or when the participants in church gatherings are more or less morally compelled to go to the Table of the Lord without a serious confession preceding it, as our Confessions encourage it. For the *exploratio* of Augsburg Confession XXIV is expressly described in the Apology in such a way that it includes confession: "In our churches Mass is celebrated every Sunday and on other festivals, when the Sacrament is offered to those who wish for it after they have been examined and absolved" (Ap XXIV 1). This confession previously took place on Saturday and still does in many a congregation. To give this up or to let it rise or fall in the general confession of sins of the congregation would be a corruption of the Lutheran Sacrament and would open the door to a false understanding of the Lord's Supper. If appeal is made to the Catholic liturgy, then it must be remembered that there also confession is to precede Communion, although it does so differently because of the different understanding of sin.

If we ask ourselves what we as pastors can do about these questions, we should take comfort from the fact that we are not the first to have to struggle with the problem of "Word and Sacrament, Preaching and Holy Communion." The church has always faced the needs indicated by these questions. So we have to beware of liturgical experiments, both the serious and the silly. The latter do exist, as when Bishop Lilje's *Sonntagsblatt* recently published a letter that reported a new way to celebrate the Lord's Supper. When the congregation sat around a table for the Lord's Supper, they left one place empty for the coming Lord.

That is a Jewish custom practiced in all pious Jewish homes in the East. At the festive Sabbath meal or some other festival a place is always kept open for the coming Messiah. What ignorance about the meaning of the Lord's Supper and the liturgy is to be found in our congregations! The need is not met by the artificial liturgical constructions of some High Church people. The great learning of modern liturgics is of no help either unless its fruits are translated into the plain language of the people, as Pius Parsch of Klosterneuberg on the Catholic side has done in splendid fashion for German-speaking people.

Why do we not explain the liturgy to our congregations, especially to the youth? That naturally presumes that we know the teaching of our church regarding the divine service, that we ourselves study the old church orders with their liturgical treasures, that we understand the Lutheran way of combining loyalty to the old liturgical heritage with the great Gospel freedom of which Article 10 for the Formula of Concord speaks. We do not mean liturgical arbitrariness but authentic Gospel freedom. We have to face the fact that a heritage that has been lost over 250 years cannot be restored quickly. We must have several forms of the divine service, just as the Roman Church has and practices in the preservation of unfamiliar rites. We need small circles and congregations in which the old liturgical heritage is preserved along with confession—*confessio* always means confession of the faith, confession of sins, and praise of God all in one—as is done in such an exemplary way, a way that puts us all to shame, in the "Brethren" congregations in Braunschweig. Moreover, in the large congregations we need extensive instruction in the liturgy. We need preaching services and special services of Holy Communion. We particularly need the divine service in the sense of the Lutheran Mass with both preaching and the celebration of the Sacrament. The sermon will then need to be short, but above all it must be authentic proclamation of the Gospel. There can be no renewal of the Lord's Supper without renewed preaching, preaching that is not just the pious talk of a man but disciplined exposition of Holy Scripture that strikes the heart. Such preaching grows out of serious study of Scripture, plumbing the depths of the divine Word. It should not be that the hearer of the text will always know exactly what is coming next because he has already heard it a hundred times.

Such are the tasks set before us, and no one can relieve us of them, neither hierarchy nor synod nor theological faculty. From the inner renewal of our office, the *ministerium docendi evangelii et porrigendi sacramenta* (ministry of teaching the Gospel and administering the sacraments), the primary office of the church, the only one that the Lord Himself has instituted, can the renewal of our church come. *Veni creator Spiritus!*

HOLY BAPTISM

Letters to Lutheran Pastors, No. 4
March 1949

(Published in *In Statu Confessionis: Gesammelte Aufsätze von Hermann Sasse*, ed. Friedrich Wilhelm Hopf [Berlin and Hamburg: Lutherisches Verlagshaus, 1966], 91–100.)

With the doctrine of *Holy Baptism* the difference between the confessions that appeal to the Reformation has become clear to many of our contemporaries. Already in the 16th century, besides the controversy over the Lord's Supper, there was a very lively, revealing debate over Baptism, above all at the Mömpelgard Colloquy between Andreae and Beza. But since Lutherans and Reformed retained and defended the practice of infant baptism against the Baptists, it was not sufficiently noticed at that time what a profound difference existed between the confessions also in the understanding of this means of grace. We have to thank Karl Barth for putting his finger on what for him was "a wound on the body of the church" ("Die kirchliche Lehre von der Taufe," *Theol. Existenz heute*, New Series 4, 1947; *Theol. Studien*, part 14, 28f.). And even if he encounters determined opposition to his charge that the Reformed churches would like to revise their teaching and practice of Baptism, it remains an open question whether Barth has not been more Reformed on this subject than the Reformed, whether he has not seen more clearly than any Reformed theologian before him certain inconsistencies of Zwingli and Calvin, who expressed themselves in terms of their opposition to the Anabaptists of the 16th century. It is necessary for us Lutherans to deal with the understanding of Baptism and with Barth's objections to infant baptism because Barth's pupils have tried to read his doctrine of Baptism into the Augsburg Confession and because considerable uncertainty about the basis of infant baptism and therefore about the understanding of the sacrament itself can be seen in current Lutheran dogmatics.

1.

Basic to every discussion about the Sacrament of Baptism is the recognition that Baptism is a *sacrament*, a means of grace in the strict sense. It is not just a more or less beautiful, more or less legitimate custom of the church just like confirmation, marriage, and burial. Thus all arguments collapse immediately that see in Baptism a symbolic action, perhaps the symbol of the prevenient grace [*gratia praeveniens*] that precedes all human action or a symbol of what makes "a church comprising all the people" [*Volkskirchentum*] in contrast with what Troeltsch calls "sects," in the sense of a second form of Reformation church that emerged out of the radical Anabaptist movement. Nowadays people speak of "free churches" rather than "sects" and maintain that the abandonment of infant baptism would destroy the *Volkskirche* and lead to the "free church."

Now in fact all the "free churches" except the Baptists practice infant baptism. Quite apart from this, however, the very serious dogmatic question must be raised, whether the Sacrament of Baptism can be used as a means of maintaining the *Volkskirche* even though infant baptism may not be theologically defensible. Baptism has been a part of Christian dogmatics since the days of the apostles. The concept of a *Volkskirche* is scarcely a hundred years old. As far as we know, this theologically illegitimate term was coined by Johann Hinrich Wichern. At any rate he gave currency to the idea from the sociology of religion. The theological nonsense of this term, which no educated theologian should utter, is apparent when the assertion is made repeatedly that one becomes a member of a free church by voluntary decision, whereas one is "born into" the *Volkskirche*.

One never becomes a member of the church by a decision or by birth. The latter is taken to be the case only in certain state churches, such as that of Zurich. In this prototype of a *Volkskirche* from Zwingli's time, one may exercise all the rights of a member of the church, with the exception of what is reserved to the clergy, even without being baptized. According to the witness of the New Testament (1 Cor. 12:13) one becomes a member of the church by Baptism. The only theologically legitimate question, on which the rightness or wrongness of infant baptism depends, is who is to be baptized, people who are able to confess their faith in Jesus Christ, that is, adults and older children, or also minor children, that is, infants in the proper sense of the term.

2.

So the question of infant baptism is a theological question and not merely a practical, sociological question. It is also not a question that can simply be answered historically. Thomas Aquinas (*Summa th.* 3, question 68, 9) answers the objection that intention and faith are necessary for the reception of Baptism, and therefore that children cannot be baptized, with a quotation from the last chapter of *The Celestial Hierarchy* of Dionysius the Areopagite, according to whom the apostles approved of infant baptism. That is a tradition that, to say the least, is beyond verification. But Joachim Jeremias (*Hat die älteste Christenheit die Kindertaufe geübt?* [1938] [translated as *Infant Baptism in the First Four Centuries* (1960)]) and W. F. Flemington (*The New Testament Doctrine of Baptism* [1948]) with an abundance of persuasive arguments have made it seem likely that infant baptism, which is first explicitly spoken of by Irenaeus (about 185), goes back to the time of the apostles. There it would have been practiced according to the model of the Jewish baptism of proselytes. This we know was performed not only on adults, but in the case of the conversion of whole families it was performed on all who belonged to the whole "house" and so included the children. The well-known examples of Lydia, the dealer in purple, and of the jailer at Philippi (Acts 16), who were baptized with their whole household after they themselves had come to faith, would be relevant. When Polycarp testified at his martyr's trial that he had served the Lord for 86 years (*Mart. Pol.* 9), that can only refer to his membership in the church. Then his baptism would have occurred in the apostolic age, before the year 70. The assertion of Justin (*Apol.* 1. 15) that in his day there were many Christians in their sixties and seventies "who had become disciples of Christ as children" can only refer to people who were baptized as children between A.D. 80 and 90. Of Ireneaus we have spoken already. He confesses that Christ came to save all, "all who through Him are born again to God: infants, little children, boys, youths, and men" (*Adv. haer.* 2. 22. 4). In the church order of his pupil Hippolytus the baptism of little children is explicitly mentioned. They are to be baptized prior to the adults, and their parents or a relative are to represent them in giving consent and in the confession of the creed by speaking for them in their place (*Apost. trad.* 46). When Tertullian in his writing *On Bap-*

38

tism explicitly opposes the custom of infant baptism, he does not speak against it as if it were an innovation. So also later when Pelagius attacks Augustine's doctrine of original sin, he lets the point stand that children also are baptized and does not contest infant baptism. Similarly Origen and Cyprian take the baptism of children for granted. Origen stated that infant baptism goes back to a tradition the apostles received from the Lord (*Commentary on Romans* 5. 9), a statement that was transmitted to the Middle Ages by Dionysius the Areopagite. Cyprian gives Bishop Fidus the well-known advice that Baptism is not to be delayed until the eighth day after birth according to the analogy of circumcision (*Ep.* 64). Jeremias is right when he maintains that a later introduction of infant baptism would have provoked a profound upset in the church and would have left distinct traces in the history of the church. What we know of the history of the church indicates much rather that in the early church both forms of baptism, the baptism of adults and infant baptism, always existed side by side, just as they do today in the mission fields. This can only mean that infant baptism must go back to the time of the apostles. It would have been included in the practice of baptizing whole families to which the New Testament gives witness, even though children are not explicitly mentioned.

3.

If we must then answer yes with the greatest probability to the historical question, whether the church of the apostolic age knew and practiced infant baptism, we have still in no way decided the theological question, whether it is right to baptize infants. Did not the church in Corinth in Paul's day practice also vicarious baptism for those who had died? We could be dealing with a very ancient misuse. Infant baptism has a theological foundation only if it can be shown from Scripture that it is a legitimate form of baptism.

The argument that once the Anabaptists and nowadays Karl Barth have raised against infant baptism asserts that to the essence of the Sacrament of Baptism belong "the responsible willingness and readiness of the baptized person to receive the promise of grace directed towards him and to be party to the pledge of allegiance concerning the grateful service demanded of him" [Barth, *The Teaching of the Church Regarding Baptism* (1948), 40]. In an article in the Berlin church weekly *Die Kirche* a pupil of Barth recently tried to support this view by referring to the account of the Ethiopian chamberlain in Acts 8, where not only the expression of the desire of the one to be baptized but also his confession served as conditions for the baptism. That theologian had simply overlooked the fact that verse 37, with its request for a confession and the giving of a baptismal confession, is an old insertion, as examination of the manuscripts demonstrates. The oldest and best manuscripts are ignorant of it, and so they are witnesses of the fact that in earliest times (cf. Acts 2:41) a baptism was known in which a creed was not spoken.

Therefore, we have to ask, What is Baptism according to the witness of the New Testament? What does it give or what is the good of it? How is Baptism related to the faith of the one to be baptized? Is it necessary for salvation or not? What we may answer first of all is that according to the clear teaching of the New Testament Baptism is the "washing of regeneration." The early church, which always simply identified Baptism with regeneration, and the church of all times, with the exception of the Reformed communities, have understood Titus 3:5 in this way—and rightly so. There Baptism is "the washing of regeneration and renewal in the Holy Spirit." In Baptism the Holy Spirit is bestowed; we are "baptized into one body" (1 Cor. 12:13). According to Rom. 6:3, the baptized are baptized into Christ's death. Those are all realities that happen not alongside of Baptism but in it. Water baptism in the New Testament, as long as it is baptism into Christ, in the name of Christ, is Spirit baptism; it is a being born anew and at the same time from above "of water *and* the Spirit" (John 3:5). The New Testament knows nothing of a being born again without Baptism or apart from Baptism. Baptism is therefore not a sign but a means of regeneration. To regard it only as a sign of a regeneration that also may take place without it or apart from it is unbiblical.

What is it that prompts the Reformed doctrine? We may observe something similar in the doctrine of the Lord's Supper. On the one hand the pure symbolism of Zwingli is rejected. He saw Baptism as merely a sign professing that one is a Christian, just as the white cross worn on the garment of a Swiss Confederate made him recognizable as a Swiss Confederate [Library of Christian Classics, 24:131]. On the other hand, along with the Roman sacramental doctrine of an *opus operatum*, the Lutheran—and New Testament—identification of sign and action is also rejected.

At the bottom of all this lies the antipathy of Calvin and his predecessors in medieval theology against the idea that an external, physical action can produce spiritual effects, such as the forgiveness of sins. This is first of all a secular, philosophical presupposition, and second, it misunderstands the significance of the Word of God in Baptism. "For without the Word of God the water is simple water and no Baptism. But with the Word of God it is Baptism, that is, a gracious water of life and a washing of regeneration" (SC IV). Also in Catholic doctrine the Word as the *forma* is inseparably tied up with the sacrament; indeed, it is what makes the sacrament a sacrament. This is in harmony with the words of Augustine, which time and again are quoted by all churches in the West: "The word comes to the element and makes the sacrament." Where Luther differs from the Catholic doctrine of Baptism he says himself in the Smalcald Articles, distinguishing himself from both the Thomists and the Scotists:

> We do not agree with Thomas and the Dominicans who forget the Word [God's institution] and say that God has joined to the water a spiritual power which, through the water, washes away sin. Nor do we agree with Scotus and the Franciscans who teach that Baptism washes sin away through the assistance of the divine will, as if the washing takes place only through God's will and not at all through the Word and the water. (SA III V 2–3)

With Luther everything depends on the intimate connection of Word and water: "God is surely a God of life. Because He is there in this water, it cannot but be the very water of life, which puts death and hell to flight and makes alive with the life that has no end" (WA 52, 102, 29). Luther has no need to demonstrate first that this presence of God or Christ can be no other presence than that which happens in His Word. All effects of Baptism are effects of the Word combined with the water for Luther and for the Lutheran Church.

The Reformed opposition to this Lutheran understanding of Baptism is therefore nothing else than opposition to the Lutheran doctrine of the means of grace as a whole. They are opposing the fact that God does not give His Spirit, and therewith forgiveness of sins, life and salvation, to anyone apart from the external means of His grace, apart from the external Word, apart from Baptism, or apart from the Lord's Supper. "The power of Jesus Christ, which is the only power of Baptism, is *not bound* to the administration of Baptism" (Barth, 14f.). The earlier Reformed theologians favored the distinction between the external baptism with water and the inner baptism with the Holy Spirit and with the blood of Jesus Christ, which cleanses from all sin. But the two are not always received together; it is possible to have the one without the other. Whether a person receives the baptism of the Spirit and blood together with water baptism depends on whether he belongs to those who are predestined or not. Hence we can understand the consistent opposition ever since Calvin to emergency baptism and in particular baptism by midwives [Niesel, *Reformed Symbolics* (1962), 270]. In the Union Constitution of the Palatinate we find the sentence: "The Protestant Evangelical Christian Church of the Palatinate accepts no emergency baptism" (E. F. K. Müller, *Die Bekenntnisschriften der ev.-reformierten Kirche* [1903], 871). Baptism then gives the person nothing that he could not also have without Baptism. Whether one is saved or not does not at all depend on Baptism, but only on whether one is predestined to salvation or not. That is the classic Reformed doctrine. Even when the old doctrine of predestination is weakened or abandoned, as by the followers of Barth, its consequence still remains: Baptism is indeed instituted by Christ—Calvin accepts the institution of Baptism by Christ in agreement with Luther and with the whole ecclesiastical tradition of the Eastern and Western church—and it must be done in the church as an ordinance of Christ, but Baptism is not necessary for salvation. One can, Barth maintains (p. 15), speak only of a necessity of command [*necessitas praecepti*], not a necessity of means [*necessitas medii*].

4.

When the Lutheran Church against this position affirms the *necessitas medii*, the character of Baptism as a means of grace in the strict sense, it is naturally not in conflict with the old Catholic statement: "God is not confined to His sacraments." That God may have other ways of saving people has never been questioned by our church, as the writings of Luther and the classical Lutherans on the fate of children who died unbaptized proves. But He has not revealed anything to us about that, and we are bound to what He has revealed to us. What we must be on our guard against is the tearing apart of Spirit and Word, of external and internal baptism. It is water baptism inseparably bound to God's Word of which Luther's baptismal hymn speaks:

All that the mortal eye beholds
Is water as we pour it.
Before the eye of faith unfolds
The power of Jesus' merit.
For here it sees the crimson flood
To all our ills bring healing;
The wonders of his precious blood

42

The love of God revealing,
Assuring his own pardon.

[*LW* 223:7; tr. © Elizabeth Quitmeyer. Used by permission.]

How the marvel of the rebirth that is worked through Baptism relates to the fact that baptized people also are lost is hidden in divine predestination, about which the Gospel has revealed nothing to us. We shall understand that much better in the light of glory, as Luther says at the end of his *Bondage of the Will*. We cling to the Gospel and to the promises that the Gospel attaches to Baptism when we confess of Baptism as the washing of regeneration: "It works forgiveness of sins, delivers from death and the devil, and gives eternal salvation to all who believe this, as the words and promises of God declare" (SC IV).

But what of the faith of the child to be baptized? With this question we come to the heart of the Reformed rejection of the Lutheran doctrine of Baptism. This rejection has its parallels in the Reformed world in the so-called Gorham controversy regarding Baptism a century ago when the denial of baptismal regeneration by the Evangelicals in the Church of England deeply troubled Anglicanism. If one stands for infant baptism, then the following alternative seems to be inescapable: Either Baptism bestows forgiveness of sins and regeneration to eternal life apart from the personal faith of the child being baptized and his personal confession—that is the answer of the Catholic Church, which lets the faith of the church take the place of the faith of the child to be baptized— or forgiveness of sins and regeneration are detached from the administration of Baptism. In practical terms this opens several possibilities of viewing Baptism. One can with the majority of the Reformed retain infant baptism, thereby seeing in it the New Testament sign of the covenant analogous to Old Testament circumcision, referring to Col. 2:11. Or one can reject infant baptism altogether as was done by the Anabaptists at the time of the Reformation and is done today by the "congregations of Christians baptized as believers" [*Gemeinden gläubig getaufter Christen*]. Or one can take a middle way with Karl Barth between these possibilities. He declares infant baptism as valid but as a violation of the New Testament order of Baptism, a false ordering of baptismal practice that rests on the erroneous presuppositions of a *Volkskirche* and must be revised by ecclesiastical decision. We need not here pursue the fact that Barth himself came to recognize that none of the large Reformed churches is disposed to follow his advice and give up the custom of baptizing infants that has been firmly established since Zwingli and Calvin. We might just ask in passing whether the position of the Baptists is not the real consequence of the Reformed doctrine of Baptism and whether the retention of infant baptism was not a compromise resulting from the power of a tradition that was a millennium and a half old and from their opposition to the Enthusiasts of the 16th century. For Baptism cannot be understood as the counterpart to circumcision, despite Col. 2:11, because circumcision lacks the very thing that makes Baptism Baptism. At the very least they are as different as the new covenant is from the old, as Israel according to the flesh is from Israel according to the Spirit. If one sticks to these parallels, then Baptism can never be more than a sign of grace. It can never be a means of grace in the fullest sense, even though the Reformed have tried to retain this term for Baptism.

As was often the case, Luther's way was the lonely way between Rome and the Enthusiasts. Over against the Enthusiasts, among whom he lumped Zwingli and his followers, as he would also have done with the Calvinists had they been part of his experience, he firmly held to the Sacrament of Baptism and everything that belongs with it: infant baptism, necessity for salvation, and regeneration. Over against Rome he firmly held to the *sola fide:* Forgiveness of sins, life, and salvation are given only to faith. Just as in the Sacrament of the Altar only *he* receives forgiveness of sins and so also life and salvation who has faith in "these words," that is, in the promise: "Given and shed for you for the forgiveness of sins," so it is true of Baptism: "It works forgiveness of sins, delivers from death and the devil and gives eternal salvation to all who *believe* this, as the words and promises of God declare." And this is not talking about some future faith that is then confessed at confirmation, so that this would be a necessary completion of Baptism.

Bucer, who first introduced pietistic ideas into the church, brought an un-Lutheran element into confirmation, which has its own rightful place, an idea rooted not in Biblical thought but in a sociological view of the church. This element ripened in the age of Pietism and rationalism. It is significant that in Wittenberg in the 18th century confirmation was introduced into the synagogue, not the church, where they were content with first communion. At that time people could only conceive of the church as an "association," a "religious society" that one joined by a voluntary decision.

Against all this for Luther the faith that is spoken of in connection with infant baptism is not the future faith of children to be reared as Christians nor is it, as many a Lutheran in the 19th century thought, a faith that is like a seed awakened to life by the act of baptism, but it is the faith with which the children come to baptism, just as with adults, except that this faith of children is not yet a conscious faith that they can confess themselves.

In the Large Catechism Luther calls our attention to the fact that the faith of an adult also can never be the foundation of Baptism:

> I myself, and all who are baptized, must say before God: "I come here in my faith, and in the faith of others, nevertheless I cannot build on the fact that I believe and that many people are praying for me. On this I build, that it is Thy Word and command." Just so, I go to the Sacrament of the Altar not on the strength of my own faith, but on the strength of Christ's Word. . . . We do the same in infant Baptism. We bring the child with the purpose and hope that he may believe, and we pray God to grant him faith. But we do not baptize him on that account, but solely on the command of God. (LC IV 56–57)

And Luther bases this on the fact that all people can lie and deceive themselves, but not God, who has given the command to baptize. That God through His Holy Spirit can also give faith to a child, just as to an adult, cannot be questioned when we remember how Jesus blessed the children and presented a child to His disciples as an example. Yes, strictly speaking, even the faith of the greatest-hero of faith, even the faith of an Athanasius or a Luther, is no greater than the faith of an infant.

Or when does the faith begin, on the basis of which we dare to baptize? Is it at the age when we nowadays have confirmation or when small children are able to make some confession of faith, as Thomas Müntzer wanted? We would be making a psychologically perceived fact out of the wondrous working of the Holy Spirit if we here set a temporal boundary on the sway of the Holy Spirit.

Here too Luther goes his lonely way between the hierarchical safeguards of Rome and the psychological safeguards of the Enthusiasts. It is the lonely way of the Reformer, who heeds only the Word of God and counts on this Word for everything, even for what is humanly impossible. Only in this way can he and the Lutheran Church hold together the objectivity of the sacrament and the *sola fide*, whereby we do not forget that justifying faith is not the matter of a single moment, but the substance of our whole lives. Such faith is not some act of our commitment to God that is particularly perceived and experienced in some isolated moments of our life. Rather, it is the constant though always clouded reliance on the Gospel's promise of grace. Repentance also, according to the Gospel, is not just a single act but goes on our whole life long. So also our Baptism is not an isolated act, but something that goes on in all our life. Being a Christian does not just mean that we were once baptized but that we live in the strength of our Baptism and again and again return to it. To the question, "What does such baptizing with water signify?" the Small Catechism gives the familiar answer: "It signifies that the Old Adam in us should, by daily contrition and repentance, be drowned and die with all sins and evil lusts and, again, a new man daily come forth and arise, who shall live before God in righteousness and purity forever" (SC IV). As we who are both sinners and righteous live by daily contrition and repentance, by the daily forgiveness of sin, so also the death and resurrection of Christ, that real though also incomprehensible anticipation of an eschatological experience that takes place in Baptism, is something that is intended for our whole life.

This is how Luther understood Baptism and the faith of those who are baptized over against Rome and the Enthusiasts. We do not simply grasp them in a moment, either in the moment when the Sacrament of Baptism is received or in the moment of confirmation or in any other moment of our lives that we might like to designate, but we grasp them, or should grasp them, throughout our whole lives, every day anew. Therefore Luther also knows no second sacrament that would have to complete Baptism, neither confirmation nor a repentance that would be anything else than a return to Baptism.

5.

The question of whether adults or infants are to be baptized, then, has become theologically unimportant, although it remains important for church practice. We can see now why this question plays no role in the New Testament or with Luther. Apart from the fact that adults to be baptized speak their consent and creed themselves, Baptism has always been done in the church "as if" those to be baptized desire it themselves and believe what is confessed in the baptismal creed. This "as if" belongs to the very essence of the matter and may not be explained away as liturgical traditionalism or ecclesiastical conservatism. We baptize children as if they were adults, just as we baptize adults as if they were children. Whatever the difference between adults and children may mean for us humans and our judgment of a person, it means nothing for God. Before Him a person is a person, either a child of Adam or a child of God, regardless of age. That is the more profound reason why all baptismal liturgies deal with the child "as if" he were an adult.

Only the Nestorian and the Reformed churches have produced specific liturgies for the baptism of children.

It was also baptismal practice until Calvin and the Reformed Church that it did not take place before the assembled congregation. In the early church the baptismal candidates received the Sacrament of Baptism outside the worship room, while the congregation was assembled to intercede for those to be baptized. That apparently did not happen just for the sake of propriety, for the Baptists administer the baptismal washing in the sight of the congregation. The place of the baptistry, whether it is an expanded baptismal well or a simple font, was always in front of the entrance to the church in former times. It is most interesting that Calvin himself, who, we believe, destroyed the dogmatic content of Baptism, brought Baptism out of the realm of the private and individual, out of the vestibule, as it were, into the sanctuary of the assembled congregation. He probably took that over, as so much else, from Bucer in Strasbourg, to whom the corresponding instruction in the Hessian church order of 1539 may be traced. That instruction is found again in later Reformed church orders, such as those of the Palatinate of 1563 and Bentheim of 1588. And so while the Reformed Church reserves the administration of baptism to the ministerial office and forbids emergency baptism by the laity, especially by women, right in the New Testament we see the performance of baptism as part of the apostolic office receding into the background. So the worship service combined with a baptism is passed off as a "sacramental worship service" in the Reformed Church and in the Protestantism of today that is considerably influenced by modern Calvinism. They forget that sacrament in the sense of a sacramental worship service purely and simply means the Lord's Supper, the Sacrament of sacraments. Luther's terminology gives abundant evidence of this. Naturally, the Christian congregation is free to perform baptism in the worship service. But Luther never designated a worship service in which a child was baptized in conjunction with the Creed as a sacramental worship service. A sacramental service for him was the Mass, the combination of service of the Word and Lord's Supper. In that he was at one with the whole church before him. Whatever reforms might be necessary to restore respect for the Sacrament of Baptism in the Lutheran Church of today, under no circumstances should our church let itself be diverted from the goal of restoring the proper sacramental service of the church of all times, also of the Lutheran Reformation. A deeper understanding and a new appreciation of Baptism is only possible through a return to what Luther's catechism, on the basis of the New Testament, in simple faith teaches about Baptism as the washing of regeneration.

"Yet I do as a child who is being taught the Catechism," writes Luther in the Preface to the Large Catechism. "Every morning, and whenever else I have time, I read and recite word for word the Lord's Prayer, the Ten Commandments, the Creed, the Psalms, etc. I must still read and study the Catechism daily, yet I cannot master it as I wish, but must remain a child and pupil of the Catechism, and I do it gladly" (LC Pref 7–8). How well it would be with us Lutheran pastors, how well it would be with our church, if we paid more attention to this word and let it become active in our life and in our office! How many false conceptions of Lutheranism would be gone from our own souls, how many prejudices about our church on the part of the world would then vanish all by themselves! Kyrie eleison!

THE LORD'S SUPPER IN THE NEW TESTAMENT

1941

(Published in *Vom Sakrament des Altars: Lutherische Beiträge zur Frage des heiligen Abendmahls*, ed. Hermann Sasse [Leipzig: Verlag von Dörffling and Franke, 1941], 26–78.)

The Sources

Paul and Mark

Historical investigation of the Lord's Supper in the New Testament begins on firm ground with the report of its institution in 1 Cor. 11:23–25. This report is the earliest literary source for our knowledge of the origin of the Lord's Supper. (It is also "the oldest document of Christianity that bears witness to Christ's words in direct speech, as Werner Elert points out in *Der christliche Glaube*, 5th ed. [1960], 361.) It was written in the mid-50s and so at least 10 years before the composition of Mark's gospel.

Prompted by the abuses that took place in Corinth, Paul reminds the congregation of what he had once "delivered" to them regarding the origin and meaning of the Lord's Supper. This is what he had taught them already when the congregation was founded in the year 50, and we may assume that not only the content but also the wording of the crucial text was already the same at that time. For the verses at 11:23–25, in contrast to those that precede and those that follow, have been

49

no more freely formulated by Paul as he dictated than the similarly introduced verses about the content of the Gospel at 1 Cor. 15:3ff. (Joachim Jeremias has shown the pre-Pauline Aramaic origin of 1 Cor. 15:3b–5 in *Die Abendmahlsworte Jesu* [1935], 72f. [*The Eucharistic Words of Jesus* (1966), 101–03].) In both cases we are dealing rather with sharply defined statements of the Pauline kerygma, and the statements about the institution of the Lord's Supper seem to have served not only catechetical but also liturgical purposes. We may suppose that in all the congregations of Paul's mission territory these words were recited when the Lord's Supper was celebrated. ("One is certainly entitled to the assumption that the oldest forms of a liturgical account of the institution underlie the corresponding narratives of the New Testament"—F. Hamm, "Die liturgischen Einsetzungsberichte," *Liturgiegeschichtl. Quellen und Forschungen* 23 [1928]: 2; cf. also J. Brinktrine, *Die heilige Messe*, 2d ed. [1934]: 18f., and A. Arnold, *Der Ursprung des christlichen Abendmahls im Lichte der neueren liturgiegeschichtlichen Forschung* [1937], 77.) They read as follows according to the oldest attainable text without the expansions of later manuscripts:

> The Lord Jesus on the night in which He was betrayed took the bread, gave thanks and broke it and said: "This is My body for you; this do in remembrance of me." In the same way also the cup after the meal with the words: "This cup is the new covenant in My blood. This do, as often as you drink it, in remembrance of Me."

What is the origin of these words? Did Paul formulate them himself for his congregations or did he find them already as an established formulation in the church? What is the origin of their content? How did Paul, or whoever formulated these sentences before him, know what happened on Jesus' last night? How did they know of the Lord's words and their meaning? The apostle himself gives the answer in the words with which he introduces that account: "I received from the Lord what I also delivered to you."

There has recently been much lively discussion of this *egō gar parelabon apo tou kuriou ho kai paredōka humin*. Lietzmann has espoused the view that is also predominantly that of Catholic and Reformation-orthodox exegesis. (For Catholic exegesis see Wilhelm Koch, *Das Abendmahl im N. T.* [Bibl. Zeitfragen IV 10], 30f. Old Lutheran theology thought that Paul learned his theology and so also his doctrine of the Lord's Supper in the third heaven [2 Cor. 12:2f.], e.g., *Kurtz Bekentnis und Artickel vom hl. Abendmal* [1574], folio E 1; Joh. Gerhard, *Ausführliche Schrifftmessige Erklerung der beyden Artikel von der hei-*

ligen Tauffe und von dem heiligen Abendmahl [Jena, 1610], 237.) According to this view, "I received from the Lord" is to be understood in accordance with what Paul says of his Gospel in Gal. 1:11f. "I did not receive it from man [*oude . . . para anthrōpou elabon*], nor was I taught it, but it came through a revelation of Jesus Christ." A contrary view is represented by Rudolf Otto, Gerhard Kittel, and J. Jeremias, the last two on the basis of their knowledge of the rabbinical principle of tradition and its terminology. "From the Lord" is then to be understood as indicating that not the risen Lord but the historical Jesus is the starting point of the tradition. In this view Paul would then mean that the tradition concerning what happened at the Last Supper and the words that Jesus spoke there came to him by way of an unbroken chain of witnesses right back to the historical event itself. Lietzmann conceives of it in this way: Paul knew the narrative from the tradition of the church. "But the Lord has revealed to him the essential meaning of this story" (Hans Lietzmann, *Messe und Herrenmahl* [1926], 255 [*Mass and Lord's Supper* (1979), 208]). Lietzmann sees in Paul the creator of a new type of Lord's Supper, but he does not challenge the fact that the apostle knew and used a tradition about the Last Supper of Jesus. Even if Paul had had the conviction, on the basis of a special revelation, of possessing a better understanding of the Lord's Supper than the church before him and the apostles who participated in Jesus' Last Supper—a question that we will have to discuss later—it would no more exclude knowledge of a human tradition regarding this Last Supper than his statement regarding the Gospel in Gal. 1:12, "I did not receive it from man," excludes the apparently contradictory statement about the content of the Gospel in 1 Cor. 15:3, "I delivered to you as of first importance what I also received," that is, the formulated teaching of the earliest church.

Even if we had no other text by which to test the reliability of the tradition reproduced by Paul in 1 Cor. 11:23–25, the following considerations would support its essential accuracy. Any statement made around the year 50 about the events that happened on Jesus' last night, no more than 20 years earlier, was subject to the judgment of eyewitnesses, that is, the original apostles who were still living. Every reader and hearer of the Pauline account knew where he could make sure of the authenticity of the statement that was offered. If Paul had taught something else than the original apostles regarding the origin of the Sacrament that formed the heart of the original Christian cultus, his Judaizing opponents would hardly have missed the opportunity to prove clearly the unreliability of what he proclaimed. (This obviates Lietzmann's suggestion that the type of the Lord's Supper observed in the original [Jerusalem] congregation was introduced in Corinth by Jewish Christians and that Paul then thought it necessary in 1 Cor. 11 to lead the congregation back to his understanding of the Lord's Supper [*Messe und Abendmahl*, 254 (*Mass and Lord's Supper*, 207–08)].)

If Paul in those verses is only handing on a tradition that was there before he was, it gains weight the older it is. If, as we assume, it was formulated for liturgical use, then it must indeed be supposed that the characteristic of liturgical language and liturgical style has influenced the formulation. The liturgy speaks neither the language of a notarized official document nor that of a history textbook. But that in no way changes the fact that it preserves historical facts in its language with great faithfulness and at its center has accurately retained the very words of Jesus.

The reliability of the tradition preserved in 1 Cor. 11:23–25, which is only presumed on the basis of internal characteristics, is substantiated through the happy circumstance that the New Testament contains a second account of Jesus' Last Supper in Mark 14:22–25 that is quite independent of the Pauline account but is essentially in complete agreement with it. We give the Marcan account, emphasizing those words that it has in common with the Pauline:

> And as they were eating, *He took bread,* and blessed, and *broke it,* and gave it to them, *and said,* "Take; *this is My body." And* he took *the cup,* gave thanks, gave it to them, and they all drank of it. And *He said, "This is My blood of the covenant,* poured out for many. Truly, I say to you, I shall not drink again of the fruit of the vine until that day when I drink it new in the kingdom of God."

A comparison of the two texts produces the following: (1) We are dealing with two different traditions. The Marcan text does not derive from the Pauline, nor vice versa. The differences are too great for that. It is impossible to see why Mark would leave out the mandate to repeat or why Paul would substitute a different reflection on the meaning of the celebration (1 Cor. 11:26) for the word of Jesus about the prospect of the messianic meal. (2) Both texts see in Jesus' Last Supper the institution of the Lord's Supper in the church; Paul says this explicitly, Mark simply takes it for granted. (3) Both texts agree on the essentials of the action and on the essentials of the explanatory words about the bread and the cup. (4) Both also differ just at the words of explanation in a way that shows the Marcan text to be an older form of the tradition. If we can here find the rule borne out that liturgical texts are prone to grow, to comment on themselves, and to improve their form, then we must award the greater age to the Marcan text of the explanatory words as shorter, less clear, and less shaped to liturgical use (contrary to J. Behm, who in G. Kittel, *Theol. Wörterbuch zum N. T.* 3:730, lines 27ff. [*Theological Dictionary of the New Testament* 3:731], gives Paul the preference because the word about the cup in him shows an "inconceivable autonomy"). The explanatory word about the bread in Mark is in the shortest conceivable form: "This is My body." The Pauline text adds: "for you. Do this in remembrance of Me." At this point we simply point this out without discussing the question of whether the expansion of the wording under consideration in Paul changes the meaning of the Eucharistic words of Jesus or simply makes them clearer. Also in the case of the word about the cup, the wording of Mark must be regarded as earlier. Both texts in fact say the same thing: The wine that is the content of the cup is the blood of the covenant, that is, the blood that was poured out to complete the covenant. Jeremias suggests, "The strangely complicated formulation of the word over the wine in Paul/ Luke ('this cup is the new covenant') was occasioned by the intention of warding off the misunderstanding that the Lord's Supper was a Thyestian meal where blood was drunk" (*Die Abendmahlsworte Jesu* [1935], 60; cf. 58 [*Eucharistic Words*, 170; cf. 168–69]). He has also shown that the Pauline formulation of the word about the bread is, insofar as it goes beyond the Marcan text, impossible in Aramaic [*Eucharistic Words*, 185–86].

In summary then we may conclude that Christianity in the forties knew several independent versions of a tradition and used them in the celebration of the Lord's Supper. According to it, Jesus at His Last Supper gave His disciples bread and wine with the words: "This is My body," "This is My covenant blood, shed for many." This makes the credibility of the reports extraordinarily strengthened. But has it been proved? We have no further sources for the period between Jesus' Last Supper and the oldest account that was later included in the Gospel of Mark. May we assume that this oldest report goes back to the testimonies of the eyewitnesses, that is, the circle of the Eleven? From the sources that we have it is simply impossible to prove this. It would, however, be methodologically impermissible to deny the authenticity of the report until exact and direct proof of its reliability is furnished. The skepticism with which even the research in our part of that tradition has been confronted does not even provide evidence of the historical sense of its representatives. In this skepticism the historian, who with

Ranke wants to know how it actually was, is no longer speaking but the prosecuting attorney, who accepts no word of the man suspected of false witness unless proof is provided by eyewitnesses or circumstantial evidence. We must be clear about the fact that it means the end of *historical* investigation of the New Testament if the rule of all historical research is no longer valid, that a report is to be regarded as reliable until there are compelling grounds—and not mere conjectures—to question its accuracy. In our case this means: The traditions at hand in 1 Cor. 11 and Mark 14 about Jesus' Last Supper have a claim to credibility where they agree until compelling grounds are produced that they are legendary and falsely report what actually happened in that Last Supper of Jesus. Whether there are such grounds is a question the conscientious historian must take quite seriously. He may not shirk the responsibility of pursuing every trace of any such grounds. When he has done this and when his investigation of the New Testament comes up with no such grounds, then he has only the one possibility: that the reliability of that tradition is established indirectly.

Matthew and Luke

A sufficient ground for doubting the accuracy of the Marcan and Pauline tradition of Jesus' Last Supper and the origin of the Lord's Supper in the church that is based on it could exist if it could be shown that there is a divergent tradition in the New Testament, one that is otherwise construed at least in hints. Even then we would still have to explore carefully whether the early church did not have good grounds for placing more trust in the tradition represented by Mark and Paul than in this other one. But then the unique position of the account standing behind Mark and Paul would be shaken anyway. In fact there are those who think they have found a completely different tradition, and this in the account of the Lord's Supper in Luke.

While the account in Matthew (26:26–29) is a simple expansion of Mark 14:22–25, in which the most important variation is the addition of "for the forgiveness of sins" to the word about the cup, the text of Luke presents us with a puzzle that has not been solved to this day. It reads as follows in Luke 22:14–20—we emphasize the words that it has in common with Paul:

> And when the hour came, He sat at table, and the apostles with Him.
> And He said to them, "I have earnestly desired to eat this Passover
> with you before I suffer; for I tell you I shall not eat it until it is

fulfilled in the kingdom of God." And He took a cup, and when He had given thanks He said, "Take this, and divide it among yourselves; for I tell you that from now on I shall not drink of the fruit of the vine until the kingdom of God comes." And *He took bread, gave thanks, broke it* and gave it to them, *and said, "This is My body* (given *for you. Do this in remembrance of Me." And the cup in the same way, after the meal, with the words: "This cup is the new covenant in My blood*, poured out for you).

The written tradition represented by Mark and Paul clearly lay before the author of this text and served as sources. The text, however, is not simply a combination of the two. Besides what is taken over from Mark (for example, the "poured out for . . ." in Luke 22:20 in comparison with Mark 14:24) and Paul, Luke contains some remarkable peculiarities in verses 15–18, of which the most striking is the blessing and the distribution of a cup before the bread. So the Lucan account, as we read it, has two cups. What is said of the fruit of the vine, which follows what is said of the cup in Mark, here is put after the distribution of the first cup. Before this in verse 15 we have a word about "this Passover" and the fulfillment in the kingdom of God.

Even if the manuscript transmission were completely consistent, one would have to ask—above all because of the two cups—whether the text is completely in order. However, verses 19b and 20, in parentheses in our translation above, are missing in the old Latin and Syrian manuscripts, as also in the Greek Codex D. Not only such a careful textual critic and exegete as Theodor Zahn but also almost all English theology and today indeed also the overwhelming majority of German theologians have decided in this case that the manuscripts just named have preserved the authentic text of Luke in contrast to the mass of the Greek codices, that therefore vv. 19b–20 did not belong to the original body of the Third Gospel. In fact, the addition of these words, which are clearly borrowed from the Pauline account of the Lord's Supper, may be easier to understand than their omission. Zahn (*Das Evangelium des Lukas* [1913], 678f.) has taken the view—and Jeremias (*Abendmahlsworte*, 44ff. [*Eucharistic Words*, 158f.]) has recently supported this view with very impressive reasons—that Luke could only write about the Last Supper in an incomplete and unclear way in view of Theophilus and other readers like him who had not yet been received into the congregation, because of the calumnies to which the celebration of the Lord's Supper was exposed. That certainly contains an accurate observation. Already in the period of the New Testament, long before the later discipline of secrecy was taught in the church, one clearly avoided saying more about the Lord's Supper in public than was absolutely necessary. The silence of John's gospel regarding the institution of the Lord's Supper, the absence of the Lord's Supper in the list of subjects that belong to elementary instruction in the church according to Hebrews 6:1f., and many other examples speak for the correctness of the thesis recently substantiated anew by Jeremias with great insight and much new material. If the shorter reading is the genuine one, there is hardly a more plausible explanation than this, and we would then have to put up with the fact that Luke gives the decisive words of the Lord's Supper, "This is My body," without any veil or circumlocution but lets them stand in their total starkness as a puzzle for the world.

But does the manuscript evidence really require that preference be given to Codex D, which is otherwise never regarded as primary? Isn't the deletion of 19b–20 perhaps just one of the manifold attempts particularly evident in the variants of the Syrian manuscripts to remove the problem that the apparent doubling of the cup at the Last Supper in Luke causes? (Details about the objections to the shorter text are found in E. Lohmeyer, *Theol. Rundschau*, New Series, 9 [1937]: 178ff.; A. Arnold, *Der Ursprung des christlichen Abendmahls* [1937], 31ff., where it is pointed out that Tatian, from whom the most important variants of D seem to come, knows v. 20.) We can scarcely agree with Zahn that if the longer reading were the original one, it would give rise to no questions or changes. Then we would at best expect that not the second but the first cup would be deleted. If 19b and 20 are an insertion, then it is indeed a very old one, for Marcion (Marcion omits "new" before "covenant" in Luke 22:20) and Justin (Justin names as his source "the recollections of the apostles," i. e., the gospels [*Ap.* 1. 66. 3; 67. 3]. His text therefore depends on Luke, not on Paul.) already know no other than the longer reading.

Since the question of the authenticity of Luke 22:19b–20 cannot be clearly settled on the basis of the manuscript evidence, we shall consider both possibilities and ask in each of the two cases what the peculiar character of the Lucan account of the Last Supper might be—we have already described its external peculiarities, the most important of which were the differences from Paul and Mark.

Common to both forms of the text, that from D and that from the *textus receptus*, is the stronger emphasis on the eschatological character of the Lord's Supper and its connection with the Passover. In doing this the tradition represented by Luke brings nothing fundamentally new, for neither Mark (14:25) nor Paul (1 Cor. 11:26) lacks their respective views of the messianic banquet and Christ's return. Both know of the connection between the Last Supper and the Passover (Mark 14:12–16; 1 Cor. 5:7ff.) What is peculiar to Luke's longer text is that he combines this eschatological outlook with the Passover, which precedes the actual Lord's Supper, and has the word about the fruit of the vine, which in Mark follows the word about the cup, spoken at the distribution of a cup that is not yet the cup of the Lord's Supper but can only be one of the cups passed in the Passover (as Procksch points out ["Passa und Abendmahl" in *Vom Sakrament des Altars*, ed. Hermann Sasse (Leipzig, 1941)], 20). The understanding of the Lord's Supper itself in the longer Lucan text is exactly the same as in Paul.

In the case of the shorter reading it appears to be otherwise. If we had no other account of the origin and essence of the early Christian Lord's Supper, we would have to assume that Jesus gave His disciples first the cup and then the bread. With the cup He spoke eschatologically of the fruit of the vine. With the bread He spoke the puzzling words of explanation, "This is My body," in isolation.

If we take this reading to be the original, we have to ask why Luke portrayed the event in this way. Does he do it because he regards the traditions of Paul and Mark, which he has before him, as false and wants to replace them with a better one? That is altogether unlikely. Then the only explanation we have is that his report does not seek to describe the institution of the Lord's Supper but only to allude to it. So he hides the cup of the Lord's Supper with its word about the blood of the covenant behind the cup of blessing of the Passover meal with its eschatological word. For the same reason then he breaks off the words of the Lord's Supper with "This is My body," leaving the explanation in the dark.

Justin proceeded in a similar way when he felt compelled to confront the slanders of the heathen with some authentic facts of the Lord's Supper. The apostles, as he tells it in *Ap.* 1. 66, report "that the following instruction was given to them. Jesus took bread, spoke a prayer of thanksgiving, and said, 'This do in remembrance of Me; this is My body,' and in the same way He took the cup, spoke a prayer of thanksgiving, and said, 'This is My blood.' " The transposition of the command to repeat and the abbreviation of the words of explanation show how the apologist was concerned not to reveal the secret completely. One does not say it all, and one at least alters the sequence if one has to speak. (That probably also explains the vague rendering of the Rule of Faith in Irenaeus and Tertullian. There too, where the content must be disclosed, the exact wording is not given. The same predicament, having to impart the holy teaching to someone else and yet being obliged to conceal it in essential matters, is found in ancient Buddhism. There too one is helped by regarding only the *literal* reporting of certain teachings as forbidden; see H. Oldenberg, *Buddha*, 8th and 9th edition [1921], 418f.) Therefore, in the shorter reading of Luke the Passover cup serves to point to the cup of the Lord's Supper and at the same time to conceal it. The reversal of the sequence of bread and cup that then results is a welcome means of veiling what actually happened. This raises the possibility that a liturgical custom in the *Didache* and perhaps already hinted at in 1 Cor. 10:16 and 21, in which the Eucharistic prayer over the cup is spoken before the Eucharistic prayer over the bread, may reflect the cup-bread sequence of the shorter Lucan reading. One may not, however, regard the traces of such a usage as proof of the historical reliability of this reading. For the very writings in which they may be found testify quite unmistakably that in the *participation* in the Lord's Supper the bread precedes the cup. (According to *Didache* 9. [5.] the prayer of thanksgiving is first spoken for the cup, then for the bread, but in the instruction it always speaks of the "eating and drinking" of the Eucharist, and the concluding prayer at 10. 3. refers to "food and drink," "spiritual food and drink." Also in Paul at 1 Cor. 10:16f.—the reference shows close connections with *Didache* 9. 4. and 10. 5.—first "the cup which we bless" and then "the bread which we break" are mentioned. That one cannot draw too far-reaching conclusions for practical use from this sequence, which in 10:21 is even used of eating and drinking, is seen by 1 Cor. 11:23–26.)

Therefore even the shorter reading in Luke testifies of no other Lord's Supper than that we know from Paul and Mark. Even someone who cannot accept the view that Luke wanted to veil what actually happened at the institution and who sees in the variations of the shorter reading a conscious correction of the other traditions is still not able to wring another meaning of the Lord's Supper from this reading. One cannot say that Luke pictures a Lord's Supper that is not an explanation and appropriation of the death of Christ but only an anticipation of the messianic banquet. For the connection both with the messianic banquet in the kingdom of God and with the death of Jesus belongs to every tradition of the Lord's Supper, even though sometimes the one, sometimes the other may be more prominent. The absence of the word about the blood of the covenant does not by itself alter the character of the

Lord's Supper. As long as the words "This is My body" are there, the account in Luke, where his own peculiarity may always remain, shares what is essential with Mark and Paul.

Some scholars, like Bultmann (*Jesus*, 30), K. L. Schmidt (*RGG*[2] 1:8), and for a time Lietzmann (*1 Cor.*[2], Handbuch zum N. T., 60; otherwise in *Messe und Herrenmahl*, 216), have gone a step further and have excised also v. 19a from the older account of the Lord's Supper as it is contained in Luke's gospel. But an operation like the deletion of 19a lacks justification either in textual criticism or in literary criticism. It is purely the product of the prejudice that the Lucan text must provide an older account of Jesus' Last Supper, one different from Mark and Paul. But is it any wonder that the Lucan account differs completely from the others if one declares that what he has in common with them is inauthentic? "What remains by this time describes how Jesus at His last meal in the circle of His disciples expressed the conviction that He would celebrate His next meal with His own in the kingdom of God" (K. L. Schmidt, *RGG*[2] 1:8). That is indeed all that remains if one has removed everything else. P. Feine is not unfair when he observes that with this method he could prove anything.

The voices that declare 19a inauthentic are heard less and less. Nevertheless, the efforts to discover in Luke's shorter reading the desired tradition about the Lord's Supper different from Mark and Paul have not ceased. Lietzmann (*Messe und Herrenmahl*, 218) finds "that Luke describes a Lord's Supper that contains eschatological hopes, and in which the bread is the essential feature" [*Mass and Lord's Supper*, 176]. But he is not able to explain the words, "This is My body." They form the strongest objection to his conjecture that the oldest, pre-Pauline Lord's Supper was only the continuation of the table fellowship that Jesus had with His disciples while on earth and of its customary breaking of bread. Lietzmann's hypothesis becomes no more acceptable by his pointing to the breaking of bread in the Emmaus pericope and in Acts. For neither the name "breaking of bread" nor the observation that the celebration was held with "gladness" permit the conclusion that there is something essentially different going on than in the Lord's Supper in the Pauline congregations. Also the absence of the reference to the death of Christ in the prayers of the *Didache* does not prove that the remembrance of the death of Jesus was lacking in this Eucharist. We could only say that if we had the complete liturgy of the church out of which the *Didache* comes. As long as the statement "This is My body" must hold good as an authentic word of Jesus, which also played a role already in the breaking of bread in the early church, we must assume that there has never been a Lord's Supper that was not also a memorial celebration of the death of Jesus and a repetition of His Last Supper.

An understanding of the Lord's Supper different from that in Mark and Paul could only be wrung from Luke's shorter account if it could be shown that the words "This is My body" have a different meaning for him than for Paul and Mark. This is what Rudolf Otto (*Reich Gottes und Menschensohn*, 2d ed. [1940], 214ff.) has tried to prove. He believes that he has discovered the oldest account of the Lord's Supper in Luke 22:17–19a and 29f. By his joining 29 to 19a, it reads: "This is my body (= this is I myself); and I appoint unto you in covenant the kingdom, as my Father has appointed it unto me in covenant, that you may eat and drink at my table in my kingdom, and sit upon thrones, judging the twelve tribes in Israel" (*Reich Gottes*, 216 [*Kingdom of God and Son of Man* (1943), 274]) But that is an arbitrary combination, and that it is untenable becomes clear from the fact that verses 28–30 are demonstrably put into the context of the account of the Lord's Supper for the first time by Luke, as is also what precedes them. (Luke includes sayings at 22:28ff. that he omitted at 18:23f., as is shown by the parallels at Matt. 19:28f. See A. Arnold, 42). Also untenable is Otto's further assumption that the words "This is My body," in Aramaic *den hu gufi*, should mean nothing more than "This is I Myself." This supposition rests on another, that the words with the cup can under no circumstances come from Jesus and that the later addition of "This is My blood of the covenant" completely changed the original meaning of "body," in the sense that only through the juxtaposition of "body" and "blood" did the word *body* receive the meaning of a physical body. But there is not the slightest clue that such a drastic change in the meaning of "This is my body" ever happened. It would have had to have taken place already in the very earliest period of the church, even before the traditions represented by Paul and Mark were formed, and therefore already during the lifetimes of the eye- and earwitnesses of Jesus' Last Supper. Such an unlikely assumption must rest on firmer ground than what apparently forms its only foundation, namely, the presupposition that the original Lucan account *must* have known a Lord's Supper entirely different than the traditions lying before Paul and Mark. In fact such an older tradition, which differed from the other accounts not only in details but in its basic understanding of the Lord's Supper, cannot be demonstrated. Luke's particular treasure does indeed furnish us with an important supplement to what is reported in Paul and Mark, but precisely not in reference to what these two tell of the actual institution of the Lord's Supper and of the words that Jesus spoke. Therefore, according to all the rules of historical research the traditions contained in Paul and Mark remain the oldest historical source.

Jesus' Last Supper

Whoever tries, on the basis of the sources just discussed, to portray what happened at Jesus' Last Supper, which the church from the earliest days has understood as the institution of the Lord's Supper, must be aware from the start of the limitations of this effort. The more reliable these earliest sources appear to be, the more the historian must be on his guard against reading more out of them than they say. It is just the nature of the New Testament tradition to display an extraordinary conciseness. The evangelists report what it seemed necessary for their first readers to know and not a word more. For the modern historian this means that he faces regrettable gaps in the tradition; that applies also to the tradition regarding the institution of the Lord's Supper. We cannot reconstruct the "night when He was betrayed" in all details, nor do we know all that went on at the Last Supper. Under these circumstances the task of the historian cannot be the hypothetical reconstruction of what we are not told but only the analysis of what has been handed down for its authenticity and its meaning. This excludes in particular every attempt to establish by way of psychological considerations what was going on in the soul of Jesus at the time of the Last Supper and what He therefore might have said and what He might have meant with His words.

There ought to be an end, once and for all, to such suppositions as those with which Heitmüller (*Taufe und Abendmahl im Urchristentum* [1911], 55f.) tries to clarify the situation in which Jesus spoke the words of the Last Supper (emphasis mine):

> The thought of a catastrophe *must* have stirred in His soul . . . considerations of what would become of His work, of what His life had labored for, of His disciples in case of His death—the struggle for faith itself, for His work, for His God. On the evening before His arrest, *presentiment* would become, if not *knowledge*, then surely *certainty*. This is *psychologically understandable*. This acceptance is supported by His word: "From now on I shall not drink of the fruit . . . ." A *mood* of farewell moves Him. Thoughts of death fill His soul. As He reclined with His own for the meal, He was sure that this was the last fraternal meal. All His thoughts about this termination of His

work *closed in* on Him again; all love for His disciples intensified vividly. He is not defeated in His struggle for faith in His God and His work. He is sure in the joyful hope that some day He would be united again with His own in the Father's kingdom. But what would become of the flock of those who were His, whose faith and weaknesses he knew so well . . . ?"

Just as untenable is what we read in Dalman (*Jesus-Jeschua* [1922], 131f.; emphasis mine):

> On this night He performed the breaking of bread, certain of His approaching death, His soul full of the destiny that His Father had designed for Him. How *natural* it was, as He set about breaking and distributing the bread piece by piece, that *the thought pierced His soul:* "This is what will happen to Me when I have to suffer death."

The text does not offer the slightest clue for such constructions, in which the exegesis of rationalism still lingers. (Cf. the interpretation of H. G. E. Paulus in 1805: "The breaking of the bread caught the mind of Jesus, filled with thoughts of death, by surprise for a moment over the similarity to a murderous dismemberment. The sight of the grapes' blood convulsed Jesus: This is to Me suddenly like My own blood" [quoted by Herman Schultz, *Zur Lehre vom Heiligen Abendmahl* (1886), 8].) They serve not to explain but to obscure the actual situation, for they squeeze the Lord, who is instituting His Supper, into the psychological categories of modern Western man.

An explicit warning about this wrong track is therefore necessary at this point because numerous interpreters of the Lord's Supper pericope have let themselves be led astray by such psychologizing tendencies. The more "naturally," the more self-evidently an exegete fits the celebration of the Last Supper into the whole life of Jesus as a farewell meal and legacy and the more this celebration has forfeited the character of the surprising, the extraordinary, and the offensive, then the more necessary it is for concerned exegesis to examine whether it has fallen victim to that danger of psychologizing. It is not historical interpretation of the pericope of the Last Supper if a historian tells us what his thoughts would have been, had he been there speaking the Words of Institution. To interpret this pericope does not mean to paint moods—neither Jesus' mood nor the mood of His disciples—nor does it mean to guess at thoughts that might have "closed in" on Jesus at that time or "pierced His soul." It means to give an account soberly and objectively of what *happened*, what was *said*, and what was *meant* by the words.

So what did happen then? Jesus sat down, or more precisely, He reclined—as was the custom at the Passover meal—at table with His disciples. The first Lord's Supper took place during a meal, and this combination of the Lord's Supper with a meal was maintained for a considerable time, as we know, in the agape meals of the early Christians. Only in the middle of the second century does Justin tell us that in Rome at that time the Lord's Supper was separated from the usual time for the meal and transferred to the divine service on Sunday morning. From this combination of the Lord's Supper with a regular meal, however, it cannot be concluded that Jesus' last meal was only an ordinary meal and not a Passover meal. The meal that Jesus as head of the house [Hausvater] had that night with His circle of disciples was much more. It was indeed a farewell meal, a last time of fellowship at table together. It was also a Passover meal, whether one understands it with the Eastern tradition and such modern scholars as O. Procksch as an anticipated celebration or with the Western church and many recent theologians as an actual Passover meal. These alternatives may perhaps never be resolved with complete certainty, but the fact that Jesus Himself understood the meal as a Passover meal should never be disputed. Jeremias has shown how Jesus' last meal in all details fits into the framework of a Passover meal. The only remaining counter-argument is the difficult problem of the date. Was the Thursday on which the Passover was eaten Nisan 14, and was Jesus executed on the first day of the high feast? Is an anticipated Passover, a Passover without a Passover lamb, on the day before Nisan 14 conceivable? However one may answer these questions, it is impossible to undo the connection between Jesus' last meal and the Passover meal without doing violence to the reports. The account of the preparation for the Passover (Mark 14:12–16 and parallels)—"one of the most beautiful in the Gospel of Mark" (E. Lohmeyer, *Das Evangelium des Markus* [1937], 298)—is utterly credible and with its local color and vividness offers no ground for critical doubt. So strong is its connection with the pericope of the Last Supper that it can only be broken by force. Even if the institution pericope can be interpreted without the report of the preparations (e. g., 1 Cor. 11), the latter only has its culmination in the former and never existed for itself alone.

In the course of this Passover meal then there occurred what Mark 14:22f. describes with the words: "And as they were eating, He took bread, and blessed, and broke it, and gave it to them and said, 'Take; this is My body.' And He took a cup, gave thanks, and gave it them, and they all drank of it. And He said to them, 'This is My blood of the covenant, which is poured out for many' " [14:22–24]. The exact moment of this action or these two actions cannot be determined with certainty. According to Mark the distribution of the cup seems to follow immediately that of the bread. According to the tradition preserved in Paul ("after supper," 1 Cor. 11:25), two things were done, of which the second, the distribution of the blessed cup, took place at the end of the meal, while the first came earlier, either at the beginning of the meal or during it. Jeremias (*Abendmahlsworte*, 41 [*Eucharistic Words*, 87]) and Billerbeck (Strack-Billerbeck, *Kommentar zum N. T. aus Talmud und Midrasch* 4:75) take the view that Jesus attached His words about the bread and wine to the table prayer that the head of the house spoke over the unleavened bread immediately before the eating of the Passover lamb and to the prayer of thanksgiving that was spoken over the "third" cup, "the cup of blessing" (1 Cor. 10:16), at the end of the actual meal before the "hymn of praise" (Mark 14:26, the Passover Hallel). This is very likely. That the connection between the first Lord's Supper and the Passover liturgy is not more clearly expressed in the accounts that we have may be reasonably explained by the fact that these traditions have been influenced by the liturgical interests of the early church. The ecclesiastical traditions had no further interest in the details of the Passover ritual. Its whole attention was concentrated on what has remained in the liturgy of the church from the first Lord's Supper (Arnold, 77f.). This also explains why in the Marcan account there is not even a hint of what went on between the distribution of the bread and the cup. That, along with all the details of the traditional Passover ritual, which Jesus doubtless observed, was irrelevant for the Lord's Supper itself. Where the Passover of the New Testament is celebrated, that of the Old Testament is both fulfilled and abolished. The early church had already perceived what was later put into words: "This new Passover's new blessing Hath fulfilled the older rite" (So Thomas Aquinas in "Lauda Sion salvatorem." Among the church fathers the thought is found in Athanasius, Ephraem Syrus, Chrysostom, Theodoret of Cyrrhus, and Peter of Laodicea, among others; cf. O. Casel, *Das Mysterien-Gedächtnis der Messliturgie*, 148, 151, 153, 155, 158.)

Jesus performed two actions during the meal: the blessing, breaking, and distributing of the bread and the blessing and distribution of the cup. Both actions belong as such to the settled way of Jewish religious table customs, and they occur not only in the Passover celebration but also at other meals, such as at the family meal with which the celebration of the Sabbath begins on Friday evening. Also of Jesus is the "He took bread, gave thanks, and broke it" attested not only at the Last Supper but also at the miraculous feeding and in the Emmaus story, which appears to allude to the breaking of bread that He practiced during His days on earth. The praise of God the Creator for the bread, the grateful recall of the blessings that God has heaped on His people, the breaking of the bread and its distribution to those taking part in the meal as a sign of their participation in the praise, the prayer of thanksgiving over the cup, and perhaps also its distribution—these are all Jewish customs practiced by Jesus in harmony with the piety of His people. They supply the ingredients of the action that He performed at the Last Supper, and that is different from similar actions in that He Himself did not partake of the bread and the wine as the head of the family usually did. That can at least explain the invitation, "Take," in Mark 14:22. (The "Take" is not there in Luke and Paul—in Matthew it is expanded to "Take, eat . . . drink." The *labete* may be compared with the inscription *labe eulogia* on a Jewish gold-ornamented glass cup; cf. Lietzmann, *Messe und Abendmahl*, 209 [*Mass and Lord's Supper*, 169f.].) But regardless of how much His action may resemble Jewish benediction rites, it can scarcely be derived from them. It is not what the action of Jesus on that night has in common with these rites that gives the Lord's Supper its character, but what distinguishes it from them. Just as the early Christian agape meals appeared externally to be interchangeable with the Jewish fellowship meals and yet according to their inner meaning were something quite new, so is it with the blessing and distribution of bread and wine at Jesus' Last Supper. What happened there was something quite new, a special action that receives its meaning only from the words that He spoke along with it.

The *words of explanation* with which Jesus accompanied His action are therefore the key to understanding the Lord's Supper. They reveal the difference between His action and that of a pious Jewish head of the house who eats the Passover with his family and speaks the traditional blessings. They not only distinguish the Lord's Supper from the Passover, but also this Last Supper of Jesus from all the meals that He had had with His disciples before. The assertion has been made that the earliest Lord's Supper of the church, "the breaking of bread" of the original Jerusalem congregation, is not to be understood as a repetition of Jesus' Last Supper at all, but as a continuation of the table fellowship that He had always had with His disciples. There is a kernel of truth in this hypothesis. In fact, there must have been something special in the table fellowship between Jesus and His disciples even before and apart from the Last Supper. The "breaking of bread" does indeed go back to Jesus' days on earth. It was performed by Jesus daily as the action of blessing before their common meals, and once, at the feeding of the five thousand, it occurred before a great many people. This "breaking of bread" that Jesus performed in the circle of His disciples lives on in the Lord's Supper of the early church. That is the element of truth in Lietzmann's thesis about the origin of the Lord's Supper. Its error lies in the fact that it does not perceive what Jesus' Last Supper means in this context. While it is the end, the culmination of the breaking of bread performed by Jesus Himself, it is also the beginning of a new celebration in which Jesus' breaking of bread was "lifted up," the celebration of a much closer fellowship than the earthly table fellowship had been. In this celebration the Lord is not only a table companion, not only the host who speaks the blessing, not only the head of the house who eats the Passover with His own, but He is Himself also the food and drink of the meal. He is the Passover lamb, the sacrificial food that is eaten, His blood the holy drink that is drunk. Thus in this meal a fellowship is established in which the old table fellowship lives on and which at the same time is a much closer and deeper fellowship. There is no analogy to this fellowship, just as there are also no parallels to this celebration. The Lord's Supper received this character as something unique, something remarkable from the Words of Institution.

The Words of Institution

We have already observed the notable fact that the Words of Institution—just like the Lord's Prayer—have not been entirely uniformly transmitted (how this diversity is to be judged in the light of the history of the liturgy is shown in the work of F. Hamm cited above), but at the same time we have established that the forms of the text essentially agree and that the original form of the words is still recognizable. Since Matthew gives the Marcan form with the addition of "for the forgiveness of sins" to the words about the cup, and since the longer Lucan text is dependent on Paul, the original form of the words of the Lord's Supper must be ascertained from a comparison of Mark and Paul. This comparison shows that the Marcan form of the text is older than the Pauline, in which the words about the cup have been touched up, and the command to repeat has been added to both of the words of explanation. We agree with Jeremias, who expresses the result of his careful examination of the Words of Institution as follows: "The oldest text of the words of interpretation obtained by a comparison of the texts agrees exactly with the Marcan text" (*Abendmahlsworte* [1935], 64 [Cf. *Eucharistic Words*, 173]). This text reads: *labete touto estin to sōma mou . . . touto estin to haima mou tēs diathēkēs to ekchunnomenon huper pollōn.* "Take! This is My body. . . . This is My covenant blood poured out for many."

What do these words, the most disputed in the New Testament, mean? We are assured that "today there is agreement from Zürich to Erlangen . . . that the decisive texts of the Lord's Supper are to be understood symbolically" (W. Niesel, *Abendmahlsgemeinschaft?* [1937], 37), and this assertion is supported by pointing to the more recent exegesis, which has shown that the words of the Lord's Supper have a parabolic character. If this is in fact an assured result of more recent research, then we would expect that these exegetes would have arrived at a consensus on what this parable should mean. But that is by no means the case.

Jülicher, the founder of the theory that the words of the Lord's Supper are a double parable comparable to the double parables of mustard seed and leaven, the lost sheep and coin, and others, understands the meaning of "This is My body" as follows:

> At the breaking of the bread into pieces He thought of the similar fate that awaited His body, and with no other perception of profound similarities between His body and the bread than what was there before His eyes, He could in view of the *klōmenon* before Him say to His disciples: This is My body; this same treatment will presently happen to My body. This they could all understand. . . . He was describing what His body would suffer, not what the disciples should do." (Ad. Jülicher, "Zur Geschichte der Abendmahlsfeier," *Theol. Abhandlg. C. v. Weizsäcker gewidmet* [1892], 242f.)

The point of comparison here is the being broken in pieces and then also the being poured out (Ibid., 244). Heitmüller (*Taufe und Abendmahl im Urchristentum* [1911], 57) objects that this symbolism may hold for the bread, but not for the cup, of whose pouring out or consumption nothing is said. Jülicher's interpretation has forgotten that bread and wine are distributed in order to be eaten and drunk:

> In view of this another interpretation may here be proposed . . . : "Just as I give all of you this one bread and you all eat of the one bread as the sign and as the foundation of a closer fellowship, so do I give you My body, that is, Me Myself, and so you are to receive Me

into yourselves as the resource for a most intimate brotherhood and fellowship." (Ibid., 58)

Here the point of comparison is in having a part in the one gift. Althaus interprets the action of the Lord at the Last Supper still differently:

> The action is first of all Jesus' last parable: He proclaims by means of a symbol together with the interpreting words His imminent death. By making the bread and wine into symbols of His sacrificial death, He portrays the meaning of His death for the life of men: "You live because I die."

The action is both "parabolic action" [Gleichnishandlung] and a "done parable [Tatgleichnis], that is, a real gift in symbolic action" (Die luth. Abendmahlslehre in der Gegenwart [1931], 43f.). For Althaus the point of comparison is separate handing over of the bread and wine as symbols of body and blood: "Only in death are body and blood separated. Jesus therefore points in the symbolic action to His sacrificial death. In going to His death He gives up His life for the disciples" (Ibid., 39). "The gift of the Sacrament is therefore not Christ's heavenly corporeality, but His death" (Grundriss der Dogmatik, part 2 [1932], 152). Lietzmann has greater difficulty in finding the point of comparison:

> A distinct problem is posed by the question: How can Jesus compare the bread to his body and the wine to his blood in a context of this kind? Where is the third term of comparison? The early comment that the breaking of the bread into pieces is a symbol of the dismembered body of the victim is obvious enough; but it is difficult to find an analogous point of comparison in the case of the wine. It is true that it is "poured out"—from the pitcher into the cup, from the cup into the throat—but everyone feels that this figure is less appropriate: the pouring out from the pitcher probably took place before Jesus spoke. . . . It is easy to see the bread as a symbol of Jesus dying as a victim for his people; this is not so in the case of the wine, yet it is the words connected in the tradition with the wine which have compelled us to adopt the dominant conception of the victim and his blood-covenant; and it is only by starting from this conception that we have come to our interpretation of the words concerning the bread. (Messe und Herrenmahl, 221f. [Mass and Lord's Supper, 180–81])

Jeremias finds it easier to explain the "double parable." After he correctly points out that touto cannot possibly refer to the action of breaking or the action of pouring out, since the words of explanation were not spoken until long after the actions, he states:

68

It was not the action of breaking the bread or of pouring out the wine that Jesus interpreted, but rather the bread and wine itself. . . . The *tertium comparationis* in the case of the bread is the fact that it was broken, and in the case of the wine the red color. . . . Jesus made the broken bread a simile of the fate of his body, the blood of the grapes a simile of his outpoured blood. "I go to death as the true passover sacrifice," is the meaning of Jesus' last parable. (*Die Abendmahlsworte Jesu* [1935], 75f. [*Eucharistic Words*, 221, 223–24]. That this death is for the benefit of others lies, according to Jeremias, not yet in the parable but in the direct statement about the meaning of His death that is added to the word about the wine [*Abendmahlsworte*, 77 (*Eucharistic Words*, 225)].)

Enough of these examples, which could be multiplied as much as you like! They show that there has been no success so far in explaining the alleged parable in the words of the Lord's Supper. The exegetes indeed assure us: "Its meaning is quite simple. Each one of the disciples could understand it" (Jeremias, *Abendmahlsworte*, 76 [*Eucharistic Words*, 224]; similarly Jülicher, 243), yet they themselves quite clearly cannot agree what that meaning should be. In fact symbolic exegesis today does not seem to have gotten beyond the situation of the 16th century, when Luther again and again had to point out that his opponents were united in only one thing: *that* the words of the Lord's Supper were to be understood symbolically, while they differed widely on the interpretation itself. What sort of a parable can it be when even learned exegetes cannot say with certainty what it actually means!

Let us suppose that after the church for so many centuries has falsely understood the words of the Lord's Supper, at least one of the modern scholars has finally succeeded in discovering their meaning. What sort of meaning would it be? "I must die" is according to Jeremias "the meaning of Jesus' last parable"; according to Althaus (*Abendmahlslehre*, 43): "You live because I die." It is difficult then to see what need there is of the Lord's Supper, for Jesus had already told His disciples that before. Had He wanted to say it once more with special emphasis in His departing hour, wouldn't a direct instruction about the imminent fulfillment of Isaiah 53 have been much more suitable than a parable about whose meaning scholars cannot agree even after 19 centuries? One could respond to this with Althaus that the Last Supper was certainly more than a parable: "In making the bread and the wine into symbols of His death and giving them to be consumed, Jesus was at the same time granting in parabolic pledges a participation in what

His death achieved" (Ibid., 43). Certainly, but all notable representatives of the symbolic interpretation of the words of the Lord's Supper have taught this, even Berengar, Zwingli, and Oecolampadius. For none of them was the Lord's Supper *only* a parable. But it might be asked whether an application of that kind might not have been much more impressive if Jesus had used a plain, straightforward statement of what He was giving His disciples, rather than an ambiguous parable.

But perhaps He did that! Perhaps His words are to be taken quite literally, just as they read! If that should be the case, then it would certainly be comprehensible that the exegetes have so far not arrived at a unanimous interpretation of the parable presumed to be in the words of the Lord's Supper. How can one explain a parable that is not a parable at all! Perhaps this failure of recent exegesis may serve to shake the dogma held with an astonishing lack of critical thought in modern Protestantism that *touto estin to sōma mou* cannot mean anything but "This *signifies* My body," especially since the copula "is" probably was not even expressed in Aramaic.

It was certainly not just a more or less respectable dogmatic stubbornness, as is supposed today, that caused Luther so decisively to offer resistance to Zwingli's understanding of the *est* as *significat*. It was also good philological reasons. It was also his superlative sensitivity to language and style, in which the greatest Bible translator that Christianity has produced far surpassed his Humanistic contemporaries.

Let us now ask once how Jesus would have expressed Himself if He had intended a parable. Lohmeyer observes, in commenting on Jeremias's attempt to understand the statements as a double parable:

> Linguistically it would have to say *homoion esti to sōma mou toutō* or something similar to *homoia estin hē basileia tōn ouranōn zumē*. Also the reference to the word of explanation with the unleavened bread [*Mazzot*], "This is the bread of affliction," proves nothing. For there a comparison is clearly indicated by the repetition of the word "bread," and this repetition is just what is altogether absent in Jesus' word. (*Das Evangelium des Markus* [1937], 306 n. 2)

No help is given here either by reference to such expressions as "I am the Bread of life," "I am the true Vine," or "I am the Good Shepherd," for in these expressions the "I am" does not at all mean "I signify." No one denies that *esti* can also be used in the sense of "signifies," but in that case the comparison must be recognizable as a comparison. That applies also to a parabolic action. Thus Agabus in Acts 21:11 makes it clear that he has acted parabolically with the words: "So shall the Jews

70

at Jerusalem bind the man who owns this girdle and deliver him into the hands of the Gentiles." Similar explanations are given of parabolic actions in Jer. 19:19ff. and Ezek. 4:1ff.; 5:1ff. (One notes the "Thus . . . . So" in Jer. 19:11 and the continuation "This is Jerusalem" in Ezek. 5:5ff.)

To understand the action and the words of the Lord's Supper as a parable is linguistically impossible. Wherever it has been tried, it has not happened for philological reasons, but—and this ought to be freely acknowledged—only from the consideration that if the Words of Institution are taken literally, they appear to state something absurd.

The words of the Lord's Supper do in fact appear to express an absurdity if one understands them literally. How can Jesus say that the bread that He holds in His hand, that He breaks and distributes, is His body, that the wine in the cup is His blood? And if He actually meant that, how could the disciples understand it? "How could Jesus give His glorified body to His disciples while He was still corporeally sitting in front of them and the glorification was still to come? . . . But above all: The disciples absolutely could not have been able to understand this word in this sense. Yet Jesus certainly did not offer them a riddle in this solemn moment" (Heitmüller, 56f.). But if, as we saw, the words of the Lord's Supper become an insoluble riddle if one tries to interpret them as a parable, how then are we to escape the absurdity? It can be done if one accepts that Jesus gave His disciples "body" and "blood" not figuratively but actually, but that the words "body" and "blood" do not mean what we in our language call "body" and "blood." And so the understanding of "body" in the sense of "person" enjoys great popularity in our day. If "This is My body" is put into Aramaic as *den hu gufi*, as is generally accepted today, then one easily understands *gufi*, "My body," in the sense in which it is often used, namely, for "I myself." (Similarly Kattenbusch, who takes *gewijjah* as the basis for "My body": "With Jesus 'my body' means 'I' " ["Der Quellort der Kirchenidee" in *Festgabe für A. von Harnack* (1921), 170 n. 1].) In a careful discussion of this question, Dalman comes to the conclusion: "It would be possible to take *guphi* in the sense of 'I myself.' However, the fact that the Early Christians did not take it in this sense, as well as our Lord's reference to His Blood at the administration of the wine, necessitates the translation 'My Body' (G. Dalmann, *Jesus-Jeschua* [1922], 131 [*Jesus-Jeshua*, 143]). In fact this understanding of "My body" would only make sense if one either could find a similar transferred meaning for blood, of which there is none, or if one with R. Otto (*Reich Gottes und Menschensohn*, 2d ed., 214ff. [*The Kingdom of God and the Son of Man*, 320f.]) and his followers (e. g., E. Käsemann, *Abendmahlsgemeinschaft*? 67f.) denies that Jesus spoke the words about the cup at all, which we have seen as impossible in another connection (see on p. 59). If "My blood of the covenant poured out for many" unquestionably means the actual blood of Jesus that was poured out on the cross, then "My body" can only mean His actual body that was given into death.

Another new interpretation of body and blood has recently been proposed by Lohmeyer. He recognizes, as we have already seen, the impossibility of understanding the words of the Lord's Supper as a parable. "Therefore we are not here involved in looking for the third factor by which bread and body can be compared with each other. . . ," but the "supposed identity between bread and body is the riddle and mystery that contains in itself the meaning of the action" (*Das Evangelium des Markus*, 306). In the statements "This is My body" and "This is My covenant blood," "this" must be taken as a predicate noun, not as the subject. These statements do not say what the bread and wine but what the body and blood now are. "Now the bread the disciples take and the wine they drink signify nothing else than the fellowship in fulfillment. Body and blood signify nothing else than the earthly life of this one Master, who is the norm and the fact of their fellowship. Through the idea of fellowship therefore an identity between bread and wine becomes possible" (Ibid., 306f.). The meaning of the action at the Last Supper and the word about the bread is then given as follows: "As My body was the means and the heart of the disciples' fellowship so far, so now it is the common eating of the bread"; to say it on the model of a familiar saying of Jesus: "Where two or three break the bread, there am I in the midst of them."

The word of the covenant blood must then be similarly understood. However cleverly Lohmeyer may carry this theory through, it is simply not tenable. To take *touto* as a predicate noun placed in front of the statement is far too artificial and needs better substantiation in view of the fact that since the early church *touto* has always been understood as subject. It founders in the setting of the word about the cup in 1 Cor. 11:25: *touto potērion hē kainē diathēkē estin en tō emō haimati*, and in Luke 22:20: *touto to potērion hē kainē diathēkē en tō haimati mou*. For here "this cup" without any doubt is understood as subject, and there is not the slightest clue for finding that it was otherwise in Mark or Matthew.

Apart from this question, Lohmeyer's thesis means a new attempt to make the identification of bread and body, wine and blood comprehensible by a new interpretation of "body" and "blood." "Body and blood," according to Lohmeyer, means "nothing else than the earthly life of this one Master," and "My body" means "the person of the Master." He does not investigate the Aramaic background. But what does "My covenant blood" mean? There is nothing said of this with the same clarity. We are told only that the word about the cup says the same as the word about the bread, and the equation of blood and wine means: "That which is the content and power of His life and death now happens in the fellowship of the eating and drinking" (Ibid., 308). So then, there is no actual identity of the bread and the wine with the body and blood of Christ, but a functional identity of both. The bread and the wine or, more precisely, the eating and drinking of the bread and wine now exercise the same function of establishing fellowship that previously Christ's body and blood or, more precisely, His bodily presence and His death exercised: "Whenever, therefore, the disciples break the bread together and drink the wine, this meal brings about the same fellowship, as much historic as eschatological, that was previously embodied in the figure of the Master. To say it more precisely, the fellowship of the brothers that is effected in the eating and drinking is the presence of the Lord" (Ibid.).

But we need only raise the question whether this fellowship, whether this presence of the Lord can not also be mediated in other ways, whether it is not wherever two or three are gathered together in His name to hear His word and to call on Him in prayer, there is He in the midst of them, and we will recognize that there is in this theory no real identification of the bread with the body, the wine with the blood. It fails to explain "the riddle and mystery" of the equation of body and bread, wine and blood; much rather it shatters this identification by its complicated efforts at explanation. For Lohmeyer, too, the bread is not actually the body nor the wine actually the blood of Christ.

There is a still weightier objection to raise against all these attempts at new interpretations. Their advocates can only explain the unquestioned fact that the church has always taken "body" to be the actual body and "blood" to be the actual blood of the Lord in such a way that this ecclesiastical understanding of the words of the Lord's Supper represents either a misunderstanding or a development of the original Lord's Supper. But when could this misunderstanding or this development have occurred? Perhaps first with Ignatius at the beginning or with Justin in the middle of the second century? Is not this realistic understanding of the words of the Lord's Supper found already in Paul, our oldest witness of the Lord's Supper, and in the four gospels? Even those scholars who are of the opinion that Jesus Himself used "body" and "blood" in a transferred sense acknowledge that in places like 1 Cor. 10 and 11 or John 6:51b-58 a realistic understanding of the Words of Institution is taken for granted. This question calls for investigation.

The Understanding of the Words of Institution in Paul and John

In what sense "is" the bread the body and the wine in the cup the blood of Christ for Paul? There is no doubt that according to Paul those who take part in the Lord's Supper actually consume bread and wine. According to 1 Cor. 10:17 they all partake of the *one bread*, and 11:27ff. confirms that the communicants actually consume bread and wine: "Whoever, therefore, eats the bread or drinks the cup of the Lord in an unworthy manner will be guilty of profaning the body and blood of the Lord. Let a man examine himself, and so eat of the bread and drink of the cup." This passage has always been legitimately quoted against the doctrine of transubstantiation (SA III 6). If the bread were *changed* into the body of Christ, it could no longer be designated as the object of the eating. And if Paul meant that it is now only figurative bread, he would express himself differently. But do the communicants receive *only* bread and wine? No, for "the cup of blessing which we bless, is it not a participation [*koinōnia*] in the blood of Christ? The bread which we break, is it not a participation in the body of Christ?" (10:16). "Participation in the body of Christ" may not be taken, as has been attempted, as a figurative expression for the fellowship of the church. In that case, what would "participation in the blood of Christ" be? It really deals, therefore, with a communion with the body given into death "for you" (11:24) and with the blood shed on the cross. Paul chooses the term *koinōnia*, communion; he avoids the word *metechein*, partake, which he uses for the participation in the bread (10:17), and he also does not speak of eating the body and drinking the blood. That these formulations are not accidental but deliberate is shown by 10:20f.: "I do not want you to be partners [*koinōnoi*] with demons. You cannot drink the cup of the Lord and the cup of demons. You cannot partake of the table of the Lord and the table of demons." One drinks the cup, one partakes [*metechein*] at the table, that is, one eats and thereby comes into communion with the demons in the heathen cult, with the body and blood of Christ in the Lord's Supper. The distinction between "partaking" and "communion" expresses the distinction that exists in the relationship the communicants have with the bread on the one hand and with the body and blood of Christ on the other hand. In order not to blur this distinction, Paul avoids, probably on purpose, the expressions "eat the body of Christ" and "drink the blood of Christ," which for some reason may have seemed dubious to him. One may certainly not understand this as though the "participation in the body and blood of Christ" is something purely spiritual and not as close and as real as the connection of food and drink to the human body. In the Bible the word *koinōnia* signifies the closest and deepest communion conceivable between God and man (1 John 1:3) and between the members of the body of Christ, a communion in which our body also takes part (1 Cor. 6:15).

It would also be a misinterpretation of Paul to suppose that the koinonia of the body and blood of Christ is established in any other way than by eating the bread and drinking the cup. There is no support in Paul for the notion that the *faith* of the recipient or the *Holy Spirit* brings about the fellowship of the body and blood during the celebration of the Lord's Supper. Nor can one read into 1 Cor. 10:16 the notion that the action of blessing and breaking the bread is what creates the koinonia. (This widespread notion is suggested by the Württemberg Bible Society to the readers of its Bible editions by their emphasizing of the words *bless* and *break* in 1 Cor. 10:16.) It stands there unambiguously: the cup is the koinonia, the bread is the koinonia.

However, from the statement in 1 Cor. 10:16 that the bread is the koinonia of the body, we may not now conclude that the bread is not the body for Paul. Certainly the identity of bread and body may not be understood as if only the bread is the body. Jesus was not saying this when He called the bread He gave His disciples His body, for His body was also beyond the bread. The identity that exists between bread and body is rather to be understood in this way with Jesus as well as with Paul: Where this bread is, there is actually the body of Christ; where this bread is given and received, there the body of Christ is given and received with it. In this sense also for Paul the bread is not only the koinonia of the body, but the body of Christ itself. That follows quite clearly from the continuation in verse 17: "Because there is *one* bread, we who are many are *one* body, for we all partake of the *one* bread." That means: Whoever partakes of the bread has koinonia with the body of Christ, "for Christ's body is that *one* loaf. . . . Christ is so essentially in the elements that, by partaking of them, we incorporate ourselves in him and so become one with him" (H. Lietzmann, *Messe und Herrenmahl*, 224 [*Mass and Lord's Supper*, 182–83]).

The reproach for the unworthy communicant in 11:29 shows that Paul understood the statement in 11:24, "This is My body," literally. The unworthy communicant does not differentiate the Lord's body, which is the only thing it can mean, from ordinary food. But if eating the bread and drinking the cup is what creates the koinonia with the body and blood of Christ, then all who partake of the Lord's Supper come into this "koinonia," both the worthy and the unworthy guests, some blessedly, others the opposite. And of course Paul knows that one cannot speak of a koinonia in the same sense for the unworthy as for the worthy and that one should rather use a different expression for them than koinonia. And he does not use the word *koinonia* in this case. In 10:16f. he is not thinking of the unworthy. The general rule in the New Testament—we observe it also in John—is that the terminology used of the Lord's Supper relates only to the normal situation of worthy reception. As seriously as the church took the problem of Judas's participation in the Last Supper, so clearly has it regarded unworthy reception as the exception, which does not touch the essence of the Sacrament. We may never forget that already in the time of the apostles only the baptized, therefore members of the body of Christ, were admitted to the Lord's Supper as the fellowship of the body and blood of Christ and that already very early we know that an act of confession preceded the celebration (*Didache* 14. 1). *What the Lord's Supper is and what it gives has always been defined on the assumption of worthy and blessed reception.* But when the circumstances in Corinth force the apostle to deal with the question of unworthy participation in the celebration, he leaves no doubt that the unworthy communicants also come into the very closest contact with the body and blood of the Lord, not, however, for their blessing but bringing judgment on themselves. And this judgment expresses itself not in general punishments but in physical consequences: "That is why many of you are weak and ill, and some have died" (11:30). In place of this characteristic formulation one could scarcely put a statement like: "That is why many have not had success in their work, and some have become quite poor." The Lord punishes *physically* those who by unworthy participation in the Lord's Supper are guilty of profaning the body and blood of the Lord. This understanding of 1 Cor. 11:27ff. is confirmed by the statements about the Old Testament types of the Christian sacraments in 10:1ff. Here Paul warns the Corinthians against a false confidence in the supposedly infallible saving power of Baptism and the Lord's Supper:

> I want you to know, brethren, that our fathers were all under the cloud, and all passed through the sea, and all were baptized into Moses in the cloud and in the sea, and all ate the same supernatural food and all drank the same supernatural drink. For they drank from the supernatural Rock which followed them, and the Rock was Christ. Nevertheless with most of them God was not pleased; for they were overthrown in the wilderness.

The parallel is obvious only if, just as once all members of God's people took part in that "baptism" as well as the supernatural food of the manna and the supernatural drink from the supernatural Rock, so now all members of the church, that is, all communicants, consume the supernatural food and the supernatural drink of the Lord's Supper, whether it be for blessing or for judgment. That is the Pauline understanding of the Words of Institution. "It is true," remarks H. Lietzmann (*Messe und Herrenmahl*, 224 [*Mass and Lord's Supper*, 182]) against the attempts of J. Weiss and G. P. Wetter to explain away the identification of "bread" and "body" in 10:17, "that sacramental theology is at variance with the usual tendency to spiritualize on the part of Paul, who is determined not to know anything of flesh and blood but only the risen Lord. But we have to recognize this contradiction and not explain it away."

The realism of the Pauline doctrine of the Lord's Supper is all the more striking as the statements of the apostle are consistently dominated by the unmistakable tendency to prevent any materialistic misunderstanding of the Lord's Supper. This becomes quite clear when we compare his statements with the formulations in the remarkable passage, John 6:51b–58 (on the following see also W. Elert, *Der christliche Glaube*, 458ff. [*The Christian Faith*, 375ff.]). This forms the second part of the long discourse on the bread from heaven, which follows the miracle of the feeding in John. The "bread from heaven"—after the Old Testament expression for manna—in the first part of the discourse, or controversy, that runs through 51a is Jesus Himself: "I am the Bread of life," "I am the living Bread which came down from heaven." To eat this bread, which comes from heaven and gives life to the world (v. 33), means nothing else than to believe in Him. "He who comes to Me shall not hunger, and he who believes in Me shall never thirst" (35). "For this is the will of My Father, that everyone who sees the Son and believes in Him should have eternal life; and I will raise him up at the last day"

(40). This part of the discourse has been properly taken as the scriptural foundation of the doctrine of the *manducatio spiritualis,* the spiritual eating of Christ in faith. But it does violence to the text if one now reads this meaning into the verses from 51b on: "And the bread which I shall give for the life of the world is My flesh. . . . he who eats My flesh and drinks My blood has eternal life, and I will raise him up at the last day. For My flesh is food indeed, and My blood is drink indeed. He who eats My flesh and drinks My blood abides in Me, and I in him. . . . This is the bread which came down from heaven." Here the heavenly bread is no longer the person of Christ but His flesh. Whoever eats the flesh of Christ and drinks His blood is to be raised to eternal life. The transition from one theme to the next is so abrupt, the tension between the statement about the spiritual eating of Christ in faith and that about the sacramental eating and drinking of His flesh and blood is so great that 6:51b–58 has been interpreted as an insertion by which the ecclesiastical doctrine of the Lord's Supper as "medicine of immortality" was introduced into the Fourth Gospel, which was originally not interested in the Sacrament and therefore ignored the institution of the Lord's Supper (thus R. Bultmann, *Das Johannes Evangelium,* 161ff.). Now this gospel, just like the synoptics, also in other respects shows traces of a complicated process of development, and it is quite conceivable that the discourses as we read them today may have come together from various sources. But to lay bare some sort of original John [*Ur-Johannes*] from the text as we have it is impossible. For it has clearly been part of the character of this gospel from the beginning that the parts that seem to contradict each other are fitted together into a whole. Thus 6:51b–58 forms an integrating part of the gospel, and even the tension that exists without a doubt between 6:27–51a and 51b–58 is something that cannot be fancied away. Again and again in the discourses of Jesus in John there are repetitions of a line of thought that at the same time are an extension of it, and an extension in a quite unexpected direction. And much as themes that sound altogether spiritual in the statements about the judgment and the resurrection abruptly stand next to expressions of a massive eschatological realism (John 5:24–29), so here two lines of thought about the bread of life stand next to each other that at first glance seem to contradict each other, and yet for the evangelist they form a contrapuntal pair. Both are true for him. Christ is the Bread of heaven, and the flesh of Christ is the bread of heaven. There is an eating of Christ as the true Bread of heaven that happens in faith. And there is an eating of the flesh and a drinking of the blood of Christ that occurs in the Sacrament of the Eucharist. Both of these truths belong together in such a way that one cannot reduce one of them to the other.

What is so striking in the statements about the sacramental eating is the realistic, even drastic, wording in John 6:51b–58: While Paul speaks of the *body* and blood of Christ, it is called *flesh* and blood in John. Where Paul speaks of fellowship in the body of Christ, fellowship in the blood of Christ, John is not afraid to speak of eating the body and drinking the blood, and he even uses for "eat," besides the ordinary word *esthiein*, the extremely harsh sounding *trōgein*, "chew." While Paul obviously consciously avoids the starkly realistic sounding expressions, John evidently delights in them. And it is just this drastic wording that has again and again prompted the suggestion that it must have a deeper, mystical meaning hidden behind it. Is it really correct to speak of the *flesh* of the Son of Man as the food of the Lord's Supper when Jesus Himself used the word *body?* Paul never would have put "flesh" in place of "body." Why was the evangelist not satisfied with the expressions that he found in Paul? That must be connected with John's interest in the word *sarx* in general. When he uses this word, either he speaks of the flesh in the sense of the transitory, sinful creature (1 John 2:16), the flesh that is at variance with the Spirit (John 3:6; 8:15) and that therefore is of no use (6:63), or he speaks of the flesh that the Logos has taken on (1:14; 1 John 4:2; 2 John 7). The statements about the flesh of the Son of Man belong naturally in this context. And now it becomes clear immediately why John does not take over the Pauline terminology but develops it in a more realistic direction. His principal antagonist is the Docetism of emerging Gnosticism (1 John 4:2), a spiritualistic Christianity that believes it is stating the highest thing possible of Jesus Christ when it regards Him as a divine being who had a heavenly body but no body of flesh. The representatives of this view would not have failed to exploit passages of the letters of Paul, for example, the statements that Christ was "in the likeness of men" and was "found in human form" (Phil. 2:7[–8]) or that flesh and blood cannot inherit the kingdom of God (1 Cor. 15:50). In the presence of the heresy of Docetism the terminology of Paul was no longer sufficient—just as later in the history of dogma newly appearing heresies again and again required the improvement of the terminology. (One thinks of the *homoousios* that had to serve as the defense against Arianism or of the development of Lutheran terminology about the Lord's Supper.) Therefore John had to define the Incarnation exactly as becoming flesh. And the same reason would have prompted the development of the terminology about the

Lord's Supper. If need be, one can understand the word *sōma* entirely spiritualistically, even though this is against Paul's meaning. Therefore, in order to accent the reality of the body unequivocally, John dares to say "flesh" instead of "body," something like the "resurrection of the dead" in the Eastern confessions of faith corresponds to the "resurrection of the flesh" in the Western Creed. In all these phrases "flesh" means nothing other than "true body." This theological use of the word *sarx* constitutes the protest against the spiritualization of redemption, against the dualistic world view that regards flesh in itself as evil, and so against the denial of the Incarnation. John 6:51b–58 is to be understood in this sense. The "flesh" of Christ here is nothing else than what the church later called "true body." Eating and drinking do not mean a physical eating in the usual sense. That would be the "Capernaitic" misunderstanding, which according to John 6:60ff. must have already very early caused people to become confused about the Christian faith, a misunderstanding that still pops up in the heathen reproach about the cannibalism that supposedly was practiced in the Christian divine service. Over against this misunderstanding the statement holds true: "It is the Spirit that gives life, the flesh is of no avail; the words that I have spoken to you are Spirit and life" (6:63). That does not mean that the flesh of Christ is of no use, as Luther already correctly saw. (Luther established the rule: "Whenever Spirit and flesh are set in contrast to each other in Scripture, there flesh cannot mean Christ's flesh but must mean the old Adam." [WA 26:375; cf. American Edition, 37:250].) Then the Incarnation would also be given up. But here flesh must refer to human flesh with its natural functions. The eating of the flesh, that is, of Christ's true body, is an eating, as far as what is eaten goes into our bodies, but it is not a *carnal* eating, not an eating that serves to build up our body. The effect of this eating is twofold: the entrance of Christ into the person ("He who eats My flesh and drinks My blood abides in Me, and I in him" [6:56].) and the possession of "life" (53), specifically, "eternal life" (54) now and in the resurrection. How this happens the Gospel does not tell us. It is simply a miracle, as much beyond human comprehension as any other of Christ's miracles and as the last things, with which this miracle goes together.

If one asks how John relates to Paul at this point, a real agreement is discovered here also. For Paul naturally did not teach a physical effect of the Lord's Supper only for the unworthy, even if in 1 Cor. 11:27ff. he only happens to speak about them. Both Paul and John would accept the expression with which the Antiochene Liturgy about the turn of the first century describes the gifts of the Eucharist (that Ignatius, *Ad Eph.*, 20. 2, did not formulate the expression himself but quoted it from the liturgy has been shown by Lietzmann, 257 [*Mass and Lord's Supper*, 210]):

> *pharmakon athanasias*
> *antidotos tou mē apothanein*
> *alla zēn en Iēsou Christō dia pantos.*

> Medicine of immortality,
> Antidote that we die not
> But live in Jesus always.

The Unity of the Lord's Supper in the New Testament

If Paul and John understood the Words of Institution literally—and the realization that this is the case has made more and more headway in the last generation—then only one way out remains for those who cannot credit Jesus with a realistic understanding. They must accept that the Lord's Supper has already undergone a development in the New Testament that has led to a different understanding of the Words of Institution, at variance with Jesus' original meaning. Now no one will deny that the Lord's Supper already experienced a history in the New Testament. Jesus' Last Supper, the breaking of bread in the first congregation, the Lord's Supper in the Pauline congregations, and the Sacrament of the flesh and blood of Christ that lies behind John 6:51b-58 are the stages of this history still recognizable today. In that history not only the external form but also the understanding of the Lord's Supper have unfolded. This development is further reflected in the expansion of the *verba testamenti* in the liturgical usage of the early church, which we have discussed, and especially in the addition of "for the forgiveness of sins" and of the command to go on doing it. While the former clearly represents only an elucidation of "for many," in regard to the command to repeat it must be asked whether it has not completely changed the original meaning of the Lord's Supper. If Jesus, as it is often supposed, gave no thought at all to a repetition of the celebration, then whoever first came up with the idea of repeating what had been a nonrecurring eschatological action would be the actual originator of the church's Sacrament of the Lord's Supper. In the same way, the transition from a symbolic to a literal understanding of the words of explanation would mean not just a development but a complete change of the original understanding of the Lord's Supper. Whoever subscribes to such a radical change must answer the question of when and for what reasons it would have happened. The transformation of a nonrecurring symbolic action into a Sacrament that can be repeated (and that means the creation of the Sacrament) could only be explained, if need be, out of the inner necessity of the early church, even if our sources give no reason for such an assumption. But this explanation breaks down completely over the question why one would have exchanged a figurative understanding of "This is My body" for a literal one. For one cannot consider Paul, John, and the church for which they speak to be so unthinking as not to realize the difficulties that the realistic interpretation brought with it. If "This is My body" must be understood literally, then that applies not only to the Lord's Supper celebrated in the church today but also more than ever to what Jesus observed with His disciples on the night before His death. It was not first a discovery of Zwingli, Calvin (*Inst.* 4. 17. 17), and modern exegesis that Jesus still stood before them physically as He gave the bread to His disciples with these words. The apostle who preserved for us the earliest report of what happened there certainly knew it also. He tells us what Jesus said, did, and ordained on that occasion.

Here lies the reason why the realistic statement of the Lord's Supper in Paul and John also cannot be derived from an influence of the Hellenistic mystery religions. That a parallel exists between the Lord's Supper and the sacrificial meals and communion celebrations of the mysteries Paul himself has noted. Even more than that, we may assume that the terminology of the apostle (e. g., the expression "the table of the Lord"; cf. H. Lietzmann, *Handbuch z. N. T.*, on 1 Cor. 10:21 and Preuschen-Bauer [Bauer-Arndt-Gingrich], *Wörterbuch*, under *trapeza*) and even his thoughts about the effects of the Lord's Supper have been influenced by his religious environment. As he, the great missionary to the Gentiles, understands Jesus as the Lord, the Kyrios, in contrasting Him with everything that bears the name "kyrios" in the Gentile world (1 Cor. 8:5f.), so he explains for himself and his congregations the koinonia with Christ that the Lord's Supper creates by contrasting it with the koinonia that is actually created between those who partake of the sacrificial meals and the demons who are there honored as lords [*Kyrioi*]. At one point, however, and that the most decisive point, this parallel is shattered. That a historical person at a historical time—"The Lord Jesus on the night when He was betrayed"—gave His disciples His body and His blood to eat and to drink is an assertion for which

82

there is nothing comparable in the heathen cults. But on this assertion everything depends. For that action of Jesus was certainly for Paul not just the promise of something that would happen only after the Lord's resurrection and ascension, but it was the historical beginning, the institution, of the Lord's Supper. The fundamental difference that separates emerging Christianity from the mystery religions around it becomes clear precisely in the Lord's Supper. The heathen mystery cult rests on a myth. That Attis or Osiris died and rose again is myth, religious-poetic garb for a timeless truth, perhaps the truth valid always and everywhere that suffering leads to joy and death to life. It is nonsense to ask when the death of Osiris took place. This death is not a historical event, for the myth tells of things that lie beyond earthly history because they are timeless and eternal. It is quite the opposite with the death and resurrection of Jesus Christ. These did not happen in the timelessness of myth but at a specific time in earthly history: "Suffered *under Pontius Pilate . . . on the third day* He rose again from the dead."

The Lord's Supper is firmly anchored in this history according to the oldest witness we have of it in the New Testament. Its historical origin is *"on the night when He was betrayed."* (Because it depends on the *historical* and not the *calendar* date, the night is designated as the night of the betrayal, not as Passover night.) It would be a serious mistake to try to understand the account of the institution as "an etiological cult legend" (e. g., K. L. Schmidt, *RGG*[2] 1:9). It is as far removed from something like that as the historical message of the death and resurrection of Jesus is from one of the resurrection myths. The Lord's Supper stands and falls on the fact that it is the repetition of the Sacrament instituted by Jesus Himself. So Paul could not have understood it in any other way than that Jesus gave His disciples at the Last Supper the same thing that is received in the Lord's Supper of the church. But that the Redeemer, who is about to die as a true Man, gave His body and His blood to those who were His own to eat and to drink is utterly inconceivable to Hellenism and therefore an idea that could not have derived from Hellenistic influences.

Nothing shows more clearly how alien the Christian Lord's Supper was to ancient heathenism than the position that the ancient world took over against it. That through the consumption of holy food one took in the deity, its life and its powers, was a concept that heathen antiquity knew. Had the Lord's Supper been nothing else than a celebration of a communion in which consecrated food and consecrated drink bound the participants in the cult to one another and with their lord, it would have been inconceivable that the ancient world would have taken such strong offense at it. The reproach of "Thyestian meals," that is, cultic cannibalism, that accompanied the ancient church through the whole period of persecution can only be explained if the Lord's Supper was something that ancient heathenism was absolutely incapable of understanding. That calumny cannot be explained as though occasionally the suspicion of ritual murder was expressed, similar to that aroused by other secret cults. Since it recurs continually, it must have its root in a possible misunderstanding of the Lord's Supper. (In the same way the reproach of indecency attached to the "holy kiss" [e. g., Rom. 16:16; 1 Cor. 16:20; 1 Peter 5:14], with which the Lord's Supper began, is explained.) But if the thought that at the Christian altar one partook of the body and blood of Christ, that the flesh of the Son of Man was eaten, and His blood was drunk, aroused such strong offense, then one cannot derive such thinking from the influence of the mysteries.

But the transition to sacramental realism also cannot be explained as a result of a development purely within the church. Neither Paul nor the church from which Paul took over the liturgical account of the institution could have replaced an older symbolic-spiritualistic understanding of the Lord's Supper with a realistic one. If Paul, as Lietzmann thinks, really were the originator of a second type of Lord's Supper, then it would be inconceivable that among the charges raised by his opponents against him one never finds one that he falsified the Lord's Supper. Of the church before Paul, however, we may only assert that it changed the original meaning of the Lord's Supper if clues could be found that there ever was a Lord's Supper that was not a commemoration of the death of Christ, not a repetition of the Lord's Supper that was instituted by Him, and in which the Words of Institution either were missing or were understood in some other way than literally. There are no such clues. Neither the breaking of bread in Acts nor the Lord's Supper in the *Didache* can be cited in support of that. If the celebration took place "with gladness" according to Acts 2:47, then it can surely be assumed that this was also the case when Paul presided over the breaking of bread as Acts 20:7–11 reports. When did the Lord's Supper ever lack the character of the Eucharist? Since when should remembering the Lord's death and joyful thanksgiving for His redemption be regarded as mutually exclusive? And if reference to Jesus' death and mention of the Words of Institution are missing from the prayers of the Lord's Supper in the *Didache*, it should not be forgotten that we do not have the complete liturgy of the church that stands behind the *Didache*. How little the argument from silence is valid in this area is shown by Paul himself. If the circumstances in Corinth had not made it necessary for him on this one occasion to speak of the Lord's Supper, then surely modern New Testament scholarship would have asserted that the Lord's Supper was not celebrated at all in his congregations. For in his other letters he does not say a word about it.

So we can come to no other conclusion than that the Lord's Supper, from Jesus' Last Supper to the Sacrament of the church, is a unity, as the Fourth Gospel testifies. Its names vary; the rite has changed; the understanding of the celebration deepened little by little. But it is one and the same Lord's Supper that sees its history in this development. What remains the same in all stages of this development are the Words of Institution. And that can not only be the wording, which preserves itself in the main except for minor variations, but must also clearly be its meaning. In the church of the New Testament it was never understood in any other way than in the sense that Jesus Christ Himself gave His disciples His true body and His true blood to eat and to drink at the Last Supper and that in the Lord's Supper of the church He still does the same. Since it can absolutely not be seen why the apostles should have introduced this interpretation of the Lord's Supper into the church, and since, as we have pointed out, the Words of Institution cannot be understood as a parable or in some other figurative sense, no other possibility remains at all than to accept that Jesus Himself intended for the Lord's Supper to be understood in this way.

Jesus Himself said and meant that the bread is His body, the wine in the cup is His covenant blood. It is a different question whether one believes Him when He says this or not, whether one regards this statement as significant or not. The experiences of New Testament scholarship of the last generation should be a warning for us against the error of answering the question about the historical authenticity of Jesus' sayings on the basis of whether one agrees with them or not. How many sayings [*Logia*], how many statements of the New Testament witnesses have been denied Jesus because someone regarded it as impossible that they came from His lips! It has been denied that He regarded Himself as the Messiah, that He spoke of the saving significance of His death. Today we know that His whole activity, suffering, and death can only be understood under the assumption that He knew Himself to be the Messiah-Son of Man and that He applied to Himself and fulfilled the prophecy of the Suffering Servant of God (see Otto Procksch, "Passa und Abendmahl," *Vom Sakrament des Altars*, ed. Hermann Sasse [1941], 25). If one looks at what historical-critical theology of the last century has at one time or another declared authentic or inauthentic in the gospels, one is almost tempted to find there the rule: Theological statements that this theology no longer understood or did not regard as correct were denied to Jesus. They were laid at the door of anonymous tradition of the congregation or of the apostles, Paul most of all, but Jesus was not credited with them. Thus Heitmüller (*Taufe und Abendmahl*, 56) says of Luther's understanding of "This is My body":

> That this understanding is very old, that it, or at least something like it, is already to be found in early Christianity, even in Paul, and that the writers and the first readers of the gospels understood the words in such a way is certain. . . . All of this, however, does not justify the view that Jesus Himself meant these words in this way. No less than everything speaks against this view.

On closer examination, this "everything" consists of three arguments: The copula "is" was probably not spoken in Aramaic; furthermore, "is" can be used for "signifies"; and third, Jesus still stood physically in front of His disciples when He spoke the words of the Last Supper. As if Paul, the apostles, and the early church had no notion of that "everything"! If Heitmüller can credit the authors of the gospels with understanding the *verba testamenti* literally after all, why can he not credit Jesus with that? Is it out of respect for the Lord, to whom he would not want to ascribe an obviously absurd statement? Or does he need Jesus' authority to authenticate his own view? In any case, the historian must be on his guard against measuring Jesus and the apostles by two different standards and declaring the ideas with which he himself does not agree to be a garnishing by the apostles. Because some have not guarded against this danger, the distance between Jesus and the early church and between Jesus and Paul could be exaggerated in recent scholarship in a way that does violence to the historical reality. As far as the Words of Institution are concerned, however, there is no serious historical basis for the assumption that Jesus meant something essentially different by them than the early church and the writers of the gospels. Least of all is that a sufficient reason for the historian as such not to understand the meaning of the Words of Institution.

The Theological Meaning of the Lord's Supper

Our historical inquiry into the origin of the Christian Lord's Supper ended with the discovery of what Jesus said and did at the first celebration of the Lord's Supper and with the well-founded supposition that the Words of Institution already at that time said nothing else than that with the bread and the cup He gave those who took part in the celebration His true body and His true blood to eat and to drink. Historical research is not able to get to the bottom of the meaning of this assertion, which at first sounds absurd. But this is not to say that it has no meaning. The disciples of Jesus obviously did not feel it was senseless. They did not, as on other occasions, say: "Explain to us the parable" (Matt. 13:36; 15:15), for they apparently knew that it was not a matter of a parable here. They also did not express the disgruntled astonishment with which the natural man has always reacted to the words of the Lord's Supper and that is characteristically expressed in John 6:60: "This is a hard saying; who can listen to it?" Certainly their understanding would only have been a very weak one, and who could expect more from them? They accepted the Lord's Supper just as they accepted Jesus' prophecy of His suffering, death, and resurrection after an initial protest. What applies to the announcements of the Passion must certainly also be accepted of the words about the Lord's Supper: the full understanding of it dawns on the disciples only after Easter. Yet already at the Last Supper they must have understood enough that this action and the words that accompanied it had a deep meaning. Under the assumption that this was Jesus, as He had let Himself be known by them, they clearly received what He said about His body and blood, words that would have been an absurdity coming from any other mouth, as absolutely meaningful. Under this assumption and *only* under this assumption was there at that time and is there now an understanding of the Lord's Supper.

Therefore, only in theological statements can what the Lord's Supper is be expressed, for theological statements in the strict sense of Christian theology are statements based on the assumption that Jesus Christ is the Son of God, who became man, true God, begotten of the Father from eternity, and also true Man, born of the Virgin Mary; that He died on the cross as the Lamb of God, who bears the sin of the world; that He rose bodily from the dead; that He is exalted at the Father's right hand; and that He will return in glory to judge the living and the dead. Because the Lord's Supper can only be understood on this assumption, it is totally incomprehensible to the world, which does not believe in Christ, and the church at all times has gotten into the greatest difficulty when it was asked by the world, and that includes historical and religious scholarship, what the Lord's Supper really is. One can just as little make it clear to a person who does not believe in Jesus Christ as one can explain to him the essence and effect of Baptism. This explains the silence with which the early church already surrounded the Lord's Supper and that was only broken when it became a question of confronting the worst calumnies. These calumnies themselves, just like the assertions of strangeness and the lack of comprehension in later times, are a confirmation that the Lord's Supper has always been a riddle to the world, the Words of Institution always an absurdity.

There, however, where one shares that faith, the Lord's Supper has always been regarded as one of the deepest mysteries of the Christian faith and the most holy part of the Christian divine service. What it meant for the church of the New Testament becomes clear if one tries to imagine the original church in Jerusalem without the breaking of bread or the Pauline congregations without the Lord's Supper. It is impossible. A Lord's Day without the Lord's Supper is absolutely unthinkable in the New Testament. Without the Eucharist the church would have ceased to be church. It would no longer exist at all. And that goes for the whole New Testament, also for those writings in which the Lord's Supper is not directly mentioned; even there it stands in the background as a fact that belongs to the essence of the church. All this is only clearly understood, however, if all that Jesus Christ is and all that He brought, His whole person and His whole work, is indissolubly connected with the Lord's Supper. That is in fact the case, and no one else than Jesus Himself has made the connection.

Therein lies the meaning of the action that we call the institution of the Lord's Supper. It is the last act of Jesus before His death, an act of unfathomable profoundness and immeasurable consequences. In the face of death, which is both the end and the fulfillment of His life's work on earth, *Jesus gives His disciples redemption.* What until then was only the object of the promise comes true in the moment when the Lord gives them His body and His blood. Without the institution of the Lord's Supper the Gospel could be misunderstood as a teaching about redemption and Jesus Himself as the greatest of the prophets of the coming Kingdom. This misunderstanding is now no longer possible. With the Words of Institution the prophetic office of Christ is fulfilled, and His high priestly work begins. From now on wherever this Sacrament is repeated, wherever the Words of Institution resound anew, there redemption is something more than the object of the promise. It is actually given to whoever receives the Sacrament in faith. Under the forms of bread and wine what Christ sacrificed as "High Priest forever" (Heb. 6:20) and as "the Lamb of God, who takes away the sin of the world"

(John 1:29) in the *one* sacrifice of the cross "for many" is received. It is actually received just as the flesh of the Passover lamb is received by all who celebrate the Passover. So the Lord's Supper is a sacrificial meal, and one could even say with the Council of Trent that it is *memoria, repraesentatio,* and *applicatio* of Christ's sacrifice if the further formulations of Trent and of other Roman doctrinal statements did not give the words *repraesentatio* and *applicatio* yet another meaning that is not compatible with the New Testament. But that the Lord's Supper is the re-presentation of Christ's sacrifice and the real bestowal of what is gained through this sacrifice is the clear teaching of the New Testament. If one wants to understand it as a sacrificial meal only figuratively, then the sacrifice of Christ on the cross would also have to be understood figuratively. The Lord's Supper confirms the sacrificial meaning of the death of Christ by again and again reminding Christendom that it is redeemed by an actual sacrifice in the sense of the words: "Without the shedding of blood there is no forgiveness of sins" (Heb. 9:22). Understood as a sacrificial meal, it forms a bulwark against the view, widespread also in modern Christendom, that the death of Christ is to be thought of only figuratively as a sacrifice, something like the heroic death of a soldier for his country or the sacrifice of a mother for her child.

That Jesus Himself understood the Last Supper as a sacrificial meal in this sense is shown by the clear connections between the action and the words of Jesus on the one hand and the Passover celebration and sacrificial thought in the Old Testament on the other. They have been expertly set forth in the first chapter of this book [Procksch, "Passa und Abendmahl," *Vom Sakrament des Altars*, 11–25]. These connections could not have been introduced only later into the Lord's Supper tradition. This is proved by the great difficulty that the idea of the blood of Christ causes in this connection. That the body of Christ is eaten, in fact *must* be eaten, as the body of the true Passover lamb is understandable if the parallel between the Passover and the Lord's Supper is really to be valid. But the idea of partaking of blood had to cause most serious offense for those whose thinking was schooled in the Old Testament. For partaking of blood was strictly forbidden in the Old Testament, and even the parallel between the covenant blood in Exodus 24:8 and the covenant blood in the Words of Institution is seriously distorted when the latter is given to the disciples to drink. The difficulty is so great that one could credit no one, least of all Paul or John, with having burdened the idea of the Lord's Supper with it after the event.

There is really no other possibility than the assumption that Jesus Himself is the originator of the idea that not only is His body taken as that of the "Lamb without blemish or spot" (1 Pet. 1:19) but also His blood. Parenthetically we may note that no doctrine of the Lord's Supper, not even the Zwinglian, can get over this difficulty, because even the representatives of the symbolic interpretation must grant that Jesus must have been speaking at least parabolically about the drinking of His blood. But if Jesus did express this idea that was so offensive to Jewish and perhaps to all human thought, then His meaning could only have been the following: Partaking of blood is forbidden in the old covenant because according to Lev. 17:11 the body's life is in the blood and because the life belongs to God. But the life of Jesus has been offered up for men. It should be for their benefit. For here men do not bring a sacrifice to God through a priest, but the High Priest offers Himself as a sacrifice to God for the sake of men. That Christ gives His blood to those redeemed by Him to drink is the strongest expression of the fact that He sacrifices Himself for men entirely, unreservedly, and completely. He gives His whole life for men without any kind of reservation. That is the sacrifice of perfect love. And wherever the Lord's Supper is celebrated, the blessing of this sacrifice is given to men. Therefore the cup in the Lord's Supper is particularly the most significant expression of the "for many," "given and shed for you for the forgiveness of sins."

Since the Lord's Supper is such an actualization, *an actual appropriation of redemption*—and not merely a promise and proclamation of it—it is *the fulfillment of salvation history*. As the redeeming work of Christ finds its fulfillment in it, so also does the great history of redemption, at whose end stands the cross of the Lord. That explains why a series of Old Testament types and prophecies points to the Lord's Supper and why it cannot be understood merely as the fulfillment of an individual one of these (see on this point Simon Schöffel, *Offenbarung Gottes in Abendmahl* [1938], 33ff.). As surely as the Lord's Supper is first of all to be understood from the *Passover*, as the act of its institution shows, so it is certainly also to be understood as the true *bread from heaven*, the manna of the end time, as is taught already in 1 Cor. 10:1ff. and John 6. Both Jeremiah's promise of the new *covenant* (31:31ff.) and what Isaiah 53 says about the *death of the Servant of God for "many"* are fulfilled in it. In the Lord's Supper the one who acts is at the same time the fulfiller and the fulfillment of all prophecies of the Old Testament about the coming redemption. Hence the Lord's Supper is the *memorial meal* of the accomplished redemption. As in the Passover one commemorated the redeeming act of God, who wondrously delivered His people from the slavery of Egypt, so the Lord's Supper should be observed "in remembrance of Me." And one can probably say that never has a command found a truer and more comprehensive fulfillment than the instruction: "This do in remembrance of Me," regardless of whether this instruction was pronounced by Jesus or whether it was included in the institution by implication. The historical character of the Christian faith, which always appeals to historical facts because it lives by the redemption that happened at a particular time in history, is nowhere more clearly discernible than in the fact that the celebration that stands at the center of the divine service is a celebration "in remembrance of Me." Where has a historical event been more faithfully remembered than is the death of Christ in the Lord's Supper of His church? There is no other event in the history of antiquity that is so imprinted in the memory of people and lives on throughout the world today. The Lord's Supper has kept this memory so deeply alive precisely because it is even more than a memorial meal. It is not only a celebration of reminiscence like the Passover, in which the human spirit recalled the past for itself, but it is a genuine, actual *bringing into the present* of God's redeeming act through the gift of the body and blood of Christ.

Like the past, the *future* also becomes present in the Lord's Supper. It is part of the essence of the Lord's Supper that it is a wonderful *anticipation of the future*. As the Last Supper was perhaps the anticipation of the Passover, which should not have been celebrated until the next day (see on this, besides Procksch, "Passa und Abendmahl," 23, also Th. Kliefoth, *Liturgische Abhandlungen* [1858], 4:186f.), so was the first Lord's Supper in any case already the sacrificial meal in which in a miraculous way—the institution of the Lord's Supper does not belong to the parables but to the miracles of Jesus—the participants actually received what was to be offered the following day on the cross. (It is never the task of theology to explain miracles [least of all to explain them away], but to state them and to expound their meaning in the light of the whole of divine revelation. In this sense the church has always pointed to the miracle of the Transfiguration in Matt. 17:2 as an analogy of the miracle of the Lord's Supper. What the anticipation involves reminds us of the words of Kliefoth [p. 187]: "One may not infer the weakness of the Lord's Supper held on the night of the betrayal from this anticipation, for as good as the blood of Christ was, before it was shed, to make the blood of goats and calves valid, so it also is with the wine in this anticipated Lord's Supper.")

91

The research of the last generation has legitimately emphasized that in the whole New Testament the Lord's Supper is the anticipation on earth of the Messianic banquet. Wherever it is celebrated, all eyes are turned toward the end. The Word of Jesus that He would not drink again of the fruit of the vine "until that day when I drink it new in the kingdom of God" (Mark 14:25) is matched by Paul's comment that in the Lord's Supper the congregation proclaims the Lord's death "until He comes" (1 Cor. 11:26). John also looks from the Lord's Supper to the resurrection of the dead "at the last day" (6:54), and it is certainly no accident that the few fragments of the earliest liturgies of the Lord's Supper that have been preserved for us are alive with a glowing hope of the Parousia. This is found in Paul (1 Cor. 16:22) and in the *Didache* (10. 6) preserved in the Aramaic *Maranatha*, which is translated at the end of the New Testament as "Come, Lord Jesus" (Rev. 22:20; that this prayer belongs to the liturgy of the Lord's Supper Lietzmann, *Messe und Abendmahl*, 237, demonstrates convincingly), and in the Eucharistic prayers of the *Didache*.

The eschatological character of the Lord's Supper may not, of course, be understood as if this Sacrament is *only* understood on the basis of Christian hope as a celebration in which the church brings its eschatological expectations impressively into its consciousness. Much rather the hope of the Lord's return and the coming Kingdom is so powerfully alive in this celebration because the Lord's Supper, as the celebration of Christ's real presence, already includes a fulfillment of that expectation. Whoever partakes of it already now sits at the table of the Lord, whose guest he will be one day in the kingdom of God. The same Lord, whose coming in glory one implores in the Eucharistic prayers, is already present in the celebration of the Eucharist. Thus the prayer "Come, Lord Jesus" retains its eschatological meaning, but at the same time it carries the meaning expressed in an early liturgical prayer (in the Mozarabic liturgy, quoted according to Lietzmann, *Messe und Abendmahl*, 105 [*Mass and Lord's Supper*, 86]): "Be present, be present, Jesus, good priest, among us, as also you will be in the midst of your disciples." Because Jesus Christ is really present as High Priest and sacrificial Lamb in this celebration, the custom, taken over from the synagogue service, of singing the Sanctus, the song of the seraphim in the presence of God, at the celebration of the Eucharist has taken on an especially profound meaning. The celebration of the Lord's Supper as the church's divine service has become the counterpart of the divine service that takes place in heaven, an idea that is expressed in Rev. 4

(cf. also 1 Clement 34:6 where, in addition to Is. 6:3, Dan. 7:10 is quoted: "Ten thousand times ten thousand stood before Him, and a thousand thousands served Him"). Thus in the Lord's Supper the boundaries of space and time are overcome: Heaven and earth become one, the incalculable interval that separates the present moment of the church from the future kingdom of God is bridged.

From this it becomes easy to understand what the Lord's Supper must mean for the church's *preservation*, as it turned out that the eschatological expectations, as the apostolic age cherished them, did not come to fulfillment. Humanly speaking, there was perhaps never a deeper disappointment than the nonappearance of the Parousia, which they had believed to be so near. How was it possible for the church to survive this disappointment? How was it able to preserve hope for the Day of Jesus Christ through so many centuries in spite of the mockery of the world and doubt in its own ranks? The Lord's Supper alone has made that possible. It is the Sacrament of the church that waits for the fulfillment of the promises. The church that celebrates it understands itself to be the new people of God, who have been freed from the slavery of Egypt but have not yet arrived in the Promised Land. It is what later came to be called food of travelers [*cibus viatorum*], eaten in haste by pilgrims like the first Passover according to Ex. 12:11: "In this manner you shall eat it: your loins girded, your sandals on your feet, and your staff in your hand; and you shall eat it in haste. It is the Lord's passover." It is food for travelers like the manna, with which Paul and John already compared it. Like Israel in the wilderness was miraculously saved by the "spiritual food" (1 Cor. 10:1ff.) manna, by the "bread from heaven" (John 6:32, 50f., 58; cf. Psalm 78:24), from death by starvation, so the church is preserved on its journey through the wilderness of this world by the miracle of the Lord's Supper. The situation of the church with the Lord's Supper is pictured in no better way than in these Old Testament types. With the traveling staff in hand, in the wilderness between Egypt and the Promised Land, as those who have been freed from the slavery of the old age but have not yet arrived in the land of freedom, in the twilight between the ages Christians eat their Lord's Passover, they live on the bread of heaven, when they celebrate the Lord's Supper. And no one can understand this Sacrament who does not understand this situation, that is, who does not himself belong to these travelers.

Finally, there is yet one more sense in which the Lord's Supper is an actualization of the redemption achieved by Christ. F. Kattenbusch

("Der Quellort der Kirchenidee" in *Festgabe für A. v. Harnack* [1921], 168f.) once raised the questions, whether, when, and how Jesus actually fulfills His promise in Matt. 16:18 that He would build His church, and he answered in this way: "The Lord's Supper was the act by which He founded His church (*ekklēsia*), His congregation." Even if we must stick to the fact that the church first entered into history on the basis of the events of Easter and Pentecost—the significance of Peter also first became clear at that time—Kattenbusch's thesis nevertheless doubtlessly contains a correct perception. For if the Twelve represent the 12 tribes of Israel and their circle is therefore the representation of the people of God who believe in Jesus as the Messiah, then they are already the church insofar as there can be a church before the death and resurrection of Jesus. Then the Last Supper, which Jesus celebrated with them as the Passover of the new covenant, is really the *organization of the new people of God*. At the same time He establishes the relationship that will exist from then on between Him and His church—"My church" [*mou tēn ekklēsian*] He emphasizes in Matt. 16:18.

The fellowship binding Him with the church that celebrates the Lord's Supper is more than a table fellowship. His presence there is more than the presence for which the prayer quoted above asked: "Be present . . . among us, as you will be in the midst of your disciples." Because He is not only the host but also the Passover lamb, therefore "what counts most is not His table fellowship with the disciples but His incorporation into the disciples under the bread and wine, as the Passover lamb was incorporated into the celebrating congregation" (Procksch, 24). Clearly, this fellowship, this koinonia, that binds Christ to His church and the members of the church to one another is something utterly unique, a koinonia for which there is no analogy at all either in the religious fellowships of the world or in human community life. Paul expresses the unparalleled nature of this fellowship when he calls the church the *body of Christ*. What does he mean by that? No explanation is needed if a form of community is called a corpus, a body in the sense of a corporation. If we find that Paul is merely applying to the church the simile common in ancient sociology of a body and its members, there is no problem at all; and it would be immediately understood if the apostle said of the church in this sense: "We, though many, are one body in Christ" (Rom. 12:5). The puzzle begins at the point where Paul no longer designates the church as a body in Christ but as the body of Christ (1 Cor. 12:27; cf. v. 13; Col. 1:18; Eph. 1:23; 4:12, 16). For the statement "You are the body of Christ" (1 Cor. 12:27) contains much more than a comparison between the church and a body. The idea that the church is the body of Christ in Paul is indissolubly bound up with his view of the Lord's Supper, as 1 Cor. 10:17 shows: "Because there is *one* bread, we who are many are *one* body, for we all partake of the *one* bread." The koinonia of the body of Christ that the Lord's Supper effects is, as we have shown earlier, the actual partaking of, the closest fellowship with, the body of Christ, which is given to us with the bread. It is at the same time, as we now recognize, membership in the church as the body of Christ. (Even if Ephesians and even—though there is no serious basis for it—Colossians would have to be regarded as deutero-Pauline, the usage "body of Christ" for the church would still be secured for Paul through 1 Cor. 12:27. It is a fabrication for H. Schlier, *Christus und die Kirche im Epheserbrief* [1930], 41, to understand "body of Christ" in 1 Cor. 12:27 as "a body that belongs to Christ" and to assert: "It should not be said as in Ephesians that they [i. e., the Christians] are the body of Christ and His members [the *autou* with *mele* is missing in Paul!]." In 1 Cor. 6:15 the bodies of Christians are explicitly called members of Christ. The progress in Col. and Eph. in the doctrine of the body of Christ lies only in the introduction of the idea of Christ as the Head of the church.)

There is then in Paul a double usage of the expression "body of Christ." Body of Christ is the bread of the Lord's Supper, but body of Christ is also the church. Both statements are to be understood quite realistically in the meaning of the apostle. Because the bread of the Lord's Supper is the body of Christ, therefore the church is the body of Christ. How are we to understand this? The *corpus Christi* that is in, with, and under the church is to the *corpus Christi* that is in, with, and under the bread of the Lord's Supper apparently as the church itself is to the bread of the Lord's Supper. As this *one* bread binds Christians to the unity of the church, so the true body of the Lord, which is received in the Lord's Supper, makes the church to be the body of Christ. We must recall that according to the view of the apostolic age the church above all comes into view in the celebration of the Lord's Supper. When the heavenly food of the body of Christ goes into us, we at the same time go into this body. When Christ embodies Himself in us, we are at the same time embodied in Him. This corresponds exactly with what is said in John 6:56 about this double communion: "He who eats My flesh and drinks My blood abides in Me, and I in him." When the heavenly body of Christ is given to us Christians in the Lord's Supper, we become the church as the body of Christ on earth. According to the New Testament, then, there is not only the body of Christ that, exalted at the right hand of the Father, is truly given to us as heavenly food in the Sacrament of the Altar, but there is also, as a result and effect of this heavenly gift, what theology later called the *corpus Christi mysticum* (the expression has been adopted also by Lutheran theology, e. g., by John Gerhard, who speaks of *corpus Christi personale* and *corpus Christi mysticum* [*Loci* 22. 3—Preuss ed., 5:263ff.]), the church, which not only *resembles* a body but *is* the body of Christ on earth. Both belong inseparably together, just as the Lord's Supper and the church go together and, rightly understood, are one. Where the Lord's true body is received in the Sacrament, it does not remain without effect in the world. There the church is built as the body of Christ on earth and grows toward the consummation (Eph. 4:12–16).

Therefore, the Lord's Supper as "Holy Communion," as one may call it in this respect (see on this Paul Althaus, *Communio sanctorum* [1929], 75ff.), creates the fellowship of the church, the deepest fellowship with God and with all the children of God that there can be for us human beings. It is a fellowship that God has established in His gracious condescension to us sinners through the incarnation of His Son and that is renewed in every celebration of the Lord's Supper. He, the *Deus incarnatus*, who for our sake took flesh and blood, stoops down to us so low that He not only lives among us but in us, and we can do nothing else than speak the words of the centurion with the old liturgies of the Lord's Supper: "Lord, I am not worthy to have you come under my roof."

This fellowship is not only spiritual, as Christian idealism has always thought, but spiritual-physical [*geistleiblich*], just as the redeeming work of Christ affects the whole person, body and soul. One can only understand the Lord's Supper of the New Testament and its meaning for the church if one does not forget what the modern Christian unfortunately has forgotten again and again, that we belong to the church not only according to the spirit but also according to the body: "Do you not know that your bodies are members of Christ?" (1 Cor. 6:15). Therefore, as the New Testament makes quite clear, the Lord's Supper stands as the future becoming present in connection with the resurrection of the body. The Bible does not tell us the how of this connection. But the fact of this connection is clearly certified for us, as we saw in the discussion of John 6: "He who eats My flesh and drinks My blood has eternal life, and I will raise him up at the last day" (v. 54). Not only our souls but also our bodies belong to the Incarnate One, who has redeemed us body and soul. So the church according to its deepest essence is the body of Christ, and the Originator of the Lord's Supper also became the Founder of the church when He gave His disciples the bread with the words pregnant with meaning: "This is My body."

THE LORD'S SUPPER IN THE LUTHERAN CHURCH

Letter to Lutheran Pastors, No. 6
May 1949

Dear Brothers in the Ministry!

1.

We are unjustly accused of having abolished the Mass. Without boasting, it is manifest that the Mass is observed among us with greater devotion and more earnestness than among our opponents. Moreover, the people are instructed often and with great diligence concerning the holy sacrament, why it was instituted, and how it is to be used (namely, as a comfort for terrified consciences) in order that the people may be drawn to the Communion and Mass. The people are also given instruction about other false teachings concerning the sacrament. Meanwhile no conspicuous changes have been made in the public ceremonies of the Mass. [AC 24 1-2]

It is good for us Lutherans of today to remember that our fathers once could have said such a thing in Article 24 of the Augsburg Confession. It makes us aware of the quite enormous difference between our divine service and that of the Reformation and how far removed our modern understanding of the Lord's Supper is.

Who of us today would still dare to state that we have not abolished the Mass, the divine service comprising the proclamation of the Word and the Lord's Supper? No Christian of the Reformation, apart from the followers of the Reformation at Zurich and Geneva, could conceive of a Sunday divine service without the Lord's Supper, just as already in the church of the New Testament there was no Lord's Day without the Lord's Supper. And no one probably would dare to maintain that this divine service was celebrated with greater devotion and earnestness than by the Catholics.

If one asks for the secret of the vitality of the Catholic Church even in our time, one would have to admit that it is not its hierarchical organization, not its cult of saints and relics, not even, as many suppose, its traditional political astuteness that gives it its inner strength and predominance, but the fact that it celebrates the Sacrament of the Altar uninterruptedly throughout the world. This determines its whole life, even its whole theology.

To be sure, this Lord's Supper has been mutilated by the withdrawal of the cup from the laity. Certainly, false ideas about man's cooperation in salvation have gotten in since the intrusion of the early Christian notions of sacrifice that were, however, alien to the New Testament. It would be amazing indeed if what we must call the great errors of Catholicism had not gained a hold right here in this Holy of Holies of the church. The veneration of the consecrated host outside the celebration of the Sacrament, which was alien to the early church and still is to the Eastern Church but which first belonged to the later Middle Ages, is one of these errors, and it primarily produced the reaction of the Reformed false doctrine. Even Catholic theologians, who stand firmly on the dogmatic foundation of their church, readily admit that the Christian place of worship is not the house of God primarily or essentially because of the presence in it of the Eucharistic Christ in the tabernacle.

Traditional Protestantism criticizes much too easily when it places these things in the foreground, which for Catholics, at least for Catholic priests and laymen schooled in the modern liturgical movement, are not really what is essential, just as it is also a dangerous prejudice on the evangelical side to suppose that the external pomp, splendor, and beauty of the Catholic divine service constitutes its essence, as if it could not also be celebrated in puritan simplicity and meagerness. What the church of the Lutheran Reformation possessed and what modern Protestantism has lost, what Catholicism before the Reformation had largely forgotten and what modern Catholicism has largely learned to understand again is the simple truth of faith in the real presence of the true body and blood of our Lord Jesus Christ in, with, and under the forms of bread and wine in Holy Communion.

Concerning that truth the congregations of the Lutheran Reformation were "instructed often and with the greatest diligence," both adults and children. The Sixth Chief Part of the Catechism was written just for the instruction of children. If one hears again and again nowadays that children cannot understand it or not yet understand it, if modern Protestant catechetical instruction has almost become the art of distilling out of these plain words written for fathers of the house and their children a doctrine that swings somewhere between Zwingli and Calvin and is presented as Lutheranism simply because it is not blatant Zwinglianism, then one certainly is no longer surprised if the instruction that Article 24 of the Augsburg Confession has in mind scarcely happens any more. Then it is even less surprising that "instruction against other false teaching concerning the Sacrament" no longer takes place and that it is regarded as nothing but tactlessness or a violation of Christian love.

However, we may also then not be surprised if people no longer know "why the Sacrament was instituted and how it is to be used," that troubled consciences are not comforted by it, and theologians hunt in vain for a means "by which people are drawn to Communion and Mass." As appealing as the efforts of modern liturgical movements such as the Berneuchener and those like them to renew Holy Communion and the evangelical divine service may be, all these movements remain a liturgical handicraft for an aesthetic-religious elite that finds refuge from the real needs of our time in the incense cloud of a religious world where one dreams of sacrifice and transformation, of the bringing into the present of the sacrifice of Golgotha, where one fears nothing except Luther's plain confession of the real presence of the true body and blood of Christ in, with, and under the elements of bread and wine. But this proves that sacrifice, re-presentation, and transformation are only words that have next to nothing to do with Catholic *doctrine*, are not dangerous to it, but at the most lead people who are tired of this rhetoric to Rome.

The teaching that goes on is neither Lutheran nor Catholic; it is not even Reformed, though it is closest to the Reformed doctrine. One really does not teach at all; one only discusses and meditates (but not in the sense of the meditation of the great Christians of the past) and has nonbinding conversations, whose results, nevertheless, are to be binding for whole churches. But the people's hunger for the bread of life remains unsatisfied. The yearning for Christ, who according to His true divinity and humanity is present with His church in His means of grace for all time to the world's end, remains unappeased. For our theologians do not know whether that is the case, and if they do know it, they talk as if they were not quite sure. The Christian congregations and the people who are today looking longingly to the church want to know. They do not want to know whether the Catechism speaks "too directly," "too unguardedly," or "not dialectically enough," but whether what it says is true.

2.

Because they knew what they received there, the people of the old Lutheran Church went to Holy Communion. Because they know that at the altar they receive the body of Christ, Catholics in our time are going to Communion in ever growing number. Because they no longer know for sure what is received in the Sacrament of the Altar, Protestants, even those who call themselves Lutheran, are going to the Lord's Table in ever smaller numbers, and all efforts to make the congregations appreciate the German Mass of the Lutheran Reformation again have so far failed, and this is not due merely to technical difficulties. The only exception where there is a growing participation in the Lord's Supper by Protestants is the custom of concluding church rallies with a common celebration of the Lord's Supper. To what extent that is actually progress in the use of the Sacrament of the Altar will be discussed later.

General church statistics of ecclesiastical Germany inform us that out of 100 communions, more than 99 are by Catholics and less than one is by Protestants. However one may explain this number theologically, it is a simple fact that the Sacrament of the Altar plays an almost vanishing role in the life of evangelical Christendom, while it has become more or less a distinctive mark of Catholicism and its divine service. The reason for this can only be that the modern Protestant, also the modern theologian, indeed even the Lutheran pastor of our day, has become uncertain in his belief about the Sacrament and accordingly in his teaching about the Sacrament and therefore unable to "instruct" the congregation "often and with great diligence concerning the Lord's Supper," as our Confession takes it for granted as self-evident.

What is the reason for this? Why could the pastors of the 16th century do it, and why can we do it no more, despite the advances in the investigation of the New Testament and of the history of the Sacrament from both the dogmatic and the liturgical sides? The error must lie in our theology, to which Goethe's profound word applies: "We have studied ourselves out of life."

All genuine theology must proceed from the principle of speaking where God's Word speaks and being silent when God's Word is silent. For this reason Luther is the greatest teacher of the church for us, because he held unshaken to this principle even when the great temptation came to him, in which even the greatest theologians have always been caught at some point, to let something else hold sway in addition to the Word of God. The most difficult temptation for him, the basically conservative theologian, was traditionalism. He had held on to the traditional liturgy of the Mass with tenacious allegiance (even the Latin language at first). He had preserved the ancient liturgical forms and thereby saved them for the Lutheran Church. But with the sure sense of feeling of a theologian rooted in Scripture, he had recognized where already in the first century before the canon was completed something foreign from Judaism and paganism broke into the church, something that no apostle had taught: the sacrifice that man offers in the Lord's Supper. All traditionalistic theologians of our time, even those who regard themselves as good Lutherans, try to revive the sacrifice of the Mass in some way. In this matter Luther was unrelenting. With the theological penetration that was uniquely his he perceived that any concession at this point would mean a surrender both of *sola scriptura* and of *sola gratia*, which belong inseparably together.

The Lutheran Church knew with the Reformer that the word "sacrifice" is also used in Scripture in the figurative sense. If every prayer of praise and thanksgiving can be called a sacrifice, why not also the *Eucharistia*, the great prayer that was spoken at the Lord's Supper, and along with it the Lord's Supper itself? Chemnitz and other theologians put this question to themselves very earnestly. Their answer was that we are not here dealing with an adiaphoron any longer because the Roman Church here understands the word "sacrifice" in the strict sense of an atoning sacrifice, and one must repel this misconception. With the same seriousness the Lutheran Church today must oppose the modern theories that this only has to do with the church holding up the unique sacrifice of Calvary before the Father. The Roman sacrifice of the Mass is more than this according to the teaching of the Council of Trent (Session 22), that is, a truly atoning sacrifice in itself, however its relationship to the sacrifice of the cross may be defined (*instauratio*, *repraesentatio*, etc.).

In contrast to Calvin, who saw in the doctrine of transubstantiation the real cause for the decline of the Biblical Lord's Supper and the root of all corruption (which is historically untenable, since the doctrine of transubstantiation is over a millennium younger than the doctrine of the sacrifice of the Mass), Luther judged this teaching relatively mildly. For him it was a philosophical aberration of theology, a "clever sophistry," which does not agree with the statements of Scripture, in which the consecrated bread is still called bread (SA III VI; cf. 1 Cor. 10:16; 11:28). He judged the doctrine of concomitance even more mildly: "We need not resort to the specious learning of the sophists and the Council of Constance that as much is included under one form as under both. Even if it were true that as much is included under one form as under both, yet administration in one form is not the whole order and institution as it was established and commanded by Christ."

Luther also clearly recognized the danger that threatens every theologian, that he might follow not only Scripture as the *norma normans* but also some philosophy, whether it be Aristotelian-Thomistic, which seeks to explain the miracle of the Lord's Supper with the philosophical miracle of transubstantiation, or the Platonic-Neoplatonic theory of image and sign, which since the days of Augustine was the great danger for the church and which was revived by Zwingli and Calvin, each in his own way. He also faced the temptation, which captured Zwingli, to understand the Words of Institution figuratively, the *est* in the sense of *significat*. He knew that there could be no stronger weapon against the Roman Church than if one could prove that the Words of Institution must be understood in this sense. However, he withstood this philosophical temptation, which also had implications for church politics: "The text is too powerfully present" [WA 15:394; American Edition 40:68]. He also withstood the final and most difficult temptation to sacrifice the complete irrationality of the miracle of the Lord's Supper for Zwingli's humanistic-rationalistic objection: *Deus non proponit nobis incomprehensibilia* (God does not put incomprehensible statements before us). On the contrary, thought Luther, all the great truths of the Christian faith are *incomprehensibilia!* He here rightly recognized that the rationalizing of the doctrine of the Lord's Supper brings with it the rationalizing of the whole dogma of the church.

However, it was not some kind of practical or theoretical considerations that led Luther to his doctrine of the Lord's Supper, but the Word of Scripture entirely alone. On the one hand, he saw the disagreement of all his opponents and their inability to offer a credible, cohesive interpretation of the Words of Institution. On the other, he saw the Word that no exegesis could shake: "This is My body."

> Consequently, you can boldly address Christ both in the hour of death and at the Last Judgment: "My dear Lord Jesus Christ, a controversy has arisen over thy words in the Supper. Some want them to be understood differently from their natural sense. But since they teach me nothing certain, but only lead me into confusion and uncertainty . . . I have remained with thy text as the words read. If there is anything obscure in them, it is because thou didst wish to leave it obscure, for thou hast given no other explanation of them, nor hast thou commanded any to be given. . . .
>
> If there should be anything obscure about these words, thou wilt bear with me if I do not completely understand them, just as thou didst forbear with thine apostles when they did not understand thee in many things—for instance, when thou didst announce thy passion and resurrection. And yet they kept thy words just as they were spoken and did not alter them. Thy beloved mother also did not understand when thou saidst to her, Luke 2 [:49], "I must be about my Father's business," yet with simplicity she kept these words in her heart and did not alter them. So have I also kept to these thy words. . . . Behold, no fanatic will dare to speak thus with Christ, as I know full well, for they are uncertain and at odds over their text. (WA 26:446f. [American Edition 37:305–06])

That is genuine theology that speaks when God's Word speaks and is silent when God's Word is silent.

3.

But, it is objected, one cannot ignore the progress of exegesis and the findings of four centuries of historical research. To that we have to answer that the Lutheran Church does not think of standing by the formulations of the 16th century without testing them. We certainly reserve the right not to consider the Bultmannian interpretation of the New Testament, just to mention the most prominent example of our time, as truly serious exegesis. According to it, Jesus did not regard Himself as the Christ at all, and the assertions about Him, such as the One born of the Virgin Mary, the Lamb of God, who bears the sins of the world, His resurrection and ascension, are considered to be myths. We do not even take this interpretation seriously as historical scholarship.

Genuine historical scholarship we take very seriously. It has pleased

God to reveal Himself in history and to give us the Holy Scriptures as the documents of a great history of salvation. But precisely on the question of Holy Communion one can study the possibility and the limit of the historical task.

There is no longer any serious historian who denies that Jesus instituted the Lord's Supper. Indeed, there are hardly any scholars who seriously deny that Jesus wished this Supper to be repeated by His people. Where in early Christendom would there have been the commanding spirit who would have thought of bridging the time between the death and the return of the Lord with such a celebration, in which past and future again and again become present, and the distance between heaven and earth is bridged? The church has been able to survive the delay of the Lord's return, for which it has been praying for 19 centuries and for which it has been waiting so long, only because Sunday after Sunday is the "Day of the Lord," the day of the anticipated parousia, the day on which He comes to His congregation under the lowly forms of bread and wine and "incorporates" Himself in it anew.

Christendom did not take this over from the Jews or from the Gentiles. Neither a congregation nor an individual contrived it, neither one of the original apostles nor Paul, who was so greatly suspect to the Jewish Christian congregations. What a weapon he would have provided for his enemies if anything unhistorical could have been found in what he reported in 1 Corinthians as a tradition about the Lord's Supper! He himself then would have fallen under the anathema of Gal. 1:8f. And what Christian of the first century could ever have come up with the idea of drinking blood, which was inconceivable to every Jewish spirit and would even have been intolerable if it was only intended symbolically. There is only One who possessed the authority for such an institution, and that was Jesus Himself.

The tradition about the Lord's Supper quoted by Paul in 1 Cor. 11:23ff. belongs to the bedrock of the tradition of the historical Jesus, which no criticism of a serious historian can destroy. That this tradition is good and reliable is confirmed by the mention of the fact that the cup was given "after supper," while Mark and Matthew are no longer interested in this not unimportant detail, which had not come into church usage even though it was mentioned in liturgical formulas following the example of Paul. Where is there anywhere in the history of religion of the ancient world a fact like the institution of the Lord's Supper by Jesus that is attested by two different traditions in different form (Paul-Luke and Mark-Matthew) but so consistent in substance?

Historical problems certainly still remain. The Aramaic wording of the words spoken by Jesus can only be reconstructed by conjecture, and the conjectures will always differ. The famous question of the relationship of the Johannine (and perhaps Pauline) dating of the Last Supper with the 13th or 14th of Nisan and with this the understanding of this Supper as an anticipatory or an actual Passover, a question with which the early Easter controversies are connected, cannot be decided with absolute certainty. And so here, as with so many questions of the life of Jesus, our natural curiosity, as well as the historian's legitimate thirst for knowledge, remains unsatisfied. Here also Holy Scripture proceeds as usual. It tells us *only* what we should know because it belongs to our salvation, but *that* it does tell us. And the great art of exegesis consists in weighing all the questions of historical research and thinking them through, making use of all the findings of history, and then saying to the historian where the boundary of his knowledge lies.

Every historian is in danger of wanting to understand the people with whom he is dealing psychologically, to enter into their situation internally and externally, and from there to interpret their words. It is one of the basic realizations of recent theology that this procedure is not possible with the person of Jesus, and that is because our sources are not sufficient. The theologian will see in the extraordinary reserve of the evangelists, which makes a biography of Jesus and a description of His soul impossible, the indication that we cannot understand the God-Man psychologically. None of us can experience what went on in the soul of Jesus in the hour of the Last Supper. Thus all efforts to experience psychologically and to describe what Jesus must have been thinking at that time and how His words must therefore be explained are frustrated. That explains the diversity of the explanations, which Luther already criticized in those who felt they had to go behind the plain literal sense.

All we have are the Words of Institution as they have been transmitted in the New Testament in Greek translation in differing forms but with a consistent meaning. Jesus really meant what He said: that the bread that He gave to His disciples was His body. He really meant what He said: that the wine that He gave them in the cup was His blood. It cannot have been a parable, or he would have given an explanation or introduced it as a parable. In reality, He would have proposed a riddle for them instead of a parable, which no one has solved to this day. Even the appeal to the Pauline figure of speech of the "partaking of the body" and to the cup as a testament does not help us over the fact that Paul, as well as John, knows of an eating of the body (or flesh) and of a drinking of the blood. One also cannot give a new interpretation to "body," for the Johannine "flesh" shows what is meant. One cannot spiritualize "body" and "flesh." The "blood" stands there too. One cannot say that "flesh and blood" or "body and blood" together mean "person," for in the institution body and blood did not even appear in the same sentence. They appear in two sentences that were spoken at the beginning and at the end ("after supper") of the meal, separated by at least an hour.

One can say confidently that in the four centuries since Luther just about every conceivable path has been followed to get around the literal sense. At the end of this path of so much toil and trouble, of so much expenditure of powers of discernment and learning modern exegesis must capitulate before the plain wording. "The text stands there too powerfully." "The path of the spirit is the detour," said Hegel. From the detour of historical, psychological, and philosophical researches, discoveries, mistakes, and wrong tracks of so many centuries theology returns, insofar as it is genuine theology, to the paradoxical doctrine of the presence of the true body and blood of Christ in the Lord's Supper, to the Real Presence.

4.

This naturally is not to say that the exegesis of the future will come with flying colors into the camp of the Lutheran dogma of the Lord's Supper. This will not happen because this particular dogma is connected with the totality of Lutheran doctrine. But it will certainly happen that Luther will again be regarded as a serious "dialog partner." It will happen in this case also, as it has happened so often in the history of dogma: A defeated army will take over something from the victorious one and then claim the victory for itself. Zwingli's doctrine of the Lord's Supper has already been severely compromised in the Reformed Church. No one really wants to be a Zwinglian any more, just as even Calvin, in spite of the Consensus Tigurinus, thought he stood closer to Luther than to the Zurich reformer. If all the signs do not deceive, modern Calvinism is about to more or less give up Calvin's doctrine of the Lord's Supper The *significat* of the Swiss reformers has very few friends left in the world, perhaps more among modern Lutherans than among theologically trained Reformed. But that does not mean a transition to the Lutheran doctrine. The great rock of offense remains the "materialistic" wording of the doctrine of the Lord's Supper of Luther and the Lutheran Church. Melanchthon, and the later Melanchthon at that, who had given up the "materialistic" wording of the Real Presence in favor of a "personal" one, seems to have become the church father of modern Protestantism in this respect.

There is an eclecticism in the making in the doctrine of the Lord's Supper that rejects Zwingli's and Calvin's spatial conception of heaven but at the same time rejects Luther's doctrine of the *unio sacramentalis*, the sacramental unity of the body and blood of Christ with the elements, and with it the oral reception of the body and blood of Christ and the reception by unbelievers. Christ in the midst of His congregation, His real presence understood in the sense of Matt. 18:20—that seems to be the winning solution to the question of the Lord's Supper toward which one aims, apparently a compromise in which Luther's concern is taken into account, but which in reality is a reformulation of Calvin's doctrine, from which certain time-bound ideas about the world and heaven have been abandoned. It is a solution that has made an impression on congregations and pastors, and yet it is a solution that is not consistent with Scripture, because Jesus did not at all say, "This is Myself," but "This is My body" and "This is My blood of the covenant."

Perhaps never has a more dangerous enemy of the Lutheran doctrine of the Lord's Supper appeared than this pure crypto-Calvinism. It is dangerous because this time it has taken hold not only of Electoral Saxony but of a great part of world Lutheranism. It is dangerous because there is scarcely a Lutheran church leader—with or without a bishop's cross—who grasps its theological significance. It is dangerous because the modern Lutheran Church no longer seems to know how to wield the weapon that alone can overcome this opponent: the Scriptural witness of the "It is written." Here lies fundamental reason why the Formula of Concord is today coming under such heavy attack. In it Luther's doctrine of the Lord's Supper is formulated in such a way that one cannot give it a new interpretation.

5.

A whole series of important questions could still be discussed here, but there is not enough space for this time. It should just be suggested that the principle of speaking when God's Word speaks and remaining silent when God's Word is silent should also consistently be brought into play when we speak of the purpose and use of the Sacrament of the Altar.

The church of the *sola scriptura* can never forget that the Lord's Supper is also a memorial meal. "This do in remembrance of Me." Has any of the great men of world history ever established such a memorial for himself as Jesus in His Supper? Has there ever been a testament as faithfully carried out as this one? "For the forgiveness of sins"? Has a church ever more faithfully preserved this than the church of the *sola fide*? According to Roman doctrine no one may receive Communion who is in a state of mortal sin, for with such a person, as Thomas (*S. th.* 3. 79. 3) explains, Christ cannot unite. Lutheran doctrine believes that Jesus comes only to such people, for He is the Savior of sinners.

Against the foolish objection that already before the Communion we receive forgiveness in the absolution Luther has already said what is necessary. We cannot receive forgiveness often enough and should receive it in all kinds of ways, for we remain sinners until we die, even though in faith we are righteous.

And finally concerning the connection between the Lord's Supper and the resurrection, which Luther loved to emphasize, he never went beyond what the Biblical teaching is. He knows the fact of the connection but not the how. One may not burden him with certain theosophical speculations of the 19th century about this how. Here too he speaks as Scripture speaks and is silent when Scripture is silent.

And if one reproaches him for dealing too briefly with the idea of the fellowship meal, the *synaxis*, then one has never read his sermons on the Lord's Supper, where the early Christian ideas about the bread made of many grains and the wine pressed from many grapes are found. Whether the Lutheran Church since then has guarded all these thoughts of the Reformer with sufficient care is another question.

Our task, dear brothers, is to stir them up again and to practice that great "instruction" that Article 24 of the Augsburg Confession requires of us. Let me, in conclusion, say a word about that.

Our first task is to celebrate the Sacrament of the Altar again and again quite seriously but also with the blessed joy of the first Christians (Acts 2:47). Moreover, we Lutherans have the great freedom that exists, as was already mentioned, in the celebration of the Roman Mass. It can take place in utter simplicity but also with the full splendor of the ancient liturgy of the Lord's Supper, which Luther preserved and the Lutheran Church kept for two centuries with such great love as a priceless treasure.

That's where the "instruction" comes in. Here we can learn from the liturgical movement of our time. On this point they are clearly right.

Our people should know the meaning of the Gloria, the Preface, the Sanctus, the Benedictus and Hosanna, the Consecration as it is expounded in the Formula of Concord, the Agnus Dei, and the Communion. We can explain it to them in special lectures, but we can also do it in sermon and Bible class. So many texts emerge totally spontaneously: the great types of the Lord's Supper in the Old Testament—Melchizedek, the sacrifice of Isaac, the Passover, manna, the miraculous feeding of Elijah exhausted to the dropping point in the wilderness. Then in the New Testament, besides the specific texts of the Lord's Supper, there are all the parables and other sayings of the Lord that speak about the future messianic banquet, the Passion history together with the farewell discourses, the first church, the liturgical formulas in the epistles and in Revelation, everything that speaks of the church, and all texts about the high priestly and kingly office of Christ.

What totally new substance our confirmation instruction would receive if it again became sacramental instruction and the Fourth and Sixth Chief Parts did not just make up a more or less unrelated appendage. And don't let anyone come up with the excuse that the children are not yet mature enough or that they would misunderstand it. Where that sort of thing is said, it may be assumed that the teacher is not yet mature enough. How one can say these things to children one can learn, with the necessary changes, from the Catholic instruction for First Communion. That is what we can do. The rest God must do: awaken the hunger and thirst for the Sacrament, which is always at the same time a hunger and thirst for the Word of God.

Something else also belongs in our instruction of the congregation about the Sacrament of the Altar according to Article 24 of the Augsburg Confession: "The people are also given instruction about other false teaching concerning the sacrament." That is not to be avoided. The condemnations cannot be separated from the positive explanation of the doctrine. Even in Barmen one can not get away from this, although one might try to ignore the Scriptural condemnations of false doctrine in the Confessions of the Reformation. The "damnamus" is not a loveless judgment against other Christians but the rejection of false doctrine that is commanded in the New Testament, a duty of pastoral care for those who are straying no less than for those who are endangered by error. If our church right at this point has always taken this most seriously and has not admitted to the Lutheran celebration of the Lord's Supper those who reject the Lutheran doctrine of the Sacrament, it has not thereby anticipated the Last Judgment. In the ancient church the communicant, to whom the consecrated elements were given with the words "The body of Christ" and "The blood of Christ," answered with his "Amen." How can one who is Reformed say Amen to the Lutheran distribution formula? He must take offense at it. Who gives us the right to mislead someone into an unworthy reception of the Lord's Supper in that he does not discern the body of the Lord (1 Cor. 11:29), and to whom would we want to be accountable for it? Is that Christian love?

We must be clear about the fact that there is a profound difference in the understanding of the Lord's Supper here. Not only is the meaning of the Words of Institution in dispute between Lutherans and Reformed, but from this difference also emerges a totally different understanding of the practice of the Lord's Supper. The Lord's Supper can and must have a different purpose in the Reformed Church than among Lutherans. It can and must, as a human act of confession, become a means toward union. That is what it has become in the Reformed and in the crypto-Calvinistic churches of our day. While for us Lutherans—just as for the Catholic churches of the East and West—the Sacrament of the Altar can only be the goal of unification, it stands firm for all Reformed churches and those churches influenced by the Reformed spirit that it is the *means* of unification that Christ willed.

Therefore the idea in the "Constitution of the Evangelical Church in Germany," specially provided for the sake of a few backward Lutherans but completely clear in its meaning, is that altar fellowship—which is basically the same as admission to the Lord's Supper—is the norm between all parts of this church. The legal restriction, practically speaking, is without any significance because this altar fellowship has been generally practiced in fact and in principle—and not just since the [constituting] Synod of Eisenach. The argument based on the need of the refugees is only an excuse, as is already shown by the fact that in the last century one used internal migration as the justification. Besides, there were hardly any Reformed in a number worth mentioning among the refugees from the East, and these have by now made contact with their mother church, at least insofar as they are religious.

Thus it is also claimed that at every churchly gathering today there must be a common celebration of the Lord's Supper, which then becomes the high point, the "unforgettable experience," for all participants at which one feels the breath of the Spirit and the presence of the Lord in a way that Zinzendorf would have been proud of.

As it is in Germany, so it is in the ecumenical realm. To be sure, at Amsterdam the concession of their own celebrations of the Lord's

Supper had to be made to the weak flesh of the Orthodox, the Anglo-Catholics, and the Lutherans, but with pride the enormous stride forward was reported in that a Scandinavian prelate participated in no less than three of the "Lord's Suppers," and Martin Niemöller announced *urbi et orbi* how this Lutheran archbishop had gone with him and the Archbishop of Sydney to the Reformed Lord's Supper, together with all manner of sectarians.

What is really the motive of such going to the Lord's Supper? Since when is the Lord's Supper a means of church politics in the Lutheran Church? What does the Christian congregation, which according to Luther is to judge doctrine, have to say to its bishops on this question? Does it have nothing at all to say any more? Then Western Christendom might just as well have spared itself the Reformation. And what does the Lord Christ say to all this? Now that is something everyone can look up in the second and third chapters of the Revelation of St. John.

In heartfelt affection I greet you, dear brothers in the ministry, in this jubilant season of the church year.

THE LUTHERAN UNDERSTANDING OF THE CONSECRATION

Letters to Lutheran Pastors, No. 26
July 1952

Dear Brothers in the Ministry!

Various inquiries from your circle suggest that I say a word about the Lutheran understanding of the consecration in Holy Communion. Among these was the question of a layman from the Prussian Free Church on how one is to understand the connection between the recommendation or introduction of the epiclesis and the withdrawal of the "for the forgiveness of sins" into the background in the recent liturgical movement. This was asserted in Letter 23 ("The Scriptural Basis of the Lutheran Doctrine of the Lord's Supper").

A further inducement came from the fact that the question about the essence of the consecration has become a main issue in the liturgical movement that is going through the Lutheran churches in America and has been the cause of considerable controversy (cf. the article "The Theology of the Consecration in the Lord's Supper" by G. Drach in *The Lutheran Outlook*, March 1952, and the quarrel between this publication and the *Una Sancta* of the circle around Dr. A. C. Piepkorn, St. Louis). It could hardly be otherwise. Nowhere do dogmatics and liturgics affect each other more profoundly than in the question of the nature and function of the consecration. The answer to this question makes quite clear whether the Lutheran doctrine of the Real Presence has been grasped or not.

1.

Let me begin with a word about the *liturgical movement* in the Lutheran Church. It is a part of a large movement that goes through all of Christendom and perhaps also touches humanity outside the church, as the political pseudoceremonies and pseudoliturgies of our time suggest. It came about, as its origin in the years just after the turn of the century indicates, with the end of the dominance of rank individualism and rationalism. Where the liturgical movement appeared in the churches, it had something revolutionary about it—not without good reason was it tied up with the youth movement in Germany. It was a kind of revolution when in Catholic churches suddenly the table [*mensa*] of the early church replaced the high altar, while at the same time in Presbyterian churches in Scotland the Reformed communion table gave way to the medieval high altar. So church governments, from the Pope to Methodist church assemblies, had much trouble, the salutary kind of trouble that church governments need so that custom and thoughtlessness do not rule the church exclusively.

If one today in the middle of the century looks back to the results of the great movement, then one would have to say that only *one* church has dealt with it, has set aside its revolutionary excesses, and has put it in its service. That is the Roman Church, which in many countries, especially in Germany and Austria, derived a real inner renewal from this movement. This has happened. The fruits will only become completely clear when languages such as German and English have been raised to the level of liturgical languages and when a Catholic "German Mass" [*Deutsche Messe*] will remind Lutheranism that it was once a "German Mass" that led the Lutheran Reformation to victory. If one compares the success of the liturgical movement in the Roman Church with the failure of all efforts to renew the liturgical life of the evangelical churches in our time, one could have serious concerns about the future of these churches.

Where does the difference lie? What is evident immediately is that the liturgical movement in the Roman Church affected all of the people from the Catholic scholars to the most unsophisticated country congregations. All efforts on the Protestant side remain limited to pastors, some church-minded lay people, and very small, sometimes almost sect-like associations. The second immediately obvious difference is that the liturgical movement in the Roman Church has remained on the foundations of Roman dogma in spite of some difficult conflicts with dogma and church order—it happened that liturgical scholars out of genuine

114

enthusiasm for its liturgy joined the Eastern Church—while on the other hand the liturgical movement in the area of the evangelical churches of Germany, including the Lutheran, has lived in continuous conflict with the church's confession. This has been all the more ominous since, besides the liturgical movement, the confessional movement in which Lutherans and Reformed were beginning to discover anew the confession of the Reformation and the doctrine of the church had been going on since the twenties. That this confessional movement has scarcely any relationship with the liturgy is in part to be explained by the fact that it received the strongest impulses from the Reformed side. Karl Barth has never understood what church liturgy is, and how should he ever know it! On the other hand, leaders of the liturgical movement were men who had never experienced the rediscovery of the Reformation and the doctrine of the church: Heiler, whose supposed conversion to Lutheranism in Uppsala was a misunderstanding, as though revolt against the Pope were already Lutheranism, and Wilhelm Stählin, who came from the Nuremberg church, influenced by Melanchthon and the Enlightenment, and from the Gnostic movement of Rudolf Steiner's "Anthroposophy." It is significant that these two men have never understood the *sola fide*. For Heiler the authentic doctrine of justification has always been that of Trent, while Stählin is a latter-day disciple of Osiander. He has always dismissed the doctrine of justification in the Formula of Concord with strong words, even though his literary statements are somewhat more cautious. One should read over his book, *Vom göttlichen Geheimnis* (1936), now translated into English [*The Divine Mystery*], putting the question, What happens here to the basic doctrines of the Reformation? His criticism of the doctrine of forensic justification, p. 67 [106], no longer leaves any room for the idea that God's forgiving and absolving verdict is our righteousness. That we have no other righteousness than the righteousness of Christ, that our righteousness is always an alien righteousness—this humbling and gladdening truth no longer has a place in a theology that regards man's "transformation" as his redemption. As a result, the *sola fide* disappears. This book speaks of faith only in the sense of the devout appropriation of the divine mystery, no longer in the sense of confidence [*fiducia*] in God's mercy in Christ. *Sola scriptura* also disappears. What's the good of all the beautiful words about the "mystery of the Word," pp. 32ff. [55ff.], and about the character of the Bible as revelation if there are also additional sources of revelation, tradition and the mystical experience? Or is it not the Catholic tradition out of which it can be said about the sacraments among Lutherans: "What we in the Evangelical Church call 'Sacraments' is all that is still left from a world of mystery that once embraced and filled the whole life of the Christian Church in its breadth, length, depth and height" (p. 49 [79])? And what else is that "meditation," without which we cannot grasp the depths of a Bible passage or other matters, than a Gnostic-mystical experience ("How does one achieve knowledge of higher worlds?" as we are reminded of Steiner's book)? Not the straightforward hearing of the Word with the assistance of the Holy Spirit but "meditation" should disclose "the divine secret" to the person. So we hear that "practice in meditation is an inestimable aid to really hearing the word, to penetrating into the secret meaning of a Bible phrase, or to experiencing in ourselves the power of a sign or of a melody" (p. 75 [118]). What a combination: Bible, sign, melody!

> All meditation originates a union, perhaps not to be dissolved, between my psychical experience and certain spiritual contents, words, pictures, signs. Every genuine meditative experience is conscious of that very strange occurrence, that I become one with the object contemplated, not so that I pass over to it, but rather that it comes to me, pulls me by the body; indeed, enters into myself so that I experience its presence even in bodily sensations. (p. 75 [117])

This meditation, whose origin from Gnostic sects is well known, should find its "most beautiful example" in what the Christmas story tells of Mary: "She kept all these things, pondering them in her heart" (p. 75 [118]). To that is added: "Luther often pointed to this." Really? He certainly did not mean this "meditative experience." He spoke in another way about the Word, about faith, and about the Holy Spirit, who works in us faith in the Word.

It is an unspeakable tragedy of German Protestantism that behind such out and out pathological and heretical movements there was a genuine longing for the renewal of the Lutheran liturgy and the sacraments in line with the Lutheran Church. It is this yearning that has led so many Lutherans in Germany into the High Church movement, above all that of the Berneuchener. Here they thought they could find what was no longer offered in the churches that no longer understood their own liturgy, neglected the prayer of the church, the daily prayer, and let the Sacrament of the Altar deteriorate. From this one must understand the success of the Berneuchener. They did something. They did much that was wrong, but at least they acted. And who would deny that they have also accomplished something good in the area of liturgical prayer and authentic church music? This is the reason that W. Stählin also enjoys respect among those who object to him theologically. But it remains a tragedy of the German church in the past generation that the confessional movement and the liturgical movement did not find the way to each other.

Confession and liturgy belong inseparably together if the church is to be healthy. Liturgy is prayed dogma; dogma is the doctrinal content of the liturgy. The placement of liturgy above dogma, for which one calls in the liturgical movements of all confessions with the well-known saying "lex orandi lex credendi" [the law of what is to be prayed is the law of what is to be believed] ("ut legem credendi lex statuat suppli-candi," Celestine I, Denzinger 139, called to remembrance by Pius XI in "Divini Cultus," Denz. 2200), has been opposed in the Roman Church by the present Pope [Pius XII] in his encyclical "Mediator Dei," in which he points out that one can also turn this saying around and that in all circumstances dogma should be the norm for the liturgy. If that is already known in Rome, how much more should it be known in the church that makes or would like to make the right understanding of the Gospel also be the criterion for the liturgy.

We Lutherans know nothing of liturgy that is prescribed by God's Word. We know that the church has freedom to order its ceremonies and that it can therefore preserve the liturgical heritage of Christendom, as long as it is consistent with the Gospel. Indeed, our church in the Reformation placed the greatest value on preserving as much as possible this heritage that binds us with the fathers. But these ceremonies do not belong to the essence of the church or to the true unity of the church, as Article 7 of the Augsburg Confession and Article 10 of the Formula of Concord teach. Löhe knew this when in his *Drei Bücher von der Kirche* [*Three Books on the Church*], right where he speaks of the beauty and greatness of the Lutheran liturgy, he protests against overesti-mating it: "The church remains what she is even without liturgy. She remains a queen even when she is dressed as a beggar" (Book 3, chap. 9 [p. 178]). Even the Pope has reminded his bishops that the Masses that are secretly celebrated in prison camps, without any pomp, in utter simplicity, come very near to the Mass of the ancient church and are not inferior to a pontifical Mass. In Lutheran Germany, however, one can today hear theologians even some who come from unliturgical Württemberg—say that there is a form of the divine service that belongs to the essence of the church, even that Gregorian chant belongs essentially to the Christian liturgy. It is high time that the liturgical movement in the Lutheran church wakes up from its romantic dreams and subordinates itself to the norms to which the whole life of the church must be subject: the *norma normans* of Holy Scripture and the *norma normata* of the church's confession. And this applies to all the Lutheran churches in the world, for the Scandinavian, in which the Anglican influence is so great, and for the American, in which the ideas of the European liturgical movement have now gained a footing. If this serious reflection does not take place, then the liturgical movement will become what it has become already for many of its adherents: the end of Lutheranism and the road to Rome.

2.

On one point the liturgical movement is right absolutely without a doubt, and here it is irrefutable. It has called attention to the fact that the Lutheran Church has more or less gone the way of Reformed Protestantism in being without the Sacrament, and thereby it has lost what belongs to the essence of the Lutheran Church. A part of the essence of the church in the Lutheran sense is the *Sacrament*, and that in a different sense than the Reformed Church claims that about itself. Lutherans and Reformed do not mean the same thing when they use the word "sacrament." For the Reformed sacrament is always only a sign of divine grace, a sign that can remain empty, that is, when it might please God to have it so, a sign of a grace that also exists without the sign. They are actions that Christ has commanded and that man must carry out; by fulfilling them we show our obedience to the Lord of the church. For Lutherans sacrament is more than a sign; it is a means of grace in the strict sense. In Baptism we receive the forgiveness of sins, rebirth, and the gift of the Holy Spirit, no matter what we may do with this grace later. In Holy Communion we actually receive with the mouth the body and blood of our Lord for the forgiveness of sins or, if we do not believe this, to our judgment.

This difference in the understanding of sacrament, however, must also work itself out in the celebration of a sacrament. So in the Reformed church every divine service is a "sacramental divine service" [*Sakramentsgottesdienst*] in which one of the two sacraments that exist according to Reformed belief is celebrated, either Baptism or the Lord's Supper. What matters is that the congregation carries out Christ's command. This explains the remarkable custom in modern Reformed churches of performing baptism before the assembled congregation in the divine service. This is probably an influence of the Baptist churches, where the baptismal tank replaces the altar and baptism is performed as an actual bath with as much water as possible, so that the poor person being baptized has to rush out of the church in order to change clothes on the outside.

The early church did it just the other way around. It had the baptism performed outside in front of the church by the deacon—just as the apostles themselves seldom baptized but entrusted it to their helpers (Acts 10:48; 1 Cor. 1:14ff.)—after which the newly baptized came into the church. For this reason the baptismal font according to ancient custom had its place at the entrance of the church. If it were not so hopelessly dreary to witness the thoughtlessness and ignorance of modern Lutheranism, one could smile over the eagerness with which the German and American Lutherans are now also taking over the custom of performing baptism in the congregational divine service—which from experience is thereby interrupted—from the Reformed churches. The Rhenish Church, the most Reformed among the provincial churches of the Old Prussian Union, has elevated this custom or nuisance [*Sitte oder Unsitte*]—it depends entirely on the outlook—to the level of church law. That is the same church in which, despite the Union, despite Barmen, despite the EKiD [Evangelische Kirche in Deutschland]—in which according to its constitution one should "listen to the testimony of the brothers"—one controversy over candles after another broke out because the Lutherans want to have their candles on the altar and the Reformed forbid them because they are not necessary for salvation, as W. Niesel was not ashamed to report in the Reformed church paper.

Naturally, the question of the place of the baptismal font and the time of day at which baptism is performed, as well as the question of the size of the congregation that is present, is just as much an adiaphoron as the question of whether and how many candles should burn on the altar. The Lutheran Church has the freedom to transfer baptism into the divine service, provided it would not be the occasion to smuggle the Reformed concept of sacrament into our congregations, as if Baptism were a sign that must be seen by as many spectators as possible, a sign that we men may discard, and not the means of grace through which a human soul is born again to eternal life. The instant the Lutheran congregations, as in the Rhineland, have to submit to a Reformed law, the new custom ceases to be an adiaphoron. Then the *casus confessionis* exists, in which there is no more adiaphoron according to Article 10 of the Formula of Concord.

But assuming that the *casus confessionis* does not exist and that our church, in the exercise of the freedom that it has in all matters of ceremony, introduces baptism into the divine service, this service would not thereby become, as Karl Barth thinks, a sacramental worship service [*Sakramentsgottesdienst*]. The only sacramental worship service in the Lutheran sense is the divine service in which the Sacrament that belongs in the Sunday divine service is celebrated, *Holy Communion*. For the Lord's Supper is still for Luther simply "the Sacrament," as his usage that again and again puts "Baptism and the Sacrament" together shows (e.g., in the Short Preface to the Large Catechism, Müller, [*Die symbolischen Bücher der evangelisch-lutherischen Kirche*], 380: "yet they come to Baptism and the Sacrament and exercise all the rights of Christians, although those who come to the Sacrament ought to know more . . ." [LC Pref 5]). Others follow him in this, e.g., Justus Jonas in the translation of the Apology (at AC VII/VIII, Müller, 154: "they have one and the same Baptism and Sacrament," which corresponds to the Latin text: *habent . . . eadem sacramenta*).

As is well known, the term "sacrament" is never totally precisely defined in the Lutheran Confessions, and that is because the concept of sacrament is not found in Holy Scripture and is only a way of thinking of later theology in order to summarize the actions instituted by Christ (Baptism, Lord's Supper, Office of the Keys) into categories. Lutherans should never have gotten involved in the polemics regarding the vacillation of the confessions on the question of what all are sacraments. Christ did not institute "the sacraments" but each particular rite. Whether one calls absolution—which does not exist in the Reformed church—sacrament or Gospel is a question of terminology and nothing more. Among these rites, however, is one that belongs to the divine service, without which there is no proper Sunday divine service in the church of the New Testament and in the Lutheran Church of the 16th and 17th centuries, even though Holy Scripture lays down no law about when and how often the command of Jesus, "Do this . . ." (Luke 22:19f.; 1 Cor. 11:24f.), should be followed. This is what the fathers of the early church called the sacrament of sacraments [*sacramentum sacramentorum*] and what Luther simply called "the Sacrament," the Sacrament of the Altar. To restore this Sacrament, which under the influence of Reformed Protestantism and the modern world has also declined in Lutheranism, and give it its proper place in the divine service dare not be an interest only of a liturgical reform movement. It is a matter of life and death for the Lutheran Church.

3.

Among the great teachers of the church there has probably been none who has understood the inner connection of *Word and Sacrament*, of *Gospel and the Lord's Supper* as profoundly as Martin Luther. The church, of course, has always known that the means of grace belong together and thus far form a unity. It is very remarkable that even for Catholicism it is the Word added to the element that first makes the sacrament a sacrament. The Word is the *forma* without which the *materia* can never be a sacrament. But what Roman dogmatics has never seen is the connection between the Sacrament of the Altar and the proclamation of the Gospel. If it had understood this, there would never have been the neglect of the sermon, which even there remains a mark of Catholicism, where one has outstanding preachers and the obligation of preaching every Sunday is impressed on the priests. In the Catholic sacrament of Ordination the priestly office, the authority to offer the sacrifice of the Mass for the living and the dead, and the Office of the Keys, authority to forgive sins, are conveyed, but not the authority to proclaim the Gospel. Now to be sure Holy Communion is a particular form of the proclamation of the Gospel ("For as often as you eat this bread and drink the cup, you proclaim the Lord's death until He comes" 1 Cor. 11:26), but it is not the only way.

The Lord's Supper without the sermon would be a misunderstood rite, just as the sermon, if it were not regularly accompanied by the Lord's Supper as our Lord instituted it, would very soon cease to be proclamation of the Gospel. Those are statements that the experience of Christendom confirms. An Abyssinian Mass and a preaching service in many a prominent, modern Protestant church in New York have in common that they are religious ceremonies from which one can no longer hear the Gospel of the crucified and returning Lord. Before this fact all other differences for theology fade away.

For the Crucified One becomes a figure of the past if His true body and His true blood, what He sacrificed for our sins on Golgotha, are not present in the Sacrament of the Altar and given to us. And the One who is coming again becomes a figure of a distant, unforeseeable future that lies beyond the scope of our life unless the church's prayer, "Maranatha," "Come, Lord Jesus," is already fulfilled now in every celebration of the Lord's Supper. There is no Gospel without the Real Presence. *The Lord's Supper is a component of the Gospel; the Gospel is the content of the Lord's Supper.* That is what Luther saw. Therefore for him the struggle for the Gospel was at the same time the struggle for the Sacrament of the Altar.

The connection between the Gospel and Lord's Supper becomes perfectly clear in the Lutheran doctrine of the *consecration*, as it is fully set forth in Article 7 of the Solid Declaration § 73ff. (Müller, 663ff.). There the decisive sentences state:

> No man's word or work, be it the merit or the speaking of the minister, be it the eating and drinking or the faith of the communicants, can effect the true presence of the body and blood of Christ in the Supper. This is to be ascribed only to the almighty power of God and the Word, institution, and ordinance of our Lord Jesus Christ. For the truthful and almighty words of Jesus Christ which he spoke in the first institution were not only efficacious in the first Supper but they still retain their validity and efficacious power in all places where the Supper is observed according to Christ's institution and where his words are used, and the body and blood of Christ are truly present, distributed, and received [*corpus et sanguis Christi vera praesentia distribuantur et sumantur*] by the virtue and potency of the same words which Christ spoke in the first Supper. For wherever we observe his institution and speak his words over the bread and the cup and distribute the blessed bread and cup, Christ himself is still active through the spoken words by the virtue of the first institution, which he wants to be repeated. Chrysostom says in his *Sermon on the Passion:* "Christ himself prepares this table and blesses it. No human being, but only Christ himself who was crucified for us, can make of the bread and wine set before us the body and blood of Christ. The words are spoken by the mouth of the priest, but by God's power and grace through the words that he speaks, 'This is my body,' the elements set before us [*proposita elementa*] in the Supper are blessed. Just as the words, 'Be fruitful and multiply and fill the earth,' were spoken only once but are ever efficacious in nature and make things grow and multiply, so this word was spoken only once, but it is efficacious until this day, and until his return it brings it about that his true body and blood are present in the church's Supper [*usque ad hodiernum diem et usque ad eius adventum praestat sacrificio firmitatem*]." [FC SD VII 75–76]

4.

If one wants to understand these statements, one must comprehend what they have in common with *Roman doctrine* and what separates them from it. At first glance it might appear that the Roman Church is done an injustice here. Does it not also teach, referring to the fathers of the fourth century, above all Ambrose, but also referring to the word of Chrysostom in *De prod. Judae* 1. 6 (Migne *SG* 49:380), that the priest performs the consecration *ex persona Christi* and that it is not human words but the words of Christ that bring about the miracle of the Real Presence? In *Summa Th.* 3, q. 78, Thomas quotes the words of Ambrose from *De sacramentis:* "The consecration happens by the words and statements of the Lord Jesus" [*Consecratio fit verbis et sermonibus Domini Jesu*]; everything else that is said in the way of prayers is a human word and does not have the effect of Christ's words: "Therefore, what Christ says, this it is that makes the sacrament" [*Ergo sermo Christi hoc conficit sacramentum*] (Migne *SL* 16:440). Yes, even the comparison between the Words of Institution and the words of creation, as Chrysostom offers it, is readily repeated in Catholic dogmatics (cf. *Deutsche Thomas-Ausgabe* 30:429).

Are the fathers of the Formula of Concord, above all is Luther, who knew Roman doctrine well, not guilty of a sin against the Eighth Commandment when they contend that that church teaches consecration through the word of the priest? Could the Reformed not say the same thing about the Lutheran view of the consecration? What sort of basic difference exists for a strict Calvinist between the Catholic priest and the Lutheran pastor, who both maintain that the Words of Institution that they speak bring about the miracle of the Real Presence as the words of Christ?

In fact, the Lutheran doctrine has a true kinship here with the Catholic. It is no accident that the Formula of Concord here appeals to the teachers of the ancient church, who are the fathers for the Roman as well as the Lutheran Church. Both churches are churches of the Real Presence; both churches believe that in every valid Lord's Supper the same miracle takes place as at the first Lord's Supper and that then as now it is the Lord's Words of Institution [*verba testamenti*] that bring about this miracle of the Real Presence. And yet there is a profound contrast between them. Where does this contrast lie?

It does not lie, as many simply assume, in the question of *transubstantiation*. The doctrine of transubstantiation is condemned by Luther and the Lutheran Church because it is not consistent with Scripture—which speaks of the consecrated bread as still bread in 1 Cor. 11:26ff.—and therefore is a false philosophical-theological theory that tries to describe the miracle, which mocks every description and explanation. But the doctrine of transubstantiation does at least want to hold firmly to the Real Presence. For this reason Luther always judged it more mildly than the Enthusiasts' and the Zwinglians' denial of the Real Presence. In this matter, despite the deep chasm that exists, the Lutherans stand closer to Rome than to the Reformed, even to the Calvinists.

And one may not, as still happens, attribute a doctrine of consubstantiation to Lutheranism and try to understand the contrast on that basis. If Luther early in his career appealed to the consubstantiation taught by the Occamists against transubstantiation, he only did it to show that even within the Roman Church the doctrine of transubstantiation was not the only option. But the doctrine that two "substances" exist alongside each other, the substance of the bread and the substance of the body of Christ, is also a philosophical method of explanation, which is not the teaching of our church. Selnecker, the contributor to the Formula of Concord, protested explicitly against this misunderstanding when he wrote in 1591: "Even if our churches use the ancient little words that in the bread, with the bread, or under the bread the body of Christ is received, no *Inclusio* or *Consubstantiatio* or *Delitescentia*—inclusion, dual essence, or concealment—is thereby fabricated" (*Vom Heiligen Abendmahl des Herrn* [1591], fol. E2). And similar protests have been made again and again.

Even the "in, with, and under" with which the three expressions were later summarized is not a Lutheran doctrinal formulation. The prepositions "in," "with," and "under" are grammatical devices to express the miracle that the bread *is* the body and the wine *is* the blood. Everything depends on this *is* being maintained. For this reason the Lutheran Church did not criticize the old word "change" among the fathers. For *mutare*, which Melanchthon still cites in the quotation from Vulgarius (i.e., Theophylact, who in his commentary on Mark at 14:22 speaks of *metaballein*) in Article 10 of the Apology, is accepted as an expression of the ancient church and is not put on the same level with the Roman Church's *transsubstantiare*, which indeed it is not. That some had doubts about this is suggested by the omission of the quotation in the German translation of Justus Jonas as well as the translation of *metarrhythmizei* in the Chysostom quotation in the Formula of Concord with *consecrare*. Meanwhile, the Lutheran Church, although it rejected the doctrine of transubstantiation, has never found the primary catastrophic error in this or any other doctrine of change.

The antithesis lies at another point. Rome's error is not that the words of the consecration effect the Real Presence but that it understands the consecration as a sacrifice. Here, in the doctrine of the *sacrifice of the Mass*, not in the doctrine of transubstantiation, lies the grievous error that devastates the church for Luther. This is clear from a comparison between the article on the Mass in Part 2 and the article on the Sacrament of the Altar in Part 3 of the Smalcald Articles. "The Mass in the papacy must be regarded as the greatest and most horrible abomination because it runs into direct and violent conflict with this fundamental article"—that is, the *articulus stantis et cadentis ecclesiae* [the office and work of Jesus Christ and our redemption]. "Yet, above and beyond all others, it has been the supreme and most precious of the papal idolatries" (SA II II; Müller, 301). That was from the beginning of the Reformation until the end of his life the conviction of the same man for whom transubstantiation was a "clever sophistry," a false speculation contrary to Scripture. Luther did not impute guilt to himself for the fact that he had believed in this theory when he was a monk but for the fact that for 15 years he had said private Masses almost every day and thereby had committed idolatry "and worshiped not Christ's body and blood but only bread and wine and held them up for others to worship" (WA 38:197). That was one of the most severe anxieties of his life. That the sacrifice of the Mass, the most holy rite not only of the Roman Church but of all the churches of the East, the center of Christian piety for so many centuries, should be a violation of the First Commandment! One must understand this in order to comprehend the deep chasm between the Lutheran Lord's Supper and the Catholic Eucharist, between the Lutheran and the Roman Mass, between the Lutheran and Roman understanding of the consecration.

What does it mean that the Mass is a *sacrifice?* Already quite early, perhaps already at the end of the first century, the Eucharist was called a sacrifice, even though the New Testament significantly did not adopt this usage. For the comparison between the Lord's Supper and the sacrificial meals of the Jews and the Gentiles in 1 Cor. 10:18ff. says nothing more than that the Lord's Supper is a sacrificial *meal* in which we receive what Christ once sacrificed for us on the cross. Heb. 13:10 also says no more if one wishes to apply the verse to the Lord's Supper, as Catholic theology does.

The New Testament knows of the sacrifices of Christians, the *spiritual sacrifices* (1 Pet. 2:5) of praise and thanksgiving and of confession (Heb. 13:15), of the *koinonia* of the gifts of love (13:16), of the surrender of one's whole life in the service of God (Rom. 12:1). Generally here the word *sacrifice* is used in a figurative sense according to the pattern of Old Testament usage (e. g., Psalm 50:14; 51:19).

When one considers that Christianity, as a religion that did not involve the offering of sacrifices, came into a world of religions that did offer sacrifice, that the Christians were accustomed to sacrifice and the Jewish Christians in Jerusalem still participated in the sacrificial worship as long as there was a temple, then one can probably understand that they sought a replacement for the sacrifices that men do and found it above all in the prayer of praise and thanksgiving. So it was with the Jews of the diaspora and with all Judaism after the catastrophe of the year 70. Was it then such a big step to speak of the Eucharist, the church's great prayer of thanksgiving, also as a sacrifice?

In his great controversy with Trent, Martin Chemnitz answers the question of whether one may call the Lord's Supper a sacrifice in this figurative sense in the affirmative. But a limit is placed on this designation. The moment the Lord's Supper becomes an atoning sacrifice, then one has left the ground of the New Testament. For there we find only one sacrifice for sins: the sacrifice on Golgotha, which was offered once for all at a particular moment in history and is therefore unrepeatable and eternally valid. There in the New Testament there is only the high priesthood of Jesus and the priesthood of the whole people of God, the church (1 Peter 2:5, 9), of which every Christian is a member (Rev. 1:6). To this day no exegesis has been able to find there a distinctive priestly office besides the universal priesthood of all believers. The passage where the Roman Church believes it has found its priesthood, the office of the priest who offers the sacrifice of the Mass, is the words of our Lord at the Last Supper: "This do in remembrance of Me." Where is there anything about sacrifice there? Where is there even a hint that this was an ordination? How can one understand Jesus' command to repeat in such a way that from now on the apostles and the priests to be ordained by them should sacrifice the body and blood of our Lord for the living and the dead? Something is being read into the New Testament that is not there.

What is the novelty that has invaded the church with this notion of the priest who sacrifices the body and blood of our Lord? It is nothing else than what has found its expression in the idea of Mary, who as the second Eve takes her place beside the second Adam, participating in our Lord's work of redemption. It is nothing but the notion of man sharing in his redemption, a notion that has found its expression in the different types of the Catholic doctrine of grace in the East and West.

126

It is the claim that man has a part to play in what belongs to God alone. It is the secret pride [*superbia*] of man who cannot bear that he is dependent only on grace, only on the sacrifice that another offers for him, only on an "alien righteousness." This is the terrible tragedy of church history, which is not to be understood only as resulting from human error but from seduction by a superhuman power, that the holiest celebration of the church, in which Jesus Christ is present according to His divinity and humanity, has been ruined by the claim of man also to be something.

No beauty of the ancient liturgies can gloss over the fact that in them a human priest treads beside the eternal high priest, a sacrifice done by man beside Christ's sacrifice. None of the finely worked out theories about the identity of the sacrifice of the Mass with the sacrifice of the cross, e.g., Trent's idea that the Mass is a *repraesentatio* of the sacrifice on the cross, a making present of what happened once on Golgotha, eliminates the fact that in the Mass man is also offering a sacrifice: "We Your servants, but also Your holy people . . . offer to Your illustrious majesty . . . a holy victim, an immaculate victim" [*Nos servi tui, sed et plebs tua sancta . . . offerimus praeclarae majestati tuae . . . hostiam sanctam, hostiam immaculatam*]. Thus states the Canon of the Mass in the prayer that follows the prayer with the Words of Institution, and then God is asked graciously to accept the sacrifice as He did the sacrifices of Abel, Abraham, and Melchizedek. At the end of every Mass the priest implores the Holy Trinity "that the sacrifice that I, though unworthy, have offered before the eyes of Your majesty, may be acceptable to You, both for me and for all for whom I have offered it; may it move You to pity and *propitiate* You" [*ut sacrificium, quod oculis tuae majestatis indignus obtuli, tibi sit acceptabile, mihique et omnibus, pro quibus illud obtuli, sit te miserante propitiabile*]. Even if one stresses that the priest acts and speaks *ex persona Christi*, that in the sacrifice of the Mass Christ offers Himself to the Father and thus "re-presents" the sacrifice of the cross or makes it present, the fact remains that the priest makes the offering not only in the name of Christ but also in the name of the church, in the name of the faithful who are present, and even in his own name.

How can man take part in Christ's sacrifice? One must then go as far as modern Catholic theologians, who see in the sacrificing church the body of Christ, so that Christ and the church, the head and the body, do the sacrifice together. But then it is still a working together of God and man, and one even comes to a dangerous deification of man.

Concerning the relationship between the sacrifice of Golgotha and the church, Holy Scripture says: "Christ loved the church and gave Himself up for her, that He might sanctify her" (Eph. 5:25). It is characteristic of Catholic synergism that Mary under the cross is now no longer understood only as the church, for which Jesus died, but that the present Pope [Pius XII] in the conclusion of the encyclical *Mystici Corporis* can say of her that Mary also sacrificed her son there. In the doctrine of Mary as the "co-redemptrix" the final consequence of that synergism becomes clear that finds expression throughout the life and thought of Catholicism and also in the doctrine of the sacrifice of the Mass—the deification of man, the obliteration of the line between Creator and creature. This is what one comes to if one, in the words of Karl Adam, teaches "the wondrous fact that not only God but also creaturely powers—according to the conditional elements of their creatureliness—have a causative role in the work of redemption" (*Das Wesen des Katholizismus*, 6th ed. [1931], 141).

5.

Only from this profound contrast between the Roman Catholic view of the creature's cooperation in his redemption and the Reformation's conviction that there is no such cooperation and that *Christ alone* is the One "whom God made our wisdom, our righteousness and sanctification and redemption" [1 Cor. 1:30] can the difference in the understanding of the consecration be grasped. It is still true, despite every appeal to the word of Chrysostom and despite the contention that the priest speaks the consecration *ex persona Christi*, that he also still acts in his own name and in the name of the faithful. "We your servants, but also your holy people" offer to the Father the sacrifice of Christ's body and blood—not just the sacrifice of praise and thanksgiving, not just the gifts of the offertory. It is no accident that the Words of Institution are fitted into the prayers of the Canon of the Mass in the form of a relative clause and thereby become a part of a *human prayer*. However beautiful these Mass prayers may be, as not only the Roman Mass but also the liturgies of antiquity and of all the churches of the East have them, they remain human prayer and take the Words of Institution into human prayer. It is characteristic of the predominance of the human prayer that since the fourth century in the Eastern Church, the epiclesis, the invocation of the Holy Spirit to change the elements, has been understood as the actual consecration in place of the *verba testamenti* [Words of Institution]. But even if one, as was probably the case in the earlier Masses, understood the whole series of the prayers, including the Words of Institution, as the consecration, it would still be the prayer that consecrates. That is confirmed by the fact that in the Roman Mass the whole Canon is prayed inaudibly so that the congregation does not get to hear the Words of Institution and has to be alerted to the moment when they are spoken by the ringing of a bell. The elevation of the consecrated host for all practical purposes replaces the hearing of the Words of Institution. One must consider once what it meant for the German people, after over 700 years of Christian history, to hear the Words of Institution for the first time in the Lutheran Reformation, and that the same is true of the other nations who accepted the Reformation at that time. Then one will understand what the Lutheran Mass in the mother tongue meant for these peoples.

Long before he created this Mass after years of the most careful theological and liturgical work, *Luther* had recognized where the decisive error in Rome's understanding of the words of consecration lay. In *The Babylonian Captivity* he declared that what makes the Mass a proper Mass in the sense of the institution of Christ is the Word of Christ [*verbum Christi*] alone, i.e., the Words of Institution. "For in that word, and in that word alone, reside the power, the nature, and the whole substance of the mass" (*WA* 6:512 [American Edition 36:36]). Everything else is "accessory to the word of Christ" [*verbo Christi accessoria*]. A year later in *The Abolition of Private Masses* he interpreted the Words of Institution as the heart of the Sacrament of the Altar. In this Sacrament is the whole sum of the Gospel (*est enim in eo summa tota evangelii*, *WA* 8:447), as Paul says with the words: "As often as you eat of this bread and drink of this cup you will be proclaiming the Lord's death until He comes" (Luther is quoting the Vulgate). In the German version of the writing (*The Misuse of the Mass*) of the same year he says:

> For if you ask, What is the Gospel? you can give no better answer than these words of the New Testament, namely, that Christ gave his body and poured out his blood for us for the forgiveness of sins. This alone is to be preached to Christians, instilled into their hearts, and at all times faithfully commended to their memories. Thus the godless priests have made words of consecration out of them and concealed them so secretly that they would not reveal them to any Christian, no matter how holy and devout he has been. (*WA* 8:524 [American Edition 36:183])

129

Hidden deep in the Canon of the Mass among purely human prayers and in such a way that the Christian people can no longer hear them, the words of the Lord's Supper, the Gospel pure and simple, are stuck. By no longer permitting them to be heard and clothing them in human prayer formulas, they have made out of this Gospel a "benediction" [*Benedeiung*], a *verba consecrationis*, as the Latin wording says. That is, they have robbed the words of consecration of their real meaning. For in the Mass they are no longer good news to the believing sinner but only a consecration in the sense in which there are other consecrations, e.g., the consecration of churches or bishops, a rite of blessing with a particular effect. In view of all this we can understand why Luther, when he began to reform the Mass, immediately made two liturgical changes: The *words of the Lord's Supper* were to be chanted *aloud* by the liturgist, and the framing of Christ's words with a whole series of prayers was completely set aside. The only prayer that Luther left in this position was the *Lord's Prayer*, which in the Roman Mass follows the Canon, while Luther put it before the Words of Institution. For him no man-made prayer seemed tolerable beside the *verba testamenti*.

Theodor Knolle has shown the profound doctrinal and liturgical meaning of the old Lutheran Mass in several works (*Luther-Jahrbuch* [1928] and in his contribution to the volume *Vom Sakrament des Altars* [1941]) and raised a warning voice against the introduction of epicleses and eucharistic prayers, which bring the Words of Institution again into a relative clause between purely human words, even if they are beautiful and venerable human words. Even when one makes the utmost effort to speak of sacrifice only in an indisputably evangelical way, what is Lutheran still becomes a Roman Mass. The pious man again puts himself alongside Christ, and the Words of Institution are no longer the Gospel. The congregation edifies itself with its beautiful prayers, but it no longer hears the Gospel in the Lord's Supper. The forgiveness of sins recedes. It is no longer seen as the great and joyous gift of the Sacrament.

Is there some connection here with the fact that confession, which according to Lutheran teaching should precede the reception of the Sacrament of the Altar, is no longer taken very seriously? It is then either a General Confession without the complete seriousness of self-examination, which was a matter of course for our fathers, or it becomes in many High Church movements a poor imitation of the Roman auricular confession. But the deep inner connection that exists between absolution and the reception of the Sacrament is no longer understood. It can only be understood when one knows that both, *absolution and the Sacrament of the Altar*, are two sides of the same thing, that both are the *Gospel* for sinners. But if anyone wonders why we should receive forgiveness twice, what it means that one should be absolved of sins and then still receive the Sacrament for the forgiveness of sins, to such a one we may answer—Luther caught the spirit of it—"You have not yet pondered how great is the weight of sin."

6.

Although Luther understands the consecration in Holy Communion as something more than the consecration itself, more than the dedication of elements, it remains *consecration* in the strict sense. The Formula of Concord says it in this sense in its doctrine of consecration, as we quoted it above. It is the doctrine as our church developed it in the struggle against the Enthusiasts, after the doctrine of the consecration determined by the sacrifice of the Mass had been overcome in the struggle with Rome. Precisely because the Words of Institution may no longer in any way be blended with human words or be hidden among the words of men because they are the words of the Lord Christ Himself, they are as powerful as God's words in creation and accomplish what they say. So the Word of the Lord in every celebration of His Supper makes the bread to be the body and the wine to be the blood of the Lord. "For as soon as Christ says: 'This is my body,' His body is present through the Word and the power of the Holy Spirit" ("The Sacrament of the Body and Blood of Christ" [1526] *WA* 19:491 [American Edition 36:341]). "How that comes about you cannot know" (Ibid., 489 [340]). "We are not bidden to search out how it can be that our bread becomes and is the body of Christ" (*WA* 18:206 [American Edition 40:216]).

In accordance with the principle that theology should speak where God's Word speaks and should be silent where God's Word is silent, Luther and the Lutheran Confessions make no dogmatic statements about the how of the Real Presence. The philosophical lines of thought that are found here and there have a purely apologetic character. They do not try to explain the Real Presence but only to confront the reproach that the Lutheran doctrine is nonsense. *The Lutheran Church does not know a dogma about the how of the Real Presence that corresponds to transubstantiation.*

This restraint on the question of the how is also observed when it comes to dealing with *practical problems*. When does the Real Presence begin? When does it end? Is it limited to the moment of reception? What is the difference between a consecrated and an unconsecrated host? Is a second consecration necessary when the consecrated elements are not sufficient, and if so, why? What happens with the elements that are left over?

When one considers Luther's statements, one notices a very realistic "Catholicizing" attitude that is downright offensive to later Protestants of all confessions. First of all, it is determined that the Real Presence begins with the Words of Institution, which effect it. "There the words make the bread to be Christ's body given for us. Therefore it is no more just bread, but Christ's body wears the bread" [*Ergo non est amplius panis, sed corpus Christi hat das Brot an*] (*Sermon on the Catechism* [1528], *WA* 30/1:53). This notion is no different from the ideas of the *Formula Missae* (*WA* 12:214 [*LW* 53:30]) and the *Deutsche Messe* (*WA* 19:99 [*LW* 53:81]). It would "accord with the Lord's Supper to administer the sacrament immediately after the consecration of the bread, before the cup is blessed." For Luther is weighing whether it might not be best to follow Luke and Paul here. In this case the consecration would also remain a consecration and would not become a formula of distribution as has happened in many modern churches.

It is not necessary here to go into the fact that for Luther only the celebration of the Lord's Supper that corresponds to Christ's institution is a proper sacrament; therefore a private Mass in which no congregation communes is not one. The consecration spoken in this Mass is ineffective, while even in the Roman Mass with communion—even though only under one kind—Christ's institution is still there, though badly deformed. *Extra institutionem Christi* (outside of Christ's institution) the Sacrament is not there; consequently, the Real Presence ceases when the celebration is over. There is no reservation of the Sacrament, no procession with the Sacrament, and naturally no veneration of the reserved host. Such a practice would be veneration of a created thing, for then only the bread is there. But during the celebration the sacramental union of the body and blood of Christ with the elements exists. From this perspective alone is Luther's discussion of the *consecrated host* to be understood. This finds expression above all in his advisory statements in the cases of Pastors Besserer in Weida and Wolferinus in Eisleben.

On 11 January 1546 Luther expressed himself in a letter to Amsdorf regarding Besserer, who had been imprisoned because he had given a communicant an unconsecrated host in place of a consecrated one that had fallen on the floor (cf. Enders 17:7 n. 2 on No. 3599). Luther opposes his imprisonment but favors his dismissal from office: "Let him go to his Zwinglians!" (Ibid., line 11). "As a mocker of God and of the people he has publicly dared to regard consecrated and unconsecrated hosts as the same thing" [hostias consecratas ac non consecratas pro eodem habere] (lines 9f.).

The case of Wolferinus, which happened three years earlier, had to do with the fact that a controversy broke out among the pastors in Eisleben because Wolferinus had put the remaining consecrated elements back with the unconsecrated, referring to the fact that the sacraments are actions [actiones], not static facts [stantes factiones—things remaining done]. In Luther's first letter to Wolferinus of 4 July 1543, which is also signed by Bugenhagen as one who agreed with Luther's judgment (Enders 15, No. 3285), the Eisleben pastor is urgently admonished to give up this dangerous practice that could lead to Zwinglianism; besides it is against the custom existing in the other churches. The elements that are left over should be consumed by the pastor and the communicants, "so that it will not be necessary to raise such objectionable and dangerous questions about the cessation of the sacramental action" (line 46). This demand corresponds with the repeated advice of the Reformer that what remains [die "reliquiae"] should be either consumed or burned. In a second letter of 20 July Luther warns Wolferinus against a misunderstanding of Melanchthon's statement, "There is no sacrament outside of the sacramental action" (Enders 15, No. 3291). Wolferinus is so limiting the sacramental action that he is about to lose the Sacrament. His definition threatens to limit the Real Presence to the consecration, which is indeed the most potent and the principal action in the Sacrament, and would lead to a renewal of the scholastic question, At which of the words does the Presence begin? The action of the Sacrament is not limited to a moment, but actually extends over a period of time. Luther then gives his definition of the sacramental action [actio sacramentalis]. He expresses it thus, "It starts with the beginning of the Lord's Prayer and lasts until all have communed, the cup has been drunk empty, the hosts have been eaten, and the people have been dismissed and have gone from the altar" (line 34), and he adds: "In this way we will be sure and free from doubts and from the offensive, interminable questions" [et scandalis quaestionum interminabilium].

These written answers of Luther correspond to his personal conduct as communicant (on that subject see Hans Preuss, Luther als Kommunikant: Festschrift für Friedrich Ulmer [1937], 205ff.) and as celebrant. In many churches in which he celebrated the Lord's Supper there remained for a long time memories of his conduct, e.g., in the Church of Our Lady in Halle during his last journey to Mansfeld. Long afterwards they were still telling of this celebration, one of the last, if not the last of his life.

> The great number of communicants had wearied his aged arms; at one point his quivering hand caused him to spill a little of the consecrated wine on the floor. Luther put the chalice down on the altar, fell to his knees, and sucked up the wine with his mouth so that it should not be trodden under foot, whereupon the whole congregation broke out in sobbing and weeping. (K. Loewe, quoted by K. Anton, *Luther und die Musik* [1928], 59; G. Kawerau offers another report, quoted by Hans Grass, *Die Abendmahlslehre bei Luther und Calvin* [1954], 115–21; Grass's careful treatment of the whole question is emphasized here.)

One may not simply explain these notions of Luther as echoes of his Catholic past. How profoundly he had freed himself from this past we have seen in the discussion of the Sacrifice of the Mass.

It all comes down to the question of whether we are here dealing with private views of Luther and his colleagues and the majority of the Lutheran pastors of the 16th century or whether the doctrine of the consecration that is involved in these views is to be regarded as *doctrine of the Lutheran Church*. For this is what must concern us here above all, not what falls under the heading of liturgy and ritual.

Against the hypothesis that the Formula of Concord confesses this doctrine the Saliger controversy over the Sacrament has repeatedly been cited. In Lübeck and later in Rostock *Saliger* had maintained that the Real Presence is there before the *sumptio*, the receiving of the elements, and he and his followers appeal to Luther. The fact that Saliger was condemned has repeatedly been brought forward to show that according to Lutheran doctrine there is only a Real Presence at the moment of the reception of the consecrated bread and wine. But other factors played a role in his condemnation, above all the way in which he pursued his cause and the expressions that he used (see on that J. Wiggers, *Zeitschrift f. hist. Theol.*, 1848, 613ff.; H. Frank, *Konkordienformel* 3:66f., 146f.; Grass, 111f.). "In this controversy those who were not followers of Saliger, even those who opposed him, did not maintain a Real Presence only in the reception. Wigand shows in his expert opinion, after he has set aside the case, that if the sacramental action is interrupted and there is no reception, there is a Presence before the eating and drinking" (Grass, 111).

In the decision, the Wismar Recess written by Chytraeus, one of the authors of the Formula of Concord, which was partially incorporated into the Solid Declaration [VII, 83-85; *Bekenntnisschriften*, 1000 n. 4], papistic expressions that let the Sacrament exist beyond its use [*extra usum*] are forbidden, but the teaching is also specifically rejected "that the body and blood of Christ are not present in the Lord's Supper until the consecrated bread and wine are touched with the lips or taken into the mouth." Here precisely that view is rejected that later orthodoxy regarded as correct. So it is also not the teaching of the Formula of Concord that the Real Presence is there only in the *sumptio*, in the reception of the elements. This view is explained by the misunderstanding that the *usus*, the use of the Sacrament, is the same thing as the *sumptio*, the reception. Thus the Formula of Concord, making use of the Wismar Recess, decides the question of the effect of the consecration in this way:

> But this blessing or recitation of Christ's words of institution by itself, if the entire action of the Lord's Supper as Christ ordained it is not observed (if, for instance, the blessed bread is not distributed, received, and eaten but is locked up, offered up, or carried about), does not make the sacrament. But the command of Christ, "Do this," which comprehends the whole action or administration of this sacrament (namely, that in a Christian assembly we take bread and wine, consecrate it, distribute it, receive it, eat and drink it, and therewith proclaim the Lord's death), must be kept integrally and inviolately, just as St. Paul sets the whole action of the breaking of bread, or of the distribution and reception before our eyes in 1 Cor. 10:16.
>
> To maintain this true Christian doctrine concerning the Holy Supper and to obviate and eliminate many kinds of idolatrous misuse and perversion of this testament, the following useful *rule* and norm has been derived from the words of institution: Nothing has the character of a sacrament apart from the use instituted by Christ, or apart from the divinely instituted action [*Nihil habet rationem sacramenti* extra usum *a Christo institutum* oder extra actionem *divinitus institutam*]. (SD VII 83–85; Müller, 665)

The definition of *usus* as *actio* is then repeated:

> In this context "use" or "action" is . . . the entire external and visible action of the Supper as ordained by Christ: the consecration or words of institution, the distribution and reception, or the oral eating." (SD VII 86)

The reception [*sumptio*] is therefore only a part of the use [*usus*]. The teaching developed here by the Formula of Concord matches exactly the one that we found in Luther. For him also the *usus* is the entire *actio*, and the Real Presence, effected by Christ's Word in the consecration, is bound up in the whole *actio* and can therefore not be restricted to the moment of reception. The consecrated bread is the body of Christ also when it lies on the altar or when the pastor holds it in his hand. This is the Lutheran view.

This view certainly does not allow one thing that the Roman teaching knows: the precise *designation of the moment* at which the Real Presence begins and the moment when it *ceases*. We have observed that Luther in one place takes into account that the Lord's Prayer, which precedes the Words of Institution, belongs to the *actio* that is attended by the Real Presence. When we say that the consecration brings about the Real Presence, we are not making a statement about what Roman theology identifies as the moment of consecration. When we say that after the celebration the consecrated bread is no longer the body of Christ, that is not a statement about the moment when the sacramental union ceases, corresponding to the Roman teaching that the Real Presence ceases when the forms decay.

The designation of these moments was the work of scholastic theology, above all of Thomas. But even Thomas could not give a Scriptural basis for it. He simply concludes from the use of the present tense *est* in the statement, "Hoc est corpus meum," that the effect of the consecration takes place at the moment in which the statement has been fully spoken. The same applies to the words about the cup—while his doctrine of concomitance allows him to assume a presence of the blood together with the body *ex reali concomitantia* (S. th. 3, q. 78, art. 6.). But this is only a rational argument. Until the middle of the fourth century the early church never knew anything of a "moment of consecration." It turns up in Cyril of Jerusalem and in Serapion (Egypt) and in the West for the first time in Ambrose (cf. Gregory Dix, *The Shape of the Liturgy* [1947], 240). But to this day the Eastern Church has not arrived at complete clarity about the "moment of consecration" (Words of Institution or epiclesis), while the influences of Latin scholasticism, from which the question was posed to the Eastern Church, are fading. Influence of the Scholastic tradition was also involved when Lutheran theologians sought to designate the moment when the Real Presence begins and the moment when it ends. Here lies the theological error of Saliger, and Chytraeus was absolutely right when he said in his criticism that for the devout heart it is enough to know from the Words of Institution that the body and blood are given to us, and it is useless to argue about the bread on the paten or the bread that is left over (cf. the Latin wording from Wiggers in Grass, 112). The same thing must also be said to the later orthodox theologians, who for logical considerations denied a duration of the Real Presence and confined it to the *moment* of the reception, like Aegidius Hunnius (quoted by F. Pieper, *Christian Dogmatics* 3:373 n. 118, from C. F. W. Walther, *Pastorale*, 175), who tried to show the logical impossibility of a duration of the Real Presence that begins with the consecration. He points to the hypothetical case of a celebration of the Lord's Supper that is interrupted by fire breaking out after the consecration but before the reception. To that we can only say that here exactly the same mistake is made as in Scholasticism. One tries to answer questions that Holy Scripture neither knows nor answers and that therefore the church also cannot answer with rational efforts. We cannot determine the moment of the beginning and the end of the real presence of Christ's body and blood in the Sacrament of the Altar with watch in hand, just as we cannot fix temporally the presence of Christ when two or three are gathered together in His name and therefore the promise of Matt. 18:20 is fulfilled for them. We may never forget that the presence of Christ, His divine and human nature, is always an eschatological miracle in which time and eternity meet.

7.

The Lutheran doctrine of the consecration assumes that every celebration of the Lord's Supper is an unfathomable miracle, just as the first Lord's Supper was not, as the Reformed Church supposes, a parabolic action but also a miracle. Every Lord's Supper that we celebrate is a miracle, no less than the miracles that Jesus did during His days on earth. The same is true, although in another way, of Baptism. As the preaching of the Lord was accompanied by His signs and wonders, so the proclamation of His church is accompanied by the sacraments. And as the deeds of Jesus were the dawn of the coming redemption (Luke 4:18ff.; Matt. 11:4ff.), so in Baptism and in the Lord's Supper we are already given what belongs to the coming world. As often as the church gathers around the table of the Lord it is already the "day of the Lord," i.e., the day of the Messiah (cf. Amos 5:18), the day of His return. This is the original meaning of Sunday as the "day of the Lord," on which John (Rev. 1:9ff.) in the Spirit could participate in the heavenly divine service, while the churches of Asia were gathered for the Lord's Supper (cf. 3:20). Sunday is an anticipation of the parousia. It is this because on that day the Lord comes to His church in the Word and in the Sacrament of the Altar. For this reason the church greets Him before the consecration with "Blessed is he who comes in the name of the Lord. Hosanna in the highest." The old Lutheran Church of the 16th and 17th centuries still celebrated the divine service in this sense, which Article 24 of the Augsburg Confession defends with the words: "We are unjustly accused of having abolished the Mass. Without boasting, it is manifest that the Mass is observed among us with greater devotion and more earnestness than among our opponents." This honor is long past, since late orthodoxy neglected the liturgical instruction of the people, Pietism destroyed the Lutheran concept of sacrament, and rationalism nullified faith in miracles.

Will the Lutheran Church recover the divine service to which its Confession bears witness? It cannot be a matter of repristinating an unrepeatable past but only of understanding anew the teaching of the Holy Scriptures about the Sacrament of the Altar as confessed in the Confession. Everything else will come of itself. It is an experience of the history of Lutheranism in the 19th century that generally, wherever Luther's doctrine of the Real Presence is again understood and believed, hunger for the Sacrament of the Altar wakens afresh, and the liturgy is renewed. We see beginnings of such an experience even today. No liturgical movement can help our church unless it is inspired with Luther's profound understanding of the consecration. In the consecration Jesus Christ is speaking and no one else. He speaks the Word of divine omnipotence: "This is My body," "This is My blood," and of divine love: "Given and shed for you for the forgiveness of sins." And this Word creates what it says, the true presence of His body and blood and the forgiveness of sins. So both forms in which the Gospel appears meet in the consecration, the spoken and the acted Gospel, the Word and the Sacrament. In this sense the consecration is the Gospel itself.

These pages have been written while in Germany the great vital questions for the Lutheran Church are considered in the convention of the Lutheran World Federation in Hannover and in smaller conferences. Whatever the outcome of these meetings may be, let us never forget, esteemed brothers, that the decision about the future of our church and the preservation of the Lutheran Confessions is made in the individual congregation. For there, in the church at a particular place, stands the altar around which the church gathers.

Sanctorum Communio

1974

(Published as chapter 1 of Hermann Sasse, *Corpus Christi: Ein Beitrag zum Problem der Abendmahlskonkordie*, ed. Friedrich Wilhelm Hopf [Erlangen: Verlag der Ev.-Luth. Mission, 1979], 13–29.)

In the old World Conference on Faith and Order, which is not identical with the Commission on Faith and Order of the World Council of Churches, the healthy rule applied that all important documents had to be published not only in the three languages used at the conference but also in Latin and Greek. As long as this rule was observed, the lack of clarity and the ambiguity that unfortunately was often desired were avoided, ambiguity that infuses modern ecumenical documents.

What did it mean for Christendom that the confessional documents of the 16th and 17th centuries, right up to the Westminster Confession, were presented in Latin and that the theologians of all denominations had the opportunity of engaging in genuine dialog with one another, an opportunity of which they made ample use? Today English seems about to become the ecclesiastical language of the Western world; even the *Osservatore Romano* has to have an English edition. Now English certainly belongs among the classical languages of Christendom—one need only think of the English Bible, of Cranmer's liturgical texts, and of the wonderful language of John Henry Newman—but modern English is too noncommittal, too indefinite for dogmatic formulations. Added to this is the dreadful inclination of modern theology to express its thoughts in ever newer terminology. Certainly, the church must and therefore theology may develop new terms when the old terms are no longer understood or are no longer adequate. Classical examples of this are the *homoousios* of the Nicene Creed and the struggle over terminology for the trinitarian and christological dogmas (*ousia, hypostasis, essen-*

tia, substantia, prosōpon, persona, physis, natura, and their laboriously formed and often dubious equivalents in Syrian, Coptic, and Armenian).

But a new terminology is only allowed when it serves to bring clarity, not to confuse the concepts or cloud the truth. Otherwise our theology is in danger of becoming what Harnack called the "systematic misuse of a terminology invented for someone's own purpose." This danger is especially great in the area of modern ecumenical theology.

Such a misfortune seems to lie behind the Leuenberg Concord, which has no less a goal than the establishment of church fellowship between the Lutheran, Reformed, and Union churches of Europe. That is in every respect a utopian undertaking, for such a church fellowship is not only impossible, but it is a logical absurdity. It would be conceivable and commendable to seek a new, closer relationship among these churches. Whatever one might call this relationship, the expression *church fellowship* is impossible because it plays a part in the doctrine and in the ecclesiastical law of the Lutheran Church and not only that, but it goes back to the earliest church and is deeply rooted in the New Testament. It is the fellowship that binds within the one, holy, catholic church all believing individuals and their congregations in the oneness of the body of Christ. It is a fellowship of the church, not of the churches, whether one understands churches to mean local congregations or dioceses, each of which is *the* church of Christ, *the* people of God at that respective place (e.g., in Jerusalem, in Corinth, in Ephesus, in Rome).

The Biblical word for this fellowship is *koinonia, communio.* This *koinonia* is distinct from all other fellowships because it is not of human origin and reaches beyond the range of what is earthly and human. This fellowship is not founded on a social contract or on natural religion, as Schleiermacher taught: "The religious self-consciousness, like every essential element *of human nature,* leads necessarily in its development to *fellowship* or communion: a communion which, on the one hand, is variable and fluid, and on the other hand, has definite limits, i.e., is a church" (Friedrich Schleiermacher, *Der christliche Glaube,* ed. Martin Redecker [Berlin, 1960], 1:41 [*Christian Faith* 1:6]; cf. 2:215 where it says that the church comes into being by the coming together of born-again individuals [2:115]). Rather, it originates in the divine means of grace, the Word of God and the sacraments of Christ. "That which we have seen and heard we proclaim also to you, so that you may have *fellowship with us;* and *our fellowship is with the Father and with His Son Jesus Christ*" (1 John 1:3; cf. vv. 6f.).

The Greek word for this is *koinonia*. Of the first congregation in Jerusalem immediately after Pentecost and the baptism of the 3,000 it says: "They devoted themselves to the apostles' teaching and fellowship, to the breaking of bread and the prayers" (Acts 2:42). Fellowship is founded in Baptism and finds its concrete expression in the Sacrament of the breaking of bread. That corresponds exactly to the usage of Paul: God has called the believers "into the fellowship of His Son, Jesus Christ our Lord." "By *one* Spirit we were all baptized into *one* body . . . and all were made to drink of *one* Spirit" (1 Cor. 1:9; 12:13). The connection with the Lord's Supper becomes quite clear (1 Cor. 10:16f.). The *koinonia* of the body and blood of Christ coincides with the *koinonia* of the church. We shall return to this passage later.

That the fellowship of the church is at the same time the fellowship of Christians with the Father, the Son, and the Holy Spirit is expressed in the apostolic blessing in 2 Cor. 13:13 [14]. The question has been asked whether the *koinonia tou hagiou pneumatos* means a common sharing of the Holy Spirit or the fellowship that is worked by the Spirit. It is of course both. 1 Cor. 12:13 confirms that it is a result of the Spirit. The word is also used for the consequence or confirmation of this fellowship worked by the Spirit. Thus the collection that Paul gathered from his Gentile Christian congregations for the poor saints in Jerusalem is called *koinonia* (Rom. 15:26; 2 Cor. 9:13), just as in Heb. 13:16 *koinonia* means the gifts of love within the congregation in contrast to the *eupoiia*, the alms one gives outside the congregation. If both are designated as *thysia*, the most solemn word for sacrifice, then we may recall that in Acts 2:42 *koinonia* probably means the bringing of the gifts in the divine service. We would then find in this passage, for the first time, the four basic elements of Christian worship: proclamation of the apostolic word, the breaking of bread, the bringing of the gifts or "communion," and the prayers of the believers. One can ask whether that is an accident.

The Biblical idea of koinonia is echoed in the Third Article of the Western baptismal creed: "I believe in the Holy Spirit, the holy catholic church, the communion of saints [*sanctorum communionem*], the forgiveness of sins, the resurrection of the flesh and the life everlasting." The phrase *sanctorum communionem*, the last addition to this creed that grew by steady development, must be understood from its context. It is not, as was thought for a long time and as Luther still understood it, an explanatory apposition to *sanctam ecclesiam catholicam* as a kind of definition of the church. The Roman Creed, in contrast to the Eastern creeds ("God of God, Light of Light, very God of very God"), has no explanatory repetitions, but with every new idea it introduces a new fact.

Sanctorum communio cannot be understood as a "congregation of saints" [*Gemeinde der Heiligen*]. In biblical Greek *koinonia* never means congregation [*congregatio*]. It designates a state of affairs within the church, the congregation of saints [*congregatio sanctorum*]. Within the holy catholic church there is the *communio sanctorum*, in which *sanctorum* can be the genitive either of *sancti*, the holy persons, or of *sancta*, the holy things, therefore meaning participation in the *sancta* as the consecrated [*geheiligten*] things.

If an expression is found in the Creed with a double meaning, then it may also—as in the corresponding case with a word of Holy Scripture—be understood in a double sense. It would then, if one thinks of holy persons, deal with the *koinonia* that exists according to 1 John 1 between the members of the church, something like the Catholic Church understands its doctrine of the fellowship within the church in its three parts: the church militant, the church triumphant, and the church suffering in purgatory. While we as evangelical theologians must oppose the doctrines of purgatory and of the invocation of the saints, which Rome bases on this concept of the *sanctorum communio*, just as certainly we must hold on to the Biblical doctrine of the *koinonia* between the members of the church in the sense of 1 John 1 and may recover it in the *sanctorum communio*. Indeed, the usage of *ecclesia* in Heb. 12:23 for the city of the living God, the heavenly Jerusalem, allows us to go beyond the scope of the temporal church and to understand with the fathers that all saints and righteous persons from the beginning of the world, indeed even the angels and authorities and powers in heaven [*virtutes et potestates supernae*] are included in the concept of the *ecclesia*, just as Niceta of Remesiana did in his explanation of the Creed (Cf. Werner Elert, *Abendmahl und Kirchengemeinschaft in der alten Kirche hauptsächlich des Ostens* [Berlin, 1954], 170f. [*Eucharist and Church Fellowship in the First Four Centuries* (St. Louis, 1966), 209ff.]; Ferdinand Kattenbusch, *Das apostolische Symbol*, vol. 2: *Verbreitung und Bedeutung des Taufsymbols* [Hildesheim, 1962], 930). He calls this church *sanctorum omnium congregatio*, the congregation of all the saints. "In this one church believe that you will reach the communion of saints" [*In hac una ecclesia crede te communionem consecuturum esse sanctorum*]. The fellowship of the saints is then an eschatological treasure in which the members of the church will take part. This church appears on earth in the form of the catholic church with which one must stand in fellowship ("cuius communionem debes firmiter retinere"). Then follows a warning against the false churches [*pseudo-ecclesiae*] of the heretics and schismatics, who no longer belong to that holy church, because they, deceived by demons, believe and live differently than Christ taught and the apostles handed on.

This understanding of *communio sanctorum*, which is based on Augustine's ecclesiology, is not the original one, however, and therefore is also not the only possible meaning of the expression. There is much evidence that it originally meant participation in the *sancta*, the consecrated elements in the Lord's Supper that had become the body and blood of the Lord. This understanding of *sancta* goes back to the liturgies of the Eastern Church, where the communion is introduced with the call: "The holy things for the holy ones" [*Ta hagia tois hagiois*] (Cf. the proofs in Kattenbusch, 927ff.; Elert, 7ff., 171–81 [209–33]). Even though the personal understanding prevailed in the West, the old meaning was never completely forgotten. Hahn reports a text of the Creed in Old Norman French that gives our passage as *la communion des saintes choses* (holy things) and points to a late explanation of the Creed in German, found in Ulm, that has the same understanding of *sanctorum communio* (August Hahn, *Bibliothek der Symbole und Glaubensregeln der alten Kirche*, 3d ed. [Breslau, 1897], 83).

If this understanding is correct, then we would have the reference to the Sacrament of the Altar that has often been missed in the Creed. In any case it is implied in "communion of saints." For the *koinonia* that according to the New Testament exists among the saints, the believers, finds its strongest expression in the fellowship of those who, gathered around the Lord's table, receive His body and blood. "The cup of blessing which we bless, is it not a *koinonia tou haimatos tou Christou?* The bread which we break, is it not a *koinonia tou somatos tou Christou?*" It is not the action of the blessing and breaking that creates the fellowship but the content of the cup and the bread: "Because there is *one* bread, we who are many are *one* body, for we all partake of the *one* bread." The Greek word for "partake" is *metechomen*, which in the Vulgate is suitably translated with *participamus*, while *koinonia tou somatos tou Christou* is rendered *participatio corporis Domini*, and *koinonia* in verse 16 is rendered *communicatio*. The passage shows how closely the idea of the church as the body of Christ goes together with the concept of the sacramental body in the Lord's Supper. It has been justifiably supposed that Paul derived the idea, unique to him, of the church as the body of Christ from the Lord's Supper. In any case 1 Cor. 10:16f. shows that both meanings of *sanctorum communio* have their root in the expression *koinonia tou somatos tou Christou*. We shall have to examine later how the connection between the *corpus Christi mysticum* and the *corpus sacramentale* is to be determined.

If these observations are correct, then one will no longer be able to say that the understanding of the Lord's Supper is not one of the articles of the faith, as the Reformed have unrelentingly emphasized since Zwingli and Oecolampadius. Luther protested against this from the beginning, above all against the Strasburgers and especially Bucer. The latter always pleaded that both Luther's and Zwingli's understanding of the Lord's Supper had their rightful place in the church and should be tolerated. At the end of the Marburg Colloquy when Bucer with great and honest pathos exhorted both parties to have such tolerance, he got to hear the catastrophic words from Luther: "You have a different spirit." For Luther the doctrine of the Lord's Supper was binding dogma of the church, although he did not find it in the Creed. The Nicene Creed has no counterpart to *sanctorum communio*, but it does count Baptism as an article of faith: "I confess one Baptism for the remission of sins." What is to be believed and confessed is that Baptism gives the forgiveness of sins. That prompts the question whether perhaps the *remissionem peccatorum* in the Apostles' Creed refers to Baptism. It has often been understood in this way, e.g., in a formula in the Gallic church: "through Holy Baptism, the forgiveness of sins" [*per baptismum sanctum remissionem peccatorum*] (Hahn, 77). A creed in a manuscript of the eighth and ninth centuries reads, "remission of sins either through Baptism or through Penance" [*remissionem peccatorum sive per baptisma, sive per poenitentiam*] (Ibid., 99).

If one wants to judge these variants and the uncertainty that they reveal correctly, one must give thought to the fact that the "Third" Article has also remained a problem in the Eastern Church. At Nicaea they were content with the words "and in the Holy Spirit." The original Nicene Creed is really a binitarian creed. Only in the great debates over the meaning of the *homoousios* did Athanasius reach the conclusion that the *homoousios* of the Son is not intelligible without the *homoousios* of the Holy Spirit. At the synod of Alexandria in 362 an agreement was reached with the Cappadocians and their doctrine that Father, Son, and Holy Spirit are of the *same* essence (*homoios kat' ousian = homoousios*), not of *one* essence, which *homoousios* originally meant. It was the great concession made by Athanasius that *homoousios*

144

could be used in both ways, so that to this day the fine distinction exists between the Eastern Church and the West in that there one understands the Trinity as three-in-one [*Dreieinigkeit*], here as threefold [*Dreifaltigkeit*]. The result of all this lies before us in the Constantinopolitan Creed of 381, our "Nicene Creed." When the Council of Chalcedon accepted both texts as equally valid and recognized the synod of 381 as "ecumenical," the Creed was brought to completion. Yet even today it bears the character of something unfinished. A clear testimony of the Spirit as *homoousios* is lacking. Only the West has made up for the omission in the *filioque* of the Nicene Creed and in the Athanasian Creed. In a version of the Creed in the Old Irish Church we read: "Credo in Spiritum sanctum, deum omnipotentem, habentem substantiam cum patre et filio; sanctam ecclesiam, abremissa (*abremissa*, the Late Latin form for *abremissio*—cf. *missa* for *missio, collecta* for *collectio*—are found in other texts; note the sequence: the Sacrament of Baptism precedes the Eucharist) peccatorum, sanctorum communionem . . ." (Hahn, 84f.). It would lead us too far afield to quote here further examples from the Middle Ages of how *communio* and *remissio* are used with reference to the sacraments.

And where else but in the Third Article would there be room for a doctrine of the sacraments? It is not only the article of faith about the church that suggests this connection, but the whole article as such, for the Holy Spirit is pertinent to the "last things." He is indeed eternal God, from everlasting to everlasting. As such He shares in the creation and preservation of the world. To Him belongs the kingdom of nature as well as the kingdom of grace. He gives man life (Job 32:8), joy (Ps. 51:14), and wisdom and leads him on a level path (Ps. 143:10). The extraordinary powers of the warrior, the special gifts of the artist and of the ruler, and above all the gift of prophecy are His work. But above all, the fulfillment of the end time will bring a full measure of the Spirit for the whole people of God (Is. 44:3; Joel 3:1f.). Even the resurrection of the dead is the work of the Holy Spirit (Ezek. 37). With the resurrection of Christ as the firstborn from the dead, the resurrection of all the dead has begun (1 Cor. 15:20ff). Since then it is "the last hour" (1 John 2:18). Now at the end of the world the Son of God has indeed appeared (Heb. 1:2). Now the prophecy of Joel about the outpouring of the Spirit of God on the whole people of God is fulfilled. Now the Spirit no longer rests on individual people, on kings and prophets, but on the whole people of God in the whole church. One can speak of church in a general sense. Church was the whole people of God, all saints and believers from the beginning of the world. But the church of Christ, church in the full sense, has only existed since Easter and Pentecost.

And to the church belong the sacraments or—in order to avoid the ambiguous and so often misused word of ecclesiastical Latin—Baptism, absolution, and the Lord's Supper. Whatever one may want to call these things, whether one speaks of sacraments with the Latin church or of mysteries with the Eastern church, or whether one simply designates them collectively with a term like "means of grace," they all have one thing in common: they have an eschatological significance. In them the future redemption is already present. They denote not only a divine, heavenly reality, but they give us a share in it already now. The forgiveness of sins that we receive in Baptism and absolution is the anticipation of the acquittal of the Last Judgment. Our death and our resurrection to eternal life have already begun in our baptism (Rom. 6:3ff.). In Holy Communion Christ comes already now and gives us a share in the "messianic" banquet in heaven. It would have been better to understand the sacraments in this way as anticipation of the redemption of the end time instead of forcing them into the scheme of the sign theory. Augustine gave it its start. The commanding authority that he won in the West bequeathed this scheme to all Western churches. Thus, to give only one example, in *De civ. Dei* (10, 5) he calls the visible sacrifice the "sacrament or sacred sign of an invisible sacrifice" [*invisibilis sacrificii sacramentum id est sacrum signum*]. Since then Medieval theology understood sacrament as sign. In the first edition of his *Loci* even Melanchthon dealt with the sacraments under the heading "On Signs." Johann Gerhard is the first one for whom sacrament is no longer "in the category of signs" [*in genere signi*] (Thomas Aquinas, *Summa theologica* 3, q. 60, art. 1) but "in the category of action" [*in genere actionis*]. How dangerous the sign theory is may be seen from Augustine's thought that sacraments belong to the essence of every religion, the true as well as the false. How much distress of unnecessary controversy, how many misunderstandings and false teachings Christendom would have been spared if from the beginning one would have remained with what Holy Scripture teaches about Baptism, the Lord's Supper, and absolution instead of forcing these holy actions onto the Procrustean bed of Neoplatonic philosophy.

But in the fourth century there was no longer anyone able to do that. By then the Christian faith had risen into the upper levels of society, and so had gotten into the hands of those whose thought was shaped by late antiquity and by the heathen religiosity of a certain

146

philosophy. What Augustine says of his own conversion applies much the same to all the heathen who found the way to Christ: "Late have I loved you." Late, in many cases much too late, did they encounter the Gospel. Thus the great Alexandrians, also the Biblical theologian Origen, read it with late Greek eyes. It is a proof of the indestructible vitality of the divine Word that it even survived this.

The East did not develop a doctrine of the sacraments in the Augustinian-Western sense, if only because it did not know the word *sacrament*. Instead, the Eastern Church spoke of mysteries. That "sacrament" is the same thing as "mystery" was not completely forgotten in the West. Hugo of St. Victor still treated his dogmatics under the title "On the sacraments" and accordingly spoke of the sacrament of the Trinity, etc. The original difference in meaning between the Latin and the Greek word consists of the fact that *sacramentum* (from *sacer*, *sacrare*) looks at the action of man, at his praying, sacrifice, etc. Thus in later Latin *sacra* becomes the designation of the cultus. The governor of Carthage warned the martyrs of Scilli not to say anything evil *de sacris nostris*, that is, about the heathen cultus of the state (*Passio Sanctorum Scillitanorum* 5, Rudolf Knopf, *Märtyrer-Akten*, 3d ed., ed. G. Krüger [Giessen, 1929], 29f. [Hardy, *Faithful Witnesses*, 29]). *Sacramentum* appears originally to have meant "dedication," later also the oath of loyalty made by recruits, a meaning that also acquired significance for Zwingli. *Mysterium*, on the other hand, designates the divine secret and what this secret suggests and imparts. In medieval Latin the words are used without distinction—probably under the influence of the Vulgate—as in the usage of modern German Catholics one can still speak of receiving communion as receiving the holy mysteries. (The best discussion of the language problem is presented in the commentary of the German edition of Thomas: *Thomas von Aquin: Vollständige, ungekürzte deutsch-lateinische Ausgabe der Summa Theologica*, ed. Katholischer Akademikerverband [Salzburg and Leipzig, 1938], 30:385ff.)

We have commented on the problem of the language history because it casts a bright light on the history of Eucharistic teachings. The uncertainty of the theological doctrines is partially a result of the ambiguity of the terminology. In what matters here, however, there is no difference between East and West. In "sacrament" as in "mystery" the thing that is meant by the body of Christ is the same. It is the body that was born of His mother Mary, that died on the cross, that was buried, rose from the dead, ascended into heaven, and is sitting at the right hand of the Father (cf. the medieval hymn "O Lord, We Praise You" [*Gott sei gelobet und gebenedeiet*], whose thoughts ring through countless liturgies of East and West and that our church still sings in many languages with the second and third stanzas added by Luther).

This and nothing else is the church's dogma of the Lord's Supper. It stands behind the *sanctorum communionem*. There are two reasons why it is not expressed in an explicit article of faith. First, there was no church or heresy that had challenged it. And second, it is there in all liturgies of Christian antiquity. There probably have been individual theologians who have questioned or challenged it—what have theologians not challenged? But there is no liturgy of the Lord's Supper that did not contain it or take it for granted. The New Testament already contains the first traces of a Christian liturgy of the Lord's Supper. The four accounts of the institution already bear clear characteristics of liturgical texts. The oldest fragment, which goes back to the Aramaic beginning of the church, is the "Marana tha" (1 Cor. 16:22). It is contained, still in its original Aramaic form, in the *Didache* (10. 6), while it appears at the end of Revelation (22:20) in Greek translation: *erchou Kyrie Jesu* (Come, Lord Jesus). It could be that behind it stands a Jewish prayer for the coming of the Messiah. This is suggested by the custom that has been preserved among Jews and Christians in the East down to our own day of leaving a place "for the Messiah" empty at solemn meals. That in Paul as well as in John (cf. also *Did.* 10) the *charis* formula ("The grace of the Lord Jesus Christ . . .") follows, with which the Eucharist still begins in the Eastern Church today, could be an indication of such a connection.

In a much later form, behind which a Greek text could stand, such a prayer for the coming of Jesus to his congregation celebrating the Eucharist is found in the Mozarabic liturgy as an introduction to the Eucharistic prayer: "Come, come, Jesus, good Priest, in the midst of us, just as You were in the midst of Your disciples. Consecrate this offering so that we may eat the consecrated things by the hand of Your holy angel, O holy Lord and everlasting Redeemer." Then came the Words of Institution and the Postpridie, which begins with the words: "Lord Jesus Christ, consecrate this living sacrifice by the light of [Your] coming." The Lord is asked to be in the midst of His congregation, as He was once in the midst of His disciples at the Last Supper, and to do what He did then, namely, bless the gifts put before Him. This "blessing" (*hagiazein, sanctificare*) is clearly more than the blessing of ordinary food with the word of God and prayer according to 1 Tim. 4:5. Here *sanctificare* means what we would call "consecrate," as in the prayer to the *sanctificator* in the Roman Offertory. (It appears that the "Veni sanctificator, omnipotens aeterne Deus, et benedic hoc sacrificium . . ." is a remnant of an old epiclesis to the Spirit. Mozarabic and Gallic forms add "Spirit" or "Paraclete." "Sanctificator" is a title of the Holy Spirit.) As it is the Holy Spirit in the East who descends in the *epiphoitesis* on the offered gifts and makes them the body and blood of the Lord, so here Jesus is the consecrator. He does the same thing that He did at the institution: He speaks the Words of Institution and thereby consecrates the elements. That is the meaning of this old liturgy.

What makes the Sacrament a *sacramentum*, the mystery a *mysterion* is the fact that bread and wine become the body and blood of Christ. This and nothing else is the church's dogma of the Lord's Supper. The body and blood of the Lord are therefore the holy things [*sancta*] that are given to the communicants in order to make them the holy ones [*sancti*] and thereby bind them to the unity and fellowship of Christ's body. It is this thought of unity, which finds its perfect expression in Jesus' "high-priestly prayer" (John 17), that Hoskyns (Edwin Hoskyns, *The Fourth Gospel*, ed. F. N. Davey [London, 1947], 494ff.) rightly calls the "consecration prayer," in which Jesus consecrates Himself as the sacrifice and presents His disciples and the church of all ages to the Father: ". . . that they may all be one; even as Thou, Father, art in Me, and I in Thee, that they also may be in us. . . . I in them and Thou in Me, that they may become perfectly one . . ." [vv. 21, 23]. That is the perfect communion of saints, *sanctorum communio* in the dual meaning of the term.

As in John 17 the gaze of our praying Lord goes from this world to that of the future ("Father, I desire that they also, whom Thou hast given Me, may be with Me where I am, to behold My glory" [v. 24]), so the gaze upward to heaven belongs to the essence of the Eucharistic liturgy: *Elevatis oculis*. In most liturgies of the East and West the Son speaks the Words of Institution to God His almighty Father, just as in John 17:1 the upward look introduces the great prayer. That heaven and earth become one, as it were, in the Eucharist is one of the fundamental thoughts in the great liturgical chapter, Rev. 4. Erik Peterson has shown (*Das Buch von den Engeln: Stellung und Bedeutung der heiligen Engel im Kultus* [Leipzig, 1935], 323ff.) how the parallels there go right down to the details. Thus the Sanctus belongs to the temporal as well as the heavenly divine service. As Isaiah heard it in the vision of his call from the mouth of the seraphim surrounding the throne of

God, so it rings in its New Testament form in Rev. 4:8 (". . . who was and is and is to come"). The Sanctus is the angels' song of praise before the face of God "in never silent theologies" (thus the Greek liturgies). It is sung in the presence of God. Isaiah heard it in the temple at Jerusalem, the earthly dwelling place of the glory [*kabod*, *doxa*] of Yahweh (cf. Ps. 26:8). John heard it in the heavenly sanctuary on the Lord's Day while the church on earth was celebrating the Sacrament. Thus its worship and its Sanctus—and this applies to all the church's liturgies—encompass heaven and earth at the same time. The Trisagion now refers to the Triune God. The Lord whose praise is sung is He who was and who is and who is to come. According to John 12:41 it was indeed Christ's glory that the prophet saw. How inseparably faith in the almighty Father and the confession of the complete divinity of Christ are connected is shown by a passage like Rev. 5:13: "To Him who sits upon the throne and to the Lamb be blessing and honor and glory and might forever and ever!" to which 4:11 ("Worthy art Thou, our Lord and God") and 5:12 ("Worthy is the Lamb") may be compared.

The Sanctus of Isaiah 6 has appeared in the Christian divine service since the second Christian century. Perhaps the example of the synagogue somehow helped to bring that about. (The best discussion of the problem of the Jewish kiddush and the Trisagion in their relationship to the Sanctus of the church is offered by Josef Andreas Jungmann, S.J., *Missarum Sollemnia: Eine genetische Erklärung der römischen Messe*, 4th ed. [Freiburg, 1958], 2:166.) 1 Clement 34:6f. shows that it was used in the earliest Roman congregation in connection with Dan. 7:10:

> Ten thousand times ten thousand stood by Him and thousands of thousands served Him and cried out: "Holy, holy, holy is the Lord of hosts; the whole creation is full of His glory." And we also, gathered with one accord and devoutly, would cry to Him emphatically as with one mouth, that we may share in His great and glorious promises. For the Scripture says, "No eye has seen and no ear has heard and it has not entered man's heart what the Lord has prepared for those who wait for Him.

That this does not yet belong to the Eucharistic liturgy is shown by the fact that there is still no mention of an identification of the Lord with Jesus Christ, and no coming of the Lord is hinted at or prayed for. The gulf between heaven and earth still exists; the Hosanna, with which one greets Him who comes (Rev. 4:8), is still missing. The text of 1 Clement 34 is older than the great liturgical chapter, Rev. 4. From this we do not say, of course, that the earliest Roman church did not know the Real Presence. The letter of Ignatius to the Romans (7:3) contains one of the passages in which the bishop and martyr speaks of the flesh and blood of Christ, clearly reminiscent of John 6:53: "God's bread is what I desire, that is the flesh of Jesus Christ, who (is descended) from the seed of David; and for drink I desire His blood, which is an imperishable love." Without the realistic understanding, the constant Jewish-heathen accusation of ritual murder and cannibalism in the Christian Agape would probably also be incomprehensible.

It would lead us too far afield if we now wanted to go further into the history of the Eucharistic liturgy, in which the dogma of the Lord's Supper found its fullest expression. One must let oneself be influenced by the stirring prayers of the earthly church, the doxologies in which the church on earth becomes one with the church in heaven, and the awe-inspiring songs in so many languages in order to understand that in this Sacrament beats the heart of the church. Who can deny that this history is also the history of serious errors, even of occasional reversion to heathenism? Who can deny that again and again reforms were necessary, in which case a necessary reformation often degenerated into an unnecessary revolution? That happened not only in the 16th century, but even in our age when liturgical knowledge and art have blossomed as never before, as the Second Vatican Council carried out a reform of the Roman Mass, in which no less a man than St. Zwingli seems to have served as its godfather. But by and large the history of the Eucharistic liturgy was indeed the real heart of church history.

Today as always people ask, What does the church actually do? It prays. The praying church [*ecclesia orans*] is one of the constantly recurring themes of early Christian art. The church prays. Thus it was at the beginning. "All these with one accord devoted themselves to prayer" it says of the first believers after Christ's ascension (Acts 1:14). "They devoted themselves to the apostles' teaching and fellowship, to the breaking of bread and the prayers" it says of the church at Pentecost [2:42]. "Day by day, attending the temple together and breaking bread in their homes, they [were] . . . praising God and having favor with all the people" (v. 46).

They founded no mission society, organized no city mission, wrote no books on "dynamic evangelism." Instead, they celebrated the Sacrament and prayed continually. "And the Lord added to their number day by day those who were being saved" (2:47). And they went on praying. The leader of the apostles was imprisoned, "but earnest prayer

151

for him was made to God by the church" until the chains fell from his hands and the door of the prison swung open (12:5ff.). And so it went on.

What does the church do? What could it do in those last years of Jerusalem to solve the problem of Palestine, which the world's political powers have been trying in vain for centuries to do? What could the church do to stop the ruin of the Roman Empire and of the inestimable treasures of ancient culture? Instead of holding world conferences and having endless debates about the boundaries between church and culture, it went on praying without ceasing and sang the Te Deum on the debris of a world that was coming to an end. None of its prayers were in vain. They rose to heaven, even though they died away on earth. Only fragments have been preserved for us of what is left of the great liturgical books of the early church in the languages of the East. Only remnants have been preserved for us and are still in use in the small fragments of early Christendom that have survived the storm of Islam. The devotional literature of the last century pales before the fervor, the brilliance, the graphic power and beauty, the wonderful language of what is still available to us of these treasures in Greek and Latin. There is no human desire that would be too small or too great to find a stirring expression in these prayers. And always it is the altar before which these prayers are uttered; it is the *Maranatha*, the prayer for the coming of the Lord in the Sacrament as the anticipation of His Parousia; it is the Sanctus and the Eucharistic prayers with the Words of Institution of the Lord's Supper that are framed by these prayers. One can perhaps understand the belief in the Real Presence completely only when one has understood these prayers. Here God is present, the Triune God, the Father, the Son, and the Holy Spirit. Here all philosophy comes to an end. Here is what the early church calls "theology," the praise of God in the sense that John did it, to whom the church has given the nickname "theologian" [*theologos*]. This is no theology of the mysteries in the sense of heathen or semi-heathen mysticism. It is certainly not "the divine," a supernatural reality that we call divine and that is idle talk about our own divinity, that is presented here. Christ does not just appear as a man like an angel in the Old Testament or an avatar in Hinduism, like Krishna in the Bhagavad-Gita, a god in a human form, which He sets aside again in order to return to the divine world of the spirit. The risen and ascended One also remains the Incarnate, as He remains the Crucified. *Quod semel assumpsit, numquam deposuit—* what He once took up, He has never laid aside, as we theologians say.

This truth of the real incarnation finds its full expression in the fact that He gives us His true body and His true blood to eat and to drink, so that the *koinonia*, the fellowship that we have with Him in the Sacrament, is not merely something "purely spiritual." That the Lutheran Church has accepted this teaching of the Greek fathers emerges already from the references that the Apology to Article 10 of the Augsburg Confession quotes: "Therefore we must consider that Christ is in us, not only according to the habit which we understand as love, but also by a natural participation" (Ap X 3; cf. the whole text with the quotations from Theophylact and Cyril of Alexandria and further literature in *Bekenntnisschriften*, 248).

We cannot go into the liturgy as a source for the dogma of the Lord's Supper here any further. Only one point still needs a brief reflection: the reception of Communion. The prefatory prayers, the formula of distribution, and the response of the communicants are an unambiguous witness to the belief in the Real Presence. A few examples must suffice. In the Liturgy of St. Mark the priest says at the communion of the clergy: "Behold, it is consecrated and consummated and has become the body and blood of our Lord, God and Savior and what is holy [*das Heilige*] is given to the holy ones [*den Heiligen*]" (F. E. Brightman, *Liturgies Eastern and Western* [Oxford, 1896], 138–39). Since the earliest time the formula of distribution has rung out: *soma Christou*, "the body of Christ" (*Kirchenordnung Hippolyts*, Edgar Hennecke, Neutestamentliche Apokryphen, 2d ed. [Tübingen, 1924], 580. Hugo Duensing, *Der Aethiopische Text der Kirchenordnung des Hippolyt* [Göttingen, 1946], 61. *Apost. Const.* 8. 13), "the holy body of our Lord God and Savior," "the precious blood . . ." (The Liturgy of St. Mark, Brightman, 140). The formula finds itself under Eastern influence also in the Latin liturgies (witnessed by Augustine in Africa; in a very similar form in the Mozarabic liturgy as well as in Milan [Ambrose, *De mysteriis* 9. 54, M*PL* 16:424; *De sacramentis* 4. 5. 25, M*PL* 16:464; cf. Jungmann, 2:481 n. 102]). The response of the communicant is in every case "Amen." Ambrose explains the profound seriousness of this Amen: "That is true; I believe it" (Ambrose, *De sacramentis* 4. 5. 25, M*PL* 16:464). In many liturgies of the East the Words of Institution, which were still spoken aloud, were originally also confirmed by the Amen of the congregation. (Cf. Jungmann, 2:482. It also happened that the first part of the *verba testamenti* was spoken softly and only the second part was said aloud. Then the Amen followed the second part. See the fragment of an old southern Italian liturgy in C. A. Swainsow, *The Greek Liturgies* [Cambridge, 1884], 198.)

How much in earnest the church was about this Amen is shown by the Liturgy of Chrysostom in the confession that preceded the reception of Communion. It was spoken by every single one, by the priest before his own Communion, then by the deacon when he received Communion from the hands of the priest, then by all the communicants together. It begins with the words "I believe and I confess" and then contains the sentence: "I believe that this is truly Your spotless body and that this is truly Your precious blood." An especially strong confession of this sort is found in a text of the liturgy of the Coptic Jacobites, which Brightman gives in English translation:

> This is in truth the body and blood of Immanuel, our God, Amen. I believe, I believe, I believe and I confess to my last breath that this is the life-giving flesh, which Your only begotten Son, our Lord and our God and our Savior Jesus Christ, took from the lady of us all, the holy mother of God, and united with His divinity without mixture, without transformation, and without change. After He had made the good confession before Pontius Pilate, He gave it also for us of His own will on the holy tree of the cross. I believe truly that His divinity was not separated from His humanity for even one moment or instant. It was given for us that it might be for the salvation, for the forgiveness of sins, and for the eternal life of those who receive it. I believe that this is truly so. Amen.

Whereupon the deacon spoke: "Amen, amen, amen. I believe, I believe, I believe that it is truly so" (Brightman, 185).

This text from an old Monophysite church shows the anti-Chalcedonian position of this church. But for the dogma of the Lord's Supper that makes no difference. It is a most remarkable fact that the Orthodox, the Monophysites, and the Nestorians, with all their other dogmatic differences, show no difference in the doctrine of the Lord's Supper of their liturgies. The Mass as it was celebrated in the Nestorian churches of the Persian Empire is essentially the same as that of the Orthodox Church of the empire.

How seriously the East Syrian church—which had even spread all the way to South India and so for centuries in the Middle Ages was the most geographically extensive of all churches—took the consecration [*Heiligung*] of the elements is shown by a recently discovered instruction of Theodore of Mopsuestia, the greatest biblical scholar of the Syrian church: "When the priest distributes, he says, 'The body of Christ . . .';

therefore you say after him, 'Amen.' You then reverence after you have received the body with your hands . . . . With great and true love impress it on your eyes and kiss it and then offer your prayers to it as to our Lord Christ, who is near to you" (Hans Lietzmann, *Kleine Schriften*, vol. 3: *Studien zur Liturgie- und Symbolgeschichte und zur Wissenschaftsgeschichte*, ed. Kommission für Spätantike und Religionsgeschichte [Berlin, 1962], 84, no. 36f. This is the Syrian text published by Mingana in 1933, introduced, translated and edited by Lietzmann [*Sitzungsberichte der Berliner Akademie*, 1933; quotation from p. 13/925]).

That is therefore the dogma of the early church concerning the Lord's Supper: Bread and wine in the Lord's Supper after the consecration are the body and blood of the Lord. Nothing more? No, nothing more. There are, of course, questions for which we would like to have an answer. The one thing that the liturgy does say beyond this is that the presence is effected by the prayer for the Holy Spirit, who, by His coming down on the gifts, "changes" them into the body and blood of the Lord. The technical term of the Greek liturgy for this is *metaballein*, in Latin *mutare*. The elements thus become something that they were not before. The early church does not know a definition of this change analogous to the Roman transubstantiation. The Eastern Church first took over this doctrine as *metusiosis* in the Middle Ages under Roman influence, but it never did become binding dogma for the East. That was already impossible because a dogma could only be accepted by the whole church represented by an ecumenical council. None of the seven recognized councils had done this, if one disregards an indirect decision of the Second Council of Nicaea in 787. This synod rejected a decision of an iconoclastic synod of Constantinople (754), which declared that the only permissible images (icons) in the church were the consecrated elements. The Seventh Ecumenical Council thereby confirmed the explanation that had so often been given by the Greek fathers that the bread and the wine before the consecration could be regarded as types [*typos*, *antitypos*] of the body and blood, but not the consecrated elements, which had actually become the body and blood of the Lord. (Thus John of Damascus says in *De fide orthodoxa* 4. 13: "When some call the bread and the wine images of the body and blood of the Lord, as did Basil Theophorus, they did not believe this to be the case after the consecration but before the consecration. They spoke this way of the offering [what the congregation had brought to the altar]." Cf. Cyril of Jerusalem, *Mystagogica Cathechesis* 1. 7, 5. 6, *MPG* 33:1071. *Antitypa* is even used in the epiclesis of the Liturgy of Basil. The use of the word does not detract from the realism.)

How this miracle is then conceivable is something the church fathers wondered about just as theologians of all times have done. They set up theological theories about it, but the doctrine of the church remained uninfluenced by them. It is a serious failure of our textbooks on the history of dogma that they scarcely make a distinction between dogma and theological opinion, between the doctrine that the church confesses *magno consensu* and the theological theories that men, more or less pious and more or less learned theologians, set up.

Since Justin and his pupil Irenaeus the miracle of the incarnation has been used for the explanation: As the Word took on flesh, so the bread and wine receive a divine quality and become bearers of the body and blood of Christ through the Eucharistic prayer (Justin, *Apologie* 1. 66, M*PG* 6:427–30) or through the epiclesis (Irenaeus, *Adversus haereses* 4. 18. 5, M*PG* 7/1:1027ff.). It is impossible to understand the thoughts that are clothed in the language and thought world of the mysteries individually as "realistic" or "symbolic" in the modern sense. Wherever Neoplatonism has determined the theological thinking, the symbolic-spiritual side may come to the fore, but we must guard against applying the categories of later centuries to Christian antiquity and its theology. It should also give one pause that the later christological schools all take the same liturgy for granted. The great Antiochene, Theodore of Mopsuestia, compares what happened at the coming of the Holy Spirit with Christ's resurrection; the one is as real for him as the other. Just as there were various views in the early church regarding the baptism of children, so there were also various theological opinions about the understanding of the Eucharist. But just as the baptismal liturgy was the same, whether an adult or a child was baptized (the only exception was the Listurian church, which had a special liturgy for the baptism of children) and no one denied the validity of infant baptism, so all received the Eucharist with the same formula of distribution, "The body of Christ . . . the blood of Christ," and they all thereupon with the church of all ages spoke the Amen of faith.

Credo sanctorum communionem. Sancta sanctis. Ta hagia tois hagiois. The whole secret of the Biblical concept of koinonia is contained in these sentences. They bear witness to the fact that the church and the Lord's Supper, church fellowship and altar fellowship, belong inseparably together. Around the Lord's table His congregation gathers in order to become one with Him by receiving His true body and blood.

156

Church fellowship is not founded "on the assembling of born-again individuals in orderly interaction and cooperation" as Pietism thinks and as the "Moravian of a higher order," Schleiermacher, formulated it (*The Christian Faith*, 2:215). It is also not based on the association of philosophical convictions, as the Enlightenment of all ages has supposed.

As the body of Christ, it is a fellowship unique [*sui generis*], which cannot be made intelligible either in psychological or in sociological categories. Even in terms of the history of religions it is without parallels. The "congregation" with which the convert to Buddhism takes "refuge" is nothing like the body of Buddha. Even the sacrifices, cultic meals, and other rites of ancient heathenism, whose similarities to the Christian sacraments were not first noticed by modern historians of religion but already by the ancient enemies of the church, explain basically nothing else than the truth that "every dogma is as old as the world."

Church fellowship is also not what modern "ecumenical" theology—also in those churches that ought to know better—reads into John 17 and Ephesians 4 in order then to proclaim it as the saving Gospel for our time, namely, the wonderful organization that will arise tomorrow when the hundreds of Christian churches and sects that belong to the World Council of Churches embrace with "this kiss for all the world." This kiss would certainly not be "the holy kiss" with which the church of the New Testament began the celebration of the Eucharist but another kind of kiss, of which the New Testament also tells us.

It would be a puzzle how so many sincere Christians of all confessions could fall victim to such an error if we knew nothing of the serious and contagious disease of chiliasm. The unity of the church of which our Lord speaks in John 17, a unity for which there are no earthly parallels and which therefore is definable in no theology, is the rightly understood, i.e., according to the analogy of faith, *ut omnes unum sunt:* "That they may all be one, even as Thou, Father, art in Me, and I in Thee, that they also may be in us, so that the world may believe that Thou hast sent Me" (v. 21). The "world" is naturally not just the sum of all people who would be living on the earth at the time of the final fulfillment of this wish. It means either the whole number of those whom the Father has given to the Son (17:2, 6) or it means the world at its end. According to the New Testament it can not be said that there will ever come a time in the course of world history when unbelief and therewith sin has disappeared from the world of men. Until then the *una sancta* and the *sanctorum communio* remain articles of faith.

WE CONFESS

THE CHURCH

Contents

Translator's Preface

We begin and end with Sasse preaching. His preaching and theology are all of one piece, and he was no trimmer. There are things of first importance and others that are not, and Sasse is of enormous help in telling the difference. "Each sermon is more important than all those sessions which spend their time discussing big church resolutions regarding the Bonn constitution, the atom bomb, or Goethe's 200th birthday."

Dr. Sasse was a churchman, not a statesman. He did not market his message according to the mood of the moment or yesterday's social survey. He knew and loved the church and her history too profoundly. We do not invent or direct the church. We are to preach what we have been given to preach, "the forgiveness and justification of sinners for Christ's sake."

For His church Christ prays. The church can no more be destroyed than Christ can be destroyed. With this confidence it is possible to face squarely what would destroy the church. Most damaging are the attacks from within, the subversion of the Gospel to the uses of power to make of the church a political force, ruled by the decisions of men. Such decisions may claim episcopal, synodical, papal, presbyterial, or congregational authority. No claim holds except it be of Christ, the Holy Spirit, and His Scripture.

Two sermons and five letters are what we have in this book, with their matter rather than their dates determining the sequence. The dates, however, are important, and with them Sasse's specific message. The first sermon was preached to a small congregation celebrating the anniversary of the dedication of its church. It was during the war, when the comforting message that "Jesus prays for His church" was particularly needed.

The letter on the Holy Spirit was written after Sasse had been in Adelaide 11 years. His grasp of the intimate connection between the doctrine and the history of the church, which had thrilled the packed lecture hall in Erlangen, moved deeper to the intimate connection between the believer and Christ, His Spirit, and His church. Sasse grieved for the loss of students, so gifted, so promising, killed in the war. With faith's "nevertheless" he carries forward the work of one of the most brilliant of his students, "meaninglessly" killed in the war. He tells us the name, and speaks of those too whose names are known only to the Lord, " . . . somewhere in China." God the Holy Spirit "brings the uncompleted work to completion."

Dr. Sasse was above all a confessional theologian, and therefore confessing the faith was of the greatest importance for him. So it is fitting that we hear what he has to say about the relevance of the Augsburg Confession's famous Article VII ("The Church") for the worldwide Lutheran Church of today.

In the 19th century the great Lutheran churchmen Walther and Löhe were unable to agree on the doctrine of church and ministry and therefore sadly went their separate ways. In Australia Dr. Sasse was able to bring together the two streams of Lutheranism which might be characterized as emanating from these two theological giants. His letter on "Ministry and Congregation" is an effort toward the same conjunction in America. Although we know the subsequent sad history, this does not rob the letter of its importance.

When our confidence does not live from what has been given to the church, then we are tempted to add things to make it more sure. Sasse gives the history of the notion of apostolic succession, and its roots in men's efforts to guarantee the church. He recalls us to the grounds of confidence which alone finally hold.

In light of this the final letter, "Last Things: Church and Antichrist," speaks for itself. There are facts to be faced, documented, and honestly dealt with "in these last days." There are confessional tasks that may not be shirked.

Sasse was a confessor involved. In 1927 he played a leading role in the World Conference on Faith and Order in Lausanne. When the Nazis kept his passport, he could no longer carry forward this involvement. He was a leading theologian involved in working toward Barmen. But in the night of May 30, 1934, he left Barmen when he was denied the opportunity to speak on the morrow. Those who were arranging things did not wish to hear him further (*Die lutherischen Kirchen und die Bekenntnissynode von Barmen*, ed. W. Hauschild, p. 98).

After the war, finding the confessional situation of Lutheranism in Germany most deplorable, He left Erlangen and eventually accepted a call to Immanuel Seminary in Adelaide, Australia, where he continued to write his "Letters to Lutheran Pastors." There are points in them where pain, anger, and passion burn through. Then it is well to remember that only as sinners forgiven for Christ's sake can any of us carry on our work. There is something to trouble everyone in Sasse. This can be avoided by simply ignoring him, or by listening only when he agrees with us. To listen when he says unwelcome things may prove most fruitful. This is not to say that he is always right, as neither are any of us. Rather it points to his helpfulness in drawing us into always deeper probing, testing, and appropriation of Christian truth.

Sasse's last words to us in this volume are from the pulpit. "When the day comes when this war is over . . . " In a situation in which there appeared to be nothing but doom, he preached about the ongoing true life of the church. He proclaimed: "Nations pass away, but the church continues . . . because the future of the church is the future of Jesus Christ. Amen."

JESUS INTERCEDES FOR HIS CHURCH

A sermon on John 17:6–23 during the war (1941/42)
for the anniversary of the dedication
of a church and a meeting
of the Martin Luther Bund

How inexhaustible the abundance of Holy Scripture! There are texts there that a man could spend his whole life studying without exhausting their depths. Yes, the labor of many centuries on the part of Christendom is required to understand such passages fully. For 1,500 years the church read the epistles of the apostle Paul to the Romans and the Galatians. Faithful Christians were nourished by them in the church service. They were explored by profoundly learned men, from the ancient church fathers to the masters of medieval theology. Then after 15 centuries the hour came when the depths of their doctrine of justification were laid bare in the Reformation.

Perhaps something similar may happen with the great texts of the Bible which speaks of the divine mystery of the church: the Epistle of Paul to the Ephesians, and this great 17th chapter of the Gospel According to St. John. August Vilmar, the great Lutheran theologian of the 19th century, repeatedly expressed the hope that out of the severe struggles of the church, out of what Christians were living through in his day, there might grow a full understanding of what the New Testament says of the church. If this could be learned, he said, such a new understanding of the Third Article might be as great a turning point in the history of the church as was the new understanding of the Second Article in the Reformation.

Our celebration today of the anniversary of the dedication of this church gives us the opportunity to ponder and probe what our text says of the mystery of the church. This is given us as we stand engaged in a great struggle for the sake of the church. Your house of God has stood here now for more than 30 years. Compared with the age of other churches that is a very short time.

11

Our text speaks to us about the miracle of the church's preservation. The preservation of the church is no smaller miracle than its founding, just as the preservation of the world is no smaller miracle than its creation. It is by no means self-evident that the church should continue. In whole regions of the world it has almost or completely gone under. Many a people among whom there was a flourishing church has rejected this church. There is no sadder sight than the ruins of old churches, such as may be seen in parts of Asia which have sunk back into heathenism.

No lesser man than Martin Luther reckoned with the possibility that the church might one day be taken from our people. "God's Word and grace is like rain which falls on one place and then goes on to fall on another, not returning again to where it once was before." He pointed to those lands which once were a part of ancient Christendom but which sank back again into heathenism, and he spoke the warning: "You Germans must not imagine that it will be yours forever. Unthankfulness and scorn of it will not let it remain."

No, it is not self-evident that the church will remain where it once has been. To the whole church of Christ the promise is indeed given that the gates of hell shall not prevail against it, but this is not something that any congregation or particular church can say of itself. Just as an individual Christian may fall away, so also whole congregations, whole parts of the church, may fall away. We can read of this already in the New Testament.

No, it is not self-evident that the church will abide. That was known also by Him who speaks in our Gospel: Jesus Christ, the Lord, in the night in which He was betrayed. What He said to His disciples in that farewell night He now says once more. But He does not say it to men, but to His heavenly Father.

The final care that moves Him is His care for His church. His work on earth is completed. "I have manifested Thy name to the men whom Thou gavest Me out of the world." " I have given them the words which Thou gavest Me." "I have given them Thy Word." And this Word was not without fruit. "They have kept Thy Word." "They have received [it] and know in truth that I came from Thee; and they have believed that Thou didst send Me." And this faith held. "While I was with them I kept them in Thy name. . . . I have guarded them, and none of them is lost but the son of perdition, that the Scripture might be fulfilled." "While I was with them"—as long as that was the case there was no need to worry about the future of the Gospel. But now that He is coming to the Father, Jesus says: "I am no more in the world, but they are in the world."

Now, however, they would no longer hear His lovely voice or look into His eyes. What would become of them? Never has such a task been given to men as was given to the apostles by their Lord at His farewell. To this little flock, the Eleven, a responsibility was given such as was never laid on any others. "As Thou didst send Me into the world, so I have sent them into the world."

Should they fail, what would then become of the Gospel? And were they really the men who were equal to this task? "Then all the disciples forsook Him and fled"; so we are told about their behavior that same night (Matt. 26:56). "I do not know the man"; so said Simon Peter (Matt. 26:72), the same Peter who made the first confession and whom Jesus therefore called blessed (Matt. 16:17). To such men as these the great work is entrusted which Jesus leaves behind: "As the Father has sent Me, even so I send you" (John 20:21).

Yes, it is these feeble men whom He sends, men who do not have any more faith than any of us. They are men who do not possess the natural gifts that would be necessary to win the hearts of humankind. And He sends them into a world that does not want to know anything about them or their message. "And now I am no more in the world, but they are in the world." "And the world has hated them because they are not of the world, even as I am not of the world." That world will not take long to finish them off! If the world can nail Him to the cross, won't it be able to dispose of this handful of men?

Jesus sees that all quite clearly. How could He have any illusions about His disciples—especially in that night? In that situation He does one thing: *He prays for them.* "I am praying for them; I am not praying for the world but for those whom Thou hast given Me, for they are Thine." "Holy Father, keep them in Thy name, which Thou hast given Me, that they may be one, even as We are one." "I do not pray that Thou shouldst take them out of the world, but that Thou shouldst keep them from the evil one." "Sanctify them in the truth . . . that they also may be consecrated in truth."

Jesus prays for them. He moves from farewell discourse with His disciples to farewell prayer. Now He speaks no more to men but to His heavenly Father. Here in this great chapter of the Gospel According to John we have the greatest of all prayers. Here it is not a mere man who is praying—no human being can pray it after Him. Here prays the eternal Son. All other prayers are prayers of men to God, prayers of creatures to their Creator. But this one prayer is prayed by the eternal Son to the Father. He, the High Priest, utters it for His church. He who is on the way to Golgotha, He speaks it: "For their sake I consecrate Myself, that they also may be consecrated in truth." And He does not think only of His apostles. Rather He looks further than the farthest times of the church's history, over all generations, over all the centuries to the end of the world: "I do not pray for these alone, but also for those who will believe in Me through their word" [NKJV]. He prays for the preservation of the church. And this prayer is heard. That is the secret of the church's preservation.

We will understand this better if we ponder what is the meaning of intercession in our lives—or what it should be. There is nothing that so holds and carries our children as the intercession we make for them. There also is nothing that more deeply binds parents and children together. There would be far less anxiety about our children if we would lay all our cares for them on the father heart of God. There is nothing that so binds husband and wife together, that so helps them bear each other's burdens, as the intercessions they make for each other.

There also is nothing in the church which so binds its members together as interceding for one another. When for years on end the apostle Paul sat in prison while his mission congregations were left without protection, helpless in the world, there yet remained this one thing that he could do for them: "For this reason I bow my knees before the Father, from whom every family in heaven and on earth is named . . ." (Eph. 3:14–15). This prayer broke through the walls of the prison, and bound the apostle and his congregations together.

Therefore we make intercession in the church also for our people and government, for all who are in need and temptation, for the sick and the dying, for the church of God throughout the whole world. We remember our brethren in the diaspora. We think of the Lutheran Church of Brazil, which has such close ties with the Martin Luther Bund and our church here in Franconia. We recall our German brothers in Australia, who have remained such faithful friends of the old homeland because the Lutheran Church has preserved the German language for them through the Bible, the Catechism, the hymnbook, and the liturgy. We think of those isolated Germans who today bow their knees with us in villages in the Kirgiz Republic [of the Soviet Union] or in the forests of Siberia. We remember all brethren in the faith, including the missionaries in prison. Today, when we are separated from them by more

14

than land and ocean, and can no longer give them any external help, we know what is the power of intercession.

If that is so of the intercession which we human beings make for one another here on earth, how much more powerful is that intercession which the Head of the church makes for His members. His prayer will truly and certainly be heard. He prays for us. "I have prayed for you that your faith may not fail" (Luke 22:32). That prayer rescued Peter.

"I do not pray for these alone, but also for those who will believe in Me through their word" [NKJV]. In this prayer we too are included, you and I and every Christian who sets his entire confidence on Jesus Christ as his Savior.

Christ prays for us, and His prayer is heard. This comes to expression in the liturgy when, before the Collect, we chant: "The Lord be with you"—and then the response, "And with your spirit." [We are saying:] "May the Lord be with you as you now pray—and may He be with your spirit as you now speak out our prayer." Jesus Christ is praying along with us. The church prays together with her Head. And this prayer is heard "through Jesus Christ, our Lord."

He prays for us. He prays for His church on earth. This is the miracle of the church's preservation. Hear Luther's confession of this fact:

> It is not we who are able to maintain the church, nor could those before us, nor will those who come after us be able to do so. It is only He who says, "Lo, I am with you always, to the close of the age." It has always been He, is He now, and will always be He. As it is written in Heb. 13, "Jesus Christ is the same yesterday and today and forever." And Rev. 1, " . . . who is and who was and who is to come." He is the Man. That is His name, which belongs to no other man, nor may it be given to any other.

Oh, if one could only believe this! Oh, if we would but learn something from this great and childlike trust of Luther's! How much less would cares for the church oppress us if we would only cast all our cares upon Him who has taken the care of the church upon Himself. How differently we would then do what He bids us do for the sake of the preservation of His church.

Only when we have this great faith in Him who wondrously preserves His church, only then do we know how the church is sustained. How is the church on earth sustained? "Sanctify them in the truth; Thy Word is truth." "Through the Word the church was brought into existence; through the Word the church is preserved." So Luther once said.

As the Word founded the church—"I have given them Thy Word"—so the Word of Christ preserves the church. Not the most brilliant of human organizing, not the most splendid liturgy, not the wisest of men, not the most splendid church buildings preserve the church. It is done by the Word alone, by the plain Word of the Gospel as the saving message of the forgiveness of sins. "Fruitful ethics can be found also in Confucianism, a resplendent hierarchy also with the Dalai Lama, scientific theology also in the synagogue, a battle against alcohol also among the Turks, and a youth movement also in Moscow—forgiveness of sins alone with Jesus Christ."

The Word of forgiveness which only Jesus Christ can speak, because it is He who has borne the sin of the world, the Word of forgiveness His church is to speak as it follows Him—that is the Gospel. And it is this Word that creates the unity of the church, the unity of all the children of God. "Where this article remains pure and active, there the church remains in fine unity. Where this article does not remain pure there is no defense against a single error or any Enthusiasm." Therefore take care that this may be the case!

In our care for those in the diaspora we have learned that everything depends on the Word, on the pure proclamation of the Gospel. That is the greatest service we can perform for the preservation of the church. Father Löhe was much mocked and resisted in his day when he began his great work for those in the diaspora by training messengers in the pure doctrine. The congregations he founded in America have to this day remained watchmen of the Gospel. In this way we also belong to the great communion of the church of all ages, along with the fathers who made confession before us, along with the teachers of the church, along with the apostles—" . . . that they may be one . . . I in them and Thou in Me."

To know this is to know something of the church. The time will come when the Third Article of the Creed will be understood. The question of the church will be one of the great questions of the future. What a blessed secret this article of faith contains, what a miracle God's church is—all this can only be known by those who themselves are among those for whom Jesus Christ prayed: "Holy Father, keep them in Thy name, which Thou hast given Me. . . . Sanctify them in the truth; Thy Word is truth."

And so we then pray to Him: "Lord Jesus Christ, have mercy on us. You are the Deliverer of Your church, the Savior of Your body. Amen."

16

ON THE DOCTRINE OF THE HOLY SPIRIT

Letters to Lutheran Pastors, No. 51
July/August 1960

This letter should have arrived for Pentecost—but then in the church it is always Pentecost, or should be. Every Sunday is not only an Easter day but also a little Pentecost. So perhaps my greetings to you are not too late. The doctrine of the Holy Spirit, which will engage us here, lies behind all the questions and all the needs of the church and the holy ministry which concern us day by day. As we ponder several dogmatic and historical questions in regard to this doctrine, may it be of help to us all.

1

"The true doctrine of the Holy Spirit has no place to call its own in the church and congregation. It appears to have become a foreign body. This state of affairs must be recognized quite objectively." With these words Otto Henning Nebe began his thesis (*Habilitationsschrift*) for the University of Erlangen, *Deus Spiritus Sanctus* (*Beiträge zur Förderung christlicher Theologie, Band* 40, *Heft* 5, 1939). He was one of our most promising young doctors of theology but was killed in the war. His small but thoughtful document has not received the attention it deserves. Even so, we should not ignore the warning given with these opening words of his.

If indeed the true doctrine of the Holy Spirit has lost its place (*Heimatrecht*) in church and congregation, then it cannot be long before the reality of the Holy Spirit is also lost to us, just as Christ ceases to be present when He is not truly taught, when His Gospel and sacraments are falsified. Here may lie the explanation of the decline of those means in the church which are to be the specific locations of the activity of the Holy Spirit.

Think of the needs of the office of the ministry! How can we explain the shortage of pastors in so many churches of every confession? Why

17

do those young men who in other times would have become pastors now turn to secular callings? Why do pastors now find that their office has become a problem—and not only in Germany, where everything becomes a problem? How are we to explain the high number of nervous breakdowns among Protestant pastors that are reported to be happening in America? How are we to explain the increasing number of women pastors in the Protestant world—and the theological incompetence, even among Lutherans, in giving an answer to this comparatively simple problem, when every confirmand knows the answer?

We are all aware of the demands and pressures laid on our office. In churches nowadays the pastor has to do so many things which do not really belong to his office, that he scarcely has time for his real office, "the ministry of teaching the Gospel and administering the sacraments" [Augsburg Confession V; Tappert, p. 31]. In Germany I knew superintendents and deans who were so frazzled by the work of the week that only on Saturday evening did they finally come to sermon preparation.

We hear something of this already in an article by August Vilmar in 1849, entitled "Power over the Spirits." He spoke of where all this would lead, all this external business, all the meetings of church groups, all this having to get the money together. Deacons are to have the responsibility for such things. They are not to draw a pastor away from what he is called to do as a pastor. Vilmar preached to deaf ears, this great pastor of pastors, for whom a consistorialized church had no place. The process of the secularization of the holy ministry was not halted by all the rethinking of the nature of the office after World War I, nor even by the Church Struggle (*Kirchenkampf*) in Germany. In pondering all this we may catch a glimpse of what a church still knows of the activity of the Holy Spirit.

What is happening with the holy ministry shows what is wrong with us. We seek the Holy Spirit where He is not to be found. We no longer find Him where He would be found. We speak of Him, but our faith in Him, in His deity, in His divine Person, has grown weak, or has even been lost. If things continue to go on like this, the outcome for our church is only too clear.

2

We modern Christians seek the Holy Spirit where He is not to be found. In doing this we are, however, certainly not the first. This is a danger which has always been there since the days of the apostles, and ever and again there have been Christians, indeed whole churches, that have fallen victim to it. In the second century there was Montanism. The question which then deeply troubled Christianity and divided it was whether it was actually the Holy Spirit, the Paraclete, who was revealing Himself in the new prophesyings. We may recall the spiritualistic Franciscans in the Middle Ages, the Enthusiast movements of the *Schwärmer* against whom Luther had to battle, and in our day the various Pentecostal movements. Earnest Christians have often felt compelled to admit what leading men in the Fellowship Movement, who once acknowledged the Pentecostal Movement's speaking in tongues, which had gone on since 1905, came to recognize: It was not the Holy Spirit.

We are now not speaking of this danger, but of the frivolous manner in which we in the modern world speak of the experience of the Holy Spirit. The roots of this are in the English Enthusiasm of the 17th century and in the Pietism and Methodism of the 18th century. When at the Berlin *Kirchentag* of 1853 in a profoundly untruthful declaration the participants declared themselves loyal to the Augsburg Confession "with heart and mouth," but also with the reservation that the unity of the confession they were making was not to be injured by the differing views on its Article X that were held by the Lutherans, the Reformed, and those from Union churches, this uniting of Evangelical Germany was regarded by many as a work of the Holy Spirit. It has become almost customary at great church gatherings, and also at the big ecumenical gatherings, to perceive and solemnly proclaim the blowing of the Holy Spirit. A sort of new Pentecost is experienced in the singing of great hymns in many languages. We need to consider the mass psychology which is going on in such big gatherings, especially at a time when the world's techniques for manipulating a crowd and its modern communications media are penetrating the church.

What is said here is not spoken against getting things organized as such, nor against the way news can now go round the world, nor against the means of communication provided by modern technology. Of such things Vilmar already observed that they are there not only for the children of this world, but are also to be brought into the service of Christ's church. But we are asking whether we are always aware that there can be mass psychoses also in the church. When the church does take for its use the techniques which can control or lead a crowd of people, then there is the most urgent need to pray for that great gift of grace, the discerning and the testing of the spirits.

We seek the Holy Spirit where He is not to be found when we take it as self-evident that the way our church is developing is altogether due to the guidance of the Holy Spirit. This is not only Rome's great error; it is an error found also in other churches. The "Message" of the Lambeth Conference of 1958 begins with the statement that the bishops there assembled wished to share with all members of their church in the world the experience "which has come to us, in a fresh and wonderful way, by the power of God's Spirit among us." "We ourselves have been knit together by the Holy Spirit in mutual understanding and trust." "Because we ourselves have been thus drawn together, God has given us a message of reconciliation for the Church and the world." This message then begins with the statement: "A divided Church cannot heal the wounds of a divided world." Then God is thanked "that in Asia and Africa, as well as in Britain and America, Christian Churches are actively moving towards a greater measure of unity" (*Report*, pp. 1, 29). There is then nothing to wonder at in the answer given at a press conference by an Anglican bishop. He was asked why the Lambeth Conference, which had previously rejected birth control, had now approved it. He answered that it was by the guidance of the Holy Spirit! At Lambeth, then, the Holy Spirit is said to have confirmed the Anglican understanding of the church as well as the unionism in India and America. What has happened here to the Biblical: "It has seemed good to the Holy Spirit and to us . . ." [Acts 15:28]? The same miracle is said to have occurred at the Barmen synod in 1934, where Karl Barth's *Bekenntnisunion* was approved, and the Lutherans, the Reformed, and those of the Union churches declared that "they sought a common message for the need and temptation of the church in our day. With gratitude to God they surely believe that a common message has been put into their mouth" (Schmidt II, 92; Cochrane, *The Church's Confession Under Hitler*, p. 237). What has happened here to "Behold, I have put My words in your mouth" (Jer. 1:9; cf. Deut. 18:18)?

What Luther has to say about all this may be found in the Smalcald Articles:

> All this is the old devil and the old serpent who made enthusiasts of Adam and Eve. He led them from the external Word of God to spiritualizing and to their own imaginations, and he did this through other external words. . . . In short, enthusiasm clings to Adam and his descendants from the beginning to the end of the world. It is a poison

implanted and inoculated in man by the old dragon, and it is the source, strength, and power of all heresy, including that of the papacy and Mohammedanism" (SA III, VIII, 5 and 9).

"It is the source, strength, and power . . . of the papacy." It is a very serious question, if we really have to choose among the Enthusiasms which go on among Christians, whether the Roman one is not perhaps the lesser evil. Rome's decisions are at least based on thorough and learned consultation, and they let the ancient doctrine stand.

3

We seek the Holy Spirit where He is not to be found when we take it as self-evident that He has to come with every sermon we preach. God's Word indeed has the promise: "It shall not return to Me empty" [Is. 55:11]. But we must always ask ourselves whether what we preach is in fact God's Word. When the sermon is a true exposition of the Scriptural text, then, in spite of all our weakness, God's Word is preached. But how many sermons are preached, also in Lutheran churches, where the Gospel is not taught fully and clearly!

We seem to suppose that it is enough to train young men for four or five years. They pass their examinations more or less adequately. They are ordained and sent to some field of service. They may gather some people who do not belong to any church, but who are interested in religious questions. These then form a congregation that receives the rights of a Lutheran congregation without understanding the Catechism or the Augsburg Confession. The same thing happens in the European churches. Young candidates equipped with Bultmann's theology are sent to the sprawling suburbs of our large cities. Or they are sent into the country, where the farmers and laborers may be fortunate enough not to understand what the young man believes, or does not believe. Do we really suppose the Holy Spirit will all by Himself build a church and congregation there? He can of course make use of such instruments too. "The Word of God is not fettered" (2 Tim. 2:9), and many a pastor has been brought to the Gospel by his congregation. Many who did not understand the Gospel and the sacraments have learned in the desert of their own theological existence what the university did not teach them. But that such things happen in the mercy of God does not relieve us of having to be quite clear about what kind of a proclamation it is to which the promise has been given that through it the Holy Spirit comes to the souls of men.

Finally, we seek the Holy Spirit where He is not to be found, when we overlook the fact that while the Holy Spirit is indeed given in correct preaching, He does not always create faith, but only "where and when it pleases God." This is the teaching of the Augsburg Confession (Art. V, 2 [Tappert, p. 31]). It is not changed by the fact that under Barth's influence the "where and when it pleases God" has been misunderstood as though it meant that the Holy Spirit has not bound Himself to the Word and that God's freedom consisted in this, that He makes the preached or written Word into the Word of God for one person but not for another. [Thence the view that it *is* not the Word of God, but may *become* the Word of God.] Against this we must hold firmly that the external Word of Scripture and correct Scriptural preaching always brings the Holy Spirit. But we must never forget the other truth, that the Holy Spirit does not always work faith. This is *the freedom of God the Holy Spirit* which Article V of the Augsburg Confession teaches.

The doctrine of grace of the Reformers is a measurement of how far modern Protestantism has fallen away from the Reformation. Whatever their differences were in the doctrine of election, Luther and Calvin were agreed that it simply does not lie within the power of man to accept the grace of God or not. Already in the 17th century "by grace alone" (*sola gratia*) began losing ground among the Reformed (Arminianism) and Lutherans (election *intuitu fidei*, "in view of a person's believing later on"). How deeply this new form of synergism had penetrated the Lutheranism of the 19th century is evidenced by the failure to recognize even today what was at stake in the controversy over the election of grace, in which the Missouri Synod in America contended for *sola gratia* as confessed by Luther. The optimism and synergism prevalent in America have made such inroads into American Lutheranism that the Augsburg Confession's "where and when it pleases God" has for practical purposes been given up.

Evidence of this is the uncritical taking over of ideas and programs of stewardship and evangelism from such groups as the Seventh Day Adventists. The pastor schools his people so that with the right kind of pious talk they will then be equipped to win other people for the church. In place of the office of preaching reconciliation comes the training of "soul winners," teaching them just the right way of talking with people, to make maximum use of the techniques of psychological manipulation. The system admittedly derives from the methods of American business. Thus people are to be brought into the church, made to feel at home there, be led to make a decision, and then all together they are to carry on their building of the kingdom of God. What the Word of God is no longer trusted to do is achieved with the psychological techniques of such modern evangelization. There is of course talk of the Holy Spirit, but one no longer knows who He is. It seems He can be measured and quantified. Such evangelism produces results. Thousands are won for church membership. On the other hand we may recall the failure of the Biblical prophets and of our Lord Himself. When one considers the latter, one begins to understand the full earnestness of the "where and when it pleases God." Jesus said: " . . . so that they may indeed see but not perceive, and may indeed hear but not understand; lest they should turn again, and be forgiven" (Mark 4:12; cf. Is. 6:9–10). Whoever is not awed by what is hidden deep in these words will never truly know the Holy Spirit.

<h1 style="text-align:center">4</h1>

We modern people no longer find the Holy Spirit where He would be sought. This has been true to a certain extent throughout the church's history, ever since the days when it was necessary for Paul to teach the church in Corinth that the quiet workings of the Holy Spirit are His greatest ones. But it is especially true of us, who no longer understand *the bond of the Holy Spirit with the external means of grace* and perhaps do not even want to hear of it anymore.

Article V of the Augsburg Confession states: "Condemned are the Anabaptists and others who teach that the Holy Spirit comes to us through our own preparations, thoughts, and works without the external word of the Gospel." Now the spiritualizers, no matter of what period, will surely deny that they seek to get the Spirit by their own preparation and works. But they deceive themselves. The "preparation" is an essential part of such "spiritual" experience, and involves some doing on the part of man. This may be observed in the directions given by the great masters of mysticism, in the way a Quaker meeting waits in holy silence, or in Thomas Münzer's self-chosen cross by which he would compel the inner word to come.

Luther saw all this with remarkable clarity, as may be seen in his classic statement on "Confession" in the Smalcald Articles [III, VIII; Tappert, pp. 312—13]. The Spirit cannot be separated from the Word, just as in Holy Scripture *logos* and *pneuma* cannot be separated, although one must distinguish between them. As the eternal Word and the Spirit of God were involved in Creation (Gen. 1:2; John 1:1–3; cf.

1 Cor. 8:5–6), so in all the great deeds of God, the Son and the Spirit belong together: in the Incarnation ("who was conceived by the Holy Spirit"), at the baptism of Jesus, and at His resurrection (1 Tim. 3:16). Here is the inner reason for the Holy Spirit's bonding Himself (as far as we are concerned) with the external words of Scripture and their preaching. He who in John 3:8 is likened to the wind that "blows where it wills" has in His freedom as Lord ("And I believe in the Holy Spirit, the Lord") bound Himself to the external means of grace, so that we may know where we can find Him. For this reason, Luther explains, the spiritualizers, who want to have the Spirit without the external means of grace, make up their own means of grace. "Even so, the enthusiasts of our day condemn the external Word, yet they do not remain silent but fill the world with their chattering and scribbling, as if the Spirit could not come through the Scriptures or the spoken word of the apostles but must come through their own writings and words" (Smalcald Articles III, VIII, 6).

The profound truth of these words is evidenced throughout history. At the beginning of this century there appeared *Religious Voices of the Peoples*. It was a time of great historical research into the books of the Bible, and yet in German Protestantism understanding of the Bible had reached its nadir. The "religious voices" were those of the classical writings of the great religions of Asia. In cultured society they became books of edification and a means for achieving the "religious experience" which the church could no longer provide. At that time Oswald Spengler made his telling comment about the modern man who, instead of taking his hymnbook and going to church, stayed at home and read Confucius on rice paper.

Everywhere we seek the Holy Spirit, only not there where He is to be found. And why not? We feel it is unworthy of the Holy Spirit to bind Himself to such unimpressive external means as the homely words of Scripture, the words of Scripture interpretation, the lowly water of Baptism. "How can water produce such great effects?" we ask. To this the Small Catechism replies: "It is not the water indeed that produces these effects, but the Word of God connected with the water" [IV, 9–10]. But we ask: "How can the lowly water in Baptism convey the Holy Spirit?" It seems beneath the dignity of the Holy Spirit to be bonded with something so elementary as water and the physical sound of human words.

Zwingli expressed this thought in contradiction to Luther when he laid down the principle that bodily eating and drinking can be of no benefit to the soul. "The soul 'eats' spirit, and therefore it does not eat flesh" [*This Is My Body*, 1977, p. 193]. The humanism and idealism of modern man are speaking through him, while Luther resolutely holds to the fundamental Biblical concept of a real incarnation. "The Word became flesh." The Spirit comes in the external words of Scripture. In the Lord's Supper the bread is the body of Christ, and the wine His blood—not only sign or symbol. This essence of the Biblical revelation is perhaps the hardest thing we modern Christians, also we Lutherans, must learn again. We are so accustomed to think of body and soul, flesh and spirit, as opposites that we no longer understand that the whole magnitude of God's love lies in this very fact that God's Son comes to us in the flesh and that the Holy Spirit binds Himself to the external means of grace.

As God outside of Christ always remains the hidden God, so His Holy Spirit remains hidden from us unless we find Him in the Word and in the sacraments. And just as the revelation of God in Christ is at the same time God's hiding in the human nature of Christ, so the Holy Spirit of God is deeply hidden in the means of grace. He is always an object of faith, not of sight. "I believe that by my own reason or strength I cannot believe in Jesus Christ, my Lord, or come to him; but the Holy Spirit has called me through the Gospel, enlightened me with his gifts . . . " [Small Catechism II, 6]. Similarly we cannot believe in the Holy Spirit except by the witness He gives of Himself in God's Word. There both are found, the Son and the Spirit. There the Spirit witnesses to the Son of God (1 Cor. 12:3). There the Son bears witness to the Holy Spirit (see the words of the Lord about the Paraclete in John 14—16).

Without the Gospel, without the apostolic witness about Christ, we would be like those disciples in Acts 19:1-7 who had only received John's baptism and did not know "that there is a Holy Spirit." We might then know of the Holy Spirit as a force, a divine power that comes upon certain people, but we would not know that He is God. Only he who confesses in the Second Article that the Son is "God of God, Light of Light, very God of very God, begotten not made, being of one substance with the Father . . . " can go on to confess the faith of the Third Article: I believe "in the Holy Spirit, the lord and giver of life, who proceeds from the Father and the Son: who together with the Father and the Son is worshiped and glorified: who spoke by the prophets" [Tappert, p. 18, 19].

5

The Holy Spirit wants to be found in the Word. There He reveals Himself to us as God, as very God. Our faith in the Holy Spirit has grown weak. We seem to regard Him as a power of God, but no longer as a person. That He is more than the power of God that comes over man we learn from our Lord Himself. Without the promises about the Paraclete one could perhaps take the passages in the Old and the New Testament that speak of the Spirit in that sense. This is the case especially since the Greek *Pneuma Hagion* is in the neuter, and not in the masculine like the Latin *Spiritus Sanctus*. The Hebrew ruach is in the feminine. This suggests the difficulty our human words have in expressing the divine mystery of the Holy Spirit. In the Farewell Discourse in John, the Holy Spirit is called the Paraclete. "If I go, I will send Him (*auton*) to you. And when He (*ekeinos*) comes, He will convince the world . . . " (16:7–8; cf. the following verses and 14:26; 15:26). That this is not just Johannine is shown by Jesus' words about blasphemy against the Holy Spirit [Mark 3:29]. Blasphemy against the Holy Spirit is more than blasphemy against a something; it is blasphemy against a person, as the juxtaposition of "Son of Man" and "Holy Spirit" shows [Matt. 12:32; Luke 12:10]. And this person is God.

God's Word witnesses to the fact that the Holy Spirit is very God, or to be more exact, God the Holy Spirit witnesses to Himself in the words of Scripture, and nowhere else. This makes clear, then, how closely the understanding of Scripture as the Word of God hangs together with the right understanding of the Holy Spirit as a divine Person. Here is one of the reasons why we have lost the correct doctrine of the inspiration of Holy Scripture. If Scripture is no longer God's Word, then the Holy Spirit is no longer a divine Person. And vice versa: Whoever does not understand the Spirit as a divine Person, but as a *motus in rebus creatus* ("a movement which is produced in things"), as the Augsburg Confession speaks of this error in Article I [Tappert, p. 28], also no longer understands Scripture as God's Word but as a collection of religious writings that may stir a sense of something divine, "a breath of the divine." As Goethe said about the gospels in his last conversation with Eckermann: "There is in them the reflection of a majesty that emanates from the person of Christ. Here is as eminently divine a quality as can be found in any appearance ever of the divine on earth."

The development of Protestant theology since the Enlightenment shows clearly that the decline of belief in Scripture as the Word of God goes hand in hand with the decline of belief in the Holy Spirit as a divine Person. We can observe this also today, even where it is supposed that the old Liberalism has been overcome. What does the Holy Spirit mean for Gogarten, to cite just one example? If we read his book on *The Proclamation of Jesus Christ* (1948), we will find evidence enough for what has just been said. Where the doctrine of the Person of the Holy Spirit is no longer rightly taught, there also the doctrine of the Person of Christ is no longer rightly understood. The fathers of the fourth century knew this very well, and that brings us to one of the most difficult problems in the history of doctrine, one that is of more than just historical interest.

6

In studying the doctrine of inspiration in the fathers up to Augustine and Gregory the Great, one cannot escape the question: "Why did these theologians, when they came to speak of the relationship between Scripture and the Spirit, always draw their ideas from the Hellenistic synagogue?" These ideas, as becomes quite clear in Philo, go back to heathen concepts about the inspiration of prophets, sibyls, and the Sibylline Books. This matter was taken up years ago in these letters in "Augustine's Doctrine of Inspiration" (No. 29; also *Festschrift für Franz Dornseiff*, 1953, p. 262 ff.). Why did the fathers not simply say the same as Scripture says about its origin, the same thing our Lord Himself said (Matt. 22:43; John 5:39; 10:35), as well as His apostles (Acts 1:16; 2 Tim. 3:16; 2 Peter 1:19–21). Instead they tried to describe the process of inspiration in terms of ancient psychology.

We must realize that all the well-known ideas and pictures that have been in use since Augustine and Gregory to describe inspiration (the "prompting" or "dictating" of the Spirit, the holy writers as "secretaries" or "pens," etc.) derive from the psychology current in late antiquity, which could know nothing of the Holy Spirit. Just as the Holy Spirit Himself is inaccessible to any psychology, so also are His workings. Psychology may indeed examine certain psychological data, such as those connected with conversions. It can also examine certain phenomena of religious Enthusiasm. The proper work of the Holy Spirit, however, lies beyond what any psychology can explain or describe: regeneration, how the genuine prophets experienced God, what God's Word and the sacraments of Christ do in the human soul. The doctrine of the inspiration of Scripture which the church confesses must be a part of the doctrine of the Holy Spirit, but such a doctrine was not yet there when the fathers struggled with the problem of inspiration.

We seldom recall how long it took until the Scriptural doctrine of the Holy Spirit was understood. Something similar may be said of the doctrine of Christ. This doctrine was there from the beginning, ever since Jesus asked His disciples, "Who do you say that I am?" [Matt. 16:15]. But it took centuries until Christendom realized what all was included in the simple confessions, "Jesus is the Christ," "Jesus Christ is Lord," "I believe that Jesus Christ is the Son of God," and until the church recognized which wrong ideas had to be rejected if faith in Christ were not to be lost. It took even longer before clarity was achieved as to the full meaning of what Scripture says about the Holy Spirit.

Meanwhile Christians were being baptized "In the name of the Father and of the Son and of the Holy Spirit." Out of the Trinitarian formula of Baptism a three-part confession grew in Rome: "I believe in God the Father . . . and in Jesus Christ . . . and in the Holy Spirit." It was the original form of our Apostles' Creed. That the Christian faith is faith in the Father and the Son and the Holy Spirit was known by every Christian. But there was no pressing reason to think about the nature of the Holy Spirit. Who thinks about the air he breathes?

Even in Nicaea, when the great controversy about Christology was raging and the first decision regarding it was reached, the Holy Spirit was not felt to be a problem. The old Nicene Creed of 325 drew on earlier Eastern confessions, which derive finally from 1 Cor. 8:6. It confessed faith in one God, the Father and Creator, and in one Lord Jesus Christ. In its Christological article that creed develops a detailed doctrine of the relationship between the Father and the Son that reaches its climax in the *homoousios* ("being of one substance with the Father"). This received further clarification in the condemnations of the Arians which were appended. There is no "Third Article" such as in the old Roman baptismal confession. Following the "Second Article" there is only "and in the Holy Spirit." Not until the Niceno-Constantinopolitan Creed, the fuller creed of the Second Ecumenical Council in 381, is more said about the Holy Spirit. This is what appears as the "Nicene Creed" in our Confessions: "And in the Holy Spirit, the lord and giver of life, who proceeds from the Father . . . : who together with the Father and the Son is worshiped and glorified: who spoke by the prophets" [Tappert, p. 19].

Why was this expansion undertaken? What happened between the years 325 and 381? In the difficult struggles in 325 about the doctrine of the true deity of the Son it had become evident that the *homoousios* ("of one substance [with the Father]") of the Son is closely related to the *homoousios* of the Holy Spirit. One cannot confess that the Son is very God without also confessing that the Holy Spirit is very God and Lord.

This great recognition came to Athanasius as he struggled against the enemies of the *homoousios*, the Arians and the mediating theologians. This may have happened during his exile in the West. Here since Tertullian and Novatian there had been more engagement with the doctrine of the Holy Spirit, and the terms for the doctrine of the Trinity were already worked out. The Synod of Alexandria in 362 faced the false doctrine of the Pneumatomachi. They, along with the Arians, regarded the Holy Spirit as a creature. Athanasius opposed them and persuaded the synod to confess: "The Spirit is of the same essence and Godhead as the Father and the Son, and in the Trinity there is altogether nothing creaturely, nothing lower and nothing later" (Hefele, I, 728).

The other patriarchates were slow in accepting this. Basil the Great became a leading protagonist, while Gregory of Nazianzus, who presided at the Second Ecumenical Council in 381, gives evidence of a remarkable uncertainty in Oration 31, around the year 380:

> Some members of our own intelligentsia suppose the Holy Spirit to be an "activity," others a "creature"; others think of him as God; yet others fail to come to a decision, allegedly through reverence for the Scriptures, on the ground that they give no clear revelation on the question. The result is that they neither reverence the Spirit, nor dishonour him, but take up a kind of neutral position—or rather a pitiable position—with regard to him. Further, of those who suppose him divine, some are reverent towards him in thought, but no further; others go so far as to reverence him with their lips also. Others, even cleverer, I have heard measuring out the godhead: they admit that we have a union of three existences, but they put such a distance between them as to make the first unlimited in substance and power, the second unlimited in power, but not in substance, while the third they represent as circumscribed in both substance and power [Bettenson, *Later Christian Fathers*, p. 113].

Here we see the intensity of the theological struggle to confess the Holy Spirit. We may observe also that what was confessed by the council in 381 was not nearly so clear as what was confessed in 362 in Alexandria. The creed of 381, which we call the Nicene Creed, does not explicitly state the *homoousios* of the Holy Spirit; it is content to use expressions that imply it. But the church in the East as well as in the West has always taken these expressions as confessing the *homoousios* of the Holy Spirit. Since the Council of Constantinople in 381 the whole church has confessed that the Holy Spirit is God without reservation. And so the confession of the doctrine of the Holy Trinity was completed 300 years after the death of the apostles.

7

But was the doctrine of the Holy Trinity and with it the doctrine of the Holy Spirit really completed? Such was the conviction of the church. In reality, however, many questions remained open, as the subsequent history shows.

The East never went all the way in its confession of *homoousios*, for this means "of the same substance." So it was confessed by Athanasius and by the church in the West. The East, represented by the three great Cappadocians, Basil, Gregory of Nyssa, and Gregory of Nazianzus, could accept *homoousios* only in the sense of "similar substance." Athanasius permitted this as long as *homoios* or *homoiousios* ["similar" or "of similar substance"] was really understood in the sense of equality of being. Like every truly orthodox theologian, Athanasius was fighting for the doctrine, not for a theology. What mattered was the doctrine that God is One and that there are three Persons, whether the mystery of the Trinity was understood in the sense that the one God is Father, Son, and Holy Spirit, or in the sense that the three Persons, Father, Son, and Holy Spirit, are one God. Still today the mystery of the Trinity is confessed in the East as three in one (*Dreieinigkeit*) and in the West as one in three (*Dreifaltigkeit*). East and West complement each other in confessing that mystery which lies beyond the reach of comprehension. They belong together. In this way some echo of Origen was acceptable in the church of the East, and also in the West.

The East made no further advance, while the West went deeper with Augustine's probing of the doctrine of the Trinity. The church in the West gave the doctrine of the Trinity full confession in the *Symbolum Quicunque*, which came to be wrongly ascribed to Athanasius and was then called the Athanasian Creed, as it is in the Book of Concord. Here we have the confession of the doctrine which found its way into the Niceno-Constantinopolitan Creed with the *filioque*, which confesses that the Holy Spirit proceeds from the Father *and the Son*.

The Eastern Church subsequently pronounced this to be a falsification of the creed, and regarded this "falsification" of its most sacrosanct church text as a grievous sin of Rome. The papacy has always acknowledged that this creed can be used in the form employed by the Eastern Church because the addition does not contradict the original text. In the efforts toward reconciliation Rome has always required only that what is confessed with *filioque* should not be denied. This question of the *filioque* is the only creedal question between East and West, and therefore it has played a great, and often excessive, role in the polemics of the two confessions. Since Photius [ca. 820—891] Eastern theology has attempted to discover a great heresy in the *filioque*.

Yet this question is not one to hinder an eventual union of Rome with the Eastern Church. The difference in the way the doctrine is confessed lies along the lines of how the Trinity is understood, as indicated above. When the Eastern Church denies that the Spirit proceeds from the Son, there is a sense in which it continues to make room for the subordination of the Son to the Father which has its basis in Origen. But it is no more than a hint of Subordinationism, for Subordinationism itself is rejected by the *homoousios* of the Nicene Creed. And yet what was inherited from the great Origen has not quite disappeared. The situation might be put this way: As in many aspects of doctrine, cultus, and polity, the church of the East represents an older tradition. The church of the East did not participate in the development that took place in the West.

Why not? Here we come upon a problem which has not been sufficiently weighed in church history. It is the question of the consequences for the history of doctrine occasioned by the downfall of the ancient world.

8

When the Second Ecumenical Council met, the migration of nations had already begun. In the course of the next century the whole Western Empire fell to its Germanic conquerors. When the Third Ecumenical Council met in Ephesus in 431, Augustine was not there. He had died the previous year in Hippo Regius as it lay besieged by the Vandals. When the Fourth Ecumenical Council met in Chalcedon in October of 451, the Huns were at the doors of Italy.

Everyone knows how the history of doctrine fared in the East in the following generations under the influence of the disintegration of the empire, but no one can tell what was lost to the church in those centuries when the ancient civilization perished. How many questions were not pushed through to resolution simply for lack of thinkers with the competence to do so! We can only marvel that so much work, thought, and discussion was nevertheless accomplished. Under what deprivations, internal and external needs, did the later fathers have to work! Anastasius Sinaiticus in the seventh century indicates how hard it was to work in the wilderness, without a library, forced to rely on his memory for quotations. How the level of theological work sank in those centuries is clear if we compare Augustine with Gregory the Great.

The lamentable consequence of all this is that the doctrinal tasks of the ancient church were cut short. It was only centuries later that the heritage of Augustine was taken up by Western theology, and in the Eastern Church this never happened. So only in the West was the doctrine of the Trinity brought to what might be called completion. Of the doctrine of the Holy Spirit one has to say that also in the West it remained unfinished. The great creed of 381, our Nicene Creed, received remarkably little attention. At that time no one seemed to realize the importance of that synod in Constantinople with its meager 180 bishops. Its great achievement, the Niceno-Constantinopolitan Creed, appears first in the acts of the Council of Chalcedon, and only thereafter does it begin to supplant the creed of 325. The great ecumenical Niceno-Constantinopolitan Creed, which East and West have in common, and which they also share with the Nestorians and the Monophysites, has always had the character of an unfinished symphony.

The *filioque*, added in the West and condemned in the East as a creedal falsification, was not the only addition. In the Armenian liturgy at the place of the Third Article we read: "We believe in the Holy Spirit, who is not created and who is perfect. He has spoken in the law, in the prophets, and in the Gospels. At the Jordan he descended, he proclaimed his message to the apostles, and he dwells in the saints." In another version of the Armenian text the Holy Spirit is confessed as "of one being with the Father and the Son." (Caspari, *Quellen*, II, 33 [Hahn, p. 153].) One must not overlook the fact that such texts were not transmitted uniformly, as is shown by the variations in the different liturgies. The one just quoted is evidence of the tendency not to rest content with only an implicit confession of the *homoousios* of the Holy Spirit. This tendency came to fruition in the West in the full statement of the doctrine of the Trinity in the *Quicunque*.

9

"Who proceeds from the Father and the Son: who together with the Father and the Son is worshiped and glorified." The second "and the Son" (*et filio*) is already there in the creed of 381 and may be recognized as prompting the first "and the Son" (*filioque*). Already in the debates prior to 381 we find "who with the Father and the Son at the same time is worshiped and glorified." Placing the Holy Spirit on an equal level with the Father and the Son begins in the liturgy. Here is a classic case of the rule, so vital for understanding the history of doctrine, that the movement is from liturgy to doctrine (*Lex orandi lex credendi*). What comes to be confessed as doctrine in the church appears first in the liturgy. The doctrine of the Trinity appears first in the Trinitarian baptismal formula. "By grace alone" (*sola gratia*), proclaimed in the Reformation, was prayed in the Canon of the Mass. There in the prayer *Nobis quoque peccatoribus* the plea is made to God "not to reckon our merits but to pardon our transgressions" (*non aestimator meriti, sed veniae largitor*). *Sola gratia* was also sung in hymns of the Middle Ages: "King of majesty tremendous, Who dost free salvation send us . . . " ([*The Lutheran Hymnal* 607:8] *Rex tremendae majestatis, Qui salvandos salvas gratis*). So also the doctrine that the Holy Spirit is truly God, a Person of the Holy Trinity, appears first in the liturgy, when the Spirit is worshiped and glorified together with the Father and the Son. Adoration belongs only to God, to the Triune God or the Persons of the Holy Trinity. Whoever honors the Holy Spirit with the Father and the Son is confessing the Holy Spirit's full deity. Here arises an interesting problem. We observe that in the liturgy, in the church's solemn prayers or collects, the Holy Spirit is always named together with the Father and the Son. When the prayer is directed to the Father, it concludes: "through Jesus Christ Your Son, our Lord, who with You and the Holy Spirit lives and reigns to all eternity." When the prayer is directed to the Son, it concludes: "You who with the Father and the Holy Spirit live and reign to all eternity." But what about prayer to the Holy Spirit? Here we confront the remarkable fact that such prayers are never, or hardly ever, addressed to the Holy Spirit.

In the Eastern church they are unknown; only when the Triune God is called upon is the Holy Spirit also called upon. When I put this to an Eastern priest, he replied, "Well, you know that we do not have the *filioque*." To which I replied, "Yes, to be sure. Old Origen still remains a force to be reckoned with among you." And he agreed quite cheerfully.

Even in the Epiclesis, the solemn act in the liturgy, it is not the Holy Spirit that is called upon but the Father. The Father is called upon to send down the Spirit "upon us and the gifts here present" to make them the precious body and blood of Christ. We quote from the Epiclesis of the Liturgy of St. James, because here we have an especially full statement about the Holy Spirit:

Send upon us and the gifts here present your all-holy Spirit, the Lord and giver of life, who with you, God the Father, and your only-begotten Son, is enthroned and rules together. He is of the same being (*homoousios*) and co-eternal. He has spoken in law and prophets and your new testament. He descended in the form of a dove upon our Lord Jesus Christ at the Jordan river and remained upon him. In the form of fiery tongues he came down upon the apostles in the upper room of the holy and glorious Zion on the day of the holy Pentecost. Him himself send, O Lord, your all-holy Spirit, upon us and these holy gifts here present . . . [Hanggi, p. 250; Jasper, p. 63].

It is impossible to make a more powerful confession of the Holy Spirit's true deity, and yet this church never took the step of calling upon the Holy Spirit Himself.

Also in the West it took centuries before this happened. Even today neither the Pentecost liturgy nor the Mass of the Holy Spirit contains such a prayer. There is only the call: "Come, Holy Spirit, fill the hearts of Your faithful, and kindle in them the fire of Your love," the *Veni, Sancte Spiritus*, which follows the Hallelujah or the Gradual and from which grew the medieval sequence and the hymn *Veni, Creator Spiritus* ["Come, Holy Ghost, Creator Blest]."

What is the explanation? Does this reticence perhaps have Biblical grounds? Holy Scripture has no calling upon the Holy Spirit comparable with the calling upon Christ that is found there. But when we consider the fact that in the Eastern liturgy (but not in the Roman Mass) a calling upon Mary has its settled place, we will scarcely be inclined to consider this a valid reason.

The puzzle grows when we consider that there was indeed a church in whose liturgy prayers were addressed to the Holy Spirit, the Visigothic church in Spain. In its liturgy, called the Mozarabic liturgy, we find: "O Holy Spirit, who proceeds from the Father and the Son (*qui a Patre Filioque procedis*), teach us to do the truth, so that You, who have undertaken procession from the Father and the Son, may with love invisible join us to them from whom You so ineffably proceed" (*MPL*, 86, 691). This is only one example from the *Breviarium Gothicum*. In Isidore's *Missale Mixtum* the Holy Spirit is called upon in the Postpridie to accept the sacrifice: "Accept, we pray, O Holy Spirit, omnipotent God, the sacrifices . . . For you are in truth that fire which divinely accepted and consumed the sacrifices of our fathers. . . ." Then before the Our Father the Holy Spirit is called upon anew: "O Paraclete, Spirit, You who continue to be with the Father and the Son one God in Trinity, so fill our minds that with You praying for us we may here on earth with great confidence say, 'Our Father . . .' " (*MPL* 85, 620 [Beckmann, *Quellen*, pp. 95 f.].)

Clearly these prayers grew out of Augustine's doctrine of the Trinity. They follow logically from the *filioque*, whose grounds were stated by Augustine and which was included in the creed as confessed in the Visigothic church in Spain (Toledo 589), from where it traveled to the kingdom of the Franks. The history that led to this development is unknown to us. It happened during the dark period of the migration of the nations which followed the death of Augustine. The prayers of the Mozarabic liturgy are what is left to us as monuments from a forgotten period of the church's history, a period when from the orthodox doctrine of the Trinity, as Augustine had completed it for the West, the conclusion was drawn that in the prayers of the liturgy the church not only may but must pray to the Third Person of the Trinity, the Holy Spirit who proceeds from the Father and the Son, who with the Father and the Son is of one being, true God from eternity to eternity.

That this liturgical development did not spread more widely through the church in the West may be explained by the fact that Rome was not aware of this calling upon the Spirit in church that was customary in Spain. Rome preserved an older type of dealing with the Trinity in the liturgy. It did not allow the liturgical consequences of the *filioque* doctrine to come to expression. This seems to explain why most Roman Catholic liturgiologists in their debates about whether and where there may be traces of an Epiclesis in the Mass have tended to overlook the fact that the Mass contains a calling upon the Holy Spirit in a way which is more than the Eastern church's calling upon the Father to send the Spirit. It is there in the Offertory prayer: "Come, Sanctifier, almighty, eternal God, and bless this sacrifice" (*Veni sanctificator omnipotens aeterne Deus, et benedic hoc sacrificium*). *Sanctificator*, the One who sanctifies, is a designation of the Holy Spirit. That this is so is evidenced by the Mozarabic liturgy, where in the same prayer the Spirit is explicitly named.

The characteristic conservatism of the liturgy is perhaps explanation enough for the prayers to the Holy Spirit not being further developed. The liturgy reaches back into the time when there was as yet no Trinitarian dogma. In the Gloria in Excelsis, for example, the Holy Spirit receives only bare mention at the end, as is also the case in the creed of 325. In the Middle Ages hymns were sung to the Holy Spirit, and the churches of the Reformation have the usage of prayers to the Holy Spirit. That there is nothing here conflicting with Roman doctrine is evidenced by the solemn prayer with which the sessions of the Vatican Council were begun. We quote a few words from the lengthy prayer addressed to the Holy Spirit: "We are here, Lord, Holy Spirit. We stand here before You held back by the greatness of our sins, but it is in Your name that we are especially assembled. Come to us and be with us. . . . As You work our judgments be also their Health, You who alone with the Father and His Son possess the glorious name. . . ." Then come further prayers, among which there is an indirect prayer for the Spirit: "We beseech You, O Lord, that the Paraclete, who proceeds from You, may enlighten our souls and lead us into all truth, as Your Son has promised, who with You lives . . ."

No, there is simply nothing that can be raised as an objection to our praying to the Holy Spirit just as we do to the Father and the Son. Is our neglect of such prayer perhaps the reason why Christianity has erred into so many false pathways? Has the place left empty of prayers to the Holy Spirit perhaps been occupied by the cult of the saints? Has Mary perhaps in practice often come to occupy the place that belongs to the Holy Spirit? And what has become of the Trinity when a pope in our day died with the prayer: "Jesus, Mary, Joseph, into your hands I commend my spirit"? And of the churches which claim to have the heritage of the Reformation, must we not also say that they, even though in different ways, show loss of the true faith in the Holy Spirit?

10

The doctrine of the Holy Spirit belongs to the uncompleted doctrines of the church. Can we find the explanation for this in the fact that, strictly speaking, the doctrine of the Holy Spirit belongs with *eschatology*, the doctrine of the Last Things? When on the day of Pentecost the Holy Spirit was poured out upon the apostles, there was fulfilled, as Peter said in the church's first Pentecost sermon, that which according to the prophet Joel was to happen "in the last days," in the days of the Messiah, at the end of the world. The Third Article of the creed indeed has to do with the Last Things, with what will happen at the end of the world. The Holy Spirit as the possession of the entire people of God, not merely as an occasional and temporary gift, is a gift of the end time.

The Holy Spirit brings blessed eternity into time now in this world, forgiveness of sins, life and salvation. So also the one holy catholic and apostolic church which we confess in this same article is a fact of the end time. The church, God's own holy people, makes its journey from one age to the next, traveling through the wilderness of this world. It has been delivered from the slavery of Egypt, the old age, but has not yet arrived in the land of promise, the new age. To this article belongs faith in the resurrection of the dead and the waiting for the life of the world to come. This article ends in eternity. Therefore it necessarily remains uncompleted.

It has often been supposed that the neglect of the doctrine of the Holy Spirit is to be explained by the fact that here we are confronted with things intangible. There is more than a grain of truth in this. However, we ought never to forget the actuality of what the Holy Spirit does. What the church of the apostles and of the early Christians experienced as the reality of the Holy Spirit was not first of all the spectacular gifts of the Spirit which occurred at that time, the gifts of healing, prophecy, speaking in tongues, and whatever else has in the church's history been regarded as extraordinarily miraculous manifestations of the Spirit. Far more important were the great and lasting workings of faith, hope, and love.

If one reads the old sermons and records of what the ancient church experienced every year in the time between Easter and Pentecost, an echo of which can still be heard in the old liturgical texts, then one can say that what was experienced at this time of the church year was an inexpressible joy. We spoke of this in an earlier letter [No. 37, *Freudenzeit der Kirche*]). This joy lives in our Lord's Farewell Discourses, which have been the source of so many Gospel readings in the time from Easter to Pentecost. It is the more-than- earthly joy that we hear from the mouths of the ancient martyrs, the joy that is a foretaste of everlasting blessedness. It was not just due to a misunderstanding of the word "Paraclete" that He came to be called the Comforter. "You have sorrow now, but I will see you again and your hearts will rejoice, and no one will take your joy from you" [John 16:22]. "Your sorrow will turn into joy" [v. 20]. " . . . that My joy may be in you, and that your joy may be full"[John 15:11]. All of this is in what our Lord promises of the Holy Spirit, the Comforter.

One of the deepest heartaches of human existence is the riddle of work cut short, left unfinished. Many of our Lutheran churches have in this century twice lost the fairest flowering of their young theologians.

We who were the teachers of one of these lost generations have often asked ourselves what sense there could be in such a tragedy. There is no other answer than faith in the Holy Spirit, He who brings uncompleted work to completion. We remember those nuns in the French Revolution who, as they were lead from their cloister to the scaffold, sang the *Veni, Creator Spiritus*. They stood in the great apostolic succession of the confessors and martyrs of all times, down to those in our own day. Somewhere in China faith in the Lord Christ is sealed with the death of nameless martyrs. No one will know their confession—one of the meanings of *confessio* is the grave of a martyr—until that day when all graves will be opened.

Our Lord, after His Farewell Discourses, prayed His High Priestly Prayer thinking of all His faithful ones, also those known only to Him. In this prayer He speaks words which no man ever prayed in the face of death, in the face of what, to all human evaluation, marked His life and work as uncompleted: "Father, the hour has come; glorify Thy Son that the Son may glorify Thee. . . . I glorified Thee on earth, having accomplished the work which Thou gavest Me to do. . . . I have manifested Thy name . . . " [John 17:1, 4, 6]

"I have glorified *You*. I have done the work *You* gave me to do. I have made *Your* name known to men." Where the church, where we servants of the Lord, can speak thus as we follow Jesus on the way of the cross: "We have glorified *You* and not ourselves; we have done the work *You* gave us to do, not what we have sought for ourselves; we have manifested *Your* name, not our name or the name of our big or little church"—only insofar as we can say this will there be a fulfillment of the promise: "I will pray the Father, and He will give you another Counselor ["Comforter" in the German] to be with you forever, even the Spirit of truth, whom the world cannot receive, because it neither sees Him nor knows Him; you know Him, for He dwells with you, and will be in you" [John 14:16–17]. Where this is a vital reality in the church, there the doctrine of the Holy Spirit is no longer an abstract dogma, for then the Holy Spirit is a living Reality. The world will never understand this; also not the world that is in the church, also not the world that is in our own hearts. But He who has overcome the world, also the world in the church and the world in our stubborn and despairing hearts, says to all who believe in His name: "The Spirit of truth . . . dwells with you, and will be in you."

We hardly need to say any more about what this faith in the Holy Spirit means for the church today and for us pastors. Without this faith the history of the church and the life of Christians would have no meaning. But where this faith is alive and truly taught, there is the one holy catholic and apostolic church, to which the promise has been given that the gates of hell shall not prevail against it.

Dear brother pastors, let us pray for this faith, and in this faith do the work given us to do for Christ's church.

ARTICLE VII OF THE AUGSBURG CONFESSION IN THE PRESENT CRISIS OF LUTHERANISM

Letters to Lutheran Pastors, No. 53
April 1961

On July 1, 1868, there was the first meeting, in Hannover, of the General Evangelical-Lutheran Conference. The meeting began with divine service in St. Mark's Church. The preacher was Luthardt, who became editor of their church paper. The text was 1 Cor. 4:1 f.; the theme, "Of the True Faithfulness of the Servants of Jesus Christ." Harless from Munich opened the sessions with an address through which there rang a deep tone of repentance. He spoke of the common plight of Lutheranism. "If we speak of our wounds and what we suffer from them, we do not speak so much of wounds which others have given us, but of the wounds which we have inflicted upon ourselves in ignorance or unfaithfulness." Then came the hymn "Lord Jesus Christ, with us abide, For round us falls the eventide." Then Kliefoth from Schwerin gave his famous address: "What Is Required of Church Government in the Lutheran Church According to Article VII of the Augsburg Confession?"

If we only had more time to attend this meeting and listen to these great men! We are in desperate need of knowing our history through the last century and a half. The accounts given in the usual textbooks show little understanding or sympathy for what happened; in some there is little more than shreds and falsification.

But we want to point out that in one of Lutheranism's most dire crises Article VII of the Augsburg Confession came to occupy the center of the discussion. What was at stake was nothing more and nothing less than the existence of the Lutheran territorial churches in Germany as

40

Lutheran. In the wars of 1864 and 1866 Prussia had annexed Schleswig-Holstein, Hannover, and Electoral Hesse. This brought the demand that the Prussian Union should be imposed also on these new provinces of the Prussian state. Nothing characterizes the situation better than the famous letter which Harless, the president of the Lutheran Conference, wrote to Bismarck in November of 1870. At the same time Bishop Ketteler of Mainz, the spokesman for the Catholic bishops in Germany, wrote a similar letter to the chancellor. Their plea that in the constitution, which was being prepared for the new German Empire, the rights of the churches in Germany should be respected, was in vain. (Documents in Th. Heckel's *Adolph von Harless*, pp. 482 ff.) Harless spoke of the profound concern of committed Lutherans in Germany that the Lutheran Church would be robbed of its place in territory after territory, with the result that it could only continue to exist in small free churches, or that Lutheranism would become only a theological viewpoint within other, non-Lutheran churches. "Only with the profoundest grief can one think such thoughts through to the end, that the Lutheran Church . . . would have her lamp cast aside in Germany" (p. 485).

In this situation the Lutherans pondered Article VII of the Augsburg Confession. It was too late. Today, after almost a century, Harless's prophecy has been fulfilled in Germany. Apart from the free churches, Lutheranism no longer lives on as a church but as a viewpoint, as a "theological school of thought," within one Evangelical Church, as both Schleiermacher and Barth said. Even the territorial churches which are nominally and *de iure* Lutheran have no longer *de facto* preserved the Lutheran confessional position.

The men of 1868 turned their eyes to Lutheranism elsewhere in the world, to the Scandinavian lands and to America. Just at that time in America the gathering together of confessional Lutherans was under way. The General Council was gathering the confessional synods which could no longer go along with the unionistic General Synod. In the Midwest, confessional synods were joining with Missouri to form the Synodical Conference (1872). At that time the first beginnings of ecumenical Lutheranism could be noticed everywhere. The question as to what creates church fellowship according to Scripture and the Confessions was always the thing that caused separations and led to new unions. A new day was dawning for the Lutheran Church.

Today the question we cannot escape is whether the way things went with Lutheranism in Germany will be the way things go with

Lutheranism elsewhere in the world. Will Lutheranism everywhere become merely a viewpoint within church bodies that are not in fact Lutheran? The confessionally committed Lutherans in Denmark, Norway, and Sweden are even more lonely today than their brethren in the faith in Germany. The churches to which they belong are now only nominally Lutheran. Things are moving in the same direction also in America, and with the same speed with which everything seems to happen in the New World. The fact that Lutheranism now faces the greatest crisis in its history cannot be hidden by the putting together of big new church bodies in America, nor by the gigantic organization of the Lutheran World Federation with its reported 60 million "Lutherans," including the atheists and Communists in whole countries that once embraced the Reformation. The crisis is evidenced theologically in the general uncertainty regarding the great article of the Augsburg Confession about the church. Whatever else it may mean, this article is the Magna Charta of the Lutheran Church. We will all do well to study it thoroughly, so that we will be up to the tasks which lie before each of us.

1

Article VII of the Augsburg Confession is the first doctrinal statement ever made in Christendom about what the church is and wherein is her unity. Before the Reformation, people were content to confess the statement of faith in the Nicene Creed: "I believe (the Greek text adds 'in') one holy, catholic, and apostolic church." What this church is and wherein lies its unity, holiness, catholicity, and apostolicity— these were questions which theologians wrote about, and which were variously thought of by the various Christian denominations in ancient times, such as the Montanists, Novatians, Donatists, and Catholics. For the word "catholic," when used as in Catholic Church (Augustine, *communio catholica*), referred to only one of the numerous groups which regarded themselves as the true church. Yet they did not feel it was necessary to have a doctrinal definition of what the church is, not even in the Catholic Church or churches (they were not always in church fellowship with each other).

Many of those who participated in the World Conference on Faith and Order in Lausanne in 1927 were astonished to hear the representative of the Ecumenical Patriarch declare at the beginning that the question "What is the church?" belongs to the open questions which theologians are free to have their disputes about. Only that is church dogma which is stated in the Third Article of the Nicene Creed. Similarly Rome. The Roman Catechism speaks of the church in its exposition of the creed, but the catechism is not dogma. So we find lively debate in the 19th century about what the church is, particularly in German Catholicism since Möhler. We cannot here speak of how the Vatican Council of 1869/70 in vain sought to complete a dogma "Of the Church of Christ" but had to leave this task to the future. All previous documents, such as the encyclical *Mystici corporis*, can only be viewed as preparatory.

Echoes of Article VII of the Augsburg Confession are to be found in all the Reformed confessions of the 16th century. Of particular significance is Article 19 of the Anglican Thirty-Nine Articles, where the definition according to the official English text reads:

> The visible church of Christ is a congregation of faithful men (Latin *coetus fidelium*), in which the pure Word of God is preached, and the Sacraments be duly administered according to Christ's ordinance in all those things that of necessity are requisite to the same.

The reason why the Augsburg Confession had to speak on this matter is clear. The article goes back to Article 12 of the Schwabach Articles, and behind that lies Luther's *Great Confession* of 1528:

> Next, I believe that there is one holy Christian ("Christian" is used here, as in the late Middle Ages, for *catholica* in the sense of embracing all of Christendom) Church on earth, i.e., the community or number or assembly of all Christians in all the world, the one bride of Christ, and his spiritual body of which he is the only head. The bishops or priests are not her heads or lords or bridegrooms, but servants, friends, and—as the word "bishop" implies— superintendents, guardians, or stewards.
>
> This Christian Church exists not only in the realm of the Roman Church or pope, but in all the world, as the prophets foretold that the gospel of Christ would spread throughout the world, Psalm 2 [:8], Psalm 19 [:4]. Thus this Christian Church is physically dispersed among pope, Turks, Persians, Tartars, but spiritually gathered in one gospel and faith, under one head, i.e., Jesus Christ. For the papacy is assuredly the true realm of Antichrist, the real anti-Christian tyrant, who sits in the temple of God and rules with human command ments, as Christ in Matthew 24 [:24] and Paul in II Thessalonians 2 [:3 f.] declare; although the Turk and all heresies, wherever they may be, are also included in this abomination which according to prophecy will stand in the holy place, but are not to be compared to the papacy (WA 26, 506 f. [American Edition 37, 367 f.]).

Even if we were to disregard the doctrine of the Antichrist, which was for Luther a part of the doctrine of the church, this quotation shows why the Reformation had to ask and answer the question: "What is the church?" The highest office in the church had rejected the holy Gospel, and those who proclaimed this Gospel had been put out of the fellowship of the church. For this reason Luther and those with him had to say why they could not recognize the papal excommunication as exclusion from the church. Thus the ecclesiological question was put, and an answer had to be given.

<h1 style="text-align:center">2</h1>

The answer which Article VII of the Augsburg Confession gives to the question of the church is best understood within its context. What it says is supplemented particularly in Articles V, VIII, and XXVIII. The whole of the Augsburg Confession is the context for Article VII, and its great exposition is given in the Apology. This does not mean that our Confessions say everything there is to be said about the church and leave no question open. They do not claim to do this.

The doctrine of the church is like other parts of Christian doctrine, both simple and inexhaustible. "A seven-year-old child," says Luther, "knows what the church is, namely, holy believers and sheep who hear the voice of their shepherd" (Smalcald Articles III, XII, 2). While a child may well know the voice of its Good Shepherd and yet the deepest thinkers through the centuries of the church have not been able to exhaust the truth of Scripture regarding the Lord Christ, so also the actuality of the church remains an inexhaustible problem for theology. There are questions which our Confessions do not answer, nor have they been answered by other churches.

One such question has to do with how it is to be understood when the New Testament speaks of the church as the body of Christ. In what sense is it a body, according to Scripture? Certainly not in the sense in which the word "body" is used of a number of people joined together in an association. Not only what we call the universal church is the body of Christ, but also "the church of God in Corinth" or in any other place. What is the relationship between the "sacramental" and the "spiritual" body of Christ?

Another question which did not engage our fathers in the 16th century is the eschatological sense of the church. There is church only in the end time. "In the last days" the prophecy of Joel was fulfilled at

Pentecost (Acts 2:16–21). John says in his day, "It is the last hour" (1 John 2:18).

For answering such questions our Confessions provide vital resources, as for example in the doctrine of the Antichrist. But unfolding them demands deep study of Scripture. In this sense Vilmar was right in speaking of the doctrine of the church as an uncompleted doctrine. There are depths not yet plumbed to which the church may be led. Throughout the whole of Christianity questions are today being asked about the church, and so also among the Lutherans around the world. Our church would be dead if we supposed that we had nothing more to learn.

3

What is the church? Our Confession gives an answer which in a noteworthy way immediately differentiates itself from the answers of other churches. Article 19 of the Anglican Thirty-Nine Articles reproduces the definition of Article VII, but makes a characteristic change by inserting "visible." "The *visible* Church of Christ is the congregation . . . " This is done in opposition to the confessions of all the other Reformed churches. These, guided by Zwingli, Bucer, and Calvin, regard the true church as invisible. The Anglican insertion was perhaps done in deliberate opposition to the Scottish Confession of 1560, which links the doctrine of the church with the doctrine of the Holy Trinity and the doctrine of the person of Christ, and then says: "This Kirk is invisible, known only to God, who alone knows whom He has chosen" [16, Cochrane, p. 175].

Our Confession does not make this distinction between an invisible and a visible church. Luther does indeed, now and then, speak of the church as invisible, but in an altogether different sense. It would have been better for Lutheran theology never to have spoken as though there were two churches, one visible and another invisible. This distinction derives from the Reformed doctrine of predestination. It goes back to Augustine, and in the Middle Ages is found in Wycliffe. The invisible church is made up of all the predestined, the visible church of the baptized. It is possible to be a member of the one without being a member of the other. The sacrament of Baptism is here then only the outward sign of the baptism with the Holy Spirit. For the person who is not predestined to eternal life the baptism with water remains only a sign without effect.

This distinction is rejected by the Lutheran Church as unbiblical. Baptism according to the New Testament is not only a sign but the means that washes away sins (Eph. 5:26), "the washing of regeneration" (Titus 3:5). So there are not two churches, one the visible fellowship of those who have received a sign of regeneration, and the other the invisible fellowship of those who have been born again of the Holy Spirit to eternal life. Our church also confesses election to eternal life and knows that those baptized may be lost, and that by their own fault. We bow before the God whose hidden decisions, which He has not revealed to us, we do not understand. We bow before the God who "desires all men to be saved and to come to the knowledge of the truth" [1 Tim. 2:4], and who yet allows so many to be lost eternally. But we can never surrender the promises that are bound up with the means of grace. We can never say that He did not mean His promises. A person can lose the blessing of Baptism by not again and again, yes daily, receiving the promise of Christ in faith. But the promise remains. Baptism remains the same.

In the controversies about Baptism between the Lutherans and the Reformed in the 16th century, which we should study far more thoroughly, our theologians liked to refer to the "one Baptism" of Eph. 4:5, which was also taken into the Nicene Creed. From this great Pauline passage, on which also Article VII of the Augsburg Confession rests, as also from the "one God . . . and one Lord" in 1 Cor. 8:6, we have the repeated "one" in the Nicene Creed: "I believe in *one* God, the Father . . . and in *one* Lord Jesus Christ . . . *one* holy, catholic, and apostolic church . . . *one* Baptism for the remission of sins." What is confessed here from the New Testament, "one Baptism," is a defense not only against the idea that Baptism can be repeated, but also against the Platonizing splitting up of this sacrament into a physical baptism and a spiritual baptism.

This is true not only of the means of grace, but also of the church. Our Confession confesses only one church, and not two. The church may not be split into an invisible one and a visible one, no matter what some later Lutheran theologians may have thought about it. Thereby our Confession follows the Nicene and the Apostles' Creed, and the New Testament. When the question is put whether Article VII of the Augsburg Confession is speaking of the invisible church, as the Reformed understood this article, or of the visible church, as the Anglicans interpreted it for themselves, we simply have to say that the question is wrongly put; the article does not know this distinction, and neither does the New Testament.

4

This great article has been taken apart in some unhelpful attempts to explain it. The first sentence is said to refer to the invisible church, since the one holy church, the one that goes on forever, is an article of faith and therefore is invisible. The second sentence, on the other hand, is taken as referring to the visible church, since the congregation of all believers, in which the Gospel is preached and the sacraments are bestowed, is made up of visible people among whom here on earth the means of grace are administered and received.

The contradictions inherent in this should have led to the realization that the question is wrongly put. The author of the Augsburg Confession was not one who was unable to think clearly and logically. Neither was Luther, for that matter, who shared responsibility for the Schwabach Articles and expressed the matter in the same way in his "Great Confession" of 1528. Can one imagine that they would not have noticed such a confusion of concepts? If we examine the debates over Article VII in the 19th and 20th centuries, we find that these controversies about its meaning do not derive from any unclarity in the Confession, but rather from the unclear thinking of its interpreters, who attempted to read into it later theological notions and the categories of their own ecclesiology.

Like other articles, so also this one basically sets down the teaching of the New Testament, where the church is always both an actual, concrete gathering of people whom one can see, and also the communion of saints, the people of God, the body of Christ which one must believe. What the Jews and the heathen saw in Corinth was a group of people who assembled together. What they did not see was the holiness of these people, was the character of this group as the people of God, the body of Christ, the temple of the Holy Spirit. Yes, also the saints in Corinth, to the extent that they were really saints and not Pharisees or hypocrites, did not themselves see the holiness that was theirs.

That your sins are forgiven must be believed. The Christians in Corinth had to believe that they were God's people and that in, with, and under their visible assembly the spiritual body of Christ was present—just as they could not see, taste, or feel that the consecrated bread and the consecrated wine in the Lord's Supper were the true body and the true blood of Christ. They had to believe that.

Also for the church of the New Testament the church was not an article of sight but an article of faith in the strict sense of the word. And so it was in the church which confessed the Nicene Creed and therein the great article of the one, holy church. Only in faith could the Catholics in ancient Christendom (already then Catholic was a confessional designation) assert that they were the true church and not the Novatians, who asserted the same regarding themselves, for they not only held the orthodox faith but also had the older forms of church discipline. Only in faith could Augustine know that not the Donatists were the true church, but rather that fellowship which he called the *communio catholica*. The church is always an object of faith.

This is basically the case also for Roman Catholicism today. The conviction that the church is and must be as visible as was the ancient people of Israel, as is any social organization of people on earth, is qualified by the fact that Rome never knows exactly where the boundaries of the church are. In what sense can those who are excommunicated be said to be members of the church, whose members they remain? When schismatic churches possess the priesthood and episcopal consecrations, when even the baptisms performed by heretics, if they are done properly, are valid, and when today heretics are called "separated brethren," where is then the exact boundary of the church? Already Optatus of Mileve [fourth century] bestowed the name of brother upon the Donatists, with exhaustive theological grounds for doing so in his seven books on the Donatist schism (Migne, *PL* 11, 962 ff., 1029 f.). The editors of the German edition of Thomas [Aquinas] speak in the introduction to Vol. 29 of "the visible church of Christ, which is visible only in and through its sacraments." Do we not here have the Catholic counterpart to the Lutheran doctrine of the means of grace, the Gospel and the sacraments as the *notae ecclesiae*, the only marks by which we can in faith recognize the presence of the church?

Basically it is the conviction of all Christianity that the church is an article of faith and so not an object of observation. Otherwise the article of faith confessed in the creed about the church would have no sense. "It is necessary that everything which is believed should be hidden," says Luther in *De servo arbitrio* (*opus est, ut omnia quae creduntur, abscondantur,* WA 18, 633 [American Edition 33, 62]).When he then draws the conclusion: "The Church is hidden, the saints are unknown" (*Abscondita est ecclesia, latent sancti* [WA 18, 652; American Edition 33, 89]), the Catholics have never acknowledged this. They must admit, however, that there is some truth here. That is shown by the quotation we have cited about the sacraments. Even for Rome the church is not quite so visible as the kingdom of France or the republic of Venice, as Bellarmine once maintained in his extreme polemics against the Reformation [Mirbt, p. 361].

5

One great truth, then, that is confessed in Article VII of the Augsburg Confession is that the church of Christ is always an object of faith. The other great truth is that it is always a reality in this world. It is made up of living people. So the Apology protests against the misunderstanding which thinks of the church as a "Platonic state":

> We are not dreaming about some Platonic republic, as has been slanderously alleged, but we teach that this church actually exists, made up of true believers and righteous men scattered throughout the world. And we add its marks, the pure teaching of the Gospel and the sacraments. This church is properly called "the pillar of truth" (I Tim. 3:15), for it retains the pure Gospel and what Paul calls the "foundation" (I Cor 3:12) . . . (Apology VII and VIII, 20 [Tappert p. 171]).

In order to grasp what our Confession teaches about the reality of the church in the world, one must learn to grasp what kind of realities the Gospel and the sacraments are for Luther and for the Lutheran Church of the Reformation. Modern man, like the educated humanistic people at that time, sees in the Gospel a religious message, the proclamation of the truths of Christendom. He understands the sacraments as holy actions which symbolically represent a deeper truth. By the power that inheres in a symbol they could be more than mere signs.

Luther goes back to Holy Scripture. There the Word of God is more than a religious message. "Behold, I have put My words in your mouth. See, I have set you this day over nations and over kingdoms, to pluck up and to break down, to destroy and to overthrow, to build and to plant" (Jer. 1:9–10). Thus the Lord speaks to Jeremiah in the hour of his call, and similarly He speaks to all His prophets. Man's word can do much, but it cannot do what God's Word can do, the Word of the Creator and Redeemer, the Word of the Judge and the Fulfiller. Therefore God's own Word has been put into the mouth of His prophets. This Word has not only created the world but also makes history. The fate of Israel as well as of the Eastern peoples and world empires is determined through this Word. "But now thus says the Lord, He who created you, O Jacob, He who formed you, O Israel: 'Fear not, for I have redeemed you. . . .

49

I give Egypt as your ransom. Ethiopia and Seba in exchange for you" (Is. 43:1, 3). "Thus says the Lord to His anointed, to Cyrus, whose right hand I have grasped, to subdue nations before him and ungird the loins of kings, to open doors before him that gates may not be closed. I will go before you . . . " (Is. 45:1–2). This is not just interpretation of history. This is a revelation of the deepest core of the world-historical events of that time, when the Neobabylonian Empire collapsed under Persian attack and Israel was saved. God's Word makes history.

That is also true of the Word of God committed to the church. Also the fates of the peoples of modern Europe are determined by the Word of God which is proclaimed to them, is believed and rejected. When in the empty churches of modern nations the Word of God is preached by a faithful pastor to a handful of people, then this Word, because it is God's Word, becomes a judgment upon people who have rejected God and the faith of their fathers. And at the same time it becomes the Word of deliverance for the "holy remnant."

In my first years in the pastoral office in the environs of Berlin we pastors often asked what would become of the villages in which, Sunday after Sunday, divine service was held with a few old women—that is, if the service was not canceled. Kliefoth often asked what might come upon Mecklenburg, where the landed gentry refused to give their day laborers Saturday afternoon off, with the result that all the work that they had to do for themselves had to be done on Sunday. Today we know how such contempt for God's Word is punished. "For the Word of God is living and active, sharper than any two-edged sword" (Heb. 4:12). That is so today, as it has been for thousands of years, and will be so also in the future until the end of the world. The recognition of this reality of the Word of God is the basis for recognizing the reality of the church.

It is perhaps even more difficult for modern man to recognize the reality of the Word when it comes to him as Gospel. The reality of God's judgment is still to some extent recognizable. But the reality of grace is impenetrable to modern man, because in losing an understanding for sin he has also lost an understanding for grace. This is evidenced by the decline of confession and absolution in Protestantism—which, by the way (something we should not forget), has its parallels in the Roman church. What does it mean to go to Confession once a year, or not for many years and then on the deathbed, for the unchurched masses of nominal Catholics in Vienna, Paris, or Rio de Janeiro? Do *we* still know the solid joy of being sure that the absolution I have received from my pastor is God's forgiveness, spoken by the mouth of His servant, and therefore valid in heaven? The heart of the Gospel is the forgiveness of sins—not a doctrine about it, that and how there is forgiveness, but the bestowing of this forgiveness in the absolution. The same is to be said also of the sacraments of Baptism and the Lord's Supper. Do we still believe what actually happens in these sacraments as we learned it in the Catechism?

Only when we again grasp the reality of the Word of God and the sacraments will we also grasp the reality of the church as confessed in our Confessions. The church is no Platonic state, but an actuality in the world. It is "the assembly of all believers among whom the Gospel is preached in its purity and the holy sacraments are administered according to the Gospel" (Article VII, German text). The administration of the means of grace happens here in this world. They are extended to people who are all quite tangible. As the Lord is active in, with, and under the dealings of men—as He baptizes, absolves, consecrates, gives His true body and His true blood, gives the Holy Spirit, faith, life, blessing—so a holy church is present in, with, and under the assembly of these concrete human beings. For the promise of God bound up with these means remains valid under all circumstances.

From this it is clear that the first and second sentences of the article are indissolubly bonded together. The one church of faith, spoken of in the first sentence, is identical with the visible assembly insofar as this church is present in, with, and under this assembly. This does not exclude the fact that there may be among them hypocrites and unbelievers, unworthy and hypocritical pastors. These belong outwardly to the church as "an association of outward ties and rites" (*societas externarum rerum ac rituum*). But hidden in this external assembly is "an association of faith and of the Holy Spirit in men's hearts" (*societas fidei et Spiritus Sancti in cordibus*), "the inward communion of eternal blessings in the heart, as of the Holy Ghost, of faith, of the fear and love of God," as the German translation by J. Jonas reproduces the Latin text of the Apology (VII and VIII, 5 [final quotation from *Concordia Triglotta*, p. 227]).

There are, then, not two churches but the one church, which the eyes of man see as a congregation or church body, but in which the eyes of God see those who actually and truly belong to the church—perhaps only a small group—and are not just "mingled" (*admixti*, AC VIII) with it. That is the church *proprie dicta*, the church in the real sense, in contrast with the church *large dicta*,) the church in the broader sense.

It is, however, always the one church that is spoken of, whether in the strict or the wider sense. God's all-knowing eye recognizes in it the "association of faith and of the Holy Spirit in men's hearts." Our human eyes see only the "association of outward ties and rites," but in faith in the Lord and His promises we know that wherever the means of grace are, there Christ has His church.

<h1 style="text-align:center">6</h1>

What is confessed of the church in the Lutheran Confessions, that the church is something believed and confessed and not something of our observation, and that the church is a reality in the world, is basic for what Article VII says of the *unity* of the church. As with the church, so also with the unity of the church: It is an object of faith. As no one can see the body of Christ, so also no one can see its unity. If we were to suppose that the whole of Christianity was united in a globe-encircling organization, on the basis of a constitution and cultus acknowledged by all, and even if the same could be said of all doctrine, this union would not yet make the *Una Sancta* visible. Even in such an "ecumenical church," which many today hold up as the ideal, there would be those who belong to it only externally and are not members of the body of Christ. Even in such a giant church, including everyone who claims to be a Christian, the *Una Sancta* would yet be hidden. It would be just the same as with any local congregation.

Paul calls the Christians in Corinth "those sanctified in Christ Jesus, called to be saints." He speaks of that congregation as "the church of God which is at Corinth" [1 Cor. 1:2]. These are statements of faith. In faith he knows that God's church, the one body of Christ, is there in that pile of sinners. They are threatening to destroy the communion of the church, the unity of the body of Christ, with their party strife, these semi-believers who are so proud of their knowledge (Gnosis) and do not even know what the Lord's Supper is and even doubt the resurrection of the dead. Without contradicting himself Paul can write to this congregation, in which there is so much for him to reproach: "I give thanks to God always for you because of the grace of God which was given you in Christ Jesus, that in every way you were enriched in Him with all speech and all knowledge—even as the testimony to Christ was confirmed among you." Because the preaching of Christ is there, and has created faith, therefore Paul is certain that he who has called them will surely sustain them to the end (1 Cor. 1:4 ff.). The same is the case with the original church in Jerusalem. Acts speaks of that congregation as being "of one heart and soul," and then with striking honesty goes on to tell of Ananias and Sapphira, who lied to God, and then of the first dispute in the church, a dispute about money [Acts 4:32; 5:1–11; 6:1].

Even where we experience Christian, brotherly fellowship, "heart and heart together united," there too the communion of saints remains an article of faith, for this communion, the *koinōnia* of which the New Testament speaks, is a work of the Holy Spirit. It not only binds the believers together, but it also unites us "with the Father and with His Son Jesus Christ" (1 John 1:3). The mystery of this communion reaches into the communion within the Holy Trinity. "The glory which Thou hast given Me I have given to them, that they may be one even as We are one, I in them and Thou in Me, that they may become perfectly one" (John 17:22–23).

This unity is always an object of faith, not of observation, even though the world may see something of its working: "Behold, how they love one another." The Apology describes the *Una Sancta* with these words: " . . . men scattered throughout the world who agree on the Gospel and have the same Christ, the same Holy Spirit, and the same sacraments, whether they have the same human traditions or not" [Articles VII and VIII, 10; Tappert, p. 170]. [Ed. note: Dr. Sasse quotes both the German and Latin texts, but they are quite similar.] Hidden under the various church bodies with their different languages and nationalities, constitutions and forms of worship, and other human traditions, lives the one church. Its unity is also hidden under the divisions of Christianity. The one church is purely an article of faith, and yet it is a great reality in the world.

7

The last-quoted passage from the Apology clearly illumines the second part of our Article VII:

> For it is sufficient for the true unity of the Christian church that the Gospel be preached in conformity with a pure understanding of it and that the sacraments be administered in accordance with the divine Word. It is not necessary for the true unity of the Christian church that ceremonies, instituted by men, should be observed uniformly in all places. It is as Paul says in Eph. 4:4, 5, "There is one body and one Spirit, just as you were called to the one hope that belongs to your call, one Lord, one faith, one baptism [Tappert, p. 32; German text].

There is hardly a passage in our Confessions that has evoked more discussion than this one, and still today it is in the middle of the debates and controversies about the church and church unity, about confession and union, about the rights and wrongs of the modern ecumenical movement.

In our discussions of the first part of Article VII we rejected the division into visible and invisible church, as though the opening sentence speaks of the one holy church which continues forever (*una sancta ecclesia perpetuo mansura*), the invisible church, and the second sentence speaks of the congregation of the saints *congregatio sanctorum*, in which the means of grace are used, the visible church. There is only one church, of which one can speak in a strict sense or in a wider sense. Thus it is here. The true unity of the church, of which Article VII speaks, is both an article of faith and a reality in the world. It is the unity which binds together all those, wherever they may be in the world from the rising to the setting of the sun, who truly believe, who have one Christ, one Holy Spirit, one Gospel, one Baptism, and one Sacrament of the Altar, whether they have or do not have the same ceremonies or traditions. They have one Christ and one Holy Spirit because they have one Gospel, one Baptism, and one Sacrament of the Altar.

That is exactly the thought in Ephesians 4, whose interpretation is given in Article VII. Also there we find next to one another "one body and one Spirit . . . one hope . . . one Lord, one faith, one baptism, one God and Father" [vv. 4–6]. The one Gospel appears in the words, "just as you were called to the one hope that belongs to your call." (Compare Luther's explanation of the Third Article: "called . . . through the Gospel.") In and through the means of grace we have the one Lord, the one Spirit, the one God and Father. Since the means of grace create the church as the people of God, the body of Christ, the temple of the Holy Spirit, the *congregatio*, therefore they are also the marks of the church, the (*notae ecclesiae*).

Luther expands the list of the marks of the church. In *On the Councils and the Church* he lists the marks by which one can recognize "the Christian holy people": the Word of God, Baptism, the Sacrament of the Altar, the Office of the Keys. "Fifth, the church is recognized externally by the fact that it consecrates or calls ministers." "Sixth, the holy Christian people are externally recognized by prayer, public praise, and thanksgiving to God." "Seventh, the holy Christian people are externally recognized by the holy possession of the sacred cross. They must endure every misfortune and persecution, all kinds of trials and

54

evil from the devil, the world, and the flesh . . . in order to become like their head, Christ. And the only reason they must suffer is that they steadfastly adhere to Christ and God's word, enduring this for the sake of Christ" (WA 50, 628, 632, 641 f. [American Edition 41, 148, 154, 164 f.]). These additional marks of the church belong with the first. Where the Word of God, the Gospel, is, there it demands to be preached; so there must be a ministry. Where the Gospel is, there people must come together for divine service in order to hear it. Where the Word is, there the cross must also be; otherwise how could the word of the cross be taken seriously? Where the Word and the sacraments are, there are God's holy people. "For the Word of God is living and active, sharper than any two-edged sword . . . discerning the thoughts and intentions of the heart" (Heb. 4:12). It is "like fire . . . and like a hammer which breaks the rock in pieces" (Jer. 23:29). It has God's promise that it will not return empty [Is. 55:10–11]. And Christ's sacraments are not just some things that men do. In them Christ Himself is present and active.

Because this is so, therefore the doctrine of Article VII immediately becomes an assignment, just as in Eph. 4 doctrine and exhortation, indicative and imperative, go together. Because there is one body and one Spirit, because you were called by the Gospel to one hope, because you have received the one Baptism of the one Lord in one faith, therefore "I . . . a prisoner for the Lord, beg you to lead a life worthy of the calling to which you have been called . . . eager to maintain the unity of the Spirit in the bond of peace" [vv. 1, 3]. So faith in the one church must immediately lead to eager preservation of that unity. The indicative and imperative go inseparably together also in Article VII. The great *satis est*, "it is sufficient for the true unity of the Christian church," involves a *necesse est*, it is necessary. As the life of the Christian is continually threatened by the temptation to sin and to fall away from the faith, and each day we are to return to our Baptism, daily repent, so the existence of the church is threatened by the devil, the world, and the flesh, in which we live also as members of the church. And the church must daily pray: "Lord Jesus Christ, will you not stay?" Daily, for the evening of the world draws on, let us plead with the hymn of our fathers which was so important to us in the church struggle in Germany:

> Lord Jesus Christ, will you not stay?
> It is now toward the end of day.
> Oh, let your Word, that saving light,
> Shine forth undimmed into the night.
> (*Lutheran Worship*, 344)

Things would be better with the Lutheran Church around the world if we all, pastors and congregations, in all church bodies called Lutheran, would pray thus every evening.

<h1 style="text-align:center">8</h1>

So then the great article of the Augsburg Confession about the church is both a confession of firm faith in the indestructibility of the church and a call quickening our consciences to preserve the unity of the church and to restore it where it has been lost among us. The Apology calls the article of faith about the catholic [or universal] church "very comforting and highly necessary" [Par. 9, German text; *Concordia Triglotta*, p. 229]. How often has it not appeared as if the church were done for? *Ne desperemus,* "that we may not despair" (Par. 9 [Tappert, p. 170), we are given the great and comforting article of faith in the actuality of God's church in the world.

It would be an utter contradiction of all that the Augsburg Confession says in confessing what God's Word says, if we would use all this as a resting ground for our complacency. The confessors of Augsburg did not rest content with the fact that, despite all that was wrong in the papacy, the church was still there. They were not content to confess the profound inner communion of all God's children which no one can destroy. They were active in doing what they could to preserve the unity of outward Christianity. They took up the emperor's words regarding the purpose of their coming together to deal with the questions of the faith at the Diet, "to live together in unity and in one fellowship and church, even as we are all enlisted under one Christ" [AC Introduction, 4; Tappert, p. 25].

The question they then had to answer was wherein the true unity of the church consists. On the basis of God's Word they confessed that it is not to be found in unity of traditions or ceremonies but in the one Gospel and in the sacraments instituted by our Lord. They declined the false view of the church's unity which sees this unity in what human beings have arranged or devised, such as a great constitution or a uniform liturgy.

Our church has never taught that in areas such as these there *have* to be differences. On the contrary, there have always been efforts to preserve unity also in these areas. The confessors raised no basic objection against episcopal polity. They even acknowledged that the office of the pope was acceptable, if only pope and bishops would honor the

Gospel and not set themselves up as more than incumbents of the office of the Word and the sacraments. There was no objection to adding to this divine office also the humanly devised office of oversight (*episkopē*) over pastors and congregations. What the confessors could not do was heed the pope and the bishops more than the Word of God.

The Augsburg Confession makes this final declaration:

> St. Peter forbids the bishops to exercise lordship as if they had power to coerce the churches according to their will. It is not our intention to find ways of reducing the bishops' power, but we desire and pray that they may not coerce our consciences to sin. If they are unwilling to do this and ignore our petition, let them consider how they will answer for it in God's sight, inasmuch as by their obstinacy they offer occasion for division and schism, which they should in truth help to prevent (AC XXVIII, 76 ff. [Tappert, p. 94]).

Thus the Lutheran Reformation ended with the division of Christendom; the efforts to preserve unity ended in the separation of those on both sides who were "all enlisted under one Christ" and so wished to live "in one fellowship and church," as was confessed in the introduction of the Augsburg Confession.

Why was no other outcome possible? We can answer this question only by referring to the deep mystery of world and church history that, in this sinful world, where lies are fathered on every hand, what is lie and what is truth cannot be known if there is no line between them. Therefore unity in the church is possible only with demarcation against heresy. Thus when our Lord prayed for the unity of all those who believe in Him, He also prayed: "Sanctify them in the truth; Thy Word is truth" [John 17:17]. The apostle John was then a servant of the truth, and so a servant of the true unity of the church, when he drew the line against those who denied the Incarnation. This was also the case when the early church drew the line against Marcion and the Gnostics, Athanasius drew it against the Arians, Augustine against Pelagius, and Luther against the pope, Zwingli, and the Anabaptists. So it has ever been with the church militant in this world. We cannot confess what is true without rejecting what contradicts it. Kierkegaard observed that truth's quotation marks are polemical.

And when here on earth the tragic case occurs, which happens again and again where the question of truth is earnestly engaged, that one confession of faith is set against another, conscience against conscience, then we must leave the decision to Him who in the Last Judgment will finally separate truth from error. We do not know God's judgments, and can and may not anticipate them. Also when we must speak the *damnamus* ("we condemn") against a false teaching, God's forgiving grace may bring the erring sinner into the church triumphant, where there is no more untruth. On the other hand, this door will be shut to many a one who has done battle for the truth in perfect orthodoxy, but has forgotten that he too was only a poor sinner who lives only by forgiving grace. Only in God's light, when we shall no longer "know in part" but "shall understand fully, even as" we "have been fully understood" [1 Cor. 13:12]—only then, and not before, will we in the full truth of God also fully understand the true unity of the church.

9

If this, in bold strokes, is the Lutheran doctrine of the church and its unity, *what does this doctrine mean for Lutheranism today?* What tasks does it impose upon us? The first great task is obviously a profound self-examination. Such an examination was evident in what we cited above from the assembly of the Evangelical Lutheran Conference of 1868. "The wounds we have inflicted upon ourselves in ignorance or unfaithfulness" are still bleeding, and they have been multiplied in the decades that have passed since then. In territory after territory Lutheranism in Germany has been displaced, until today it lives unambiguously only in the free churches. Who is responsible for this?

The Lutherans in the Lutheran territorial churches have gone the way of the Lutherans in the Union churches who banded together (*Vereinslutheraner*) and committed themselves to confess the Lutheran faith. They declared that when this or that demand would be made upon them, that then the occasion for confession (*casus confessionis*) would have arrived and they would not yield. But then they did yield, saying that this was not the right *casus confessionis*. That is how it went every time. They gave up one position after another. They claimed they were indeed always ready to confess; yet when it came to it, they accepted everything. It was a tragic history, this history of the efforts to recover the Lutheran Church in Prussia. Many hearts were broken, and not only because of sorrow over a course of events they could not stop, but also because of shame at their own failure.

They then set their hope on the territorial churches that were still Lutheran: Saxony, Hannover, Bavaria, Württemberg. But even there what was Lutheran was in rapid decline. One generation ago there was still a scattering of confessional Lutherans in Württemberg. Where are they today? And what of Hannover and Bavaria? The German Evangelical Church Federation turned out to be what was prophesied by a shrewd leader of the Union churches. He called it "the sleeping car in which the Lutherans are traveling into the Union." It did not have to be that way, but the man knew the condition of Lutheran confession in the nominally still Lutheran churches.

There came the year 1933, and with it the German Evangelical Church, under Nazi compulsion. But who can compel a bishop to deny his faith? In the following year the Lutheran bishops in Barmen ratified this church, which for Barth and all the Reformed, for Niemöller and all the Union people, was a genuine union. Barth called it a confessional union (*Bekenntnisunion*).

Then came the day when Hitler's thousand-year *Reich* came to an end. It was the last occasion when the Lutheran bishops in Germany might have confessed with their deeds. They missed also this opportunity, and their churches were swallowed up in the new union called the Evangelical Church in Germany (*Evangelische Kirche in Deutschland* [EKiD]). In Eisenach, at the foot of the Wartburg, the Lutheran Church in Germany was buried in 1948. Löhe's nightmare of the Lutheran Church being buried by its own pastors became a reality. From the sleeping car of the Church Federation it was still possible to get out. One can leave a Church Federation. From the grave of the EKiD no one rises again.This hybrid between federation and church, a federation which calls itself a church and acts as a church, a church which would be a federation—"federationist church" (*bündische Kirche*) they said in 1933—recognizes no right of secession. The VELKD [Vereinigte Evangelisch-Lutherische Kirche Deutschlands, United Evangelical Lutheran Church of Germany], which was formed within the Evangelical Church in Germany, cannot get out of the larger structure, even if it wanted to. It does not want to, because it knows it cannot.

Meanwhile the Lutheran churches of the world have been looking on as spectators. They do not realize that by their being content to be deedless spectators they seal their own fate. In Sweden the slumbering conscience of a minority awakened when the demand that women be ordained was voted approval by a majority of the bishops and the church assembly. But what was there to do? The state used pressure to bring it about, and so on every hand we hear lamentation over the tyranny of the state. The state, however, can point out that the church made no use of the possibility of rejecting laws decided by the state. Opposition has been shown by the Assembly for the Church (*Kyrklige Samling*) and the bishop of Gothenburg, Bo Giertz. They are carrying on the struggle in exactly the same way as did the Lutherans in Germany and in the Prussian Union, hoping that, after winter, spring must come. The rule for the seasons is not, however, the rule in church history. A confessional church does not happen if one does not actually confess. It is not enough to work out a casuistry of how pastors and laity are to react when one of the new priestesses appears in church. Nothing less will do than taking the stand that all such ordinations are contrary to God's Word and invalid, and that all official acts done by these ladies are done by lay persons. Baptisms done by them stand as those done by a midwife. Those who walk the corridors of power will not be slow to react to such a stand. When they apply their disciplinary measures, there may then be such joy as Görres expressed in his *Athanasius* upon the imprisonment of the archbishop of Cologne: "Praise be to Jesus Christ; now there is violence!" Thus churches are saved.

Such hope dies when men are silent as our Confession is dismantled piece by piece, as the place for being a Lutheran in the traditional structure of the Lutheran Church is constricted more and more, as God's Word is set aside. Such silence means the end of the Lutheran Church. No one would claim it to be a fact that the churches of Germany, Sweden, Denmark, Norway, and Finland are inwardly held together by "great unanimity" [AC I, 1] in "the teaching of the Gospel and the administration of the sacraments" [AC VII, 2]. There is no longer a consensus in these churches regarding what God's Word demands, what the Gospel actually is, what Baptism and the Lord's Supper are. What holds them together is the setup they have inherited, their constitutions and their apparatus for running things, their property and the money that the state provides or collects for them. These are the "human traditions or rites and ceremonies" [AC VII, 3]. They are not what Article VII of the Augsburg Confession says creates the true unity of the church.

In the Prussian Union and then in the other churches it was at first said that what everything really depends on is the preaching of the Gospel and the administration of the sacraments. It was said that no pastor was being prevented from preaching the Gospel in truth and purity and from rightly administering the sacraments [AC VII, 2]. On the contrary, that was said to be what was desired.

Whatever one may think of the details in Kliefoth's address in 1868, he was surely right in rejecting the view that what is said in Article VII of the Augsburg Confession applies only to pastors, with those who govern the church excepted. For what else does it mean to govern the affairs of the church than to exercise the pastoral office in areas that extend beyond the local congregation? A bishop is one who preaches and administers the sacraments. He ordains in the name of the church. He puts the vows to the ordinands that they will be faithful to Scripture and the Lutheran Confessions. What sort of hypocrisy is it when I obligate a man to a confession which I myself do not believe! That is what used to go on in Prussia, although today it is generally regarded as intolerable. It was the way of the Prussian Union also in the Rhineland, in areas where there were both Lutherans and Reformed. Those who were training to be teachers of religion had to learn both Luther's Catechism and the Heidelberg Catechism so that they could teach the one or the other as needed. And what of those training to be pastors, when they are taught by men who do not confess their church's confession? What of their preaching of the Gospel and administration of the sacraments, and their ordination vow?

Let no one say that confession is not mentioned in Article VII as a mark of the church. No, not expressly. But what is a confession if it is no longer the declaration of the church: This is what we believe, teach, and confess, because it is the true doctrine of the Gospel, because it is Biblical truth to be preached from every pulpit!

If our fathers of 1868 could speak to us today, what a preaching of repentance that would be for the whole Lutheran Church, or what is left of it.

10

This call to repentance would go out not only to the Lutherans of Germany and Europe, but certainly to them first. They allowed the Lutheran Church to disappear as church in one territory after another until little more is left than a viewpoint or a school of thought in theology—until this also dies. For schools of thought in theology soon pass away; they disappear with their teachers and leaders. Is it conceivable that ever again in Sweden, and perhaps also in Denmark and Norway, a man might become a professor or a bishop if he saw the ordination of women as defection from the Word of God? Is there any German university today where men would be tolerated who reject the Unions, including those of Barmen in 1933 and 1934, and the Evangelical Church in Germany (EKiD) in 1948, declaring them not only false in theory but actually breaking off fellowship with such Union churches? Such questions can be put in ways appropriate to each of the European state and territorial churches, also where they are no longer governed directly by the state, but where the church authorities are at the pleasure of the mass of indifferent and nominal church members. It is the tragic but irreversible outcome of European church history: A state church can no longer be a confessional church. But a church can be Lutheran only as it is a confessional church.

This is a fact for our brothers in the faith in *America* to ponder. Are they even aware of it? Do they recognize the great crisis of the church of the Lutheran Confession? If one looks closely at the Lutheran churches in America and studies their development, one finds little awareness of the crisis. Where was their witness in 1933 and 1934 to warn and to encourage us? What was their witness in 1948? Many sat by quietly; they thought it unloving to get mixed up in the affairs of other churches. The representatives of the Missouri Synod felt they should not repeat the mistakes of earlier times and give criticism that was not always well informed or loving. But it is never a service of love if one does not help a sick man out of his sickness, but says to him that all is well. We are all responsible for one another, we who have before God and the whole church confessed the Unaltered Augsburg Confession or the Book of Concord. We are not unknown to each other. Most of the Lutheran churches in America are members together with the European Lutheran churches in the Lutheran World Federation. They see, or they ought to see, what is going on there. They cannot but see how the Confessions have become little more than a formality for many. They cannot be ignorant of what is taught in the member churches. Have things gone so far that our American brothers in the faith recognize the ordination of women? Or is this to be regarded as an internal matter for each church by itself? What has been heard from the Lutheran churches of America as they have watched one church after another welcomed into membership in the Federation, some of whom do not call themselves Lutheran, some who quickly put on the name? Subscription to the constitution of the Federation may be lightly done; many churches have no intention of considering the doctrine of the Augsburg Confession as that doctrine, and no other, which is to be preached and taught, have no commitment to guard this doctrine or repudiate what contradicts it.

Such a commitment might honestly be expected. No one can expect that all pastors become paragons of Lutheran confession and preaching by tomorrow. In every church there is weakness and theological ignorance. Yet of those churches which declare that they are Lutheran one can expect that they will learn, live, and grow from the resources of the Lutheran Confessions, and so will become what they confess themselves to be. The sickness at the heart of the Lutheran World Federation is the untruthfulness which appears symptomatically in so many of its decisions. For too many modern church leaders, church politics comes first, and then the Confessions become a tool of church politics.

This is what the Lutherans of America should have seen. Why did they not notice it? A hundred years ago they saw such things quite clearly. The '60s of the last century saw a great decision in American Lutheranism. It is connected with the name of Samuel Simon Schmucker (1799—1873). He was the first president of the first Lutheran seminary in America (Gettysburg, founded in 1826), and he held that office for four decades. He was prominent in the General Synod, a product of the pietistic and unionistic Lutheranism in Pennsylvania influenced by August Hermann Francke. In general American church history he is known as one of the prophets of the Ecumenical Movement in the United States. He is the father of what was called "federative union," a combination of churches that retain their identity and yet enter into church fellowship. For such a combination with the Reformed, the Methodists, and other Protestants, he wrote a confession of 12 articles. It was composed of pieces taken from the Anglican articles, the Methodist Discipline, Lutheran and Reformed confessions, and from the articles of the Brethren. His influence in the efforts to achieve church unions in America seems to have been greater than was formerly supposed. He is one of those who prepared the way for today's National Council of the Churches of Christ in the U.S.A.

In Lutheranism he is not highly regarded. In 1854 he published his *Definite Platform,* a watered-down Augsburg Confession from which the specifically Lutheran doctrines had been removed. His goal was an "American Lutheranism," indigenous and living in harmonious fellowship with the Reformed Churches. At this all the Lutheran synods, also his own, turned away from him. Whatever differences there were among them, here they stood united: They would not let themselves be robbed of the Unaltered Augsburg Confession. That was the great decision which happened in the '60s only a hundred years ago.

Could something like that happen now? The situation is again fraught with heavy debate of weighty church issues. Is it possible to repeat what was done a hundred years ago? And if it did happen again, would it be more than an action of church politics in which for practical reasons an old confession would once more be formally affirmed without thereby making a decision of faith? To accept a confession, when this is seriously done, means to make a decision about what is believed, for the individual and for the church body.

Do we still understand our ordination that way? When a congregation or church in America espouses the Augsburg Confession, is this still understood in the sense of a decision as to what is believed? Or have things gone so far also among the Lutherans of America that the church's confession is only something that has to be said if you are writing up a constitution? To be sure, the Confessions should be preserved, and why not? Who would want to throw out such a precious old piece of furniture? If the Anglicans pledge all their ministers to the Thirty-Nine Articles, the Presbyterians to the Westminster Confession, and Roman Catholics to the Profession of Faith of the Council of Trent, why should we Lutherans not do the same with the Unaltered Augsburg Confession? There was once in Oxford a wise and much-honored Anglican churchman. When he was asked how he could accept the Thirty-Nine Articles along with his Catholic convictions, he replied, "I also accept the gas company of Oxford, but I do not approve of it."

Have we Lutherans also reached this level of wisdom, resignation, or despair? In any case, this is something we ought to be quite clear about: Our church was the last of the Reformation churches still loyal to its Confessions. For innumerable Christians the Augsburg Confession has been truly their confession. If it should now sink to the level of being only a historical document, a formality to be put in a constitution, then we ought to know that the Profession of Faith of the Council of Trent and the doctrine of the Vatican Council will continue to stand as the confession of innumerable millions of human beings. There the faith confessed at the Reformation is included—but among the false doctrines that are put under the anathema!

That the foregoing picture is not overdrawn is clear from the facts which are there for anyone to see. In America the Lutherans are now mostly in three large groups. The Lutheran Church in America is putting itself together out of the United Lutheran Church, the Augustana Church (Swedish origins), plus one formerly Danish and another Finnish church. That adds up to one third of the Lutherans. This church characterizes itself by its participation not only in the Lutheran World Federation but also in the World Council of Churches and in the National Council of the Churches of Christ in the U.S.A., in which American Protestantism finds its unity. The churches in the middle are now united in The American Lutheran Church (The ALC). This church also belongs to the World Council of Churches, but not yet to the National Council of the Churches of Christ in the U.S.A. With the first-named church it forms the National Lutheran Council.

In all these churches there are still faithful Lutherans. To what extent they form a viewpoint that has become a minority is not clear. Those from the former Evangelical Lutheran Church who took their confession seriously were not able to halt the entry of the new American Lutheran Church into the World Council of Churches. What the "left" [LCA] and the "center" [The ALC] have in common in spite of all existing differences is that they recognize all the European state and territorial churches, even the most liberal, and beyond what is Lutheran extend their recognition to churches that in fact operate as Union churches. They work together with all of them in the Lutheran World Federation. Beyond that, they acknowledge the World Council of Churches and work with it, holding prominent positions. To what extent the confessional consciousness of these churches has been shattered is shown by every issue of their church papers, every decision these churches make. The number of pastors whose pledge to the Book of Concord is without reservation (*quia*) becomes less from year to year; or if they do it, they do not know what that means. Among the young pastors in all these churches there is a growing discussion of the question whether the old Confessions can still be accepted as their fathers accepted them a generation or two ago. It is openly stated that this is no longer possible.

What is happening here is tied up with the loss of the doctrine of Holy Scripture as the Word of God inspired by the Holy Spirit. Those on the left no longer dare say that Scripture is the Word of God, as is evidenced by the explanation accompanying the union documents. The old doctrine is still there in the constitution of The American Lutheran Church; those who did not want it there kept quiet so as not to hinder the union. Pietism once made its way through Europe traveling from west to east, from one church to another, undermining the doctrinal substance of the confessional churches, and so preparing the way for the Rationalism that brought the dissolution of the Christian faith. Similarly we may observe the deadly disease of a new, doctrinally indifferent Enthusiasm running its course in America. It draws strength from religious and intellectual thought in the United States and from the ever-more-powerful Ecumenical Movement. We know enough about such spiritual epidemics from the history of our own time! The sickness which has ravaged Lutheranism in the Eastern states now takes its course in the Midwest, traditionally a fortress of confessional Lutheranism. Iowa and Ohio have already fallen victim to it; the symptoms are evident in their faculties.

Now the sickness rages in Missouri, and unless there are signs and wonders this last great church of confessional Lutheranism will succumb. The churches of the left and the middle are simply waiting for Missouri. They see that the Synodical Conference with its continual internal tensions cannot last much longer, and their hope is that Missouri will then move into the National Lutheran Council, and from there into the Lutheran World Federation and the World Council of Churches. No one can tell what would then happen with the remaining Lutheranism (Wisconsin, the Norwegians, and the Slovaks of the Synodical Conference), or what might split off from Missouri and from other churches. Everything is waiting for the fall of Missouri. Then the way would finally be open for a Lutheran world church without a confession.

11

Without a confession? Yes, without a confession. For what most Lutherans in America understand by a confession is not what the confessing Lutheran Church has always understood by that term. Rather it is what Schmucker meant by it, what Dr. Fry and perhaps most of the leaders of world Lutheranism mean by it: sentences in which Christians or churches express the convictions they share. It is indeed important to know how much we share. This is especially true in this time of chaos in churches and theologies. We must know what we share with others, and what we do not share. We must pursue serious doctrinal discussion with those from whom we are separated, in order that on the basis of Holy Scripture we may be brought to one common doctrine.

Such theses, however, are still no confession. To suppose that they are is a notion which can be traced back to a fatal misunderstanding of Article VII that one encounters again and again. It goes something like this: For church unity it is enough "to agree concerning the teaching of the Gospel and the administration of the sacraments" (*consentire de doctrina evangelii et de administratione sacramentorum*). If we find that we agree with others regarding our understanding of the Gospel and the administration of the sacraments, then we can establish church fellowship with them. This may happen church with church, or even congregation with congregation and individual with individual. This last comes under the heading of "selective fellowship," as it is called in America. Two pastors or congregations of different churches who live together

66

in one place find that they believe the same, and on the basis of this consensus they enter upon church fellowship with each other. Since tomorrow one or both of the pastors may be called elsewhere and the makeup of the congregations is changing, this means the atomizing of the church. This is especially the case when both sides are weak in faith and theology. What is regarded as a consensus in doctrine may in fact be a consensus of ignorance and poverty of doctrine. There are even those who suppose that they can establish degrees of unity. The degrees match the level of agreement reached so far in the discussions. The consensus one tries to read out of Article VII is in all such cases a purely human arrangement.

It is a remarkable fact that until quite recently there was no translation of the German text of the Augsburg Confession, or at least not one that was widely known. The English text of the *Concordia Triglotta*, the three-language edition of the Book of Concord, takes into account both the German and the Latin versions in the case of all the other confessions, but not so with the Augsburg Confession. Here only the Latin goes into the English text. In the English translation of the Book of Concord which was recently published in Philadelphia [the Tappert Edition], a translation is given of both the Latin and the German versions of the Augsburg Confession. The German version, however, has not been quite fully understood. The great "It is enough" (*satis est*) is clearly directed against Rome. For the unity of the church Rome required more than unity in the faith; it required the acceptance of human traditions and ceremonies. *Satis est* does not then postulate a minimum of agreement, a consensus, which we achieve in the course of our discussions, but a maximum: " . . . that [with one accord, *einträchtiglich*] the Gospel be preached *in conformity with a pure understanding of it* and that the sacraments be administered in accordance with the divine Word" [italics Dr. Sasse's]. Not the agreement in doctrine—the Roman church has a consensus in doctrine, the Baptists also have one; every church has some sort of consensus, even if it is a consensus in agreeing that doctrine is not important—but only the consensus in the *pure* doctrine and in the *right* administration of the sacraments is the consensus demanded in the Augsburg Confession. That is the "great unanimity" (*magnus consensus*) with which the first article of the Augsburg Confession begins, a consensus not made by men but given by God, the consensus in the right faith, which only the Holy Spirit creates.

If it were only a human consensus, then the doctrinal decisions of the Confession would have validity only for Lutheran Churches. Then it would only claim to be the doctrine of a particular church, just as other churches have their own particular confessions. There is nothing of this said anywhere in the Book of Concord. It has no notion of any such thing as a Lutheran Church. We do not believe in the Lutheran Church, but in the one, holy, catholic [or universal] church. The Book of Concord actually became the confession of a particular church. It was first called Evangelical, then Evangelical Lutheran, and also Lutheran. But that only came as a consequence of the way things developed in the Reformation's history. It was a consequence of the church division which could not be stopped.

We believe that the true church is wherever the Gospel is still heard and where Christ's sacraments are present. Thus the archconfessionalist Philipp Nicolai believed that Christ's church was present among the Muscovites, the Ethiopians, and in the churches of the Jesuits in America [Werner Elert, *The Structure of Lutheranism*, pp. 391 ff., Note 8]. But to establish church fellowship with those who mix this Gospel with false doctrine, that we cannot do, not even with Lutherans who deny the faith of their fathers, as little as Philipp Nicolai could have church fellowship with the Muscovites and the Jesuits.

This does not mean that our Confession can claim to have some sort of infallibility. It does not mean that all Christians must first accept the Book of Concord before we can have church fellowship with them. We are bound together with the true church of all ages in the great consensus of what is believed, taught, and confessed, also with those who did not yet have or need an Augsburg Confession. We are also bound up in the unity of the true church with those who after us will confess the true faith even to the end of the world, whether they use the words of our Confession or say it in other ways. But it must be the same faith, for there is only one Gospel. This faith embraces the great Biblical truths which were set down in our Confession in defense against false doctrine and in obedience to the Lord who looks to us all to confess His everlasting truth, until He confesses before His heavenly Father those who have confessed Him and His Gospel in this world.

Evening is falling also upon the Lutheran Church. But in the evening the Lord of His church is perhaps most near.

MINISTRY AND CONGREGATION

Letters to Lutheran Pastors, No. 8
July 1949

1

One of the most grievous events in the history of the Lutheran Church in the 19th century was the fact that the two great churchmen Wilhelm Löhe and Ferdinand Walther went separate ways after the great theological leader of the Missouri Synod had in 1851 had a most promising meeting with Löhe in Neuendettelsau.

That the theological faculty at Erlangen had small regard for both of them means little. However great the achievements of the old Erlangen School, however great its representatives as men and as scholars, there was yet a weakness there which rendered them incapable of being a resource for a lasting renewal of the Lutheran Church. They were unable to hold themselves clear of the insidious poison of Schleiermacherian subjectivism. Although they were dedicated to discern and defend the objective truths of revelation, Schleiermacher's way of doing theology had infected and weakened them. What at the time was already recognized by some clear-sighted men became only too obvious by the end of the century. If "I the Christian am to me the theologian the most proper matter of my study" [J. C. K. von Hofmann of the Erlangen School, *Schriftbeweis*, I, 10], then no power on earth could keep theology from becoming a study of things in man, a "science of religion."

The other great weakness of the Erlangen School was their being so bound up in the little world of Germany's territorial churches. Their horizon reached from their small town in Franconia toward the south as far as Nürnberg and Munich, and northwards to Leipzig, Dresden, Rostock, and even as far as Dorpat [Tartu in Estonia]. How vastly farther-reaching was the vision and engagement of the little village pastor in Neuendettelsau. How much more clearly Löhe and Walther

69

saw what faced the Lutheran Church in the world—beyond a Lutheran Church run by a bureaucracy that was watched over and guided by the state. For them the church was not just a department of the state. No one could imagine that out of the laborious work of organizing these congregations on the fringes of civilization would come the great churches in whose hands, so far as it lies in human hands, today rests the future of Lutheranism. So also no one could foresee the consequences of the break between Walther and Löhe, between Missouri and Iowa. We see these consequences today and are faced with the question whether the agreement which failed to happen at that time might come in our day.

2

What separated Löhe and Walther, and so what separated Missouri and Iowa, was not by any means only the relationship between church and ministry, but this was certainly a primary point in which they could not find agreement. Nor was it a matter which separated only these two men and the churches they represented. The separation ran right through Lutheranism. In the second third of the 19th century Lutherans were drawn, in their own way, into the deep-going discussion which at that time involved all of Christendom, from the Roman Catholics before the Vatican I to the strangest sects of the Reformed world (for instance the Irvingites and the Disciples of Christ), and profoundly affected Anglicanism.

One can at first only marvel that Lutheranism could have been so disturbed by this question, even to the point of causing divisions in the Prussian Free Church and her daughter church in Australia. For the Lutheran Church, matters of church government belong to the adiaphora, to the "rites and ceremonies, instituted by men" (Augsburg Confession VII), concerning which there may and must be freedom in the church. Christ is not the legislator of a human religious fellowship, and the Gospel has in it no law which prescribes the only right way of organization and polity for the church.

One must be clear as to what this means. Other churches have "an order by which the Lord wills the church to be governed," as Calvin put it [*Institutes*, 4, 3, 1; LCC 41, 1053]. This is true of all Catholic churches, both of the East and of the West, and of all Reformed churches. Their differences have to do only with what that order must be—the universal monarchy of the pope, the episcopal-synodical government of the church as in the Eastern churches and Anglicanism, a ruling senate of presbyters among whom there must be no differences of rank, or the autonomy of the individual congregation as in Congregationalism and among the Baptists. These are just a few notable options, all of which claim to represent what the New Testament requires for the polity of the church.

Luther's entire greatness and the boldness of his basic theological principle of the strict separation of Law and Gospel become evident when one sees how beyond all these possibilities he goes his lonesome way: Christ gave His church no such law prescribing one right organization, government, and polity (*de constituenda ecclesia*). Any way of organizing things may do, so long as the means of grace are going on and are not frustrated.

One thing the Lord gave His church, however, belongs not only to its well-being *bene esse* but to its very being *esse:* "In order that we may obtain this faith, the ministry of teaching the Gospel and administering the sacraments was instituted," says Article V of the Augsburg Confession. In order that we may obtain the justifying faith of which the previous article has spoken, the Gospel must be preached, the sacraments must be administered. Therefore God has instituted the ministry, the service through which this happens. Wherever the means of grace are rightly administered, there God fulfills His promise that the Word will not return empty, there faith is created, there is the church, the congregation of saints, of justified sinners.

How the congregation organizes itself, for this no prescriptions are given, just as there are none for how the church's ministry is to be organized. The apostles came to recognize that it would be helpful for their ministry if they were relieved of the work of caring for the poor and attending to money matters. So the office of the deacons was created as an auxiliary office. But the church was the church already before this office was created. So the church can at any time create auxiliary offices to meet the needs of the time. Examples of this in the history of the church are the office of an episcopate, or superintendency, or any other offices, whatever they may be called. But all these offices have their right of existence only insofar as they serve the one great office of the preaching of the Gospel and the administering of the sacraments. A bishop may be entrusted with the task of seeing to the running of a great diocese. But the meaning of such an assignment can only consist in this, that he thereby gives room and support to the church's ministry. His actual office is the office of pastor, also when he is a pastor for

71

pastors. By human arrangement he may have the work of superintendency. By divine mandate he has solely the office of preaching the forgiveness and justification of sinners for Christ's sake.

3

If this is something on which there is agreement in the whole Lutheran Church, if the Lutheran Church can live with a consistorial or an episcopal constitution, if, as in America, it can live with a presbyterial-synodical or sometimes even an almost completely congregational organization, how are we to explain the differences of opinion which exactly in the question of ministry and congregation, and thereby in the question of church organization, have repeatedly split our church since Löhe and Walther went their separate ways?

This is a hard question to answer. It seems to me there is no doubt that Lutheranism was infiltrated by the organization and polity problems of other churches and confessions. No church in the 19th century was able to stay clear of such problems. We have only to name Möhler, Newman, Pusey, Vinet, and Chalmers. All confessions of Christendom were affected. It was a time when the old Christian Europe seemed to be coming to an end, and the question was what would take its place.

We Lutherans have much to learn from the passionate struggle of Roman Catholicism to be free from the fetters of the state shaped by the Enlightenment. This church's struggle, for instance in Cologne, has instructive parallels with the confessional battle of the Prussian Lutherans, just as later the brave struggle of the Hessian *Renitenz* [a confessional Lutheran movement] has parallels to the *Kulturkampf* at the time of Bismarck. We do well to study the tragic story of the Tractarian Movement in England, the gripping history of the Disruption in Scotland, and parallel movements on the other side of the Atlantic Ocean.

With all of this going on, Lutheranism did not remain wholly true to the glorious freedom of the Reformation. If everywhere the question was being urged as to what is the authentic way of organizing the church, the way prescribed by Christ, the way required by the Bible, then our church was caught in the danger of wanting to give an answer to this question. With all their faithfulness to the Lutheran Confessions, neither Walther nor Löhe (to name just these two) succeeded in escaping this danger.

It is similar to what happened with our classical dogmaticians in the Age of Orthodoxy. They were drawn into answering questions which came from Calvinism or Roman Catholicism, without recognizing that these were falsely put. Take for example the question of the visible and invisible church, which still continues to plague us. The fathers in the Age of Orthodoxy, as well as the fathers in the 19th century, were drawn into Reformed terminology on this question. They failed to recognize that Luther's *ecclesia abscondita* [cf. "The Church is hidden" (WA 18, 652; American Edition 33, 89)] is not quite the same as the *ecclesia invisibilis* ["invisible church"] of the Reformed. The Lutheran dogmaticians would therefore have done better to have kept to the expressions used in the Confessions and by Luther. To be sure, when we confess the church we are not confessing what we see (*Sehartikel*) but what we believe (*Glaubensartikel*). Our eyes cannot now see the church as the kingdom of Christ. As the Apology confesses (along with Luther) in expounding Articles VII and VIII of the Augsburg Confession, it is "hidden under the cross" (*sub cruce tectum* [18]). No human eye sees the church as the body of Christ. It is an eschatological fact which must be differentiated from the "association of outward ties and rites" (*societas externarum rerum ac rituum* [Apology VII and VIII, 5]) which we see. Insofar as this is so, the church may be spoken of as invisible. The expression "invisible church," however, comes from Augustine freighted with his ecclesiology, and further freight has been loaded onto it by Reformed theology. There are things here which we do not and cannot confess.

Why did they not stay with Luther's simple teaching of the "hidden" church? Here, as in some other points, our orthodox dogmaticians allowed themselves to become far too dependent on their opponents, and the theologians of the 19th century simply took this over. After all, they had no better Lutheran books of dogmatics than those from the Age of Orthodoxy. Where could they have found any such?

There is also something else to be considered. It is certainly true, as the Smalcald Articles confess, that "a seven-year-old child knows what the church is, namely, holy believers and sheep who hear the voice of their shepherd" (III, XII, 2). And yet the theologians of the last century were correct in expecting (as A. Vilmar repeatedly expressed it) that they might be led more deeply into the doctrine of the church as they were called upon to face the colossal catastrophes in the political and social life of their day and the impending future. From the beginning the church knew all that is confessed in the Nicene Creed, but it was by way of the gigantic struggle against ancient heathenism that the church of antiquity came to confess with such clarity that Jesus Christ is truly God and truly man. It is only in this way, and in no other, that we may speak of advance in the understanding of the faith.

Why the two great Lutheran streams in the last century did not flow together was clearly seen by Vilmar: The Lutheran Church had not yet come to full clarity as to what the articles in the Augsburg Confession about the church mean for the *life* of the church. So it came about that the great Lutherans of the last century left us a heritage not yet exhausted or made our own. This is especially true of those who did not just sit at their desks and think theoretically about the nature of the church, but were actively engaged in gathering and caring for congregations. The task which is given our generation cannot be to repeat the formulations of both sides and to take up the discussion where it came to a stop a century ago. Rather our task is again to think through what at that time remained unresolved. For this task we have the help of what the church has experienced since then and of what may have been given of deeper insight into the teachings of Holy Scripture.

4

It is truly remarkable how modern historical research into the beginnings of the way the church was organized has confirmed Luther's exegetical insight that the New Testament tells of no specific single way of organizing the church, and so no such single way can be canonized. As in the history of the liturgy so also in the history of the church's organization, the beginning was marked not by uniformity but by diversity. Therefore it was also possible to read into the New Testament the most diverse ways of organizing the church, and then to derive satisfaction in discovering them there!

Thus the doctrine of papal primacy was read into the Peter passages, although it had grown out of quite unbiblical soil. What Acts 15 tells us of the meeting of the council in Jerusalem has been burdened with the theory of the infallible synod, whose roots are not to be found in Scripture but in ancient sociology. The Catholic doctrine that while one may err but that all together cannot err is a notion that runs through the ancient world, from the Stoics right on to Mohammed. What do Calvin's presbyters have in common with the presbyters of the New Testament? What does "the church of God which is at Corinth" have in common with what Congregationalists nowadays understand by "congregation"? Paul would simply not be able to understand what the doctrine of the body of Christ as expressed in Pius XII's encyclical *Mystici*

Corporis has to do with what he teaches of the church as the body of Christ.

It is not surprising, then, that there is some uncertainty throughout Christendom as to the Scripturalness of the various church polities. Among the Reformed we no longer find the same certainty with which Calvin was able to find in the Bible "the order by which the Lord wills the church to be governed." We hear rather of a few basic lines laid down there that are viewed as obligatory (a presbytery as church senate or council of brothers, a synod as the final court of appeal, rejection of the office of bishop—even when, as in Hungary, this title is used because of state-church considerations). Even in Catholic dogmatics we find the attempt being made to soften the stark statements of Trent and Vatican I in order to bring them more into harmony with the historical facts recorded in the New Testament.

In this respect M. Schmaus's *Katholische Dogmatik* (1964) is most instructive. He observes "that Paul can describe the celebration of the Eucharist without any express mention of a particular priesthood (1 Cor. 11:17-34)," and then continues, "It is an action of the whole congregation in Corinth" (IV, 1, 728). After reading what the same dogmatician says so splendidly about the priestly character of the church (the priesthood of all believers), what he says about the special priesthood obtrudes like a foreign body in the whole context of his presentation. In support of the priesthood of all Christians numerous Bible passages are given; in support of the particular priesthood not a single one. There could not be a more convincing presentation of the unbiblical character of the Roman Catholic doctrine of the priesthood.

At another place we read of the relationship between presbyters and bishops: "The New Testament terms *presbyteroi* and *episcopoi* do not yet express different levels of order as do our words 'priest' and 'bishop,' which derive from these Greek designations. The separation of the one office, referred to with two names, meets us first in Ignatius of Antioch. Here for the first time we have clearly the division into three orders (deacons, priests, bishops). This may be traced back to about the year 100. Its seeds lie in the apostolic period" (p. 729). So only its seeds! To say it bluntly, the Catholic hierarchy is not yet there in the New Testament. At most it is a development of New Testamental seeds. Here we see how cautious a Catholic theologian, strictly bound to Roman dogma, has become when he deals with the Biblical foundations of the Roman doctrine regarding how the church must be constituted (*Kirchenverfassung*).

Today no one who takes seriously the Scriptural evidence would be so rash as to assert that there is to be found in the New Testament a set way of organizing the church which is obligatory for all time. This fact would surely be acknowledged by the Lutherans of the 19th century, although in their day they were not able altogether to resist the temptation to find an answer to the question as to how the church must be organized, even though they hedged their answers with all kinds of reservations and provisos. Today they would simply bow before the fact that in the church of the New Testament there were several possible ways of ordering the holy ministry and the church, the congregation of saints.

<h1 align="center">5</h1>

Which has the primacy, ministry or congregation? Is the office the product of the congregation, or is the congregation the product of the office? Löhe stood for the office, and in a different way also Vilmar and Kliefoth. Walther stood for the congregation. (Von Höfling does not fit in here; neither side took him seriously, and despite all his other accomplishments, he did not make a serious contribution in this matter.) There is more to this than is suggested by likening it to the question whether the hen comes from the egg or the egg from the hen. What is involved here is in fact of enormous theological importance. The entire understanding of the church depends on it.

When Walther and Missouri contended for the priority of the congregation, they could justly call on Luther and the old Lutheran Church as witnesses. In his *To the Christian Nobility* Luther gives the following well-known illustration of the doctrine of the priesthood of all believers. Some Christians find themselves in the desert. There is no ordained priest among them. They elect one of their number to the holy ministry. By this election he has whatever rights and responsibilities belong to one who occupies the church's ministry (WA 6, 407 [American Edition 44, 128]).

We may compare the certainty with which Luther speaks here with the uncertainty and indecision with which Thomas More dealt with the same problem a few years earlier in his *Utopia*. After an account of the tolerant Enlightenment religion of the Utopians and its kinship with Christianity as the enlightened humanist understood it, he relates that many joined their religion and were baptized. Then he continues: "There was unfortunately no priest. Initiated into everything else, they further

76

desired those sacraments which, among us, are conferred by none but a priest. Yet they understand them and desire them with the greatest eagerness. They zealously disputed among themselves whether, without the authority of the Christian pontiff, one selected out of their number might attain the character of the priesthood. It seemed likely that they would have such an election, but, to tell the truth, they had not yet done so by the time I departed" (Lupton, pp. 269 f.). Such is the uncertainty with which the humanist speaks, the friend of Erasmus, the Englishman not prone to making decisions in matters of doctrine. It follows quite naturally and logically that this early representative of Enlightenment religion was executed as a martyr for papal primacy, and in our day has been canonized as a protagonist of the papacy.

The question whether such isolated Christians as pictured by Luther and by More can, as a Christian congregation, rightfully put a man into the office of the holy ministry reveals whether a person thinks evangelically or not. There has never been an evangelical theologian who basically disagreed with Luther in such a case, not even A. Vilmar, the most "high church" among the Lutherans of last century, and certainly not Löhe. Vilmar regarded the situation put by Luther as rather fanciful, as a borderline case that could scarcely occur in real life. But should such a case actually occur, then he would agree with Luther that the congregation has the right to act as they did in Luther's story. And so Vilmar remains within the boundary drawn by the Evangelical faith. [He says:] "In situations of necessity, such as when little congregations (*ecclesiolae*) are cut off without contact, they can indeed have one from among them be their emergency shepherd (*Nothirte*). Although this is possible, it does smack of storytelling. But never may such a case be used to establish the regular way of doing things" (*Die Lehre vom geistlichen Amt*, p. 74).

The regular way in Vilmar as in Löhe is that shepherds are ordained by shepherds, which is also regarded as the normal thing in the Confessions of the Lutheran Church and its church orders. Here our church expressly acknowledges the ancient catholic practice. The church of the Lutheran Reformation, however, has never been in doubt regarding the possibility of the office being bestowed without the traditional ordination by an ordained servant of the Word. Herein is agreement also among all those who do not simply regard the exercise of the holy ministry as the priesthood of all believers performing its function. What makes a priest a priest is the offering of sacrifices. In the New Testamental and Evangelical sense this means the bringing of the spiritual offerings of the whole church [1 Peter 2:5]. The preaching of the Gospel and the administering of the sacraments are connected, to be sure, with such spiritual sacrifices, but they are not in themselves the functions of a priest.

6

That the great freedom of the Reformation is truly the freedom of the Gospel is shown by the fact that the Office of the Keys is given three times in the New Testament: in Matthew 16 to Peter, in John 20 to all the apostles, in Matthew 18 to the whole church. These three bestowals of the office may not be separated. One may not be selected as the chief one, and then played off against the others. To the Twelve Jesus gave the office of preaching the Gospel to every creature and making disciples of all nations by baptizing them. To them He gave the mandate at the Last Supper: "Do this in remembrance of Me." Who were the Twelve? They were the first ministers (*Amtsträger*). From them proceeds "the ministry of teaching the Gospel and administering the sacraments" [AC 5]. But they are at the same time the church, the *ekklēsia*, the representatives of God's new people of the end time.

It is therefore in fact impossible in the New Testament to separate ministry and congregation. What is said to the congregation is also said to the office of the ministry, and vice versa. The office does not stand above the congregation, but always in it. In Acts 13 Paul and Barnabas are sent out as missionaries by the congregation in Antioch. They were already sent by the Lord. What more could this congregation give to Paul with the laying on of hands than what he had already received by the direct commissioning of the risen Lord, who appointed him to his work? Nevertheless the sending is quite deliberately repeated with the laying on of hands. Office and congregation belong inseparably together.

Church history confirms this. Only where there is a vital ministerial office, working with the full authority of having been sent, only there is a living congregation. And only where there is a living congregation is there a living ministerial office. Vilmar's pessimism about the congregation can be explained by the fact that he did not yet know a living congregation. . . . [We omit a few sentences in which Dr. Sasse deplores the lack of living congregations in German Protestantism.] Of all Lutheran churches there can hardly be another in which the office of the ministry is so highly honored as in the Missouri Synod, where the congregation is so much the center of churchly thinking and activity. Office

78

and congregation are piped together. The life of the one is also the life of the other. If the office falters, so does the congregation. If the congregation falters, so does the office.

Already for this reason the alternative "ministry or congregation?" in the 19th century was falsely put. Löhe himself saw this, by the way, as Hebart has shown in his illuminating book about him. What was lacking was the strength to draw the consequences of this recognition, and instead there was misapprehension in diagnosing what lay behind the other's position. The position taken by Missouri had nothing to do with the American propensity to do things democratically, as Mundinger has shown in his penetrating study *Government in the Missouri Synod.* After all, Walther and those like-minded with him were all antidemocrats. And Hebart has shown that no conservative political notions distorted the concept of the church for Löhe, who was never so dominated by nationalistic motives as were Bezzel and the later representatives of Neuendettelsau. On both sides there was an overemphasis on one aspect of Biblical truths which in the New Testament belong together. This happened because each party took one side of the New Testament passages as the important one, under which the other had to be subordinated.

7

Much light is thrown on the whole matter by an examination of the question of how the office of the ministry is bestowed. There is an *immediate call.* Here God calls directly without human intermediary. So it was with the apostles, prophets, and teachers. (We are not here taking into account those who were given gifts of healing and other such charismata.) Only Christ can make a man an apostle. When a man was called to replace Judas, He did it through the casting of lots. God has reserved for Himself the right of calling a person to be a prophet. Neither in the Old Testament nor in the New does a man cooperate in his being called to be a prophet. So also a teacher was regarded in the early church as being called in this way. To him was given the particular gift of expounding Scripture, which was then the Old Testament. The offices of those who were thus directly called by God belonged to the whole church. Those to whom these offices were given could exercise the functions of their office anywhere. The church, the congregation, had only to recognize them as having been given the gifts of their office—or to recognize them as false apostles, false prophets, or false teachers. This was a difficult task, which could be accomplished only through the gift of discerning the spirits.

There is also the *mediated call* for the offices of a particular congregation. These offices also are bestowed by the Lord Christ, but He does it through men. Such were the bishops and deacons, who were already there in the Pauline congregations (Phil. 1:1). They were chosen by the congregation. Similarly the presbyters, where this institution of the synagogue was maintained. It was determined by the decision of the congregation who should belong to this body of "honored ones" who sat in the first seats, the places of honor in the divine service (Matt. 23:6). Clearly there were some congregations where the arrangement was episcopal-diaconal, and others where the arrangement was presbyterial (Acts 20:17 ff.). This diversity was not something Paul thought important to set aside. Not until the Pastoral Epistles do we see them growing together into a unity. We are also not told in the New Testament who it was that elected these congregational officers. Was it the whole congregation or was it done by the "honored ones," a part of the congregation, as was the case in Rome at the time of the First Epistle of Clement—although the whole congregation was certainly involved in giving its approval.

Nothing is more misleading than to read the notions and rules of modern political or social theory into the ways things were ordered in the New Testament. The church (*ekklēsia*) is not a democracy in our sense of the term. It is not a collection of individuals, each of whom may claim the same rights. But one also dare not picture it as aristocratic. It is a body whose members are joined together in different ways and with different rights and functions. Even the body of presbyters, which was itself a unity, had different grades within it, for outstanding among them were those "who rule well . . . especially those who labor in preaching and teaching" (1 Tim. 5:17), that is, those who were also bishops. Also the laity (the Christian people) were an order, below which there were the order of the catechumens and still lower orders (*Stände*).

A person was usually placed in the orders and offices of the congregation by the laying on of hands with prayer. This laying on of hands could be done by a single person, as the apostle Paul did (2 Tim. 1:6). Or it could be done by the presbytery (1 Tim. 4:14), or by both, as was apparently the case with Timothy, or by a whole congregation through their representatives (Acts 13:3).

It is important to observe that the idea of a succession of the laying on of hands did not yet exist in the second century. The oldest succession

80

list we have is that of the church in Rome, recorded by Irenaeus. But this is not a list of successive consecrations but a list of those who occupied the office of bishop, with no attention paid to who laid hands on each one. Here also, certainly in the early days, there was considerable diversity. None of the Catholic theories regarding ordination and consecration can claim any other support from the New Testament than that with the laying on of hands and the accompanying prayer in the name of Jesus a charisma for the office is bestowed.

It should be noted that the laying on of hands, which played a large role in the church at the time of the apostles (Heb. 6:2) and was not confined to the bestowal of an office, does not belong to the essence of ordination (cf. John 20:21 ff.); that is to say, it does not have a special mandate of Christ. It is rather a usage taken over from the Old Testament, such as we find in Moses' ordination of Joshua (Num. 27:18; Deut. 34:9), and used to place into office those who were to serve the church. It is neither a sacrament, nor merely a gesture. It accompanies, and expresses the prayer, which is promised to be heard, that the Holy Spirit be present and graciously bestow His gifts. God is the One who does this, the Lord Christ, the Holy Spirit. He does this through men, whether through one, through a collegium, or through the whole congregation (Acts 20:28). This is His usual way, though He may also give such gifts directly, and with them an office.

In the light of the foregoing we may then recognize, as our Lutheran fathers did quite clearly, the impossibility of making an *essential* difference between call and ordination or even making this difference divisive of church fellowship. It is God who calls into His ministry, usually through men. The how is not the decisive thing. Whether He does it through one person, through a collegium, or through a congregation assembled in divine service, it all happens in the name of the church, the whole church, which is the body of Christ, and so it happens in the power of the Holy Spirit.

8

When one has come to recognize this, then the differences between the theological theories of the 19th century become small indeed. Then one begins to understand the glorious freedom of the Lutheran Church, which knows no law about how ministers must be placed into office (*de constituendis ministris*), because Jesus Christ did not give such a law, either directly or indirectly. When the holy ministry is received and instituted as given by the Lord, not *over* the congregation but *in* the congregation, then it becomes very large and can be received and rejoiced in as the great gift it is. Then the question how it is bestowed gives place to what is bestowed. The more or less dubious theories of its apostolic origin give place to its apostolic content. This is nothing other than what was committed to the apostles, that they should be proclaimers of the pure Gospel and servants of the sacraments instituted by Christ—this and nothing more. Herein is the apostolicity of the office of the holy ministry.

Only from this deep understanding can the spiritual office be revitalized. How unimportant then becomes all that has grown onto this office through the modern overorganization of the church; one has only to think of the church politics with which modern bishops kill their own time and that of others. Each sermon then becomes more important than all those sessions which spend their time discussing big church resolutions regarding the Bonn constitution, the atom bomb, or Goethe's 200th birthday.

Conversely: The more seriously we take the holy ministry, the more seriously we take the Christian congregation. If we did this, we would be freed from the aberration, from which our territorial churches (*Landeskirchen*) suffer so deeply, that one can draw a line around an area on the map of a city (a police district) and suppose that within that line is what the New Testament calls a congregation, and that some modern methods of caring for souls are all that is necessary to bring it to life. To think that by reporting oneself to the police station in that area as a resident one becomes a member of a Christian congregation is a notion that cannot be fitted into any Christian understanding of the church! Taking the ministry and the congregation seriously would put an end to the misunderstanding that the church taxes which the government extracts more or less painlessly are the offerings from which the church of Christ lives. It would also mean the end of the notion that what the Confessions say of church government is fulfilled by having a clever— alas, all too clever—central church bureaucracy running things not by the Word but by force (*non verbo, sed vi*).

All of this must pass away and will pass away, just as church government by princes as *summi episcopi* disappeared overnight. But the holy ministry, preaching repentance and forgiveness, and the congregation of the faithful, who in faith are justified sinners—that will remain. The future may involve forms which we today do not know about, but which the Lord of the church is preparing amid the thousandfold suffering of contemporary Christianity. He is His body's Savior even when we see only dissolution. Still true are Luther's great words about God's way in history: "By putting to death He makes alive" (*occidendo vivificat*).

This faith in what God is doing does not exclude our responsibility, but rather includes it. This means renouncing everything that is destructive of the genuine holy ministry instituted by Christ and the genuine congregation instituted by Him, everything that makes of what Christ has instituted a place for exercising our lust for power, whether clerical or congregational. The office of the holy ministry is not lord over the congregation (2 Cor. 1:24); the congregation is not lord over the office of the holy ministry (Gal. 1). Both are under Him who alone is Lord; in Him they are one.

These are just a few thoughts about church and ministry which may help you read with new awareness what God's Word has to say on this subject.

APOSTOLIC SUCCESSION

Letters to Lutheran Pastors, No. 41
April 1956

1

Apostolic succession is an ancient concept, and yet the particular implication with which it is used nowadays is, as far as I can see, a quite recent product among Christians. In 1833 appeared the first of the "Tracts for the Times," calling for a renewal of catholic thinking in the Church of England. It was a powerful summons to the Anglican clergy to ponder the responsibilities of their office. The author reminded his brother clergy that the Anglican ordination liturgy contains "the doctrine of the Apostolic Succession." He was the same John Henry Newman who 12 years later gave up this view and converted to the Roman Church.

His appeal had to be to the liturgy, since none of the confessions of the ancient church, or the Thirty-Nine Articles, contain such a doctrine. Noteworthy is also the fact that the Roman Church has no particular doctrinal article concerning the *successio apostolica*. There appears to be only one doctrinal document in which the expression is used, and that, significantly, in what the Holy Office wrote to the Catholic bishops of England in 1864 (*apostolicae successionis praerogativa*, Denzinger, 1,686).

In the Roman textbooks of dogmatics the matter itself is dealt with in the doctrine of the apostolicity of the church and in the doctrine of priestly ordination. Trent speaks of it, rather in passing, in the doctrine of the priesthood, when it says the bishops succeeded to the place of the apostles (*in apostolorum locum successerunt*, Session 23, ch. 4). In the following canons, in which the doctrines of the Reformation are rejected, there is no mention of any succession at all.

There are two places in the Interim of 1548 which approach the way in which the term is used nowadays. The Interim is not a doctrinal statement, and yet it does give a good indication of the thinking of the Catholic reform theologians at that time. Catholicity is said to be a "sign of the true church, that is, that it is universal, poured out through all places and times through the apostles and those who followed them right up to us and in continuing succession to the end of the world." Similarly the article concerning the sacrament of ordination speaks of the succession of the church: "When the bishops lay on hands and ordain to these offices, they are acting in this always continual transmission and succession of the church." [Melhausen, pp. 66, 94].

What nowadays is called apostolic succession is regarded in the Catholic churches as so self-evident that there is scarcely need to talk about it. It is quite simply given with the sacrament of priestly ordination. When the Church of England and its daughter churches (recently also certain Lutheran churches, and union churches such as that of South India) make so much of their apostolic succession, one is prompted to ponder the fact that we are most apt to speak of those virtues which we do not possess. It is hardly by chance that this overemphasis on apostolic succession emerged in a church which indeed claims to be catholic and to possess the three offices of bishop, priest, and deacon, and yet is unable to say what these offices actually are.

We would have no need of engaging the Anglicans and their unclarity (the product of the sorry history of their Reformation), if they were not continually beating on the doors of all other churches, demanding from Rome the recognition of their orders and from Protestants the receiving of their "apostolic succession." Prussia repeatedly looked with longing eyes at the Church of England, from the first king, mightily impressed by "no bishop, no king," to romantic Frederick William IV [1840—61] and his failed attempt to found a Jerusalem bishopric under the auspices of Prussia and England. The plans for this bishopric were what finally drove Newman to Rome. They contained the thought that the Church of England would help those churches "less fully organized."

In our lifetime we have seen a renewal of this friendly offer. It was made—to the dismay of all serious English theologians—by certain English bishops as Hitler's millennium was breaking upon us. In all seriousness they said to us that our struggle against Ludwig Müller and the other "German Christian" bishops was hopeless. The thing to do was for the German "bishops" to have themselves consecrated from England. That would bring everything into proper order. We were invited to consider the example of certain Nordic churches which enjoyed a good standing with the Church of England.

We will speak later about the fateful consequences for Lutheranism throughout the world which resulted when the churches of Sweden and Finland entered upon joint consecrations with the Anglicans. They should have said not only that such consecrations by the Church of England are null and void in the eyes of Rome, but that the notion that something more is given by them than is given to the ministry of Word and sacrament also runs counter to the Lutheran Reformation, according to the understanding of Article V of the Augsburg Confession.

The baleful consequences are plain for all to see in the mission fields of Africa and India. There we are now blessed with two groups of Lutheran missionaries. The one has "apostolic succession," the other does not. Both are more or less in church fellowship with a whole range of churches, but no longer with one another and no longer with whatever Lutheran Church faithful to the Confessions is still left in the world.

To what an extent this matter has become a problem in Germany can be seen by the shocking case of Friedrich Heiler, a professor of theology in the Evangelical faculty of Marburg. He had himself secretly consecrated bishop. Secretly he bestowed priestly ordination on Evangelical pastors so that they now secretly (their congregations were not informed) would be able to effect the "change" in the celebration of the Sacrament of the Altar. Were there ever before in Christ's church sacraments and ordinations at which what was given and what was received was not clearly stated, but kept secret, not done in the presence of the Christian congregation? The church governments in Germany would do well to keep a watchful eye on such surreptitious Romanizing, as well as on the open Calvinizing of the Lutheran heritage. Instead they make special laws and take measures against those who are again taking seriously the old heritage of genuine Lutheran catholicity, the only weapon against Romanizing.

2

In any attempt to understand all the talk nowadays about apostolic succession, we must begin with the fact that apostolicity is integral to the church. Therefore any church, any collection of people that claims to be church, claims apostolicity in its own way. Roman Catholic theologians are in the habit of dividing between apostolicity of origin, apostolicity of doctrine, and apostolicity of succession (*apostolicitas originis, doctrinae, successionis*). Every church claims the first two. Every church finally traces its origin back to the apostles and so to Jesus Christ Himself.

So it is nonsense to say that the Lutheran Church and the other Protestant churches came into being in the 16th century or even later, while the Roman Church goes back to Jesus and the apostles. The Eastern Church is evidence and protest enough against such an idea. Where was the papal church before there was a papacy? Whether any church has its origin in the church of the New Testament or not is simply a matter of faith. The Baptists and the Disciples of Christ make the claim that their church was *the* church at the time of the New Testament. Our Lutheran fathers never had the idea that they were founding a new church. They were of the conviction that Christ's one church was being renewed with the pure apostolic doctrine in contrast with Rome, which had fallen away from the Gospel.

These are matters of faith, and one should not try to settle them by appeals to historical proofs. How this goes may be seen in the polemics between the Anglicans and the English Roman Catholics. Both attempt to prove that they are the legitimate continuation of the medieval church in England. We Lutherans have no part to play in that sort of dispute, although it has often been suggested that we should.

To provide the proof for the identity of any historical construction is always enormously problematical. One may, for example, speak of an English nation and of a German nation that continue through the centuries. But if one looks more closely, one notices how great are also the differences. In what sense are the English people of Henry VIII's time identical with the 10 times as many English people of today? In what sense are today's German people identical with the people of Luther's time? Was it anything more than a fiction when it was thought that the Holy Roman Empire of Byzantium was living on in the empire of Charlemagne and the German empire of Otto the Great until it expired in 1806? Is there more of an identity between the Roman Church of today and the church of Peter's day than there is between the Roman Empire of the first century and the Holy Roman Empire around 1800? It has been observed that the difference between the church before Constantine and the church after Constantine is greater than the difference in the Western Church before and after the Reformation. Here the historical proofs of identity simply fail.

The apostolicity of origin, the claim that the church to which I belong is identical with the church of the apostles, is a matter of faith. The answer has to do with whether I consider the doctrine of my church to be apostolic. The claim of the Lutheran Church to be apostolic stands or falls with the claim that it has faithfully preserved the doctrine of the New Testament. For Lutherans certainly everything depends on the question: "Where today is the doctrine of the apostles?"

Naturally, every church claims to be apostolic also in the sense of the apostolicity of its doctrine. Now it is especially worth noting the enormous difficulties the Roman Church has gotten itself into through its development, especially since the Reformation. At the beginning of his work Luther could still—within the Roman Church—appeal to *sola scriptura*. Beside it there had long been the view of those who regarded tradition as an expansion of Scripture. How old and widespread this was we may observe in the Eastern Church, but it had never been made into dogma. It was first at Trent that tradition was set beside Scripture as a second equivalent source of revelation.

When this happens, when, to speak with the Smalcald Articles (II, II, 15), Scripture no longer alone sets up articles of faith, then Enthusiasm has forced an entry into the church. It pushes beyond the doctrine of the New Testament, destroys it, and abolishes the church's apostolicity. It is one of Luther's profoundest recognitions, also expressed in the Smalcald Articles (III, VIII), that Enthusiasm is engendered by scorn of the external Word, the words of Scripture read and preached. Enthusiasm leads to the religion of the natural man, fallen man who puts himself in God's place. Luther saw that this is the great heresy which the Enthusiasts, the pope, and Mohammed—the three forms of the Antichrist known to him—had in common.

All three cited the much-misunderstood words of our Lord in John 16:12–13: "I have yet many things to say to you, but you cannot bear them now. When the Spirit of truth comes, He will guide you into all the truth." These words find welcoming ears with the pope, the archbishop of Canterbury, the Quakers, the liberals, and all sorts of heretics. Not so much, however, the words which follow, the rule by which one can recognize whether it really was the Holy Spirit whom one has heard or whether it was only the spirit of man or a still worse spirit: "He will glorify Me, for He will take what is Mine and declare it to you" (v. 14), that is, interpret the Gospel of Christ ever more deeply and thus glorify Jesus.

How far things can go when this is not heeded we may see in the history of the Roman Church—Christianity's greatest tragedy. At first tradition is like a tethered balloon, more or less held by the apostolic witness. But with the declaration of two equivalent sources of revelation—Scripture and tradition—the rope is cut and the balloon sails with the wind, no one knows where. The answer came in the course of time.

By the 19th century it was so clear that the best Catholics were filled with anxiety. Neither in Scripture nor in the tradition of the first centuries can the grounds be found for any of the modern dogmas, from the Immaculate Conception of 1854 through the 1870 Vatican Council's papal dogma to the Assumption of Mary [1950]. None of these were known to the early church.

The doctrine of the Roman Church is no longer apostolic. Even in 1854 and 1870 it was still possible to claim to be reaching back to relatively old traditions, or to what were regarded as such. Passages of Scripture could be interpreted so as to be persuasive for faithful Catholics. With the dogma of 1950 this is at an end. The Assumption of Mary is a late legend, and only "conclusion theology" can produce Mary as *mediatrix* of all graces and *coredemptrix*.

At work here has been the "theory of development." This was proposed by J. H. Newman and has been avidly put to use. By the way, one can find it already in Möhler. This theory, which is supposed to justify the modern dogmas, is the product of Romanticism and of the 19th century as a whole (the obvious parallels are Darwin and Marx). The picture is that of a seed. At the beginning of the church all its doctrines were contained within the seed, and these then unfolded from century to century. Was not this the case with the doctrines of the Holy Trinity and the Person of the God-man?

To be sure, the understanding of these doctrines progressed through generations. They were, however, already there from the beginning in the apostolic witness. The New Testament declares that Jesus Christ is not a creature but the eternal Logos. The New Testament declares that Jesus Christ, true God and true man, is one Person. What unfolds in the church is the ever deeper understanding of the apostolic words. But nothing can unfold if it is not there in the apostolic words.

In Roman Catholic theology today we find such questions dealt with as, "Did Mary ever die?" Questions do arise which call for answers, such as, "What is the essence and the extent of papal infallibility?" Since Bernadette has been canonized and solemnly exalted "to the honor of the altars," can any good Catholic have doubt about the genuineness of the appearances at Lourdes? If we further probe the question of the authority of the papal teaching office, do we not reach the point where, in addition to Scripture and tradition, there appears a third source of doctrine, namely Christ's regent on earth?

We can only rejoice in all that is done in the Roman Church in honor of Scripture. In all doctrinal explanations attention is given to Scripture and tradition. Many a Protestant church could find much to learn here. But what are we to make of private revelations when they are claimed not by some unknown person but by the pope himself? If he experienced the miraculous sun of Fatima also in Rome, or had a vision of Christ, why does he not keep this to himself, which would be the proper way? Why is it proclaimed through the media to the city and to the world? Why does the believing Catholic accept the pope's every word in questions of faith and morals? Because he has tested it against Scripture and tradition? Certainly not, but because the pope has said it!

"The pope's word is God's word." This could be read during the war on the doors of the cathedral in Salzburg in a Lenten letter of the archbishop. Now Christians all know that human words can at the same time be God's words. "Do you believe that the forgiveness I declare is the forgiveness of God?" At Confession this question is put [Small Catechism V, 27]. But only the Word of God, the Word of the Gospel, the Word of the living proclamation of the apostolic message today—only this can be God's Word.

Into what airy heights does the balloon of supposed tradition float off when the line with Scripture is severed! When *sola scriptura* is left behind, left behind also are God's revelation and its authority. One can only think with horror of the fearful fate the Roman Church is readying for itself. After all, it is still Christianity's largest and most influential church. Is it still the church in which our fathers lived during the Middle Ages? Is it still an apostolic church? Has it not lost the apostolicity of doctrine? Not as though the apostolic witness had died out within it. That is still there. Otherwise Rome would be no church. Also in the Roman Church there are people who still believe in the Savior Jesus Christ as the only Mediator between God and men. Also in this church Christ is still present in the means of grace, to the extent that these are still there. Also in this church people are born again to eternal life. But there is also in this church that horror which Luther saw, the anti-Christian exaltation of man, whether in the cult of Mary or in the revering of the pope.

If we recognize this, we can do so only in the spirit of penitent self-examination. Perhaps the same disease, Christianity's mortal illness, lurks also in us and our church, ever ready to break out. How is it said by Luther at that place in the Smalcald Articles?

> In short, enthusiasm clings to Adam and his descendants from the beginning to the end of the world. It is a poison implanted and inoculated in man by the old dragon, and it is the source, strength, and

90

power of all heresy, including that of the papacy and Mohammedanism. Accordingly, we should and must constantly maintain that God will not deal with us except through his external Word and sacrament. Whatever is attributed to the Spirit apart from such Word and sacrament is of the devil (III, VIII, 9–10).

This is an earnest warning to every church. We cannot be discovering this heresy in other churches without earnestly asking also of ourselves, "Is it I, Lord?"

3

The doctrinal locus concerning the apostolic church has, beside the apostolicity of origin and the apostolicity of doctrine, also the apostolicity of *succession*. This is what looms most largely in Christian affairs nowadays. We must first ask what it actually is, this apostolic succession, which the Anglican churches esteem themselves as having, which the Church of Sweden believes it possesses, and which the Eastern churches and the Roman Church regard as their own possession.

In his famous *Symbolism* [English translation 1906] Möhler attempted to clarify the meaning of tradition for modern Catholicism. He found himself in remarkable agreement with Newman and his friends in England as well as with Russian thinkers such as Chomjakov. Möhler's view of tradition has been traced to contemporary philosophy and Romanticism's understanding of society as an organism. Thus J. Ranft, the dogmatician from Würzburg, in his learned work *Der Ursprung des katholischen Traditionsprinzips* (1931). Other Roman Catholic scholars agreed. (Cf. the collection in honor of the 100th anniversary of Möhler's death, *Die Eine Kirche*, ed. H. Tüchle, 1938.)

Möhler finds the law of tradition, which binds together the different generations of a people or of a religious society, in the life of all such societies.

> The Divine Founder of our Church, when he constituted the community of believers as his permanent organ, had recourse to no other law than that which prevails in every department of human life. Each nation is endowed with a peculiar character, stamped on the deepest, most hidden parts of its being, which distinguishes it from all other nations and manifests its peculiarity in public and domestic life, in art and science, in short, in every relation. It is, as it were, the tutelary genius; the guiding spirit transmitted from its progenitors; the vivifying breath of the whole community (*Symbolism*, pp. 279 f.).

91

Just as there is a national spirit for peoples which sustains a people in its peculiar wholeness through the generations, so there is also such a spirit in religious communities. As examples of this we are given not only the Chinese, the Parsees, the Moslems, and Hellenic heathenism, but even Lutheranism:

> Lastly, let us contemplate the religious sect founded by Luther himself. The developed doctrines of his Church, consigned as they are in the symbolical books, retain, on the whole, so much of this spirit, that on the first view, they must be recognized by the observer as genuine productions of Luther (*echt lutherisch*). With a sure vital instinct (*Lebensgefühle*), the opinions of the Majorists, the Synergists and others were rejected as deadly; and, indeed (from Luther's point of view, *Geist*), as untrue, by that community whose soul, whose living principle he was; and the Church, which the Reformer of Wittenberg established, proved herself the unerring interpretess of his word (pp. 280 f.).

What revealing sentences these are! Plain for all to see is the utter distortion of Lutheranism, and so a lot of words are not called for to show that the Lutheran Church is not a religious association founded by Luther, having as its principle the spirit of Luther. What is most significant is that this way of speaking about a church is not put right even if we cross out "Luther" and substitute "Christ"; instead of what was allegedly established by the Reformer of Wittenberg, the church established by Christ; instead of the Lutheran Church as "unerring interpretess" of the words of Luther, the Roman Catholic Church as "unerring interpretess" of the words of Christ. In the tradition of doctrine and the succession of teachers there is said to be an inherent spirit at work infallibly revealing things. We hardly needed the specific references to the Chinese, Greeks, Parsees, and Moslems to recognize that such an idea is no product of the Christian faith and the witness of the apostles. Such an idea did indisputably exist throughout the ancient world, Hellenic and Asiatic, and it has certainly not died out. But what has to be decisively disputed is that the idea is a Biblical and Christian one, although there are indeed traces here and there of its influence on the *language* used in the Bible, and we may observe how later it infiltrated Christ's church and helped form the idea of the "catholic" church.

The Holy Spirit, who creates unity of faith and confession, is not the collective spirit of the Christian religious association. The church as the people of God is something completely other than the people of Mani or Mohammed. The church as the body of Christ is not an organism such as a secular association, a family, a nation, or any other kind of "body." Möhler's misunderstanding, and that of the whole Romantic movement, cannot be excused by pointing to the ancient church's use of terms from ancient sociology of religion in speaking of the church of Christ. One must never forget that the church fathers came out of ancient heathenism and continued to carry some of its concepts around with them for a long time, for instance in their apologetics. The vital distinction to be made is between what is truly Biblical and what was brought into the church from that ancient heathen world. Clearly the catholicity and apostolicity of the church are taught in Holy Scripture. The same cannot be said of the way catholicity and apostolicity were understood through the centuries of the development of the Catholic Church.

We have only to look at the sentence Augustine penned to overthrow the Donatists: "When the whole world passes judgment, that judgment is sure" (*Securus iudicat orbis terrarum*). He refers to the church everywhere; the Donatists were to be found only in Africa. This is the sentence that began to shake Newman's faith in the catholicity of the Church of England. Ever and again it has deeply impressed Catholic and high-church circles. It does not come, however, from Scripture but from the religious thought of the non-Christian world, perhaps from very early forms of religion which are still alive within us or could become so. "The voice of the people is the voice of God" (*Vox populi vox Dei*. [Cf. Seneca the Elder, *Controversia*, 1, 1, 10; Homer, *Odyssey*, 3, 214 f.]). This is Stoic philosophy, and at the same time a piece of ancient wisdom—or foolishness. "My community will never agree in error" [*Haddith. Muctamad*, 458—76. Cf. Lammens, *Islam* (1968), p. 93]. Thus from Mohammed the doctrine of *ijmā'*, the consensus of all Moslems.

Möhler is quite right in observing that here we are dealing with doctrines which appear also outside the church. What he failed to observe is that they do not come from Holy Scripture, and indeed cannot be brought into agreement with Scripture.

How useless, indeed impossible, it is to understand the doctrine of the church from such principles is shown by the impossibility of putting into practice the well-known dictum of Vincent of Lerins. According to this dictum, that doctrine is to be regarded as catholic, and thus orthodox, "which has been believed everywhere, always, and by all" [*quod ubique, quod semper, quod ab omnibus creditum est*). Of the geographical catholicity of "everywhere" we have already spoken. It is difficult to say anything better regarding the temporal catholicity of "always," or what is often called apostolicity. Here, however, we come upon the heart of the doctrine of "apostolic succession." What is this heart? It is the conviction of all the great schools of wisdom and established religions of Asia and the Hellenistic world that in the beginning there was truth and that it was handed down in purity from generation to generation, from father to son, from master to disciples, as from hand to hand, without anything being added or taken away. The *quasi per manus tradita* ["as though passed on by hand"] which appears in the fourth session of Trent (Denzinger 783) is an age-old technical term for this.

Now how much of this can be found in Holy Scripture? In 1 Cor. 11:23 and 15:3 Paul uses the technical terms for the receiving and passing on of a tradition (*parelabon, paredōka*). (We may note in passing that this has no adverse effect on the independence of his apostleship, which he so strongly emphasizes in Galatians.) In the New Testament we do have tradition in the sense of the message of the Gospel, or some particular message, being faithfully kept and handed on (1 Tim. 6:20), without addition or subtraction (Rev. 22:18–19). This "tradition," however, whether it be the oral proclamation of the apostles or whether it was already written down, has nothing to do with a tradition which was later placed in opposition to Scripture. The apostolic witness cannot be divided into what was preached and what was written down. These are one and the same. The authentic doctrinal tradition of the church in the sense of the New Testament is never anything else than the living transmission of this witness in preaching and instruction. It can never be an independent source of revelation. Authentic apostolic succession, then, is always and only the succession of doctrine. It may be known by its identity with the witness of the apostles in the New Testament. In this way the content of what is proclaimed by any and every church is to be weighed.

There is indeed also a succession of teachers who have faithfully proclaimed the apostolic message. But who these surely are only God knows, just as He alone "knows those who are His," who are truly His church [2 Tim. 2:19].To set down lists of such succession is an understandable desire. It is a human desire which in the ancient world produced lists of teachers, chains of transmitters of a tradition, in many schools and religions. It was therefore a piece of ancient non-Christian religion that penetrated into the church with the setting up of lists of those who held office and were transmitters of tradition. People sought in human books what is written only in the books of God.

4

The problem with these lists of succession may be illustrated by two examples, touching the Old and the New Testament. How rabbinic Judaism understood the handing down of what was taught in the Old Testament is shown by the chain of tradition with which the Mishna tractate *Pirqe Abot* ("Sayings of the Fathers") begins. "Moses received the Torah from Sinai and transmitted it to Joshua, Joshua to the elders, the elders to the prophets, and the prophets transmitted it to the men of the Great Synagogue." The line then continues through Simon the Just (ca. 300 B.C. or a century later) to the rabbis of the later period. We need not enter upon the question whether the Great Synagogue ever actually existed or whether it was a fiction developed out of Nehemiah 8—10. It is enough to consider the inclusion of the prophets in the list of those who transmitted the Torah to recognize the fiction. This artificial construction was intended to show the transmission of divine truth through the generations. The history of Old Testament revelation is pressed into a scheme whose origin is not Biblical and which cannot be brought into agreement with the Biblical record.

Our second example is the understanding of New Testament revelation to be found in 1 Clement. There we read in chapter 42:

> The apostles for our sake were given the Gospel as proclaimed to them by the Lord Jesus Christ. Jesus the Christ was sent from God. Christ, therefore, is from God and the apostles from Christ. . . . When they had received their instructions, having been filled with certainty by the resurrection of our Lord Jesus Christ and strengthened by the Word of God, they went out full of confidence in the Holy Spirit, proclaiming the Gospel that the kingdom of God was about to come. Through the country and the towns they preached, and appointed their firstfruits, after testing them by the Spirit, to be bishops and deacons of those who would believe. Nor was this any new thing, for a long time ago there was mention of bishops and deacons in Scripture. For there is somewhere in Scripture a passage which says, "I will appoint their bishops in righteousness and their deacons in peace."

Where is this written? Nowhere. The author probably had in mind Is. 60:17, where the Septuagint (literally translated) has, "I will give your rulers (*archontas*) in peace and your overseers (*episkopous*) in righteousness." Do we have here only a lapse of memory, or is it a "spiritual" interpretation of the passage? In that case, though, it should somehow be indicated. As the text stands in 1 Clement it is a spurious quotation.

There is much to ponder in the fact that such a falsification or whatever one may call it (perhaps our norms are not applicable to an earlier time) occurs in the first document of the Roman Church, near the end of the first century. The document sets up as a law that those who bear churchly office are undeposable without evidence against them, and this is imposed upon another church with the demand of obedience [59:1] and the claim to be giving a decision given by the Holy Spirit [63:2]. This was at a time when there was not yet a monarchic episcopate in Rome, let alone a papacy. Clement was one of the bishops in Rome, and we learn from the Shepherd of Hermas that he had the responsibility of correspondence with congregations elsewhere [Vis. II, 4, 3]. What he gives out as a binding decision has as its basis a falsification. Where this all leads to we may see in its fruition in the *Donation of Constantine* and the *Pseudo-Isidorian Decretals*. We here observe the first instance of that viewpoint which Cardinal Manning summed up in connection with Vatican I and its undemonstrable and untrue historical assertions about the place of the Roman bishops in the ancient church: "Dogma must prevail over history" [*Vatican Council* (1969), pp. 125 ff.].

Quite apart from the problem of the spurious quotation, we have to ask, "What is the meaning of the way history is pictured in Clement?" We find a mixture of truth and fantasy. Revelation does indeed have a chain of succession. The Father sends the Son, the Son the apostles. The apostles hand their commission (*Auftrag*) on to those who bear office (*die Amtsträger*) in the church. That is Biblical. "As the Father has sent Me, even so I send you" [John 20:21]. And the commission to proclaim the Gospel to every creature, even to the ends of the earth and until "the close of the age," was in fact given the apostles by their Lord. And of this we are told in Holy Scripture, that the apostles appointed office-bearers, both to help them and to take their place. Thus Paul put Timothy in office. According to Acts 14:23 Barnabas and Paul "appointed elders" for the mission congregations in southern Asia Minor. This historical fact was then dogmatically simplified in 1 Clement, as also by such writers of the second century as Irenaeus and Tertullian, yes, by the whole church of that time.

There is first the fact that it was not always the Twelve who founded and organized the churches, yes, not even apostles in the real meaning of the word. Indeed the greatest of the ancient churches, Antioch and Rome, were founded by unknown Christians. It is simply historically not the case that Peter and Paul were the *founders* of the church in Rome, as Irenaeus claims at the beginning of his list of Roman bishops.

96

It is further simply not the case that the office of the ministry [*das geistliche Amt*] always arose in the same way, namely by being received from the apostles. The Didache (15:1) gives admonition to congregations as to what to do in case there are no wandering apostles, prophets, or teachers among them:

> Elect therefore for yourselves bishops and deacons worthy of the Lord, men mild and not greedy for money, truthful, men who have been tested. They do the same service for you as the prophets and teachers. Therefore do not think less of them, for they are the honorable ones among you, along with the prophets and teachers.

What was always at first manifold is later brought into unified forms. This may be observed from the beginning of the church's history (for instance in the liturgy), and it is the case also with polity. It is the simplifying, dogmatical view which leads to such simplified constructions of history as we saw in Judaism's scheme of succession in the "Sayings of the Fathers" and in its counterpart in what Clement of Rome did for early Christianity.

5

It is well known how the great struggle against the Gnostic sects, which the church had to carry on in the second century, brought toward victory the idea of the apostolic succession of bishops and thereby created the Catholic office of bishop. From the standpoint of the Reformation we may regret that in this struggle the church was not content to trust its defense to the Rule of Faith (the early form of the Apostles' Creed) and to Holy Scripture. However, we must not forget that it was not so easy to stand by *sola scriptura* at a time when the canon of the New Testament was not yet in existence and when Holy Scripture was the Old Testament. Our New Testament had not yet emerged from the various writings which claimed to include the genuine apostolic witness. We need to consider what it meant in the year 180 for the martyrs of Scillium in North Africa that they were able to recognize the Pauline Epistles only as worthy documents but not yet as Holy Scripture [Owen, *Some Authentic Acts of the Early Martyrs* (1927), p. 72]. At that time it was not possible to draw Scriptural proof from the Epistle to the Romans. We must consider this situation of the church in order to understand what weight was then attached to the "apostolic" office of the bishops as guardians of the pure doctrine.

To explore the problem of the oldest succession lists, we turn to the work of Erich Caspar, the great historian of the papacy, whose lifework remained unfinished. From the *Schriften der Königsberger Gelehrten Gesellschaft* (1926) we have his *Die älteste Römische Bischofsliste*. Although much has been said in criticism of details of this work, its essential result remains, namely that the names Irenaeus gives in the list of bishops (*Adv. haer.* III, 3, 3) are genuine.

As Hegesippus traveled among the churches of the East and the West, he made lists of successions. He operated according to a dogmatic viewpoint which had the false presupposition that one could prove the transmission of the pure doctrine by the succession of the bishops, but his researches have given us highly valuable historical material [Eusebius, *Historia ecclesiastica* IV, 22, 1–3].

The Roman list which Irenaeus brings up to his time has nothing but authentic names. Its age and authenticity are evidenced by the fact that, in contrast with the current official list of popes, Peter does not appear as the first Roman bishop. Peter and Paul are presented as the founders of the church in Rome. They are said to have committed the episcopate to Linus. The whole following list with its numbering of the third, sixth, and ninth bishops is constructed on the presupposition that Linus was the first bishop, and that Peter and Paul put him in this office. In Rome in the third century Peter and Paul were still always named together as of equal rank.

It is clear from 1 Clement, as also from Ignatius' Epistle to the Romans, that at the beginning of the second century in Rome there was still no monarchic bishop, but rather a college of bishops. It would appear that it was the incursion of the great Gnostic sects into Rome which produced the need for a unified government of the church by one bishop. Pius, the brother of the author of the Shepherd of Hermas, seems to have been the first monarchic bishop in the chief city of the world.

Also here the rule proves true that things moved from East to West, not only the Gospel but also church institutions. Already in the Revelation to John we see that toward the end of the first century every church in the East had its own bishop ("To the angel of the church in . . . write . . . "). What then were Linus, Anacletus, Clement, Evaristus, Alexander, Sixtus, [Telesphorus], and Hyginus, who appear in the list prior to Pius? They were, as Harnack already saw, obviously outstanding members of the college of bishops, men who were renowned as teachers of the church. The list, we must judge, indeed has nothing but genuine names, and yet it is an artificial construction, similar to the succession list in the Mishna tractate.

And what was the list intended to prove? Nothing except that in Rome there was a tradition of doctrine, that the apostolic message was faithfully handed on from generation to generation. The point of the list is that there was a succession of teachers and therefore of doctrine. Others could have been named, for all these "bishops" had colleagues associated with them. These names may have been chosen because of the reputation of these men, but a "succession" in a strictly historical sense it was not. Without historical foundation are also the "years of reign" with which they were later supplied. There is no solid evidence for dates until the middle of the [second] century.

6

The greatest difference between the old Roman list of bishops and other lists of bishops on the one hand and what is today understood by "apostolic succession" on the other hand is the following. These lists, such as the official Roman list of popes, and the list of the archbishops of Canterbury or of Cologne, give the names of the incumbents of a particular bishop's seat, one after the other. They do not speak, and do not intend to speak, of a succession of *consecrations*. The incumbent of a bishop's seat is not consecrated by his predecessor. Succession of office must be strictly differentiated from succession of consecration. This latter only gradually began to play a part in the church. Yet today this is the idea of apostolic succession that is so insisted on: A bishop receives his consecration from another bishop, whose consecration goes back to other bishops, right back to the first bishops who were consecrated by the apostles.

How historical is this succession? In later times it can certainly be demonstrated or accepted with confidence, for after the year 200 the old usage stood firm that a bishop was chosen by the clergy and people of his church but that he could receive consecration only from one or (very soon) several bishops. [A presbyter might consecrate a bishop (*Canons of Hippolytus* II, 10).] It also became settled practice that only a bishop could ordain presbyters and deacons [Council of Ancyra, Canon 13], as also that ordination was done with the laying on of hands. But does this tell us that all consecrations go back to the apostles? Timothy was ordained by Paul with the laying on of hands (2 Tim. 1:6). In 1 Tim. 3 and 5 he was given instruction for appointing bishops, deacons, and widows (deaconesses), where the laying on of hands is explicitly mentioned. But were bishops everywhere ordained in this way? How were things done in Rome in Clement's day? We do not know.

The historian may regret a gap in our knowledge of what went on, but for one who believes Scripture to be God's Word there is a deeper meaning in the fact that we nowhere have a mandate of our Lord to carry out an ordination, let alone instructions as to how it should be done. We have the mandate to baptize. We have the mandate to repeat the Lord's Supper, and there is the institution of the Office of the Keys. This last, we do well to note, in threefold form: Matt. 16 to Peter, Matt. 18 to the assembled congregation, and John 20 to the Twelve (more precisely the disciples who were gathered on the evening of Easter Day). But no one has been able to show when Jesus ordained the Twelve. The Catholic churches have to resort to the command to repeat the Lord's Supper. With the words "This do in remembrance of Me" Jesus is said to have ordained the apostles to be priests.

It cannot be without significance that we hear of no laying on of hands. Jesus laid His hands on children and on the sick, but not on the Twelve. Where we might most expect it, when He gives them the Office of the Keys, there at John 20:21 ff. we read: "Jesus said to them again, 'Peace be with you. As the Father has sent Me, even so I send you.' And when He had said this, He breathed on them, and said to them, 'Receive the Holy Spirit. . . .' " One almost gets the impression that here, as whenever He sent out the apostles, Jesus intentionally avoided the laying on of hands. Such an avoidance may have been due to the fact that ordination by laying on of hands was rabbinical usage. That is how a rabbi ordained his disciples. Pondering what Jesus said against the scribes in Matt. 23 may suggest why Jesus did not follow their usage. Does He not say that among those that are His the title "rabbi" is not to be used, "for you have one Teacher (*didaskalos*), and you are all brethren" (v. 8)?

This did not prevent the title "teacher" from being used in the church for the great office of expounding Holy Scripture, at first the Old Testament. This office, along with that of the apostles and prophets, was foundational in the beginnings of the church, recognized not only in a particular congregation but throughout the church. And, after all, the title "teacher" was not directly prohibited by the words of our Lord. (Cf. also "master" (kathēgētēs, v. 10.)

However that may have been, it was certainly bad that, under the pressure of age-old Eastern custom, and against the express will of

Jesus, the church again took up the title "father" in place of "teacher" and first of all addressed the bishop thus (*pappas, papa,* cf. *abbas* in monasticism). (Cyprian of Carthage was still addressed thus; today the title is restricted to the bishop of Rome and the patriarch of Alexandria.)

The suggestion that Jesus was acting in deliberate contrast and opposition to the rabbis when He avoided the laying on of hands in what we might call ordination is strengthened by the noteworthy fact that the rabbis no longer followed the usage of the laying on of hands when in the second century it had become a characteristic of Christian ordination. So the laying on of hands is an early usage in the church (Heb. 6:2), with an Old Testament background (Moses laid his hands on Joshua, Deut. 34:9; cf. Num. 27:18), but it cannot be said to be something that Christ commanded us to do, let alone be called a sacrament. It was a way of bestowing a blessing, and that it certainly did.

It is also clearly not something that was reserved to the holder of a particular office. Beside the laying on of hands done by the apostles was also that done by the elders. Elders were men of special standing, not incumbents of a specific office. Thus it was in the synagogue, in the church of Jerusalem, in the Pauline congregations, and still so in Rome at the time of Clement. Elders were elected by the congregation as "honored ones," as *prōtokathedritai* ("having the first seats"), as they are still called in the Shepherd of Hermas [Vis. III, 9, 7; cf. 1 Clement 1:3; 21:6]. Because of their age, because of what they had done for the congregation, or for some other reason, they occupied the first places in the divine service. They represented the congregation. From among them the bishops were chosen, the group of officers who led the congregation, in particular to perform the office of preaching the Word or of saying the liturgical prayers, especially during the Eucharist. They did what was otherwise reserved to the prophets. Elders who then also performed such offices were to be "considered worthy of double honor, especially those who labor in preaching and teaching." What is said in 1 Tim. 5:17 matches perfectly what is said of the situation in Rome in 1 Clement. The elders as representatives of the congregation participated in the ordination of Timothy. They laid their hands on him (1 Tim. 4:14), as also did the apostle [2 Tim. 1:6].

How free was the usage of the laying on of hands in the early church we may see from the noteworthy passage Acts 13: 1–3, where the church ordains an apostle. Here in Antioch we find prophets and teachers officiating, among them Barnabas (from the sound of the words a prophet) and Paul (the schooled scribe) as "teacher," that is, as one who expounds

101

the Scriptures. During the liturgy the Holy Spirit by way of prophetic statement (as in the case of Timothy) instructs them to send out Barnabas and Paul on a special mission. "Then after fasting and praying they laid their hands on them and sent them off" (v. 3). In the early church there are more examples of a teacher becoming a missionary. There was Pantaenus, who gave up the office of teacher in Alexandria in order to go as a missionary to "India" [Eusebius, *Historia ecclesiastica* V, 10, 2].

Who laid on hands here? The congregation, perhaps through its elders. I have never been able to understand how learned Catholics, such as Tixeront in his well-known work on ordination [*Holy Orders (1928)*, p. 142] can read Acts 13:3 in such a way that the laying on of hands by the congregation could be taken as little more than a sort of godspeed for a good journey. The problem here is that the later Roman Catholic idea of ordination is being read back into a time when it had not as yet developed, or to say the least, into a time when there was greater diversity of forms in the life of the church. One has only to study such forms as they have survived on the fringes of ancient Christianity, in Ethiopia or in old Ireland, to see how at the beginning there was always diversity, which under the influence of the great metropolitan centers was reduced to unified forms.

7

What emerges from the foregoing? Here so much could only be pointed to, and yet what help have we found for dealing with the problem of the "apostolic succession" today? From a doctrinal point of view it can only be seen as a soap bubble, on which no church can be built. The Roman Church has the wisdom to put the whole matter in its doctrine of the priesthood. Rome knows that apostolic succession, in the double sense of a sequence of bishops and a succession of consecrations, has never guaranteed what the ancient church wished to have guaranteed, namely purity of doctrine, the apostolicity of the church. Rome also knows how many bishops, consecrated with every proper rite, have fallen away in persecutions or into heresy. The church in the East knows this too.

Bishop Lilje, then, is crashing through open doors when he charges that it is heresy to affirm that the apostolic succession guarantees pure doctrine. Rome does not affirm this. For Rome the purity of the doctrine, the apostolicity of the church, is guaranteed by the office of Christ's infallible vicar as successor of the "Prince of the Apostles." The significance of the succession of consecrations/ordinations for Rome is simply and only that which is expressed in the liturgy of ordination to the priesthood: the power to offer the sacrifice of the Mass for the living and the dead (*potestas ordinis*) and the power of the Office of the Keys (*potestas iurisdictionis*). The silken thread upon which the Roman doctrine of office hangs is the notion that when our Lord said: "Do this in remembrance of Me," He wanted to ordain the apostles to be priests. If these words are to be understood differently, namely in the sense that the Twelve here as in other passages are the representatives of God's people as a whole, then the entire special priesthood simply collapses. The New Testament knows that in the new covenant there is only one high priest, Jesus Christ, and the priestly people of God, whose members are kings and priests.

If the Reformers, indeed also the fathers of the Reformed churches, including the Anglican, saw one thing clearly, it is that it is quite untenable to hold this interpretation of our Lord's bidding that His Supper be repeated. In addition Matt. 18:18 makes it clear that the Keys are not the sole prerogative of the clergy. Evidence of their belonging to the whole church may be found in the early church and for a long time thereafter. There is the lovely story related by Melanchthon in the Treatise on the Power and Primacy of the Pope (67 f.), ascribed to Augustine and to be found also in Gratian's *Decretum*, where it appears as an illustration for a point of canon law. Two shipwrecked Christians were together in a boat. One was a catechumen. Him the other baptized, and then by him was absolved. The view of the Lutheran Confessions that the keys have been given to the whole church is in harmony with Scripture and the ancient church.

If one accepts the Roman view, then the apostolic succession makes some sense: The power to make the sacrifice of the Mass and the power to absolve is bestowed. If one does not accept this view, then there is no apostolic succession. Leo XIII was then quite right in declaring Anglican orders to be null and void, because their form, that is, the words of ordination, was invalid and because the right intention was lacking.

The words of ordination of the Anglican ritual are indeed ambiguous. One must probably be an Anglican in order not to see that they are therefore impossible.

> Receive the Holy Ghost for the office and work of a Priest in the Church
> of God, now committed unto thee by the imposition of our hands.
> Whose sins thou dost forgive, they are forgiven; and whose sins thou

dost retain, they are retained. And be thou a faithful dispenser of the
Word of God, and of his holy sacraments.

These words can mean ordination to the Gospel office of proclaiming
the Word and administering the sacraments. "Priest" then means presbyter, in the general sense which was the usage for a long time in North
Germany and is still the usage in Scandinavia, where the parson is called
"priest." This is the way the formula is understood by evangelically
minded Anglicans. Among the High Church and Anglo-Catholics, however, "priest" means *sacerdos*, one who offers sacrifice at the consecration in Holy Communion. As to right intention, what the ordaining
bishop may be thinking he is doing is left up to him. This is also the
case with what is meant by the formula for consecrating a bishop, whose
office is said to be "the office and work of a Bishop in the Church of
God." What is essential to this office is not said.

This way of doing things is characteristic of Anglicanism. We may
look for its roots in the character of the English people, as well as in
the inexpressibly sad story of the English Reformation, which was at
first an event of national politics rather than a religious event. This is
not to deny all that has been and is great in this church; there is much
for us Lutherans to learn from it. Its "apostolic succession" we cannot,
however, acknowledge; it is an empty form.

For us there are different grounds than those of Rome for rejecting
Anglican "apostolic succession." For us the matter is not decided by
whether the consecrating of Archbishop [Matthew] Parker [in 1559] was
adequately done: Two bishops with Roman Catholic consecration (but
without office), plus two Reformed bishops participated. This is also not
the direction of the Roman arguments against the validity of Anglican
orders. As we have seen, these attach to the faulty formula of ordination
and the lack of the intention to make the one ordained into a priest in
the Roman Catholic sense. Against these considerations the laying on
of hands, be it ever so canonical, is of no avail. When our Anglican
friends would make us in our "less fully organized churches" into suc-
cessors of the apostles by their laying on of hands, we will have to teach
them that the genuine succession of the apostles is that which lives by
the pure proclamation of the Gospel and celebration of the sacraments,
and not by the myth of an unbroken chain of consecrations going all the
way back to the apostles.

Not to see this clearly is for Lutherans a grievous failure. Of the offered "apostolic succession," we must ask what is its nature and what are the consequences of accepting such an ecclesiastical myth. The sooner the answers, the better. We may recall the answer given by Archbishop Söderblom at the World Conference for Faith and Order at Lausanne in 1927. Whatever else may be said of his limitations, it was surely a piece of his Lutheran heritage which came to sober expression when he said that the Church of Sweden has preserved the apostolic succession together with other things inherited from the ancient church, but that such a succession is according to Lutheran doctrine an adiaphoron. This he did quite unforgettably. He threw aside the printed text of what he had intended to say, for he felt compelled to speak even more clearly. For that all Lutherans were grateful.

If one looks more closely at the Swedish succession, it is really much better than the Anglican one. The critical link was a man who had just been consecrated by the pope himself in Rome, or, as Luther might say, the succession was received directly from the Roman Antichrist. But just this circumstance shows what nonsense it is to regard succession as more than time-honored custom and to consider it as theologically necessary or important. As an old ecclesiastical form, as an adiaphoron, it can be borne with that humor with which Söderblom carried his bishop's staff. Once, during a visitation, he realized that he had forgotten to pack it. It was quickly replaced by one cut from a birch tree. Is it possible for a Swedish Lutheran seriously to suppose that a pope who rejected the doctrine of the Lutheran Reformation as heresy could be the one to guarantee that the Church of Sweden has indeed true bishops and pastors?

Yet even there the old, healthy view of succession, the view in harmony with the Lutheran Confessions, seems to be losing ground in influential circles. In the official statement about itself in the handbook of the Lutheran World Federation, *The Lutheran Churches of the World*, ed. A. R. Wentz (1952), p. 171, we read that the Church of Sweden accepted the Unaltered Augsburg Confession in 1593 and that since 1686 the Book of Concord is the church's confession. Then on p. 174 we read: "Sweden's apostolic succession has opened the way for intercommunion with the Church of England," an intercommunion that has meanwhile been raised by both parties to the level of church law.

About the consequences of all this for Lutheranism around the world more than enough has already been said in these letters. We can only ask why others did not raise their voices while there was still time. Where was the voice of the bishops of Norway and of Denmark? Where was the voice of the Lutheran churches of Germany and of America? Where was the voice of the Lutheran missions? They looked on complacently when Lutheran bishops were consecrated with the assistance of Anglican bishops and archbishops. They were silent when it was up to them to raise their voices in warning; they owed this brotherly service to the Lutheran churches of the world. The old Archbishop Johannson of Finland was the first to see where this path would lead. His voice died away unheard.

We all reassured ourselves at first with the fact that the "apostolic succession" is an adiaphoron—and that it is, if it is understood in the Lutheran manner as simply a form from the ancient church. But there comes a time when an adiaphoron ceases to be an adiaphoron. This is said with all necessary clarity in Article X of the Formula of Concord. This article was a beacon and banner for us in the church struggle in Germany, and we were privileged to experience that it is still a weapon with which one can fight for the church of God. "In a case of confession or scandal nothing is an adiaphoron." Where the pure doctrine of the Gospel is at stake, there toleration of adiaphora ceases. There it is the duty of "the entire community of God . . . and especially the ministers of the Word as the leaders of the community . . . to confess openly, not only by words but also through their deeds and actions . . . " (Formula of Concord, Solid Declaration, X, 10).

We are not in a position to tell the Lutherans in Sweden who hold to the old heritage of their church (it is a truly great heritage) what they should do in order to preserve the pure Gospel of justification by faith alone and the pure administration of the sacraments, to which pure proclamation about the sacraments also belongs. We can pray for them. What we cannot do is acknowledge the Church of Sweden as a church of the Unaltered Augsburg Confession when it has altar fellowship with Anglicans and has Anglican bishops, who reject "by faith alone," participate in the consecration of Swedish bishops. The same must be said of other Lutheran churches when they put themselves into a similar situation.

Here the Lutheran World Federation would have a great task, the task of saying clearly what the Lutheran Confessions still mean for our day and wherein the true unity of the church resides. But can we expect anything else from it than that it simply offers justification for what has already been happening? Can we expect that it will commit suicide? It is at the outset committed to the principle that churches which are in church fellowship with the Reformed and the Anglicans are to be recognized as churches of the Unaltered Augsburg Confession, in spite of the latter's Articles VII and X, not to speak of the Formula of Concord.

The witness of the Lutheran Confessions will then have to be heard outside the Lutheran World Federation. May this happen only in humility and love! However conscious we may be of our poverty and weakness, this is the great service that is ours to do for those who have lost the confession of the Lutheran Reformation or are in danger of losing it. It is the task of those whose ordination to the Lutheran ministry gave them the authentic apostolic succession. This is no mysterious something that rests on a myth of consecrations. Rather it consists in the clear commission which our Lord gave to His whole church, to proclaim the pure apostolic doctrine and administer the sacraments according to the Gospel.

That is the great responsibility which today is given to the Lutheran pastor. It cannot be taken from him by any bishop, any church government, or any ecumenical organization. We may and can confess, also if those remain silent who are in the first instance called to do this. In faithful confession lives the whole glory of our office, even when this glory is hidden under the cross.

Last Things: Church and Antichrist

Letters to Lutheran Pastors, No. 24
March 1952

1

A few years ago, in the time of Germany's collapse, it was reported of a German pastor that he boasted of preaching only on the Revelation of St. John. Probably his poor congregation soon made it clear to him that that would not do. Yet, in his way, he was attempting to make good what had been neglected by the church and by us pastors: *eschatological proclamation.*

In our day the Biblical doctrine of the Last Things has come alive for us as a gift given in the midst of what the church has had to endure. At the beginning of this century a complacent church regarded the Last Things as an element of the first Christian proclamation which more or less belonged only to that first period, a form of the Gospel which was for us of only historical interest. Or, alternatively, it was thought of as something that might be of significance for the future, at the end of our lives, or at the end of the world, something we needed to study only in preparation for such an end. That there is for the church no more vitally relevant doctrine than that of the Last Things was brought home to Christians in Europe by all they were called upon to endure. It was not quite the same for Christians in other parts of the world, although in America some first indications can be observed of a new interest in eschatology.

There was perhaps some dark foreshadowing of what was to come when, at the beginning of the century, historical theology again discovered the eschatological character of the Gospel—much to the discomfort of the "systematic" theologians and the representatives of practical theology. No one can tell us, who have endured the judgments of God's wrath, that the fearful pictures of apocalyptic tribulation shown us in

108

Holy Scripture are but the product of Eastern fantasy. We can no longer read these passages the way they were expounded in earlier centuries. The old expositions seem like the work of a connoisseur who stands before some old paintings as if he had all the time in the world, and expounds what he finds so enchanting about them. He is quite at peace with himself and his expert knowledge—or his expert ignorance. The paintings mean absolutely nothing decisive for his existence.

For us these are realities of which we have had some experience. We are like those people in the East for whom Mereshkovski speaks in the introduction to *The Brothers Karamazov* (Munich, 1921).

> They are like men who stand upon some height and looking over the heads of those around them see what is coming upon them, what at the moment is not yet seen by the multitude below. Thus have we, beyond all the coming centuries and whatever could possibly happen, caught a glimpse of the end of the world's history. . . . We may indeed be the weakest of the weak. Our "power is made perfect in weakness." Our strength is in this, that we cannot be won over by any seductions of the most mighty of all devils, by any seductions of the everlasting "normality" of unending "progress." We cannot be bought by any averaged philosophy that is neither hot nor cold. Our faith is set on the end; we see the end; we long for the end. . . . In our eyes there is an expression which never was before in the eyes of men. In our hearts there is a feeling that has not been felt by men for 19 centuries, not since the vision was seen by that lonely exile on the island that is called Patmos: "The Spirit and the Bride say, 'Come.' And let him who hears say, 'Come.' . . . He who testifies to these things says, 'Surely I am coming soon.' Amen. Come, Lord Jesus!"

It is by living the Last Things that we are given a new understanding of the fact, and why it is so, that always involved in the Gospel and the proclamation of the Gospel are the Last Things, the end, Christ's return. There is preaching of the Gospel in the world because we are in the world's evening (Matt. 24:14). The reddening dawn of the daybreak of the kingdom of God is signaled by the lame walking, the blind seeing, that "lepers are cleansed and the deaf hear." Finally the nearness of the kingdom of God is signaled by the fact that "the poor have good news preached to them" [Matt. 11:5]. All preaching is preaching of the Last Things when it is preaching of the Gospel. And no preaching is preaching of the Last Things if it is not preaching of the pure Gospel—even if it were the exposition of nothing else but the Revelation of St. John and the other eschatological texts of Holy Scripture. How can anyone proclaim the Lord's death without a thought of His coming again?

How can the word "justification" come from our mouths without a thought of His coming again to judge the living and the dead? How can one say "Amen" at the end of the sermon without thinking of that great Amen at the end of the Bible: "Amen. Come, Lord Jesus"?

<h1 style="text-align:center">2</h1>

In the light of the foregoing we shall take up a single part of eschatology, a not unimportant part, *the doctrine of the Antichrist.* In dogmatics it appears, because of its nature, in two places, in the doctrine of the Last Things and in the doctrine of the church. Yet both belong together, for the doctrine of the church, when seen clearly, that is, seen in the light of God's Word, is actually only a part of eschatology. There is church only at the end of the world (1 Cor. 10:11). "In these last days," according to Heb. 1:2, "He [the Father] has spoken to us by a Son." At the end of the world the Son calls the faithful from among all nations to the true people of God, the church. All that happens in the church is fulfillment of the prophecies of the end, for example the whole activity of the Holy Spirit (Acts 2:16 ff.; Joel 2:28 ff.). The sacraments of Baptism and the Lord's Supper anticipate what happens at the end and in eternity (Rom. 6:2 ff.; 1 Cor. 11:26; John 6:54). So also Holy Absolution and the justification of the sinner anticipate what happens on the Day of Judgment. Even the liturgy on Sunday is an anticipation of the liturgy of heaven (Rev. 4), as every Sunday celebrated as "the Lord's day" anticipates the Parousia (cf. the expression "the day of the Lord," Amos 5:18). Only from this vantage point is it possible to understand the church of the New Testament and its hope anchored in the end.

The first Christians were not Adventists. Had they been, they would not have survived the Parousia's delay. In fact, the early Christian "Adventists" did fall from the faith (2 Peter 3:3 ff.). Nor were the first Christians Catholics, for whom institutionalization of the church becomes a substitute for the kingdom which has failed to come. Nor were they like some modern Protestants, for whom the kingdom of God becomes a kingdom of this world in social ethics and religiosity. Rather they lived in the great actuality of the Last Things, in the church of the living God. They were not a religious association with certain eschatological convictions. They were the holy people of the end time, the saints, who still lived in this world but no longer belonged to it. While for modern Christians, whether Catholic or Protestant, it might only be a matter of pictures and parables, for them it was a reality they actually lived when they designated themselves the people of God, the body of Christ, the temple of the Holy Spirit.

To the reality of the church, however, belongs the reality of the Antichrist. "Children, it is the last hour; and as you have heard that Antichrist is coming, so now many antichrists have come; therefore we know that it is the last hour" (1 John 2:18). Because the church lives at the end time of the world, therefore the prophecy of the coming Antichrist is being fulfilled. And because the prophecy of the Antichrist is being fulfilled, the church knows that it is the last time. So the appearance of the Antichrist must run through the whole history of the church. The Antichrist is always coming, and he is already here. Similarly in Paul, who does not use the word "Antichrist," "the man of lawlessness . . . the son of perdition, who opposes and exalts himself . . . " is coming, but in such a way that "the mystery of lawlessness is already at work." But it will only then be fully revealed when "in his time" he comes "by the activity of Satan . . . with all power and with pretended signs and wonders" (2 Thess. 2:3 ff.).

Both apostles agree that the Antichrist is on his way, insofar as his appearance belongs to the end time. Both see him active in the present and in the future. While Paul looks more to the future, John focuses more on the present. This matches what they say elsewhere about eschatology. Their unity is not diminished by whether the emphasis is on the present or on the future in an end time that embraces both the present and the future. We must not bend Paul to John or John to Paul. Rather we must recognize how in them both we have the one harmonious doctrine of the Antichrist.

We may not use our notions of time to make measurements of the last time as we are told of it in Scripture (2 Peter 3:3–9). There seems to be a contradiction between the fact that the Lord is coming soon and that 19 centuries have now passed since this was proclaimed. This we simply accept, as we also do the fact that at the time of John it was already "the last hour," in which the Antichrist was in the world, and that the time of his being revealed still lies ahead.

One cannot weaken this apparent contradiction by explaining it away in terms of a development from the comparatively harmless antichrists of the early time to the anti-Christianity which comes to consummation at the Parousia. First of all, Holy Scripture does not know our concept of development; it was first read into Scripture by the evolutionistic 19th century. Furthermore, what John tells of anti-Christianity is no less satanic, no less dangerous, than what Paul sees. Both derive from the same source: the devil. Both have the same goal: to cast Jesus Christ from His throne and to destroy His true church. Both fight with the same weapons: the power of the lie, and deceptions which seduce to falling away from the true God (1 John 2:22 ff.; 2 John 7; 2 Thess. 2:3, 9 ff.). The difference is only in the outward appearance. In John the Antichrist appears in the shape of many men who are called antichrists, in Paul in the shape of "the man of lawlessness." What we are told of is the same, whether in one form of appearance or the other.

The language in 2 Thess. 2:3 is clearly picturesque and apocalyptic. That he "takes his seat in the temple of God" is apocalyptic picture language ever since the desecration of the temple by Antiochus Epiphanes, as seen by Daniel. Similarly, that Christ "will slay him with the breath of His mouth" belongs to the picture language of the Messianic hope in the prophets (compare 2 Thess. 2:8 with Is. 11:4 and Rev. 19:15, 20).

Hence it must remain an open question whether the prophecy of "the man of lawlessness" will be fulfilled in the form of one individual man. Elert has a telling comment on the apocalyptic visions in the Bible: "Not the pictures themselves but what is meant by them provides us with what we believe" (*Glaube* [1956], p. 518). In this case the fulfillment can also be in the form of a collective person. This is clearly what John has in mind when he sees the Antichrist in many antichrists. The fulfillment could also be thought of in this way, that the collective person will find his final expression in an individual person.

There are questions here which we cannot answer because Scripture does not give an answer. Scripture tells us that the Antichrist belongs to "the last hour" and is therefore there in some form at all times of the church's history. It is "the last time" ever since Christ, the Firstfruits, rose from the dead and so began the resurrection of all the dead (1 Cor. 15:23). It was already a part of the end of the world when Jerusalem, according to our Lord's prophecy, was destroyed in the year 70.

Only an utterly unbiblical way of looking at history could suppose that the Last Things belong altogether to the future, whether near or distant. As surely as the church never ceases to pray, "Thy kingdom come," and "Amen. Come, Lord Jesus," so surely it believes what the Lord says: "The hour is coming, and now is"(John 5:25), and also the warning of His apostle: "Children, it is the last hour" (1 John 2:18). Because this is so, the church knows that the Antichrist is in the world.

3

If it did not know about the mystery of the Antichrist, the church would not be able to exist. It would not be able to arm itself against him, to fight against him, to stand against him. When it is taught that the devil does not exist, he has achieved the propagation of his most dangerous triumph. Similarly there is no greater strengthening of the Antichrist than the view that he is only an apocalyptic figure who will later someday make his appearance—indeed a most sinister being, but nevertheless a useful warning before the end.

If the Antichrist is not yet on the scene, then the readying alarm has not yet been given. What an assurance of "All's well" is given by such thinking! This is true of the whole system of successive notifications which has been read out of Scripture: conversion of the Jews, resurrection of the martyrs, and so on. Those who think this way don't seem to realize that thereby the signs of the end, for which our Lord commanded us to watch, have been turned into their direct opposite. One may acknowledge that the Lord will come as a thief in the night, but one also knows that it is not yet night, even though it may be evening, and perhaps even late evening. The church will only be at the ready if it knows that the Antichrist is already in the world, and that it is at every moment exposed to the full force of his attacks. If it does not know this, then it is hopelessly defenseless against him. That is the meaning of the apostolic warnings.

What then is *the mystery of the Antichrist?* What does he want? What does he do? What he wants is to seduce Christians to fall away from the true God, the God revealed in Christ. In the place of the truth of the Gospel he puts the lie, the way of falsehood. Here the passages in John are in full agreement with 2 Thess. 2. And there is another point of complete agreement. In contrast with the devil, the Antichrist is religious. According to John he comes with a message which sounds quite Christian. He affirms the Gospel, but he falsifies it. According to 1 John 4:3 this falsification is done by denial of the Incarnation.

John was clearly writing vis-a-vis emerging Gnosticism. This powerful movement in the early days of Christianity was able to win over great numbers of Christians, notably in Egypt and Syria. In the middle of the second century the orthodox church, the church whose faith was in the incarnate Christ, appears to have been a minority. Yet in its way how pious was this honoring of Christ as a heavenly being that appeared here on earth with only the semblance of a body! Against this John wrote his gospel with its central theme: "The Word became flesh."

The religious character of the Antichrist, as described by Paul, is disclosed in the cult of man. This appears in the church, this religious exaltation of man. The voice of the serpent at the beginning in Paradise is heard again in the message of this Antichrist: "You will be as God." This is the oldest heresy in human history, and it appears in ever new forms to the end of the world. This is clearly the sense of the prophecy of the enemy who "exalts himself against every so-called god or object of worship, so that he takes his seat in the temple of God, proclaiming himself to be God" (2 Thess. 2:4).

Whatever forms this divinization of man may take in the future— and certainly such an error always gets worse—one would have to be struck blind not to recognize the appearance of this original heresy ever and again in Christian history. The natural man always has the inclination to use religion for his self-glorification, also the Christian religion. From ancient India we hear: "Atman is Brahman" (the soul is divine). Every missionary to India knows that the greatest hindrance to the Gospel is this divinization of man. This same divinization of man is to be found also in the idealism of the Greeks and of the Germans of the classical period, and it permeates the theology of the Greek fathers, of medieval scholasticism, and of modern Protestantism.

This is what the Antichrist wants. This is what he does. He leads men away from the worship of the one true God, the God who in Jesus Christ became flesh. He leads them to serve the human "I," exalted to the place of God. He does this from the days of the apostles down to the Last Day. This is something that happens in the church. Therefore the Antichrist is more dangerous than all other enemies of the church. No Roman caesar, no modern dictator is so dangerous as the enemy of Christ within the church.

When Pliny wrote to Trajan, he reported the measures he had taken against the Christians. These went so far as the execution of the "obstinate" ones who refused to recant. In the same letter he tells of Christians who had fallen away from the church 20 years previously. Such falling away in time of persecution is not the worst thing Christendom has experienced in this regard. This was recognized when the way of repentance was opened for those who had lapsed under pressure of persecution. It was the way the first denier, Simon Peter, had gone. Antichrist's great art is that he can bring Christians to fall away without persecution. When Islam was sweeping over Christians lands, there were Christians who almost clamored to become Moslems. Many of them could give religious reasons for doing so. The Islamic rulers even tried to forbid such conversions to Islam, or at least made them difficult, for the sake of the head-tax which Christians were required to pay. The highest art of the Antichrist is that he can make falling away a work of religious piety.

<h1 style="text-align:center">4</h1>

In Christian history there is no one who has so deeply probed the mystery of the Antichrist as Martin Luther, no one who so shuddered before it. In Roman theology, even in the greatest teachers of the Roman Church, the Antichrist has always appeared as a comparatively harmless being. This figure of the distant end time may indeed be painted with the most frightening colors, but one need not be too frightened when one knows that this monster will rule for "not too long" a time, that is, three and a half years (Scheeben-Atzberger, *Handbuch der katholischen Dogmatik*, IV, 904). It belongs to the essence of the Roman Church that it puts into a more or less distant future what Holy Scripture says about the events of the end time. For the present, then, Christians need not be much concerned about it.

For Luther the Antichrist was not so innocuous. Why did the Antichrist loom so large for him? Is this to be explained by the influence of the apocalypticism of the Late Middle Ages, nourished by a mood born of the feeling that a dying world was going under, as well as by the despair of pious people in regard to the ever-more-decadent church? This certainly was an influence upon Luther and upon the whole century of the Reformation. He, along with most of his contemporaries, was convinced of living in the eventide of the world. He never supposed that the world would last much longer. In his *On the Councils and the Church* he is prompted by Nicaea's Easter canon to speak of the planned reform of the Julian calendar, and he declares it unnecessary.

> What does it matter to us Christians? Even if our Easter should coincide with the day of St. Philip and St. James [May1] (which I hope will not happen before the end of the world) and move still further, we still celebrate Easter daily with our proclamation of Christ and our faith in him [WA 50,557; American Edition 41, 65].

Of the old calendar he says:

> The old garment with its great tear has stayed on and on, and now it may as well stay until the Last Day, which is imminent anyhow. Since the old garment has endured being patched and torn for approximately fourteen hundred years, it may as well let itself be patched and torn for another hundred years; for I hope that everything will soon come to an end [WA 50, 557; American Edition 41, 65].

Vilmar once said that it would have been better if Luther had not been so sure that the end of the world was about to happen. He would then have given more thought to the future of the church. Even if this be so, we must remember that Luther was not just captive to the way the Late Middle Ages thought about the world, but that more than any of his contemporaries he had immersed himself in the eschatology of the New Testament. For him, as for the church of the apostles, ecclesiology was a part of eschatology. Unlike the men of the 19th century who saw the church as one of the great social constructions of human history, he saw the church as the holy people of God of the end time, attacked by the devil, led by the Antichrist into the great temptation to fall away, and protected and preserved by Christ.

Therefore the Antichrist fills a far different role for Luther than for the men of the Middle Ages. He is not just a frightening figure who announces the Last Day; he is the great antagonist of Christ in the drama of the church's history. No one can know what the church is, what the kingdom of Christ is, who does not know the Antichrist. Therefore the Antichrist can only be understood from the vantage point of the Gospel, and not from that of the Law, as the Middle Ages tried to do. When the 12th century gave way to the 13th in the apocalyptically minded Middle Ages, there were voices to be heard, at first hesitatingly and softly, and then with mounting strength up to the days just before the Reformation, asking "whether the pope is the Antichrist." The reasons given for this thesis were always those of the Law. The pope was the guardian of God's law on earth, but he did not keep it; he cast it aside. He did not keep the law of Christ, for instance the command of poverty. He is the greatest and most frightful sinner of all because of his scandalous life, because of his greed and his tyranny.

Luther also knew of these sins and blamed the popes for them, but as Hans Preuss has observed: "An utterly scandalous life, no matter how bad, would never have persuaded him that the pope is the Antichrist" (*Vorstellungen vom Antichrist*, 1906, p. 152). Luther always warned the Evangelicals never to claim a higher level of morality than their opponents. We are all of us sinners, and there is no sense in quarreling about who is the biggest one. In his Table Talk Luther made a comparison between his battle with the pope and that of Wycliffe and Hus.

> Doctrine and life must be distinguished. Life is bad among us, as it is among the papists, but we don't fight about life and condemn the papists on that account. Wycliffe and Huss didn't know this and

116

attacked [the papacy] for its life.I don't scold myself into becoming good, but I fight over the Word and whether our adversaries teach it in its purity. That doctrine should be attacked—this has never before happened. This is my calling. . . . to treat doctrine is to strike at the most sensitive point . . . (WATR 1, 294 [American Edition 54,110]).

For Luther the pope is the Antichrist because his doctrine is anti-Christian. With his doctrine he casts the Lord Christ from His throne and puts himself there, there in the place which is Christ's alone. Christendom, then, must choose between the Gospel and the doctrine of the pope.

In light of this we can understand why Luther time and again spoke of his lifework as the battle against the papacy. He spoke of his room in the tower in Wittenberg as his "poor little room from which I stormed the papacy, and for that it is worthy of always being remembered." His thus identifying his lifework needs no more quotations, but we may note that he does this whenever he solemnly confesses his faith. So in the Great Confession of 1528, in the Smalcald Articles, and in the Brief Confession of 1544. For him to confess the Evangelical faith meant also to confess that the pope is the Antichrist. It pained him that this confession was missing in the Augsburg Confession. Hans Preus has pointed out that just in those hours when it seemed he was about to die he confessed his commitment to the battle against the pope as the Antichrist. In 1527, when he was very ill and expected to die, he was sad that he had not been found worthy of martyrdom, but he comforted himself with the fact that so it was even for St. John, who had written a "much harder" book against the Antichrist. Ten years later, when he was grievously ill at Smalcald, he said similar things. Finally, there is the gripping prayer he prayed the night of his death. He thanked God that He had made known to him His Son, "in whom I believe, whom I have preached and confessed, whom I have loved and praised, and whom the wretched pope and all the godless abuse, persecute and blaspheme" (cf. G. Köstlin, *Martin Luther*, Vol. II, 1903, pp. 170, 632; H. Preus, p. 146). Also in the wills which Luther made we find the thought expressed that the battle against the Antichrist was the battle of his life.

This battle cannot be explained by reference either to his temperament or to political motives. The former may apply at most to particular expressions which betray the irascibleness of an old man. These the Lutheran Church has rejected, as also have non-Lutheran critics who recognized them for what they were. The battle was not occasioned by moral outrage or by personal dislike. Of these we find more than enough

117

not only in the Late Middle Ages but also among good Catholics at the time of the Reformation. On the contrary, Luther had a sort of human sympathy for Leo X. The recognition that the pope is the Antichrist is for him much rather the other side of the knowledge of the Gospel, and the battle against the pope as the Antichrist is therefore the other side of the battle for the Gospel. To understand this profound connection is to understand what the Gospel is and who the pope is. Here is the reason why the Evangelical Lutheran Church accepts what (not how) Luther taught of the pope as Antichrist and why it proclaims in its Confessions as church doctrine that the pope is the Antichrist.

<h1 style="text-align:center">5</h1>

It should never have been questioned that this really is *church doctrine* and not merely a theological opinion of Luther's and of early Lutheran theology. On what grounds could one remove from the Confessions the large article on the Antichrist in the Smalcald Articles (II, IV)? The same is true of Apology VII and VIII, 24; XXIII, 25; XXIV, 51 (in all of which the German text uses the word "Antichrist," while Melanchthon's Latin text is content with citing Dan. 11) and in the Treatise on the Power and Primacy of the Pope, 39: "It is plain that the marks of the Antichrist coincide with those of the pope's kingdom and his followers." Yet if these passages are not in accord with Scripture, they should be removed. First, however, it would have to be shown that they are not in accord with Scripture, and second, if that were shown to be the case, the doctrine expressed there would have to be solemnly retracted before all the world.

One cannot, however, do it the way August Vilmar suggests: "That the pope in Rome is not the Antichrist, as used to be supposed in the Evangelical Church, is now so self-evident that any refutation of such an unclear notion is quite unnecessary and would indeed seem quite foolish" (*Dogmatik*, II, 306). Vilmar himself would likely have revised this statement, and many another which he wrote regarding the Roman Church, had he lived to witness Vatican I. That there may be no doubt about our position, let it be clearly said: A theologian who merely because it happens to be in the Confessions lets the doctrine stand that the pope is the Antichrist, and is not solidly convinced that it is so, cannot truthfully be called a Lutheran. He cannot escape the charge of slandering the papacy.

Why did the Lutheran Church accept Luther's teaching on this point? What is the meaning of this doctrine? We must first clearly recognize what the church did not accept. There were items in Luther's view of history which were not accepted, specifically that the end of the world would come not later than within the next century. With such presuppositions Luther could not possibly answer the question as to what new forms the Antichrist might assume in subsequent centuries. The church can have no doctrine which answers such a question. The church can and must teach that all the eschatological prophecies of Holy Scripture come to fulfillment. How that may happen lies beyond its knowing. We can never say with certainty how what Scripture says in apocalyptic picture language will be realized. The fulfillment of all prophecies is greater than could be grasped by those who heard them, even by those who heard them in faith. The Lutheran Church teaches nothing in its Confessions as to how God may let the prophecy of the Antichrist come to fulfillment in the hidden future, that is, what form the Antichrist may take in the final terrors of the end time. What our Confessions can teach, and do teach, this and no more, is that in the "last time" which we can see, in the time of the church until the present day, the prophecy of the Antichrist has found fulfillment in the papacy.

Luther himself never supposed that there was nothing to be seen of the Antichrist beyond the papacy. In his Great Confession of 1528 he says:

> The papacy is assuredly the true realm of Antichrist, the real anti-Christian tyrant, who sits in the temple of God and rules with human commandments, as Christ in Matthew 24 [:24] and Paul in II Thessalonians 2 [:3 f.] declare; although the Turk and all heresies, wherever they may be, are also included in this abomination which according to prophecy will stand in the holy place, but are not to be compared to the papacy (WA 26, 507 [American Edition 37, 367 f.]).

This always remained his conviction, and Lutheran theology always followed him in this matter.

But why is the pope the "true" Antichrist? The Smalcald Articles give the following answer:

> [He] has raised himself over and set himself against Christ, for the pope will not permit Christians to be saved except by his own power, which amounts to nothing since it is neither established nor commanded by God. This is actually what St. Paul calls exalting oneself over and against God (II, IV, 10).

It is really unnecessary to quote the passages in which overzealous devotees of the pope have predicated of him what belongs only to God.

This they did and were not excommunicated for it. Among them were the medieval canonists Augustine of Ancona and Zenzelinus of Cassanis. (Documentation is given [in Tappert, p. 300, and] in *Bekenntnisschriften*, p. 431.) Among them also were the Ultramontanists of the 19th century who so flattered Pius IX. What the Confessions teach is that when the pope promulgates a dogmatic decision, one which has no basis in Holy Scripture, and makes men's salvation or damnation depend on their obedience or disobedience toward it, then he is setting himself in the place of Christ, in the place of God. This is what Luther, with sharp prophetic vision, saw as the essence of the papacy, even though he could not yet know the Council of Trent or Vatican I.

If there was any doubt on the part of some Lutherans as to the correctness of Luther's judgment, then this was removed when Pius IX, with the consent of the Vatican Council, on 18 July 1870 promulgated the constitution *Pastor aeternus*. In it eternal salvation was denied to those who consciously oppose the dogma that the pope has the exercise of direct episcopal power over the whole church, over the infallibility with which Christ has equipped His church, and that his *ex cathedra* decisions in questions of faith and morals are, "of themselves, and not from the consensus of the church," true and irreformable (*ex sese, non autem ex consensu Ecclesiae irreformabiles* [Denzinger 3074]). And when the first of these new *ex cathedra* decisions was proclaimed—the dogma of the Assumption of Mary, in 1950, on All Saints' Day, the day inseparably connected with the Reformation—the shock wave hit all Christendom. Here became visible something of the reality which Luther had recognized with deep dread—the reality of the man who puts himself in God's place and proclaims his fantasies as divine revelation.

The pope is either Christ's vicar or he is the Antichrist. That is the alternative which Luther recognized quite clearly. Either the papacy is indeed instituted by God or it is an institution "instituted by the devil" (Luther: *vom Teufel gestiftet*). This institution is not merely human. It is more than a heretical institution. It is also something fundamentally different from the great non-Christian powers. They launch their attacks against the Christian faith from the outside, and will continue to do so. Whatever devilish attacks may be made against the church by the fearful totalitarian powers of the world, no representative of these powers has yet claimed to be Christ's vicar and to speak and act in His name. They set up their temple next to the church and seek to displace it. In the papacy, however, the man who deifies himself has worked his way into the church. This is what is so horrendous in the papacy.

And since 1870 the church, insofar as it has placed itself under the papacy, can never get free of this. Not only are the dogmas which the pope produces irreformable (among them the constitution *Pastor aeternus*), but there is no power above him. "No one shall judge the supreme see." This fundamental law is adduced in the Treatise on the Power and Primacy of the Pope (50) as evidence of the anti-Christian character of the papacy. It is now set in concrete in Canon 1556 of the Codex of Canon Law (*Codex iuris canonici*). No council can ever judge the pope or in any way stand over him. If the pope dies during an ecumenical council, the council is at the moment of his death interrupted, and can only be begun again, or not begun again, by the new pope (Canon 229, *Codex iuris canonici*). Both according to [canon] law and according to the doctrine of the Roman Church, this institution can never be removed from the church or be deprived of its claims. Of all the great persecutions which Christianity has endured, those words apply which we hear from the faith of the ancient church, "It is a little cloud; it will pass." Of the sinister temptation which the Antichrist is for the church, it can only be said that he will continue until the returning Christ destroys him.

6

In Letter No. 13, "Is the Pope Really Still the Antichrist?" we pointed out, over against the position taken by Hans Asmussen, that the papacy today is essentially the same as the papacy which confronted Luther. Responses came also from some Roman Catholic readers of that letter. Among them was a venerable Jesuit Father [Cardinal Bea] who for decades has worked for better understanding between our confessions. They sought to persuade the writer that a revision of the old Lutheran judgment of the papacy is made necessary simply by the fact that a common front of all Christian churches is called for against the militant atheism of modern Communism. And it is a widely held notion that the judgment of Luther and the Confessions on this point is only of temporary significance, that it cannot be maintained in the modern world if only because the papacy is not in the hands of such morally vulnerable characters as in the time of Luther. At that time one may have observed the power of "lawlessness" [2 Thess. 2:3], whereas nowadays, on the contrary, the papacy is a stronghold of God's law and the Christian religion. It has also been said that the first pope to die a martyr's death will put an end to the talk about the pope being the Antichrist. Now we must respond to these objections.

Concerning the morals of the popes, Luther long since put an end to the notion that here are the grounds for recognizing the pope as the Antichrist.

As to the papacy being the guardian of God's law and the Christian religion in the modern world, it all depends on what is meant by law and by Christian religion. We have already observed that it is hardly by chance that the great, bloody revolutions took place in Catholic lands. The Catholic countries of Europe and South America have tumbled from one revolution to another. There seems to be only one Catholic king left in the world, in Belgium, and his throne is none too sure. What of Russia? One cannot call it a Protestant country. The mausoleum of Lenin stands next to the Chapel of the Iberian Madonna—a warning as to where the path of giving reverence to men can lead, even if it begins in the refined rites of the cult of Mary. Whoever knows the inner history of Europe's Catholic countries, in particular of the ecclesiastical principalities, and above all of the Papal States, will recognize the fearful consequences for God's church of not having heeded the Lutheran Reformation's warning against mixing church and state—something that can also be observed in the Lutheran Church itself.

The statement that the papacy is the stronghold of God's law in the world has its context in the confusion and ignorance of the modern world as to what is law given by God. Is it to be regarded as divine law that the supposed vicar of Christ makes the demand that all mankind shall be obedient to him in all decisions concerning faith and morals? Don't people see that here we have the source of the totalitarian systems of our day?

Mussolini and Hitler were sons of the Roman Church. Stalin even got as far as candidate of theology. There have certainly been absolute states before, and they came out of Spain and France. Modern totalitarianism is characterized by its claim to have power over the souls of men. This was not so in the world empires of antiquity. A citizen had indeed to go along with the state cult, but he was left to think about it what he liked. That souls can be compelled to a faith, that was first discovered by Catholicism, and secular imitators of the Roman Catholic church-system have made use of this discovery. Without an infallible pope there would never have been an infallible Hitler. The total state was born along with the total church on July 18, 1870.

How deep this connection is can be seen in the history of the last generation, whose documents are now more and more coming out of the archives. Fascism could not have happened in Italy without the pope.

The history of the '30s reveals how close was the tie between them, as well as what all was included in the Lateran treaties. The moral responsibility for all the horrors of the Abyssinian war, if it can be called a war, is shared by the Vatican. And it was not only the Madonna of Fatima who rescued the Iberian Peninsula from Bolshevism or what was so called.

We Germans who lived through it, those who had their eyes open in the fateful year of our people, the fearful year 1933, know who it was that helped Hitler to power. Without that help he would not have came to power except by violent revolution. It was not only the foolish Evangelical pastors, not only the decadent German citizenry, but the Vatican that did this. To the horror of thinking German Catholics, the Vatican ordered the dissolution of the Center Party because National Socialism was needed for the struggle against the East. For that the German people were sacrificed. Then, to be sure, when the concordat was broken (that gentlemen's agreement between two parties of whom each was convinced that the other was no gentleman), and it became clear in Rome that the stronger cards were in the other hand, then all of a sudden there was staunch defense of the very holy human rights which had not long ago been betrayed to Hitler.

We mention these things here only to refute the pious legend that the papacy is the stronghold of civil order and God's law in the world. The Roman Church is the continuation of the Roman Empire with other instrumentalities. It is the empire in the form of a church, at bottom a synthesis of church and world, of divine and human, and therefore it is that temple where man has put himself on the throne of God.

The Roman Church is indeed the defender of the Christian religion, but of what sort? In this Christian religion God is not the only Lord who is served. Our Lord Christ said clearly that one cannot serve two lords. Putting another lord beside Him, or another lady, like Mary Queen of Heaven, has in it a fatal propensity to displace Him. In theory it sounds fine when it is said that grace is superior to nature and the human will, Christ to His mother, the Redeemer to the coredemptrix, the single Mediator of the New Testament to the mediatrix of all graces. But when Catholic people are taught that the way to Christ is by way of Mary, then she has practically become the savior. Then one has to say of the pope as Luther did in his last confession: "What good does it do him greatly to exalt with his mouth the true God, the Father, the Son, and the Holy Spirit, and to make a splendid pretense of living a Christian life?" (*Brief Confession Concerning the Holy Sacrament*, 1544 [WA 54,

160; American Edition 38, 310]). But we have already discussed this aspect of Catholicism in Letter No. 13, and so need not repeat what was said there of the organic connection of the institution of the papacy with synergistic doctrine and the cult of Mary.

Only one thing more. A modern pope simply cannot be a martyr for the Christian faith like the old bishops of Rome. He would die not only for faith in Christ, but at the same time also for the superstition of Fatima; not only for the doctrine of the Gospel, but at the same time also for those errors which have been proclaimed as divine revelations necessary for salvation, such as the dogmas of the Immaculate Conception and of the Assumption of Mary, and the universal episcopacy and infallibility of the pope. He would die also for the false claim that he is Christ's vicar on earth, to whom every human being, on pain of losing his salvation, owes obedience in all dogmatic decisions, as though to the Lord Himself. This is what has to be said to those who maintain that Luther's judgment on the papacy is no longer current.

7

Among theologians it should not be necessary to spend many words to make it clear that the judgments which the Confessions of our church make about the papacy are statements of theology and doctrine, the opposite of those outbursts against individual popes and against the Roman Church that are produced by human anger and hatred. Luther's judgment against the pope has nothing to do with that of French or Italian Freemasons. It is also quite different from that of German politicians who from time to time tell of the injuries done the German people from the end of the time of the Staufers [13th century] up to the present. The judgment of the Lutheran Confessions is also something quite different from what was heard from German Protestantism during the *Kulturkampf* [in the 1870s], from the Evangelical League in Germany, from the Away-from-Rome movement in Austria [early 20th century], or from the anti-Rome movement in the United States unleashed by the proposal that the United States have an ambassador to the Holy See. What do any of these movements know of the Antichrist? They can know nothing of the Antichrist, for they do not know what the Gospel is and what the means of grace are, which have been given by Christ.

It was Luther's deep understanding of the Gospel that enabled him on the one hand to recognize its fearful perversion in the papacy, and on the other hand to give a positive evaluation of those elements of the true church of Christ that still live on in the Roman Church. The same Smalcald Articles which so sharply delineate the doctrine of the Antichrist also acknowledge that "the sublime articles of the divine majesty" "are not matters of dispute or contention," and give a considerable list of those matters which they wish to discuss with the Roman theologians. In the eyes of the world, which knows not the Gospel, this is an inexplicable contradiction. To understand it, one must know much about the reality of the church—of the church as Christ's kingdom which must always struggle against the kingdom of the devil in this last and evil time.

It is not only human beings who are engaged in this drama. It was not only Eugenio Pacelli who proclaimed the false doctrine of the Assumption of Mary as a revelation given to Christianity. It was not actually and not alone Giovanni Medici who cast Luther out of the church. It was not actually Alexander Farnese who repudiated *sola fide* and so also the Lord Christ Himself. Rather it was the Antichrist who spoke and acted in and through them. For this reason we, as also Luther did, can have some human, sympathetic understanding for those men who bore the fearful office of the papacy. This is especially true in the case of those popes who, as far as human eyes can see, were noble figures in the history of the papacy.

As did our fathers before us, so we too know ourselves to be bound together in the one holy church of Christ with all those who live within the true church also in the Roman Church—those who are born of the means of grace, the Gospel and the sacraments, which have not yet entirely perished in the Roman Church. We Lutherans should also be shamed by the true and living faith in Christ that is present within the Roman Church in spite of the Antichrist and his seductive wiles. In the Roman Church there are Christians who truly live from the Gospel that is still there, from the Gospel in the prayer in the Canon of the Mass itself, "not judging our merits, but forgiving our iniquities." We know of Christians there who, when it came to die, knew nothing save Christ and Him crucified, and who died in faith in Him, forgetting about the whole churchly apparatus and the world of saints: "King of majesty tremendous, Who dost free salvation send us, Fount of pity, then befriend us" [*The Lutheran Hymnal*, 607:8]. To recognize this is to see why Luther laid such weight on the fact that the Antichrist would not be the Antichrist unless he were actually seated "in the temple," the church of God.

We are aware, honored brethren, of what a responsibility we take upon ourselves when we today repeat in such a way the old doctrine of the Lutheran Church concerning the pope as the Antichrist. We know that we shall have to answer for this before the judgment seat of Him who someday will judge the claims of all churches, the doctrine of all confessions. His judgment is the decisive one for us, not the opinions of men.

The majority of Western Christians today, and their theologians, including Lutheran ones, show no knowledge of this doctrine of the Reformation. And why is this? Because our generation has to a large extent lost any grasp of the great realities of the faith. One is struck here in Australia, on the edge of the Asiatic world, when meeting Christians from the "younger churches" of the mission fields, by how entirely different is their relationship to the New Testament and to the realities given us there. For them this is all new, fresh, and alive, while for us Europeans or Americans it is covered with a layer of dust centuries thick. The Epistles and Gospels which are read in church on Sunday we already know, or think we know. The hymns we sing once poured out of hearts made glad by the newly discovered Gospel—but that was long ago.

Here lies the deepest reason why Luther's doctrine of the Antichrist has become strange to us. One must know much about the reality of Christ, about His real presence, about His actions, dealings, and sufferings in today's world, in order to see the Antichrist in his manifold appearances, also the most splendid and powerful ones. One must literally live from the Gospel as the message of the sinner's justification in order to know what it means to exclude this Gospel from the church in the name of Christ and to deny salvation to those who teach, believe, and confess it.

God grant us all, pastors and congregations, teachers and students of theology, open eyes and an ever deeper understanding of His Word, and thereby an ever clearer view of the reality of the Antichrist, wherever and in whatever form we may encounter him, even if it be in our own Lutheran Church!

With this wish I greet you, dear brothers in the ministry, in these Easter days, in the unity of the faith.

THE CHURCH LIVES!
A Sermon on Acts 2:42-47 for the First Sunday After Trinity

June 27, 1943

When this war is finally over, then the question will be heard again, echoing over the scorched earth and through the exhausted people of the West: "What about the church of God?" Thus it has always been when a great war had thoroughly devastated the natural fellowships of birth and history. So it was after the Thirty Years' War, after the Napoleonic wars, and after the First World War. At such times Christians have remembered what they confess Sunday by Sunday before the altar: "I believe in the holy Christian church, the communion of saints." What kind of a reality is meant by this? Whoever has ears to hear already perceives this question struggling to be heard in the world and among our German people.

Yes, what sort of a reality stands behind this confession? Perhaps none at all? Is it perhaps just an old formula that has lost any meaning, when in the midst of the most dreadful of all wars, which has long since stopped being an honorable, knightly battle, when in the midst of this war, Sunday after Sunday, yes day after day, the confession is made in a thousand languages: "I believe in the Holy Spirit, the holy Christian church, the communion of saints"?

No, it is no mere formula. Here is a reality. It may, to be sure, be overlooked or forgotten. It may be hidden from our eyes as is the sun when it has gone down in the evening sky. But it is a reality that is still there, as surely as the sun which has set is still there, even if our eyes do not see it. No, it is much more sure than that. For whether the sun will rise again tomorrow, that I cannot know with certainty. But that God the Father, the almighty Creator of heaven and earth, is still there—that I surely know. That Jesus Christ is Lord, to whom all power has been given in heaven and on earth, that the Holy Spirit, who proceeds from the Father and the Son, moves over the chaos of this time as He did in the beginning over the dark depths—that I know. And therefore I also know that there exists the church of which the creed speaks: the church which is the people of God, the body of Christ, the temple of the Holy Spirit. What better place can there be for deepening our understanding of the reality of the church than where the church first makes its appearance before our eyes in human history, at least insofar as it can be seen by our eyes?

So God's church comes before our eyes in our text which brings to an end the great Pentecost chapter in the Acts of the Apostles. The scene begins with the Pentecost miracle, followed by Peter's sermon and the baptism of the 3,000. Then the life of the congregation is described in a few matter-of-fact words, and yet they vibrate with what happened in the transforming events of those days: the inexpressible joy of the newly baptized, the simplicity of faith with which they devoted themselves to the apostles' teaching, the awe of their hearts before the wonders of the Spirit, the brotherly love which is ready to offer everything, the prayers, the celebrations of the Sacrament, and the praise of God.

It is not difficult to see why this text has always been so profoundly moving, and has prompted so much in the history of the church. The way it has stirred people may be compared with the account of the rich young ruler, which ever and again has turned people around and brought them to the commitment of all their earthly possessions. So also Jesus' charge to the Twelve as He sent them out (Matt. 10) was ever and again used as a mirror in which the church of the Middle Ages recognized its sin and apostasy. So then also what Luke reports of the first congregation in Acts 2 and 4 has been heard ever and again since the early days of the church as a call to repentance. "They devoted themselves to the apostles' teaching and fellowship, to the breaking of bread and the prayers." And we? "All who believed were together and had all things in common." And we? " . . . continuing daily with one accord . . . " [KJV]. And we? ". . . with glad and generous hearts, praising God . . ." And we? Such questioning has ever and again been prompted by the account of the first congregation, and so it must be. Here a mirror is held up to the church of all times, a call to repentance.

It is this only, however, when it is rightly understood. It can be misunderstood, just as the account of the rich young ruler and Jesus' charge to the Twelve have been misunderstood. It is understood falsely when one sees in it only Law. How often this has happened! [People have said that] the church today should be as it was then, and therefore we must again make it like that. How often in the history of the church has the attempt been made to copy it! We see it in the Anabaptists at the time of the Reformation, in the Philadelphian societies and other fellowship constructions of Pietism, in Irving's Catholic Apostolic Church in England, in the large Disciples of Christ denomination in America. There seems to be no end to the sects and fellowships which make this attempt.

The view is widely held among them that in the original church all property was held in common, a sort of noble communism. The New Testament tells us nothing of this. In the case of Ananias and Sapphira we are told explicitly that everyone could keep his property if he wished. There was no law. What we are told is that no one said of his property that it was his. Rather, they disposed what they had for the benefit of others, for those who were poorer. We are told that "they (not all) sold their possessions and goods and distributed them to all, as any had need"—a sort of common chest. Probably these were those who came from Galilee to Jerusalem to await Christ's return. Of the mother of John Mark, who wrote our oldest Gospel, we are told in Acts 12 that she owned a house in Jerusalem.

The idea of communism (mark well, the communism of love, which does not say, "What is thine is mine," but rather "What is mine is thine") is a very idealistic notion. And this ideal is read into the account in Acts. It then becomes an example to be emulated by organizing Christian associations in which private property is abolished. What eventuates can be seen in some of the saddest stories in church history: congregations that began as a fellowship of Jesus ending up as a synagogue of Satan.

The urge to make a copy of the original church has prompted some to fasten on "they devoted themselves to the apostles' teaching . . . and many wonders and signs were done through the apostles." How can a copy be made of the original church without its most important office, the office of the apostles? Therefore let us make some new apostles! Such is the folly arrived at in England in the last century by Edward Irving. So first there was the Catholic Apostolic Church, and later another one called the New Apostolic Church.

Or it could go like this: In the original church the Christians were not called Lutherans or Reformed, Presbyterians or Congregationalists, Methodists or Baptists, Catholics or Orthodox. They were called disciples. So let us have a church of the Disciples of Christ. Such was the thinking of a pious American pastor a hundred years ago. Disciples of Christ is what all Christians want to be. Here is quite the simplest way, then, to overcome the divisions of Christianity. But naturally this movement also did not renew the one church, but only made another new one, even though very large and respectable. If I should attempt, my dear Christian hearers, to give you only a sketch of all such attempts, we would still be sitting here in church at noon. All these fellowships resulted from attempts to understand and obey our text as a law for the renewal of the church.

Our text is perverted when it is used as a law for shaping the life of the church. When men do that, they end up where all men of the Law end up—either in deep despair or in titanic arrogance.

Many, many Christians have ended in deep despair, because they did not attain the blessed state of this first congregation. I remember such a one from the time when I was serving as a pastor in Berlin. He was a popular preacher, something of a revivalist, who had the gift of giving his testimony of the Lord Christ to mass gatherings of Berlin workers. He had at one time, as a Red sailor and as a member of the Soldiers' Council in Kiel, participated in the revolution. Then he was converted to the Christian faith and became a missionary at large (*Volks-missionar*). He wanted to reform the church by turning into reality what was said of the original church. This man finally went to Russia and became a Bolshevist agitator. He had despaired of being able to renew the church today according to the model of the original church, and so to reform it.

The other way things go with men of the Law is the titanic arrogance of those who imagine that it will be easy to renew the church in the ideal form of the church at its beginning. The arrogance which here comes to expression is a hidden or unspoken faith in man. It should not be hard [they say] to be and to achieve what the first congregation was and achieved. The first Christians were only men, but what splendid men they were! Men of such splendid faith, men of such splendid brotherly love! What can hinder us from being such as they?

What hinders us is the same as hindered them. This is something we must be quite clear about, dear congregation, if we would be honest and not a prey to false illusions. As at all times, so also in that first time the church was a little group of poor sinners. If you want to understand the original church and its meaning for the church of all times, then you must first recognize that they were such as we are, poor sinners. They had no other strengths than we have. They were no better than the Christians of all times. If they were holy, then it was not in any other way than that way in which poor sinners at any time are holy—holy by the fact that Christ died for their sins. He was made "our wisdom, our righteousness and sanctification and redemption" [1 Cor. 1:30]. Our wisdom is Christ. Our righteousness is Christ. Our sanctification is Christ. Our redemption is Christ. So it was in the first congregation, a congregation of nothing but poor sinners.

So the New Testament tells of it. It was the congregation in which the wicked case of Ananias and Sapphira could happen. It was the congregation, as we are told in Acts 6, in which, in spite of love communism, in spite of the splendid caring for the poor, it could happen that "the Hellenists murmured against the Hebrews because their widows were neglected in the daily distribution." The first quarrel in the first congregation was about money, about how it was allotted from the church's treasury. There was, if one may say so, something not quite straight in the way the gifts collected in the congregation were being allotted.

Then follow the controversies in the church between Paul and Barnabas, between Paul and the first congregation, between Paul and Peter, and then between Paul and Peter on the one side and James on the other. And so it goes on and on in the early church. No, the early church was anything but a church of saints who are to serve as examples of splendid Christians to be emulated through all subsequent centuries. The church of the first century is a communion of saints in the same sense as the church of every century: It is a congregation of justified sinners. The first Christians also lived from nothing else than the daily forgiveness of their sins, as we confess in the Small Catechism: "In this Christian church he daily and abundantly forgives all my sins, and the sins of all believers." The holiness of the church is the holiness of Christ. We correctly understand what our text tells us about what happened in the first church, the congregation of saints in Jerusalem, when we hear not the praise of men but only "Holy, holy, holy is the Lord," the everlasting song of the church: "You only are holy; You only are the Lord; You only . . . are Most High."

So the church is never something made or put together by pious people, but it is the church of the Lord Christ. Not in the religion which men do, even if it is the highest and most beautiful blossoming of human religious activity, not in the faith of a Peter or a Paul does the church's glory have its source. Of that source we are told in our text: "They devoted themselves to the apostles' teaching and fellowship, to the breaking of bread and the prayers." Doctrine of the apostles, fellowship, breaking of bread, prayers—in these four things is hidden the secret of the church.

"They devoted themselves to the apostles' teaching." They did not grow tired of hearing the words spoken by the apostles, the witness to Jesus Christ, His incarnation, His deeds and words, and that He "died for our sins in accordance with the Scriptures, that He was buried, that He was raised on the third day in accordance with the Scriptures." In these words, transmitted by Paul (1 Cor. 15:3–4), we have the oldest formulations of the apostolic proclamation, the first steps of the later creeds: ". . . dead, and buried . . . the third day he rose from the dead." That was the doctrine of the apostles. That was what they repeated day by day.

"We are witnesses to all that He did both in the country of the Jews and in Jerusalem. They put Him to death by hanging Him on a tree; but God raised Him on the third day and made Him manifest; not to all the people but to us who were chosen by God as witnesses, who ate and drank with Him after He rose from the dead" (Acts 10, 39–41). It was always the same message, repeated with sublime monotony by the apostles, who were eyewitnesses, and then after their death by those to whom the apostolic proclamation was committed. The church of all times lives from the doctrine of the apostles.

But does it really? Must not the church adjust its message to the contemporary situation? The reproach of not moving with the times was heard in Germany through the 18th and 19th centuries from those who held a naive faith in progress. Why go on preaching the same as Peter did in the Acts of the Apostles? How many theologians, indeed whole churches, finally had enough! They did not continue in the apostles' doctrine. They preached something else. Forty years ago they preached sermons on Goethe and Schiller. They preached the current view of the world, although most world views are lucky if they last as long as 30 years. And the churches did not become fuller, but emptier. And rightly so. For since 1848 any member of German society could read in the newspaper every morning as he drank his coffee what the latest and only acceptable world view is. For this I do not need to go to church. But where the church continued in the apostles' doctrine, there the congregation remained.

To the world it is inexplicable that the church lives on, always preaching the same old thing. In fact, it is because the same old thing goes on being preached, the apostles' doctrine, that the church goes on living. This is because the apostles' doctrine is the everlasting Word of God to all men, to all nations, to all times. It is the Gospel of Jesus Christ, the eternal Son of God, "who for us men and for our salvation came down from heaven . . . and was made man." He "was put to death for our trespasses and raised for our justification" [Rom. 4:25]. He "is seated at the right hand of the Father . . . and His kingdom shall have no end." The apostolic doctrine witnesses to the Word of God become flesh. In this witness, in the simple words of the apostles, in the straightforward words preached in the church, Christ, the eternal Word, is Himself present. *Therefore* the church lives from the apostolic doctrine.

"They devoted themselves to the apostles' teaching and fellowship." Also in this word "fellowship" something of the deep, divine mystery of the church lies hidden. For this word means something else than what we human beings otherwise call fellowship. Of human fellowship we have two kinds. There is the natural fellowship into which we are born. This is there before we are, and we are born into it without our consent. Such is the fellowship of our family and people. Then there is the fellowship which occurs because we wish it to, a fellowship we enter voluntarily. There is such a fellowship when we more or less voluntarily join a gymnastics club, a party, an association that has a purpose with which we sympathize.

But the fellowship which binds together the members of the church never arises in such a way. We are not born into the church, nor can we join it. These are two very serious misunderstandings. "Those who received his word"—the words of Peter's Pentecost sermon having gone into them working faith—"were baptized, and there were added that day about three thousand souls" [Acts 2:41]. They "were baptized"—passive voice. They "were added"—passive voice. The One who added them was the One who called them by the Gospel and kindled the light of faith in their hearts.

In this way, and in no other, did we also become members of the church. You also were added by the Holy Spirit when you were baptized. Baptism is not some symbolic action, an initiation rite done or devised by men. It is a sacrament of Jesus Christ. And in the sacraments God is already now at this time doing something with us which He plans to do at the end of all things. In a sacrament the future becomes a present reality; it is eternity that has become time. So it is in Holy Absolution, as that doctrine is confessed in our church. Already now the forgiving words, which free us from sin, speak to us the verdict of the Final Judgment. So in Holy Communion we are given the fellowship of the body and blood of Christ, which will not come to consummation until the end of all things.

Your resurrection began when you were baptized. "We were buried therefore with Him [Christ] by baptism into death, so that as Christ was raised from the dead by the glory of the Father, we too might walk in newness of life" (Rom. 6:4). With Christ you died at that time, with Him you were buried, with Him you shall rise. With Him, for you have been made a member of His body. That is the deep secret of the fellowship of the saints. So we, "though many, are one body. . . . For by one Spirit we were all baptized into one body" (1 Cor. 12:12–13). And again: "Because there is one bread, we who are many are one body, for we all partake of the one bread" (1 Cor. 10:17). That is certainly a fellowship which the world does not know and can never understand. It is the imperishable communion of saints.

Perhaps some of you are thinking that this is all some theological theory, some theology pushed too far. Such thoughts come to us because we are children of the modern world, which no longer knows of the profound reality of the living Christ. The church of which our text speaks knew about it. It lived thereby. Our fathers in the church of the Reformation also lived thereby. Whatever there is of genuine, deep brotherly love in the church of all times has grown out of this love. Let me mention only one instance, that of the church's loving service (*Diakonie*). This was the ancient church's claim to fame, even among the heathen. "See, how they love one another!" There was then such a caring for the poor and the sick, for the lonely and helpless, as the world had never known before. For the ancient civilization was a civilization without mercy, just as our world is threatening to again become a world without mercy. But all that loving activity would never have happened without the Lord's Supper. For all loving service proceeds from the altar. So it was in the early church, when the deacons and deaconesses brought the consecrated bread and wine to the sick, the lonely, the helpless, those who could not come to church. With this they brought along the congregation's gifts of love, and thereby the comfort, the help, and the fellowship of the Christian brotherhood. When in the 19th century there was a revival of the Christian diaconate, we again see such loving service going out from the altar. In Neuendettelsau the deaconess houses became places of renewed liturgy and renewed celebration of Holy Communion. You have only to attend a divine service in Bethel [a well-known home for the handicapped at Bielefeld, Germany] to realize why

134

Father Bodelschwingh [its founder] maintained the Lutheran liturgy with such great faithfulness.

But the diaconate is only one evidence of the profound connection between the sacraments and the works of practical service in the communion of saints, that communion which is inexplicable to any human reason, because it is the fellowship of the body of Christ. This fellowship goes with Holy Communion, which in our text is called by its ancient code name, "the breaking of bread." ". . . breaking bread in their homes"—they had no other place for this. "They devoted themselves to the apostles' teaching and fellowship, to the breaking of bread. . . ." These together.

For the church today, and also our Lutheran Church, there is nothing more needful than pondering this fact. When fellowship is separated from Holy Communion both are diminished. Today Holy Communion has been pushed into the background—the celebration which was the core of the divine service for all Christians until the Reformation, and still was so in the first two centuries of the Evangelical Lutheran Church. Now we often find that it has been removed from the service. Certainly not every member of the congregation can or should receive Communion every Sunday, but the Sacrament is to be celebrated in its midst.

But is there not a danger of this becoming one of those laws that ever and again have been taken from our text? No, this is no law, no more than the admonition to continue in the apostles' doctrine and the fellowship, and to be steadfast in prayer. Also *prayer*—our text uses the plural—is profoundly connected with the celebration of the Lord's Supper. Without these prayers, without the joy and rejoicing of the congregation overflowing with thanksgiving, without the irrepressible praise of what great and marvelous things the Lord has done, without the worship of the present Lord Christ, there can be no church.

They praised God "with glad and generous hearts." All liturgy of the church, all praying of the church, is only an echo of this praise of God, of these soaring-to-heaven prayers of Christianity's first Pentecost season. Then the Spirit of God enlivened hearts, enabling them to pray. For it is true also of the church that "we do not know how to pray as we ought, but the Spirit Himself intercedes for us with sighs too deep for words" (Rom. 8:26). And not in vain do we call upon the Holy Spirit as follows:

> You are the Spir't who teaches
> How one should pray aright.
> Your prayers are ever answered,

135

Your songs are ever bright.
To heav'n goes up Your call,
And for our help is pleading,
Till He the help is giving,
Whose aid is there for all.

The picture of the first church given in our text is a gripping picture indeed. But we must not forget that the light which shines about the first congregation in Jerusalem is not only the daybreak red of the church's morning, but also the sunset red of an earthly people. They were a perishing people, and a generation later that judgment was fulfilled which goes out over every nation that rejects Christ. The Jewish Christian congregation fled across the Jordan, prompted by a prophetic utterance. Their role was over, bound up with the history of their people.

But Christ's church did not come to an end. The call of God's Holy Spirit went out to the peoples of the heathen world, and then they in their day were alive with the truth of these words: "They devoted themselves to the apostle's teaching and fellowship, to the breaking of bread and the prayers." Nations pass away, but the church continues. And where there is a people which no longer has a future, there the church still has a future, because the future of the church is the future of Jesus Christ. Amen.